UNNERVED

Unnerved

ANXIETY, SOCIAL CHANGE, AND THE TRANSFORMATION
OF MODERN MENTAL HEALTH

Jason Schnittker

Columbia University Press
New York

Columbia University Press
Publishers Since 1893
New York   Chichester, West Sussex
cup.columbia.edu

Library of Congress Cataloging-in-Publication Data
Names: Schnittker, Jason, author.
Title: Unnerved : anxiety, social change, and the transformation of modern
mental health / Jason Schnittker, University of Pennsylvania.
Description: [New York] : [Columbia University Press], [2021] | Includes
bibliographical references and index.
Identifiers: LCCN 2020045611 (print) | LCCN 2020045612 (ebook) | ISBN 9780231200349
(hardback) | ISBN 9780231200356 (paperback) | ISBN 9780231553568 (ebook)
Subjects: LCSH: Anxiety–Social aspects. | Anxiety disorders.
Classification: LCC BF575.A6 S36 2021 (print) | LCC BF575.A6 (ebook) | DDC 152.4/6–dc23
LC record available at https://lccn.loc.gov/2020045611
LC ebook record available at https://lccn.loc.gov/2020045612

Cover design: Elliott S. Cairns

CONTENTS

CONTENTS

UNNERVED

Chapter One

THE SIGNIFICANCE AND MEANING
OF ANXIETY

If ever there were an age of anxiety, it seems to be now. As a category, anxiety disorders are the most common psychiatric disorders in the United States, exceeding mood disorders, impulse control disorders, and substance use disorders.[1] The lifetime prevalence of *any* psychiatric disorder—that is, the share of Americans who have experienced any disorder in their lifetimes— is just over 46 percent, but the lifetime prevalence of anxiety disorders alone is just under 30 percent.[2] Anxiety constitutes a significant part of the total mental suffering in the United States. Anxiety disorders are often directed at something in particular, though the high prevalence of anxiety disorders is not driven by a pervasive fear of a single thing, such as public speaking. The two most common anxiety disorders are specific phobia, related to an object or situation, and social phobia, related to everyday interactions, each with a lifetime prevalence of over 12 percent.[3] The two most common specific fears are of animals and heights, with about one in five Americans suffering from a significant fear of one or the other, whereas the most common social fear is public speaking (21 percent), followed closely by meeting new people (17 percent).[4] Although some anxiety disorders are episodic and might appear only once in a person's lifetime, the prevalence of anxiety disorders in any given year is high, too. About one in five Americans suffer from an anxiety disorder in a year, relative to about one in ten from a mood disorder.[5] Furthermore, anxiety is often regarded as a medical matter and treated as such. Many people take antianxiety medications to alleviate their suffering, and despite controversy and a waxing and waning in their popularity over time, the use of antianxiety medications remains common. One of the top-selling psychiatric drugs, best known by its brand name Xanax, is used primarily in the treatment of anxiety.[6] Similarly, the use of benzodiazepines, from the category of drugs referred to as minor tranquilizers, has increased over time. In total, in 2013 about 8 percent of U.S. adults used an anxiolytic, sedative, or hypnotic medication.[7]

As high as these numbers are, they are only the tip of the iceberg. If we move beyond anxiety *disorders*—formal psychiatric categories denoting severe anxiety—and simply consider basic anxiety, fear, and worry, the percentage who suffer to some degree is much higher. And here, too, anxiety stands out among other negative emotions. Americans report feeling anxious, for instance, more than they report feeling sad or angry.[8] Furthermore, no topic dominates, as might be the case if Americans worried a lot about a particular current issue like climate change. Indeed, exactly *what* people worry about has little relationship with *how much* they worry. Although people who suffer from generalized anxiety disorder certainly worry more than people who do not suffer from this disorder, the subjects of their worries are similar. And even if those who suffer from generalized anxiety disorder worry about certain topics more frequently, their excess worry is hardly over esoteric matters or so broad as to be entirely fanciful.[9] For instance, those who suffer from generalized anxiety disorder worry more about their health than do those who do not suffer from this disorder, although they worry somewhat less about their finances.[10] In short, everyone has something he or she worries about or could worry about, and people usually have something they could at least in principle worry about a lot.

Of course, anxiety is hardly a new emotion. An "age of anxiety" does not refer to the creation of anxiety itself or to new semantics for a subtle emotional experience, as might be the case for something like "artistic appreciation."[11] Indeed, anxiety is an elemental emotion, and it has long been the subject of public, philosophical, and medical discussion. It is hard to imagine a life without some degree of worry or fear, and indeed, it is easy to regard anxiety as necessary to a life well lived. Yet, for at least the last one hundred years, each generation has staked a claim on being more anxious than the one preceding it.[12] The specific claims vary in what exactly they are referring to, though they are thematically consistent. As common as claims about an especially anxious generation are claims about an especially anxious era. W. H. Auden staked one of the more visible claims to this title with his poem *The Age of Anxiety*, published between the end of World War II and the beginning of the 1950s. Although *The Age of Anxiety* is a complicated poem focused on industrialization and identity more than anxiety per se, it has nonetheless served as a benchmark of sorts, motivating other artists to further explore the topic of anxiety. And the poem perhaps accurately marked the beginning of a qualitatively different era. Auden was certainly on to something—midcentury America was, in fact, an anxious time. The period saw the rise of the pharmacological treatment of anxiety, especially the drug Miltown. Objectively there was much to worry about, including some entirely new threats, like the specter of nuclear annihilation, the emergence of the Cold War, and the enduring trauma of World War II. Concerns over anxiety were hardly limited to poets. The era also saw an increase in academic interest in anxiety. Psychologist Rollo May, for example, published *The Meaning of Anxiety* in 1950, finding no reason to dispute the widespread idea that anxiety was the signature disorder of the time and, indeed, doing much to cement it: "Every alert citizen of our society realizes, on the basis of his own experience as well as his observation of his fellow-men, that anxiety is pervasive and profound phenomenon in the middle of the twentieth century."[13] He went on to catalog some of the reasons for this pervasive anxiety, including radical political upheavals, threats of war, and the invention of the atomic bomb.[14] To these global and political forces he added more personal and psychological considerations, including "inner confusion," "uncertainty with respect to values," and "psychological disorientation."[15] Whatever the specific source of their worry, people in the middle of the century were, according to May, primed for fear and psychologically unsteady.

Invoking a not entirely dissimilar set of influences, subsequent generations have cast their own eras as particularly anxiety prone. Baby boomers, for instance, point to the social and occupational squeeze placed on such a large birth cohort, matched by the cultural upheaval associated with rejecting the lifestyles and conventions of earlier generations. Generation X, meanwhile, points to growing uncertainty, declining trust in institutions, and rising individualism, trends that have slowly set people against one another.[16] And millennials point to both new and long-standing challenges, including economic instability, growing housing costs, and job insecurity.[17]

Although it is popular to counterpoise one generation against another, the big picture of generational differences is not lost on people. In thinking about the future, parents, too, worry about many of the same things their children worry about.

At the moment, the world is in the grips of the COVID-19 pandemic. This, too, has occasioned a good deal of anxiety, much of it novel and unprecedented, but other aspects of it drawing on more familiar concerns. The economic worries of young people have been heightened by mass unemployment and the uncertainty associated with schools and universities convening online. Those with preexisting health conditions face a greater risk of complications from COVID-19, heightening the anxiety already experienced by those with diabetes or heart disease. Social isolation has suddenly become common, even among generations who, by virtue of life stage, might ordinarily be enjoying a great deal of time with their friends. And behind all this, of course, is the risk of infection itself, the danger of passing it on to others, and the uncertainty of when exactly the pandemic will end.

There is no shortage of potential ways to understand anxiety between eras and generations, though there are empirical data to support the idea that anxiety has increased over time. Recent generations are, in fact, more anxious, at least based on the sort of data scientists can compile. Using over two hundred surveys of American college students and children conducted between 1932 and 1993, Jean Twenge documents a steady increase in anxiety between cohorts.[18] The magnitude of the increase is hardly trivial, amounting to a standard deviation increase between 1952 and 1993. Even in less statistical terms, this is a very large difference. As Twenge points out, the average child in the 1980s reported more anxiety than the average child psychiatric patient in the 1950s.[19] She also finds that, of all the things that might explain a person's anxiety, the generation in which they are born is among the most important. Birth cohort explains about 20 percent of the variation in anxiety, which is more than is usually accounted for by the entire family environment.[20] The prevalence of formal anxiety disorders follows a similar pattern. The lifetime prevalence of anxiety disorders among adults sixty and older is about half the prevalence among adults age eighteen to twenty-nine, at 15 percent relative to 30 percent.[21]

Some of these patterns are not terribly controversial (nor are they simply the conceit of one generation regarding themselves as different from every other generation). Furthermore, whatever the scientific merits of his claim that anxiety is pervasive and profound, Rollo May was probably right to point out that the twentieth century at least felt like a more anxious time. But even if we accept that anxiety has increased, it remains unclear why it has increased—and there are good reasons to expect anxiety to fall, especially over the long arc of the modern era. Many of the most common worries are hardly unique to the twenty-first century. People have long worried about their safety, economic well-being, and the fate of their children. The weapons of war have changed, but violent deaths have gone down over the long term.[22] Furthermore, life expectancy improved more over the course of the twentieth century than it did in any century prior.[23] Although we are in the grips of global pandemic that has already claimed over 400,000 lives in the United States, deaths from infectious disease have generally declined over time. In 2017, influenza and pneumonia accounted for about 2 percent of all deaths in the United States, whereas cancer and heart disease accounted for about 44 percent.[24] A characteristic feature of modern mortality improvements is the slow tempering of crisis mortality—sudden spikes in mortality from famine, war, and plagues—diminishing the significance of causes of death that in earlier eras might have seemed capricious and devastating. Objectively speaking, many conditions have improved over time, for both societies and individuals. More people in the United States can expect to live to old age. Life is more predictable. The standard of living is much higher. So why are people so anxious?

This book is dedicated to understanding the social, cultural, and medical origins of the modern age of anxiety, up to and including the twenty-first century. This involves more than exploring the causes of anxiety or thinking about what people worry about now relative to what concerned them in the past. It requires advancing arguments along three parallel lines, including simply what it means to claim to have entered an age of anxiety, a claim that appears specific but is rarely cast with precision.

THE GRADUAL ASCENT OF ANXIETY

A core argument of this book is that the rise of anxiety has been slow, reflecting the gradual accumulation of long-running social trends rather than discrete traumatic events or seismic transitions. This slow change hardly makes the growth of anxiety unusual. Many social transformations happen slowly. The rise in life expectancy was an unprecedented achievement of the twentieth century, though it happened steadily, over a series of decades through a robust economy and improvements in public health and medicine, rather than abruptly, through one or two especially significant medical breakthroughs. But anxiety has often been cast as responsive to sudden transformations, traumatic events, or technological innovations. In the mid-1800s, George Miller Beard argued that the apparent nervousness of Americans was due to technologies that had suddenly brought much of the world closer to home, from train travel to long-distance communication.[25] Beard cast particular blame on the inventions of Thomas Edison. In the 1950s, scientists focused on global conflict and the existential crises that surrounded them.[26] Following the events of September 11, 2001, scientists presented evidence that the psychological effects of the events spread well beyond their immediate geography and stretched over long periods of time.[27] Thinking about anxiety in terms of cohorts occasions the same type of speculation. When thinking about anxiety among younger generations, for instance, critics are quick to focus on character more than circumstance, including a cohort's unusual sensitivity, intolerance of discomfort, or perhaps narcissism, and in all these instances critics seem to assume that these qualities are not characteristic of other cohorts as well.[28]

Anxiety lends itself to these kinds of specific interpretations. People, after all, worry about *something*. Based on past experiences, they might worry about something happening again in the future. Trauma can certainly spark anxious apprehension about the future. Furthermore, the scope of worry has perhaps grown larger over time, now that individuals have enormous amounts of information available at their fingertips. Rare and unusual events have a way of assuming outsized significance, especially when they are reinforced in the media. Events can appear seismic in effect. And anxiety can be enduring, even when characterized by episodes of panic or alarm. Anxious people are often chronically fearful, reflecting an enduring pattern of perception and behavior sparked by something in the past.

Yet the rise of anxiety is best understood as the accumulation of slow-moving transformations, spanning eras and generations. This requires a shift in focus, from the abrupt and episodic to the gradual and structured. Many interpretations of anxiety have a way of neglecting larger social currents. Those who favor an existential interpretation of anxiety, for instance, often cast anxiety in terms of a loss of meaning, a crisis of confidence, or a failure to deal adequately with the responsibilities of freedom or modernity.

Religion is certainly related to the meaning individuals derive from their lives, as many have pointed out, but trends in religious participation are much slower than the idea of a crisis suggests, and furthermore, they are much more complicated than a simple rise in secularism.[29] Meaning is rarely lost so much as transformed. By the same token, some observers cast blame for rising anxiety on social media, purportedly pulling younger generations away from deeper friendships or more consequential forms of engagement.[30] But young people, then as now, report a good deal of social support and significant social attachments. A delay in the average age of marriage, for instance, does not mean that younger generations are forgoing marriage altogether. In fact, older people often report more isolation than younger people. What has changed, though, is how cohorts view social relationships generally, especially with respect to their attachment styles. Americans are still connected, and in many ways they are even more socially engaged than they were in the past, but their sense of security in those attachments has deteriorated, and for this reason younger cohorts are able to derive less security from their friendships. Understanding the rise of anxiety requires a broad perspective on how these trends have evolved and how they intersect.

THE AGE OF ANXIETY OR THE AGE OF DEPRESSION?

One weakness of previous accounts of anxiety is their general failure to characterize anxiety vis-à-vis other emotions, especially depression. Those who argue for an age of anxiety are rarely so precise as to argue that it is not also an age of depression. There are, in fact, good reasons to elide a distinction between the two: anxiety and depression are highly correlated, so much so that some popular measures of psychological distress blend the two with little loss to psychometric validity. In fact, the popular scientific concept of "nonspecific psychological distress" captures nicely what most people feel when they feel emotionally unwell: they feel nervous, restless, depressed, and unmotivated, all at once. Furthermore, anxiety and mood disorders are highly comorbid, meaning the risk of major depression, for instance, moves hand in hand with the risk of generalized anxiety disorder. If one is to focus on anxiety—to claim that we are truly and specifically in an age of anxiety—it is necessary to make a case for why at least some of the things that increase anxiety do not also increase depression, or to argue why thinking of anxiety as the sine qua non of mental health is more compelling than thinking of depression in that way.

In both conceptual and empirical ways, I will make the case that anxiety and depression are distinct and ought to be treated as such. Furthermore, I will argue that one of the reasons the idea of an age of anxiety has such enduring resonance is that anxiety is more responsive to environmental changes than is depression—some social environments are able to cleave the two. The resonance of claims of an age of anxiety is, in part, driven by the fact that, in the face of stress or dislocation, what individuals often feel first is anxiety. Several chapters will address this empirically, exploring the sources of worry that are now common. Status anxiety, for instance, is real, both in the sense that individuals worry about their standing relative to other people and that concerns about status impact anxiety much more than they do depression. Status anxiety is prospective more than retrospective. It reflects a fear of falling as much as confidence in what one has achieved. But the greater sensitivity of anxiety is not limited to adults or to the domains of work and professional attainment. Childhood events also have a stronger relationship with early-onset anxiety than with early-onset depression, setting the stage for anxiety in adulthood.

Beyond differences with respect to the pathways to anxiety and depression, I will argue that anxiety and depression differ in more elemental ways. The evolutionary dimensions of anxiety and depression, for instance, are likely very different, which has implications for thinking about the social origins of anxiety and mood disorders, as well as their overall prevalence. Although there are good reasons to suspect that evolution has retained the risk for both mood and anxiety disorders, the evolutionary foundations of anxiety disorders are likely stronger. By the same token, the latent risk for anxiety disorders is likely far more common than the latent risk for mood disorders. Many people will go through life with no real risk of major depression—never experiencing its key symptom of a profound loss of interest or pleasure—but most of us will experience significant anxiety or fear at some point. The pathway to an anxiety disorder is, for this reason, shorter than to a mood disorder.

At the same time, the phenomenology of anxiety and depression differ in important ways, which has implications for how the disorders may or may not be treated once they occur. Anxiety and mood disorders involve different emotions, of course. There is no mistaking the sadness of depression for the apprehension of anxiety. They simply feel different, and each can be plainly identified and named. But the two emotions also shade perceptions in different ways. The cognitive biases associated with anxiety disorders are very different from those associated with mood disorders. The biases associated with anxiety are also probably stronger and more comprehensive, affecting how anxious people interpret their environments and experiences in a more wholesale fashion. At the same time, the stigma associated with each disorder is unique, giving anxiety fewer of the negative connotations associated with depression and thereby increasing its appeal as a clinical target. Anxiety can be accepted both as common and as grounds for treatment.

THE CLINICAL AND SCIENTIFIC ASCENT OF ANXIETY

A related aspect of this book is to argue that anxiety has assumed much greater significance as a topic of scientific inquiry, as well as much greater relevance as a medical condition. This is different from arguing about the causes of anxiety or depression and how they have shifted over cohorts, though it is no less important for understanding the rise of anxiety as an idiom of distress. It is critical to understand how anxiety became a *disorder* and why patients might present its symptoms to physicians more frequently than they did in the past. Over the last two centuries, anxiety has often assumed a liminal position. On the one hand, anxiety has almost always been regarded as at least an element of emotional suffering, appearing in virtually all discussions of what constitutes mental illness, and featured as an essential symptom in many once popular disorders and syndromes, ranging from neurasthenia to a nervous breakdown. On the other hand, observers have struggled with determining the point at which anxiety becomes dysfunctional, and even with whether to regard anxiety as harmful at all. Anxiety is, after all, ordinary, in the sense that it is natural, adaptive, and part of the human experience. An important aspect of anxiety, for instance, is that it requires self-awareness.[31] Although other vertebrates demonstrate behavioral corollaries of fear, including the fight-or-flight response, only humans are capable of *feeling* anxiety. Furthermore, anxiety might very well be critical to human adaptation in a way that other aversive emotions are not. Consider, as a contrary example, sadness, and whether to regard a particular level of sadness as dysfunctional. One way to think about whether a given level of sadness constitutes a case of major depression is to determine how appropriate the sadness is relative to the person's experience. Some have proposed that major depression, if it is to be regarded as a true dysfunction, ought to be disproportionate to the putative cause.[32] The fact that someone seems to be depressed for no reason, or is more depressed than is warranted given the event that occasioned the depression, can be taken as a sign that the depression is not a normal reaction to stress and is, therefore, a disorder. Although determining what is proportionate is not always simple, such a determination is probably easier for depression than it is for anxiety. Anxiety and fear muddle the distinction between normal and abnormal in less tractable ways. Fear has an object, which itself can be assessed. Furthermore, fear represents the apprehension of some potential harm. Though the risk of that harm might be overstated, the fear itself means that something—heights, animals, or enclosed spaces—is a potential threat. This aligns fear with rationality in at least two ways. First, precisely because anxiety reflects apprehension—an orientation toward the future—it is far more difficult to adjudicate the reasonableness of anxiety than depression, for which any accounting is usually retrospective. Developing major depression after the loss of a small possession, for example, might seem excessive, but regardless of whether it is, the reason for the depression can be evaluated vis-à-vis an actual history. Anxiety over the potential loss of a job involves some supposition, because the outcome is, as yet, unrealized. Second, because fear has an object, it can be evaluated as a potentially adaptive response to a specific danger. Our evolutionary ancestors lived when predators were a real threat to survival and the inability to escape presented a mortal risk. In this context, a fear of snakes, strangers, or enclosed spaces was reasonable and could aid survival. Such threats might not be as common today as they were then, but the value of fear remains insofar as it continues to promote the avoidance of danger.

Anxiety is, in fact, associated with intelligence. In the middle of the twentieth century, the psychologist Howard Liddell aligned anxiety with cognitive ability in an article reviewing the literature on neuroses in animals.[33] In highlighting differences between humans and other animals, Liddell argued that some of the things that make humans unique are also those that make humans anxious, including, especially, the ability to plan and anticipate. Recent evidence, too, indicates that among those who suffer from generalized anxiety disorder, those with more severe symptoms tend to score higher on intelligence tests.[34] And even short of regarding anxiety as a sign of intelligence per se, it is at least common to regard anxiety as something to be learned from, in a way that is not as obvious for depression. A long-running theme in the anxiety literature is that anxiety can teach us about *ourselves* as much as our world. Freud famously regarded anxiety as a sign of an underlying conflict, providing a prod to search the subconscious for the source of the real problem.[35] One need not accept Freud's theory to see how anxiety can occasion growth. Overcoming anxiety is often regarded as a sign of maturity and grit, learning that one's fear might have been unwarranted.

This tension in how anxiety can be interpreted—desirable or undesirable, rational or irrational, normal or abnormal, aversive emotion or environmental signal—is reflected in how scientists and clinicians have historically approached anxiety disorders. As a topic of study, anxiety has not always been front and center. Within psychiatry, anxiety has remained, for the most part, a second-order concern. At the very least, the relevance of anxiety has been highly unstable, waxing and waning in relevance over time, and frequently drowning in a sea of other symptoms that assume much greater significance. I argue that this has occurred not because psychiatrists regard anxiety as irrelevant, but rather because anxiety has carried with it the legacy of earlier frameworks that psychiatrists were keen to dispel and, at times, because the medical armamentarium has strongly favored one symptom over another. To be sure, there have long been some good scientific and clinical reasons to focus on other psychiatric disorders. Psychiatrists could rightly claim that anxiety disorders, though common, were not nearly as disabling as other disorders, including major depression. Professionals could also claim to know more about depression than anxiety and thus perhaps to feel more confident in their treatment of depression. Major depression, for instance, has attracted more scholarly attention than any specific anxiety disorder. To the extent that anxiety and depression are related, one could treat one and, in the process, treat the other as well. Mental health professionals have not acted alone in this regard. The public, too, generally regards depression as more significant than anxiety.

But things have changed. Patients are increasingly granting anxiety more weight and presenting the symptom to their physicians, either in tandem with depression or on its own. Parallel to this change has been a growing willingness on the part of physicians to treat anxiety. Physicians have more pharmaceutical tools with which to treat anxiety disorders, some of which are old but newly appreciated. Benzodiazepines, for instance, are prescribed with growing frequency, though they have been available for decades. All this has occurred in the context of more scientific research on anxiety and fear as independent and unique emotional experiences. As a clinical and scientific target, anxiety is beginning to stand out in ways that it did not before. It can be studied discretely. Its biological, neurological, and behavioral signatures can be studied on their own, and they are plainly different from those of depression. Clinicians are beginning to apprehend anxiety independent of depression. In short, as a language of distress, anxiety has growing and broad-based resonance for clinicians, scientists, and the general public.

Given the multidimensional nature of this book's argument, it is useful to point out a number of things upfront. The general approach of this book is to combine an investigation of the causes and origins of anxiety with an exploration of the emergence of anxiety as a public issue, that is, as something broadly concerning in the public sphere in ways that it was not before. Other studies have taken a similar approach to explaining, for instance, the rise of drunk driving as a social problem or the shift from regarding behavioral problems as "badness" to regarding them as "sickness."[36] The chapters that follow explore the ascent of anxiety in a variety of ways, including but not limited to what causes anxiety. Indeed, one argument for why anxiety has become so prominent is that it has a unique capacity to absorb and reflect social and environmental change, refracting the social situation of individuals through fear and apprehension. Anxiety, for instance, is attached to changes in the family and household composition. It is attached to the decline in religious participation, though in complicated ways, as I later show. And it is attached to changes in social relationships and social status. The concept of status anxiety, for instance, is remarkably precise in aligning social status with anxiety (and not, by contrast, the many other possible dimensions of emotional well-being). Exploring all these fronts—the causes of anxiety, the scientific study of anxiety, and the clinical apprehension of anxiety—is necessary for understanding the present moment. I will begin, though, by considering the early modern history of anxiety, corresponding to the nineteenth century through the early twentieth century.

Chapter Two

A LATE MODERN HISTORY OF ANXIETY

Although it is possible to view the history of anxiety through a much deeper lens, the late modern period—corresponding to the nineteenth and early twentieth centuries—provides a good starting point for thinking about where anxiety stands now. Indeed, a history of anxiety in the nineteenth century will look strikingly familiar from the vantage of the twenty-first century. More than a century ago, medical professionals were grappling with distinctions that remain important today, including understanding the difference between anxiety and depression, struggling with whether to regard anxiety as a symptom of disease or a dimension of character, and cataloging similarities and differences among types of phobias. Beyond this, scientists and physicians were struggling to define the role of the environment in anxiety, especially in light of significant social change, as well as offering insights into the kinds of predispositions that might render some people more anxiety prone than others. Then, as now, some observers advanced the idea that anxiety was, whatever else it might be, necessary for the further development of civilization.

The parallels between eras are deeper still in the sense that, even in the nineteenth century, one could already see how anxiety was slowly being subsumed by other symptoms, disorders, and categories. Anxiety was certainly appreciated as a symptom of mental illness. Indeed, it was occasionally put forward as the most important symptom, central to virtually all psychiatric disorders, most famously by Freud. Yet anxiety was also placed in proximity to other symptoms that would eventually overshadow it, whether with respect to heart palpitations that could be diagnosed as problems with the cardiovascular system or sadness that could be construed as melancholia. This trend continued for much of the century as psychiatric nomenclature changed. In the late twentieth century, major depression would become the signature psychiatric disorder, absorbing much of the attention once focused on its progenitors, including nerve problems. At a variety of junctures, anxiety was both elevated as a critical element of suffering and set within a portfolio of other symptoms that could easily take its place. And all along psychiatrists struggled with how to *interpret* anxiety—whether to regard it as a sign of weakness or a sign of refinement, as the mark of an overactive mind or an insufficiently robust one, as an affliction of the upper class or a disease of the lower class, as a natural state or an artifact of modern life. The early modern history of anxiety can be read as an iterative attempt to resolve the ambivalence surrounding the concept.

In this chapter and the next I trace the evolution of anxiety disorders through their two most significant antecedents: neurasthenia and problems of nerves, including the nervous breakdown. Neither neurasthenia nor the nervous breakdown is considered scientifically credible today, and much of the history of these two disorders has been discussed before.[1] Yet there are still lessons to be learned from considering why the concepts were so popular, as well as the ways in which some of their key ideas presaged current debates about the meaning of anxiety in particular. I hope to extract several arguments from this history. First, I will argue that the language of anxiety, whatever specific form it takes, has long served an important function for the lay public. At times, some disorders are elevated over others and the signature disorders have changed. In the mid- to late twentieth century, reporting stress and depression became the dominant means of conveying feeling unemotionally unwell.[2] Throughout all this change, however, anxiety has remained important within the vernacular of suffering. Furthermore, anxiety has long provided a specific kind of language, notably providing the terms for talking about the personal consequences of social transitions. Anxiety features prominently whenever societies undergo rapid social, cultural, or technological change. Anxiety was discussed frequently, for instance, during the industrialization of the nineteenth century. In the mid-twentieth century, anxiety emerged within the context of fear of nuclear annihilation. And in the twenty-first century, anxiety is again seen as a natural outcome of rapid technological change and economic uncertainty. I will start with neurasthenia, an especially critical diagnosis in the modern history of medicine.

NEURASTHENIA AND THE CHANGING CHARACTER OF NERVOUSNESS

In 1869, George Miller Beard sketched the characteristics of neurasthenia in an article appearing in the journal that would later become the *New England Journal of Medicine*. He subsequently expanded on that definition in his books *Neurasthenia (Nervous Exhaustion)*, published in 1879, and later, *American Nervousness*, published in 1881 as a supplement to *Neurasthenia*.[3] His work received a good deal of attention, and Beard himself was not content to keep his ideas limited to the pages of medical journals. Among other outlets, he published articles on neurasthenia in the *Atlantic*, slowly establishing an international reputation as a social critic and scientist.[4] A neurologist by training, Beard characterized neurasthenia as the "exhaustion of the nervous system," advancing nerves as a vital force that could be filled or depleted based on the balance between a person's reserves and demands.[5] From this general definition Beard cataloged a wide variety of symptoms indicative of the disorder, especially in the context of *American Nervousness*.[6] In that work, the list of symptoms of neurasthenia was especially detailed, all the more so given that, after describing many symptoms enumerated over numerous pages, he stipulated that his list was to be regarded as incomplete and only "representative," to be finished when physicians learned more about the disease, and even then, a "exhaustive catalogue" of the symptoms was probably impossible because, as Beard put it, every case of the disorder was somewhat different.[7] The symptoms spanned multiple systems and experiences. Neurasthenia involved, for instance, symptoms now more consistent with major depression, including fatigue, a lack of motivation, and insomnia. Neurasthenia also involved a wide variety of somatic symptoms arrayed over multiple organs, including symptoms related to the skin, joints, heart, vision, and mucous membranes. Neurasthenia also involved the kinds of worries and anxiety ordinarily associated with the "nervousness" of the title. Beard was particularly comprehensive and florid on this score, describing the fear of the neurasthenic person as pervasive and all-encompassing, including, as described in one passage, a "fear of lightning, or fear of responsibility, of open places or of closed places, fear of society, fear of being alone, fear of fears, fear of contamination, fear of everything."[8] In assorted case studies, Beard further delved into the nature of fear, situating neurasthenia primarily in the context of social fears, though once again describing fear in capacious terms. In *Neurasthenia*, for instance, he described one patient as suffering from a morbid "fear of man or society," leading the patient to dread going anywhere other people expected something from him.[9]

By contemporary standards, the diagnostic criteria for neurasthenia were too broad and unspecific to be useful. Beard was keen to cast neurasthenia as the most significant disorder of his time, and with his definition, it is difficult to imagine anyone not suffering from at least some symptoms of the disease. Yet there is nothing that can be typified in neurasthenia's encyclopedia of symptoms and, for this reason, it is difficult to draw lessons about the disease by examining putative cases. Beard was not a terribly rigorous or critical scientist, a point that is easy to grasp in hindsight but apparent even at the time.[10] From a different standpoint, however, Beard was on to something important, at least in broad strokes, and the appeal of his work was not born from nothing. He articulated the basic idea that people were probably more nervous in the middle of the nineteenth century than their predecessors had been. The concept of neurasthenia would never have garnered as much attention as it did were it not for the fact that many in the United States were nervous about changing social conditions. In a later period, the idea of a nervous breakdown would address the same social need as neurasthenia, as would, later still, the idea of major depression.

Furthermore, Beard anticipated, in broad strokes, a model of the character and causes of anxiety that would not be out of place in the twenty-first century. He also succeeded in putting nervousness within the remit of medicine. Beard was keen to cast mental illness as a physical problem as well as a mental one. This was a significant accomplishment in itself, one that has led some medical historians to conclude that neurasthenia was, whatever else, one of the most important labels in the history of medicine.[11] At the time of Beard's writing, scientists debated whether mental illness was organic or psychological, a divide that was both consequential and strictly enforced. The prevailing framework of medicine implied that the mind could be sick only insofar as the body was sick, and diseases were allocated to one side or the other, as mostly psychological or mostly physical.[12] In this context, anxiety was downplayed, as it seemed so naturally a product of psychological, cultural, or spiritual matters. Beard spent much of his effort casting neurasthenia and all it encompassed as a physical problem, bringing the entire corpus of symptoms of "nervousness" into the bailiwick of medicine. If describing a wide variety of symptoms diluted the power of the neurasthenia as a specific diagnosis, it at least put anxiety in the same orbit as, for instance, heart palpitations and pain. In *American Nervousness*, Beard asserts that "nervousness is a physical not a mental state," one that does not come from "emotional excess or excitability."[13] If medicine accepted Beard's thinking, anxiety could not be dismissed as a product of personality or weakness, as it was when attributed to hypochondriasis or hysteria. In the twenty-first century, scientists have continued efforts to cast anxiety as biological or neurological in origin.

Beard's thinking about the causes of nervousness made another contribution. He formulated a way of thinking about the relationship between the person and environment, effectively introducing the concept of a diathesis-stress, and in the process casting neurasthenia as both a product of civilization and, at least at the time, particularly American. Beard argued the causes of nervousness could be expressed algebraically over a set of influences, as the sum of "civilization in general" plus "American civilization in particular" plus an "exhausting climate" plus "overwork or overworry" plus "the nervous diathesis."[14] Some of the elements in this formulation were, to be sure, not entirely new. The idea of a diathesis was, in fact, very old, originating in a temperamental view of illness.[15] And, though often credited to Beard, the specific conjunction of "diathesis-stress" was coined later, at a time when researchers were focused more on stress than diathesis.[16] Nonetheless, Beard effectively joined the two concepts in thinking about of the causes of neurasthenia, and he worked to advance a definition of the diathesis for neurasthenia that was more specific than what had come before. Furthermore, through the framework of a diathesis-stress, Beard effectively advanced an argument for why neurasthenia was so common, basing it not only on what he saw as profound changes in the American social environment but also a rise in the latent risk for nervousness. Both the person and the environment were changing.

Usually the term "diathesis" is a placeholder for describing a more specific vulnerability, whether biological or psychological. Today the diathesis for anxiety would be understood largely in terms of genetic factors. In his account, though, Beard zeroed in on a specific set of dispositional characteristics. This, too, was revealing, especially in highlighting some of the complexities of anxiety. Many of the characteristics Beard put forward as part of the diathesis might ordinarily be regarded as desirable and, indeed, Beard argued that the rise of neurasthenia was mostly a transitional moment in the ongoing evolution of American civilization. The diathesis for anxiety, for instance, involved "a fine organization," characterized by a strong intellect and emotional sensitivity. Such an organization was "civilized, refined, and educated," increasing with the "progress of civilization," and occurring in parallel to a shift from "labor of the brain over that of the muscles."[17] For Beard, such sensitivity offered numerous benefits. He proposed, for instance, that the nervous diathesis offered protection against fever and inflammation, arguing that the rise of brainwork was directly implicated in the decline in infectious disease.[18] Yet the nervous diathesis also involved a vulnerability to "varied and recurring attacks of diseases of the nervous system" stretching back to infancy and continuing to old age.[19]

Beard's formulation of the nervous diathesis was psychological, though it necessarily involved the environment as well. Here, too, Beard was not the first to propose that anxiety was a product of environmental strain. History is replete with examples scholars arguing for a relationship between anxiety and changing social conditions.[20] Beard did, however, highlight the significance of the *pace* of change, and he formulated the rise of neurasthenia in terms of the rise of modernity. In addition, Beard was explicit in arguing that neurasthenia was "originally American," in the sense that the forces conspiring to produce neurasthenia were most pronounced in the United States (though they could be exported elsewhere).[21] In the mid-nineteenth century, the United States was changing rapidly with rural to urban migration and the proliferation of technologies that reduced the figurative and literal distance between people. With this in mind, Beard attributed the increase in nervous exhaustion to a variety of general and specific influences, including the rise of science and its many technological innovations, such as steam power, the railroad, the steam-powered rotary printing press, and the telegraph.[22] In *American Nervousness*, he identified an even more specific culprit: "The experiments, inventions, and discoveries or Edison alone have made and are now making constant and exhausting draughts on the nervous forces of America and Europe, and have multiplied in very many ways, and made more complex and extensive, the tasks and agonies not only of practical men, but of professors and teachers and students everywhere."[23] In this context, the idea of nervous exhaustion captured the idea that many people seemingly could not keep up with the pace of modernization.

For all of Beard's emphasis on neurasthenia as the physical and psychological manifestation of change, and for all his thoughts on neurasthenia's social and psychological determinants, the therapeutic implications of his ideas were decidedly ambiguous. On the one hand, the concept of neurasthenia encouraged the serious treatment of anxiety. Beard regarded his work on neurasthenia as significant, not least because he thought it would help doctors and patients see the problem clearly. Neurasthenia would help physicians understand the sort of complaints they saw routinely in their practices and patients might welcome a diagnosis that could explain their suffering without the connotations of "insane."[24] No less significant was the possibility that patients stood to benefit from treatment. Among the medications used in the treatment of nervous conditions were potassium bromide, codeine, and morphine,[25] the appeal of which was partly based on the speed with which these drugs could alleviate the "exalted irritability" of the nerves.[26] On the other hand, Beard's emphasis on the role of temperament encouraged a more sanguine reading of midcentury nervousness. In Beard's formulation, the idea that neurasthenia involved thinking too much coexisted with the idea that proper brainwork was conducive to health.[27] From this he argued that neurasthenia could be alleviated by directing thought in productive ways and, indeed, that nervousness would eventually diminish as American culture advanced to a higher level:

The higher we rise in the atmosphere of thought the more we escape the strikes, the competitions, the worryings and exhausting disappointments—in short, all the infinite frictions that inevitably attend the struggle for bread that all must have, and the more we are stimulated and sustained by those lofty truths for which so few aspire. The search for truth is more healthful as well as more noble than the search for gold, and the best of all antidotes and means of relief for nervous disease is found in philosophy.[28]

He went on to note that failing to reach such a rarified atmosphere was the explanation for why America "has developed a larger variety and number of functional nervous diseases than all other nations combined."[29] All was not lost, though, and Beard was optimistic that American nervousness would eventually recede:

The evil of American nervousness, like all other evils, tends, within certain limits, to correct itself; and the physical future of the American people has a bright as well as a dark side; increasing wealth will bring increasing calm and repose; the friction of nervousness shall be diminished by various inventions; social customs with the needs of the times, shall be modified, and as a consequence strength and vigor shall be developed at the same time with, and by the side of debility and nervousness.[30]

Although Beard was perhaps the most prominent voice arguing neurasthenia was the product of social change, he was not alone in using nervousness as a lens for understanding fit and adaptation in a changing society. The basic themes Beard developed were used much more broadly. Richard von Krafft-Ebing, for instance, was a psychiatrist active in the late nineteenth century, focused mostly on sexual behavior and psychopathology. Krafft-Ebing viewed homosexuality as a kind of social and biological degeneration.[31] Other scholars at the time resisted this view by highlighting, for instance, the tolerance for homosexuality in ancient Greece, but these attempts at historical reclamation were largely unsuccessful, and the idea that homosexuality is a psychological disorder would linger for most of the twentieth century. Krafft-Ebing himself, however, went on to espouse a surprisingly modern view of sexual orientation, even while allowing that homosexuality caused a good deal of psychological suffering. He noted the cruelty with which society treated sexual minorities and advocated for a more tolerant approach, especially in the legal arena.[32] And in making the case for the cruelty of the larger culture, he described the suffering among sexual minorities in terms of nervousness. In his case studies, Krafft-Ebing described patients fearing, for instance, that their secret sex lives would be discovered and that they would be unable to confide in others; he described how nervous symptoms moved in tandem with sexual instincts, with desire feeding anxiety; and he described the fits, spasms, "constant anxiety," and "nervous debility" from patients habitually concealing their desires.[33] These are, of course, very different challenges from those articulated by Beard, though they no less reflect the psychological trials of individuals living in a not yet fully modern culture. The language of anxiety conveys the psychology of discontent.

THE DEVOLUTION OF NEURASTHENIA AND
THE ECLIPSE OF NERVOUSNESS

Although nervousness certainly never went away, neurasthenia as a concept eventually dwindled. There were several reasons for this. For one, Beard's definition of neurasthenia was increasingly out of step with the diagnostic ambitions of medicine. Neurasthenia was certainly a popular diagnosis and enjoyed broad cultural appeal, but what the concept achieved in terms of unifying a disorganized body of symptoms it lost in terms of scientific and clinical value.[34] Medicine was increasingly governed by the principle of disease specificity, insisting that explanations for disease satisfy in an exact and proximate fashion at the level of microbiology, anatomy, or cell function. Neurasthenia involved far too many symptoms to be properly studied, as well as too many causes spread across too many systems. Neurasthenia also came be regarded as too mild to warrant much attention.[35] In an article appearing in the *Boston Medical and Surgical Journal*, Charles L. Dana argued that neurasthenia was merely "a kind of understudy of some particular type of insanity" and, further, that neurasthenia often failed to develop into any other kind of psychiatric disorder, meaning it was likely ephemeral.[36] By his count, about 50 percent of patients diagnosed as suffering from neurasthenia likely had no real disorder.[37]

But physicians never regarded *all* the symptoms of neurasthenia as irrelevant. From the ashes of neurasthenia physicians advanced other disorders they saw as more important and, at the same time, worked to prune Beard's list of incidental symptoms and focus instead on its most morbid elements. In his critique of neurasthenia, for instance, Dana went on to outline five types of insanity that, for clinical purposes, were more useful. Among them was what he termed phrenasthenia, a type of neurasthenia that was more severe than what Beard proposed, involving "perversions, hysterias, phobias, abulias, amnesias, as well as the compulsions and impulsions, the dipsomanias, morbid fears, and the psychic tics."[38] In addition, psychiatry began to more precisely conceptualize some of the specific fears Beard cataloged in a more indiscriminate fashion, producing early versions of panic disorder, generalized anxiety disorder, and agoraphobia. Carl Westphal, for instance, described agoraphobia as a social phobia involving an intense fear of entering public spaces.[39] Similarly, the idea of a panic was formalized in 1879 by Henry Maudsley in the context of describing a "melancholic panic," closely associated with depression.[40] Parallel to these efforts, some psychiatrists were attempting to unify the various anxieties and fears under a more general framework (if not as a single disorder). Pierre Janet, for instance, divided anxiety into two core types, one featuring disturbances in conscious experience and another involving unconscious processes.[41]

For the most part, though, the new diagnoses created in neurasthenia's wake were shorn of nervousness.[42] If, as Beard anticipated, nervousness would evaporate as Americans developed the right mindset, it was less clear exhaustion or general distress would do the same, and, by the end of the nineteenth century, neurasthenia itself had devolved into a disorder mostly entailing fatigue.[43] One offshoot of neurasthenia, for instance, involved "simple" fatigue, in reference to the fact that it contained few, if any, psychiatric symptoms.[44] In a similar vein, other psychiatrists put forward different types of chronic fatigue, some with other symptoms; one involving, for instance, minor depression and another free of other psychiatric symptoms.[45] Ewald Hecker described a class of neurasthenic patients who experienced the somatic symptoms of anxiety, including dizziness, but not the psychological symptoms, effectively complicating Beard's efforts to cast anxiety as both emotional and physical.[46] In the twenty-first century, we know the two types of symptoms are distinct, which is one reason why modern anxiety researchers insist on respecting the difference between the behaviors associated with anxiety and the conscious manifestation of anxiety.[47] In the nineteenth century, however, the distinction provided yet another reason to discard Beard's concept of neurasthenia.

In moving toward reducing the significance of nervousness as a symptom, these new diagnoses were simply picking up a long-standing thread in psychiatry. Psychiatric nosology had long been ambivalent about anxiety. In his influential 1812 textbook, *Medical Inquiries and Observations Upon the Diseases of the Mind*, Benjamin Rush argued that anxiety played a largely secondary role in psychiatric disorders.[48] In Rush's framework, many of the somatic symptoms Beard aligned with neurasthenia could be understood instead as manifestations of depression, including hypochondriasis. Rush minimized anxiety in other ways as well. He distinguished among different types of fear, relegating many to simple urges and instincts. These instincts might occasionally be overblown, but they presented no real problems. In this vein, he grouped fear with other "derangement[s] of the passions," including love, grief, and anger.[49] Anticipating a theme that would be taken up in the twentieth century, he further characterized some fears as more reasonable than others, noting "there is so much danger and evil in our world that the passion of fear was implanted in our minds for the wise and benevolent purpose of defending us from them."[50] To the extent that he regarded fear as a symptom necessitating treatment, Rush called for simple environmental fixes, even for fears that had moved well beyond warranted. With respect to reasonable fears that progressed to derangements he recommended avoidance, remediation, or exposure, including, for instance, installing a roof rod for a fear of lightning or compelling children to go to bed without a candle for a fear of darkness.[51] For a fear of death, he argued that work provided the best relief, for fear "is the offspring of idleness."[52]

If disregarding nervousness as a symptom was easy given prevailing views of its causes, disregarding sadness was decidedly less so. Melancholia, a historic contemporary of neurasthenia, deserves special attention, especially as a concept that blended anxiety and depression and, thus, reveals how psychiatrists at the time conceived of differences between the two. Perhaps the most influential discussion of melancholia appeared in Richard von Krafft-Ebing's *Text Book of Insanity*, published in 1905 as an English translation, though influential in its German edition before that.[53] For Krafft-Ebing the essential symptoms of melancholia were sadness, a lack of energy, and a general withdrawal from the world, not unlike major depression today. He differentiated among types of melancholia, however, in ways that invoked anxiety and fear in different measure. For instance, one form of melancholia, *melancholia with precordial distress*, involved significant "tension" occasioned by the sudden emergence of "undefined fear" from which the individual sought relief.[54] He described the characteristics of such an episode of melancholia as involving the combination of "all psychic processes," as well as "remarkable disturbances of respiration and circulation."[55] In addition he described *melancholia with delusions and errors of the senses*, characterized by a profound lack of self-confidence and a feeling of persecution. He located these delusions specifically in anxiety, even if the delusions themselves were the characteristic element (anxiety on its own need not be delusion). In such a disorder, distress and "anxious emotional states" gave rise to "the delusion that some danger actually threatens."[56]

Following the same line of thought, he described *hypochondria melan-cholia*, wherein the patient's fears pertained to health and safety, including a fear of infection, accidents, or animal attacks.[57] In these descriptions, anxiety was important but mostly as a diagnostic adjunct. It was relevant either because it pointed to more significant symptoms, like delusions, or because it helped identify especially severe cases of melancholia. Melancholia involving anxiety, for instance, was often more degenerative, involving a worse prognosis, relative to melancholia without anxiety.

Other textbooks regarded anxiety in much the same fashion, even as they pushed further in the direction of diagnostic specificity. Much of the foundational work behind contemporary diagnostic taxonomies like the *Diagnostic and Statistical Manual of Mental Disorders* (*DSM*) lies in the work of Emil Kraepelin, a contemporary of Krafft-Ebing. Kraepelin's textbook, *Clinical Psychiatry*, published in English in 1902, was an especially important step in the direction of modern specificity.[58] Kraepelin was a hospital-based psychiatrist, and much of the material for his textbook stemmed from his experiences with inpatients. *Clinical Psychiatry* cataloged a remarkable variety of disorders, but even across this broad corpus, anxiety appeared mostly as a second-order and cross-cutting theme. Anxiety, for instance, figured prominently in *dementia paralytica*, but under its so-called "depressed form."[59] Patients with this disorder experienced episodes of intense anxiety and restlessness, but not for long: ordinarily they were placid and despondent.[60] Melancholia, too, was characterized by anxiety, especially anxiety over personal identity, social relationships, past misdeeds, and religious faith. Yet, as befits the diagnosis of melancholia, the principle and overriding emotion remained "uniform depression."[61] At times Kraepelin regarded anxiety as more diagnostically significant, but mostly as a tool for distinguishing among types of disorders and not as a symptom worthy of treatment on its own. For instance, he regarded anxiety as a way to distinguish melancholia from manic-depressive illness, arguing that in the former the patient's actions were "all the natural expression of the anxious and irritable state of the emotional attitude," whereas in a manic-depressive illness the patient's behavior was stunted, and anxiety, if apparent at all, was directed inward.[62]

Clinical Psychiatry was emblematic of the prevailing approach to anxiety in the way it simultaneously elevated anxiety as a form of suffering and diminished its significance relative to other conditions. In prefatory comments discussing a variety of emotions, Kraepelin characterized fear as "by far the most important persistent emotion" across psychiatric disorders.[63] This is a remarkably strong statement, later echoed by Freud. Yet in the same context Kraepelin provided an explanation for why fear should not assume more significance in diagnosis, arguing that fear is common, to the point that "even among normal individuals [fear] affects sympathetically the entire mental and physical condition."[64] Kraepelin also pointed to the role of milder anxieties in the development of later disorders, potentially granting anxiety special significance as a predictor of other problems. Yet here, too, he emphasized the secondary nature of anxiety. What he called "lighter grades of fear," including "timidity and cowardice" and a "lack of self-confidence," are the most frequent symptoms of psychopathic states, though at best they only provide the "favorable soil" for the development of compulsions.[65] Casting fear as the soil is not, of course, the same as casting it as the seed. Other psychiatrists were keener to do so, although they assumed a more radical stance in other respects.

SIGMUND FREUD AND THE CENTRALITY OF ANXIETY

Although nineteenth-century psychiatry was well aware of the special significance of anxiety, it never put the symptom at the center of psychiatric disorders. Perhaps the figure who most advanced the idea that anxiety deserved preeminence was Sigmund Freud, who famously regarded anxiety as an enigma "whose complete solution would cast a flood of light upon psychic life."[66] Much of Freud's approach to neurosis has not withstood scientific scrutiny, and it is tempting to disregard his thoughts on anxiety just as much as his thoughts on, for instance, the oedipal complex.[67] Yet Freud's views of anxiety were, in many ways, prescient. In several ways, he helped pave the way for the contemporary view of anxiety disorders. He succeeded in elevating the significance of anxiety as a symptom, specifying why anxiety should be under the purview of psychiatry, and advancing the idea that anxiety was shaped in significant ways by the environment.

Like his immediate predecessors, Freud focused considerable effort on unpacking the idea of "nervousness" and separating it from related experiences, including especially neurasthenia. In a statement published in 1894, well before his more well-known work was published, Freud argued for focusing on anxiety, doing so on the basis of what he regarded as anxiety's unique character and specific causes.[68] The symptoms he most wished to extract from the concept of neurasthenia were those associated with *anxiety neurosis*, a hallmark of "genuine" or "proper" neurasthenia.[69] He characterized anxiety neurosis by its symptoms, including general irritability, anxious expectation, and, short of chronic anxiety, a tendency toward anxiety attacks.[70] Freud also listed assorted somatic symptoms, including sweating, respiratory disturbance, and arrhythmia. All these sound like symptoms of neurasthenia, though unlike Beard, Freud regarded these symptoms as secondary to anxiety. In other contexts, he was even stronger on this point, arguing that anxiety was the root of other psychological symptoms. For instance, he regarded anxious expectation as the "nuclear symptom," one that could latch itself indiscriminately to "any suitable ideational content."[71] In the same vein, he positioned anxiety near the center of other disorders by arguing that anxieties could compound, as when, for instance, an already anxious woman gained additional symptoms, spanning other types of disorders, when yet another stressor appeared in her marriage.[72] For Freud, anxiety represented a kind of energy, sometimes discharged in a healthy fashion, and sometimes repressed, though providing the fuel for other kinds of affective and somatic symptoms.[73]

Although Freud recognized the role of anxiety in the onset of other disorders, he was more ecumenical regarding the origins of anxiety than many of his contemporaries. He distanced himself, for instance, from the more purely biological models of hysteria. He also recognized the quotidian dimensions of anxiety, eventually moving away from his idea that anxiety was an expression of incomplete repression. In early work Freud famously argued that repressed sexual energy was the root of anxiety—involving sexual frustration, the stress of sexual debut, abstinence, masturbation, and so on—but in later work he considered the role of trauma more generally.[74] Later still he moved away from trauma to focus on more mundane fears, opening up the causes of anxiety even more. For instance, he eventually argued that separation anxiety in children was not the result of birth trauma, as his student Otto Rank had argued, but rather a reflection of the unusual dependence of human infants on their caregivers. In addition, Freud focused less on the repressed or inadequate discharge of sexual energies and more on the many ways in which individuals reacted to dangerous or threatening situations.[75] At the same time, Freud came to regard anxiety as mundane, in the sense that anyone could experience it when the environment overwhelmed the capacity to cope. In this framing, anxiety involved a feeling of helplessness as much as fear. Whereas in earlier work anxiety was largely retrospective, in the sense that it reflected past traumas that forced their way into present consciousness, in later work anxiety was more forward looking, in the sense that it involved potentially threatening circumstances.

Freud's followers moved even further in this direction, locating the sources of anxiety in psychosocial and environmental influences, many of which could be construed as threatening.[76] Movements along these lines did much to secure the idea that anxiety was a social condition, endemic to modern life. In *The Neurotic Personality of Our Time*, for instance, Karen Horney put social and economic considerations front and center.[77] Although she identified the significance of childhood in shaping adult anxiety, she pinpointed the inability of families to provide sufficient caring as the cause of anxiety. She also identified the specific dilemmas facing American women, who lacked the kinds of opportunities that would allow them to pursue meaningful activities outside the home. American psychiatrist Harry Stack Sullivan advanced Freud's ideas in a similar fashion, in his case setting the stage for a focus on interpersonal dynamics.[78] Like Horney, Sullivan saw anxiety as rooted in early interpersonal experiences, especially inconsistent relationships. Over the life course, individuals develop interpersonal models in interaction with others, such that secure relationships early in life lead to secure relationships in adulthood, though anxious relationships led to the opposite.[79]

This expansion of the study of anxiety along social, political, and cultural dimensions was hardly limited to Freud and neo-Freudians. It was part of a more general trend in the sciences. From the end of World War II to the 1970s, there was a broadly interdisciplinary period across the social sciences, characterized by a focus on the social and cultural underpinnings of personal experiences.[80] A mode of explanation had captured the zeitgeist, reflected in the development of social psychology. During this time, Samuel Stouffer published the widely influential *The American Soldier: Studies in Social Psychology in World War II*, part of which was devoted to the combat experiences that produced psychological distress in returning soldiers.[81] Social psychology was not limited to explaining the experiences of soldiers. This was also the era that produced *The Lonely Crowd* and *The Organization Man*, books that put social arrangements and social problems front and center in explaining psychological difficulties.[82] In all these works, anxiety was featured prominently, in part because anxiety and the approach of social psychology went hand in hand: the rise of a social approach to the study of psychology was firmly rooted in trying to explain the apparent rise in anxiety specifically, as had become clear in the 1950s.

The intellectual character of the era was perhaps best depicted in Rollo May's *The Meaning of Anxiety*, published in 1950.[83] May's thoughts on the causes of anxiety were not so different from other scholars writing at the time. Indeed, he found the causes of pervasive anxiety "obvious," including "the threats of war, of the uncontrolled atom bomb, and of radical political and economic upheavals," as well as personal sources, such as "inner confusion, psychological disorientation, and uncertainty with respect to values and acceptable standards of conduct."[84] What was perhaps more unique about May's analysis was his contention that midcentury America was different from earlier eras in the way that anxiety had become more explicit, more codified, and clearer to ascertain. Whereas earlier eras might have contained "covert" anxiety—perhaps even the kind that was buried under the mix of symptoms in neurasthenia—midcentury American anxiety presented a more overt condition, apparent in popular media, literature, science, and news reports.[85] Americans talked about anxiety in a different way, adopting the general language of nerves. A new era was forming.

NERVES AND THE TRANSITION TO TWENTY-FIRST-CENTURY ANXIETY

The idea of "nerves," and in particular of a "nervous breakdown," provides a bridge between neurasthenia and twenty-first-century anxiety disorders. In the middle of the twentieth century, nerve problems were common: patients and clinicians used the term "nervous breakdown" with regularity and pharmaceuticals were used widely to treat the problem. The term is still used today, though in professional settings it has been supplanted by the formal nomenclature of the *DSM*. It is useful to revisit the middle of the twentieth century, though, to see how the public and medical professionals began to grapple with the medical treatment of worries and troubles. In many ways, the concept of nervous problems is not so distinct from the concept of neurasthenia.[86] Like neurasthenia, nervous problems involved physiological manifestations of distress, including fatigue and other somatic symptoms. A nervous breakdown also involved a host of psychological symptoms, including anxiety, but also mild depression and obsessions. When Americans were concerned about their mental health, they adopted the language of nerves to convey either the depletion of mental reserves or the energy of an overagitated state. And like neurasthenia, the nervous breakdown—the most extreme manifestation of a crisis of nerves—eventually faded from clinical relevance as its diagnostic value became suspect. Yet the backlash against problems with nerves was different from the backlash against neurasthenia. And a big difference between the eras was in how the two problems were treated. Although perhaps crude by today's standards, the pharmaceuticals available for the treatment of anxiety in the mid-twentieth century were more plainly effective than the treatments deployed in the nineteenth century. Pharmaceuticals were also prescribed widely, well beyond the offices of specialists. When presented with a viable treatment, the public had to grapple with questions about the meaning and significance of anxiety in a way they perhaps did not have to before: with the question of the severity of anxiety as a medical disorder; with the question of whether anxiety was worthy of treatment; with the question of what it means to be a consumer of anxiolytic drugs; with the question of what an ambitious and successful person ought to feel; and with the question of how anxiety's causes, including the ordinary difficulties of work and family, may or may not be relevant to thinking about anxiety as a medical condition. Of course, the public still struggles with these questions, but the types of debate surrounding the idea of a nervous breakdown were different from what had come before. And some of the answers to these questions hinged on thinking about different kinds of anxiety, some warranting more attention than others.

The rise of nerves as a medical condition was driven both by the availability of pharmaceutical treatments and patient-level demand for those treatments. During the 1950s pharmaceutical companies developed the first mass-marketed anxiolytic drugs, starting with minor tranquilizers, the most popular of which was Miltown.[87] Not unlike prescription psychiatric medications today, general practitioners wrote the bulk of prescriptions for Miltown.[88] Other medications soon followed, including Librium and Valium, both of which were less sedating than Miltown, though also more powerful. These, too, were successful, and as before, general practitioners wrote the bulk of the prescriptions.

Part of the demand for anxiolytics surely reflected that the 1950s were, in fact, an uneasy time. But if the 1950s were especially anxious, it was a particular kind of anxiety, one that, at least in the short term, lent itself to a pharmaceutical approach. Incomes rose in the 1950s, alleviating some financial concerns and reducing material deprivation. The average employee could expect a steady rise in income over tenure with an employer. But a rising standard of living also coincided with the rise of a more consumerist culture, increasing the demand for luxury goods and driving some consumers further into debt.[89] In this context, anxiety had mixed connotations. Andrea Tone documents in detail the meaning of anxiety during this period, showing how anxiety was simultaneously interpreted as a medically credible sign of internal tension and a sign of ambition and determination, echoing the type of refinement noted by Beard nearly a century before.[90] In no small measure, a nervous breakdown signaled the achievements of the person suffering from it rather than a failure to cope. Consistent with this, some of the earliest proponents of Miltown were celebrities and prominent cultural figures who described the pill as both glamorous and routine. Their enthusiasm for the drug walked a careful line between regarding anxiety as a bona fide medical condition worthy of specific treatment and regarding Miltown as valuable quite apart from the presence of any psychiatric disorder. For proponents, tranquilizers were both a medical necessity and a means of self-improvement, entirely consistent with meeting the demands of a modern life.[91] Most prescriptions for Miltown at the time were not associated with an identifiable psychiatric disorder.[92]

The scientific study of anxiety blossomed during the same period, and scientists also had a difficult time characterizing anxiety vis-à-vis illness, casting it as a mix of the medical and the personal and struggling to interpret its relationship with social standing. In *Social Class and Mental Illness: A Community Study*, August Hollingshead and Fredrick Redlich concluded that anxiety was not a problem confined to the upper class.[93] In fact, they found that rates of mental illness were generally greater within the lower class, even if members of the upper class sought treatment more frequently. Yet the idea that anxiety reflected ambition was widespread at the time, and it affected how Hollingshead and Redlich interpreted their results. The idea surfaced, for instance, in their discussion of what kinds of disorders the lower class suffered from. Adopting a framework that was not atypical for the time, Hollingshead and Redlich divided psychiatric disorders into two types: neuroses and psychoses. They further divided neuroses into several subtypes: antisocial and immaturity reactions; character neuroses; phobic and anxiety reactions; depressive reactions; obsessive-compulsive reactions; psychosomatic reactions; and hysterical reactions.[94] With this division, Hollingshead and Redlich were able to explain the greater prevalence of anxiety among the lower class while retaining the implication that anxiety reflected ambition and success. In their interpretation, specific types of anxiety were evident in specific social classes: whereas antisocial and immaturity reactions were more common among the lower class, character neuroses were more common among the upper class. Differences among these subtypes were stark, as Hollingshead and Redlich were keen to demonstrate. Antisocial and immaturity reactions were characterized by acting out and the inability to maintain "adult emotional balance and independence."[95] In the extreme, reactions of this sort were encompassing of an entire disposition, involving, among other things, "infantile personalities" and "individuals who are inadequate socially and emotionally."[96] Many of those suffering from these reactions lacked insight into their conditions and were "relatively unaware of their problems."[97] Character neuroses, meanwhile, involved a mix of milder symptoms, and Hollingshead and Redlich further softened the description by claiming difficulty in identifying any sort of typical pattern. According to their description, patients with character neuroses did not seem to suffer from any single type of reaction, instead exhibiting "mixed symptoms" of "relatively mild character" and "some behavioral disturbances."[98] Differences of this sort were accentuated by differences in how the assorted disorders responded to treatment, once again premised on the amount of self-awareness a patient showed. Whereas patients in the upper class demonstrated a better knowledge of psychotherapy and were better able to accept treatment, patients in the lower class "remained so upset that real participation in exploratory psychotherapy was never possible."[99] To the extent that lower-class patients accepted treatment, they did so in entirely passive ways. They accepted treatments that had "no meaning to them" and were "unable to understand that their troubles [were] not physical illnesses."[100] The concept of anxiety is often multivalent, but subtypes of this sort made the work of interpretation easier, allowing scientists to separate real disorder from poor character.

Other research reinforced the idea that, even if anxiety was ubiquitous in midcentury America, some kinds of anxiety carried entirely different connotations. In *The Meaning of Anxiety*, Rollo May argued that much of the anxiety found in the upper and middle class reflected a gap between their ambitions and circumstances, in this case not limited to material aspirations. The predominant cause of anxiety reflected "the needs of men in our society to appear strong, independent, and triumphant in the competitive struggle," a struggle that grows more acute as people move into adulthood.[101] The gap between aspiration and circumstance was, according to May, especially pronounced in the middle class, whose standards were higher than those of the lower class but not especially easy to realize.[102] Whereas the middle class might struggle with feeling thwarted, within the lower class "there was no cleavage, no contradiction between expectation and reality."[103]

Following a steady ascent in popularity, the use of anxiety drugs eventually declined. Much of this decline reflected growing awareness of the potential for abuse, though this concern was more powerful when coupled with the critique that anxiolytics were merely "lifestyle drugs," of little clinical value.[104] Anxiolytics ultimately fell out of favor not because they were harmful or addictive, but rather because they were being used to treat something that was not regarded as a genuine illness or, at least, was regarded as a problem whose resolution lay elsewhere. In 1957, the Committee on Public Health of the New York Academy of Medicine published a report on the use of tranquilizers.[105] The short but critical report was sweeping in its conclusions. It asked, rhetorically, whether it was necessary to have a drug "for every mood or occasion" and counterpoised the "exceedingly useful" role of tranquilizers in custodial settings against their role in "relief from anxiety and tension."[106] In support of the idea that anxiety did not represent an appropriate pharmaceutical target, the report highlighted the unusual frequency of tranquilizer use "among persons in certain occupations," especially those involving public appearances, including "toastmasters," as well occupations involving "tension" and "excitement," including journalism and advertising.[107] Professionals in certain occupations were not the only culprits in the rise of tranquilizers. The report also highlighted the "tendency among some persons to regard more and more of life's situations as emergencies."[108] Latent in much of the report's discussion was the idea that anxiety existed on a spectrum and that determining the level at which anxiety could properly be considered a disorder was difficult. Yet, these professed difficulties aside, the report struggled little with the question of appropriate use. It reported pervasive misuse of tranquilizers among patients and "expansive, extravagant and indiscriminate" claims regarding indications in materials sent to physicians.[109]

Criticisms of this sort resonated, and skeptics of the pharmaceutical treatment of anxiety went to great lengths to speak beyond the appropriateness of the drugs themselves to the nature of anxiety itself. For some critics, anxiety was not merely a natural if unpleasant condition—for them, the major achievements of society could not have been possible without some degree of anxiety to motivate breakthroughs.[110] Not unrelated to debate about whether anxiety could ever truly be an illness was the Food and Drug Administration's growing insistence that pharmaceuticals be used only in the treatment of specific conditions. At the time, the use of tranquilizers did not fit well within this framework, both because psychiatry had yet to fully develop the sort of diagnostic instruments that would lend credibility to the claim of specific disorders and because it was already quite clear that tranquilizers were being used to treat risk, especially stress and tension, rather than disease.

It was not long before a more attractive target came along. Major depression provided a cleaner therapeutic target with a more compelling clinical remit. As a state, depression occasioned fewer debates about its value to society. It was more widely accepted as disabling and undesirable. Changes in the formal classification of psychiatric disorders further elevated the significance of depression over anxiety. The era of nerves, tension, and the nervous breakdown was giving way to the era of major depression.

THE RISE OF MAJOR DEPRESSION

In the latter half of the twentieth century, major depression became the signature psychiatric disorder.[111] Whereas people once discussed nerves and tension, by the late 1980s they were discussing sadness and depression and seeking medical treatments for major depressive disorder rather than nervous breakdowns. Prescribing patterns were consistent with this switch. Between 1980 and 1989, antianxiety drugs still accounted for the largest share of physician visits involving psychiatric medications, exceeding, for instance, visits involving antidepressants, antipsychotics, stimulants, and lithium.[112] Since then, the share of visits involving antianxiety drugs steadily declined, while the share involving antidepressant drugs increased. Over a decade beginning in the early 1990s the use of antidepressants increased more than fourfold.[113] Between 1996 and 2001, the number of users of antianxiety medications increased from 5.5 million to 6.4 million, but the number of antidepressant users increased far more, from 7.9 million to 15.4 million.[114] Of the 23 million users of psychiatric medications in 2001, over 60 percent were using antidepressants. In 2005, just over one in ten Americans over the age of five used an antidepressant.[115]

In many ways, the ascent of depression—especially on the heels of the nervous breakdown—is remarkable. The symptoms of depression would not, of course, be foreign to people in the 1950s, any more than they are to people in the twenty-first century. Both neurasthenia and the nervous breakdown include elements of depression. Yet before the rise of depression as a disorder, anxiety did, in fact, stand out in the sea of symptoms, even to professionals. A study of the clinical records of those receiving psychiatric services in the middle of the twentieth century found far more references to anxiety than depression, to the point that depression barely seemed to appear at all.[116] To the extent that depression was included as a diagnosis, it was usually regarded as a rare disorder, more akin to psychosis than to everyday distress.

A simple way to account for this shift is in terms of a change in treatment rather than a change in prevalence. Perhaps the most significant development during this period was the promulgation of selective serotonin reuptake inhibitors (SSRIs), including, most prominently, Prozac. The widespread availability of a new treatment played a role in shifting depression from being regarded as a rare and not especially well-treated condition to a serious though manageable disorder.[117] To be sure, SSRIs are not indicated only for major depression. They are indicated for both mood and anxiety disorders, and, allowing for off-label use, could be used as a sort of catchall medication for emotional suffering. Nonetheless, SSRIs were billed primarily for their therapeutic effects on mood disorders and, with some understanding of SSRIs' clinical indications gleaned from pharmaceutical advertising, patients themselves began to seek SSRIs for depression rather than for other conditions. The rise of SSRIs was swift. Prozac was introduced in 1986. By 2001 the number of annual physician visits for depression increased from 14.4 million to 24.5 million, with a parallel increase in the therapeutic dominance of SSRIs relative to other treatments.[118]

The rise of depression was also fostered by the introduction of formal diagnostic criteria that created better ways to identify major depression while simultaneously complicating the identification of anxiety disorders. The watershed moment in the classification of psychiatric disorders was the publication of the third edition of the *Diagnostic and Statistical Manual of Mental Disorders* (*DSM-III*) in 1980.[119] *DSM-III* achieved many things, but above all it provided clinicians and scientists with more specific diagnostic criteria for identifying disorders. None of the previous editions of the manual had provided the symptomatic detail of *DSM-III* or the precise rules for determining when a set of symptoms constituted a disorder. The publication of *DSM-III* was enormously consequential. It fostered greater reliability in diagnostic practices among mental health professionals. It also spurred a wave of new research on psychiatric disorders, allowing researchers to speak a common language and identify similar cases for purposes of research. And it changed how the public talked about psychiatric disorders, fostering a more formal lexicon of distress. But not all disorders fared equally well in this process. Even as *DSM-III* helped to better identify major depression, it complicated the identification of anxiety disorders, creating a sharp fissure between the two types of disorders and, at least implicitly, downplaying the significance of anxiety. It did so in several ways. For one, *DSM-III* in effect eliminated the implication that anxiety could be the root of other disorders. This represented a sharp break from the edition immediately preceding it, not to mention from how anxiety was viewed by many in the field of psychiatry. Anxiety was central across much of *DSM-II*. What would later become anxiety disorders were categorized in *DSM-II* as neuroses, for which anxiety was the chief characteristic.[120] Even among psychiatric disorders fundamentally involving depressed mood, anxiety was central in *DSM-II*. In the case of involutional melancholia, for instance, melancholia was accompanied by "worry, anxiety, agitation, and severe insomnia."[121] *DSM-II* further elevated the relevance of anxiety by stipulating that anxiety need not be consciously expressed to be a symptom. Although anxiety certainly could be "felt and expressed directly" to a professional, the manual also allowed that anxiety could be controlled "unconsciously and automatically" by mechanisms such as conversion and displacement, concepts drawn from psychoanalysis.[122] *DSM-II* further allowed that anxiety need not lead to the "gross distortion or misinterpretation of external reality" to be significant, as was the case with psychoses.[123]

Other details in *DSM-III* and subsequent editions, though finer and seeming less consequential, further helped to downplay anxiety. The diagnostic criteria for mood and anxiety disorders, for instance, differ considerably in terms of their duration. The diagnostic criteria for a major depressive episode, for instance, require that the symptoms be present during a two-week period.[124] This definition captures those suffering from chronic depression, but it also casts major depression as potentially episodic. By contrast, the diagnostic criteria for anxiety disorders generally require a longer duration. This duration requirement is either expressed in terms of a specific window of time that is longer than that defined for major depression or more generally in terms of requiring "persistent" fears.[125] Both specific and social phobias require a duration of at least six months for those under the age of eighteen, and for those eighteen and older, the symptoms must be persistent. Generalized anxiety disorder requires six months of symptoms experienced "more days than not," with no age qualification.[126] The diagnostic criteria for some anxiety disorders refer to how frequently anxiety occurs following exposure to the feared situation or object, requiring consistency in the connection. In social phobia, for instance, the social situation should "almost invariably" provoke anxiety.[127] To be sure, the specifics and value of these criteria are debatable. Depending on the disorder, there could be value in criteria that have a shorter or longer time frame, and, indeed, it might be better to demand more of anxiety than depression. One could argue, for instance, that even a short episode of depression is consequential for the lives of those suffering from it, especially with the possibility of self-harm. Yet one could also argue that sudden and unanticipated anxiety is consequential, as in a panic attack. Nonetheless, these differences in criteria effectively identify different things and increase the number of people potentially suffering from depression relative to anxiety disorders. The diagnostic criteria for major depression will effectively include episodes of depression brought on by transitory circumstances, whereas the diagnostic criteria for anxiety disorders will capture more enduring traits, seemingly less tied to current circumstances. Allan Horwitz and Jerome Wakefield focus on this point in arguing why depression became the signature psychiatric disorder in the United States not long after the publication of *DSM-III*.[128] The diagnostic criteria in *DSM-III* allowed major depression to better absorb the kinds of experiences that drove people to seek mental health services. Following a stressful life event, an individual might meet the diagnostic criteria for an episode of major depression, even as that person fell short of the threshold for an anxiety disorder. In this way, the lens of *DSM-III* tilted the clinical manifestation of stress toward mood disorders, thereby priming the market for SSRIs like Prozac. SSRIs pushed the trend further along.

DSM-III also undercut anxiety disorders by creating a more variegated set of targets. There are a remarkable variety of anxiety disorders, including specific phobias, social phobias, panic attack disorder, and generalized anxiety disorder. These disorders not only differ in their symptoms but also in their subjects. Those who meet the diagnostic criteria for a social phobia, for instance, fear social encounters. The fears of those who meet the diagnostic criteria for a specific phobia, meanwhile, fall into different subtypes, including an animal type, a natural environment type, a blood-injection-injury type, and a situational type (which includes things such as a fear of flying, enclosed places, tunnels, bridges, and so on). To be sure, there exist a variety of mood disorders, too. The category of mood disorders includes major depressive disorder, dysthymic disorder, and bipolar disorder. Yet relative to the set of anxiety disorders, the set of mood disorders in the *DSM* is considerably less diverse in its content. For one, unlike in anxiety disorders, the source of the depressed mood is not an element in the diagnosis of mood disorders. Furthermore, across the different mood disorders, the disturbance in mood has a similar character, involving depression, an inability to experience pleasure, or a loss of interest or pleasure. Moreover, as a single diagnosis, major depression effectively consolidates the entire category of mood disorders, serving as an appropriate synecdoche for scientific and clinical research on moods. No other mood disorder consumes as much attention as major depression.[129] And major depression itself was the consolidation of several different subtypes of depression.[130] Before *DSM-III*, psychiatrists drew distinctions between endogenous depression, exogenous depression, and neurotic depression.[131] To the extent that these distinctions are apparent today, they appear only as historical artifacts. By 2000, citations to major depression exceeded citations to its nearest competing mood disorder, dysthymia, by a factor of more than seven to one.[132] Not surprisingly, diagnoses that were eliminated from the *DSM* altogether were left even further behind. Citations to major depression exceed those to endogenous depression, for instance, by a factor of more than sixty to one.[133]

The category of anxiety disorders is perhaps best represented by generalized anxiety disorder (GAD), although the category is not represented by GAD quite as well as major depression represents mood disorders. GAD is characterized by worrying excessively and indiscriminately about a variety of things. Yet within its category, GAD is nowhere near as dominant as major depression. In *DSM-III*, GAD was little more than a residual category for anxiety. The disorder was effectively diagnosed by exclusion: individuals could only be diagnosed with GAD if they did not meet the diagnostic criteria for another anxiety or affective disorder. Defined in this fashion, the diagnosis did not foster a good deal of reliability, and tests of agreement between two independent interviewers found especially low agreement for a diagnosis of GAD relative to other disorders. Indeed, of the major mood and anxiety disorders, GAD showed the lowest overall interrater agreement.[134] Recognizing the inadequacy of the *DSM-III*'s criteria for GAD, the authors of *DSM-III-R*—a significant revision of *DSM-III*—defined the disorder in a more positive fashion, in terms of the presence of symptoms rather than their absence.[135] But in doing so, they ironically brought to the fore even more elementary problems with categorizing anxiety. In *DSM-III-R*, they designated the primary symptom of GAD as apprehensive expectation, defined as unrealistic or excessive worry. Apprehensive expectation was not included in the other anxiety disorders, and while included in the *DSM-III* criteria, it was only one of four symptoms, of which three were required for a diagnosis. In addition, the authors of *DSM-III-R* increased the threshold for the disorder. They did so in several ways: they increased the duration criteria from one month to six, they added that a minimum number of somatic symptoms must also be present, and they added that the worry must occur over two or more areas. Although the *DSM-III-R* revision increased the reliability of the diagnosis, it laid bare problems that had long plagued the entire category of anxiety disorders. Among other things, for instance, it is difficult to count worries. In attempting to specify what potential areas of worry might be considered, the criteria listed two examples: worry about potential misfortune for one's child and financial problems.[136] It is difficult, however, to neatly place worries into bins of this sort. It is certainly possibly to have two or more separate worries about finances, including losing one's job and losing one's house. When people worry about their children, they rarely worry only about their physical safety. Subsequent research has further complicated the issue by questioning not just how to count worries but the appropriate scope of a worry. Research has shown that the number of worries and even the types of worry are not strongly predictive of the severity of a disorder.[137]

Subsequent attempts to clarify these issues have not been especially useful and, as a group, anxiety disorders suffer from a lack of diagnostic consensus. The *DSM* is the dominant diagnostic tool for scientific research, but it is not the only one. The *International Classification of Diseases* (*ICD*) provides its own diagnostic criteria.[138] Over the years, the *DSM* and *ICD* have tried to articulate a common view of psychiatric disorders, but these efforts have not been entirely successful. The two manuals articulate highly disparate views of anxiety. The *DSM* relies on the concept of "excessive" worry, whereas the *ICD* does not; the *DSM* identifies more chronic disorders, whereas the *ICD* identifies more acute disorders; and the *ICD* uses the concept of "free-floating" anxiety, whereas the *DSM* considers anxiety over multiple domains.[139] All told, these differences are not as slight as they might appear to be. With these differences, the two manuals identify very different disorders, even if they yield approximately the same overall prevalence of anxiety.[140] If psychiatry has largely hit the mark with respect to major depression, it has failed to resolve the phenomenology of anxiety, at least in the *DSM*. Disentangling anxiety and depression would require considerably more scientific research, as the next chapter discusses.

Chapter Three

THE EVOLVING SCIENCE OF ANXIETY AND DEPRESSION

Understanding the place of anxiety in the twenty-first century requires an understanding of how the study of anxiety has evolved. Moreover, it requires an understanding of how the science of anxiety has gradually separated anxiety from other emotions and elevated its significance. As a dimension of mental health, anxiety has historically been liminal, as the previous chapter attempted to show. Anxiety has at least been an aspect of mental health, but it has often been superseded or obscured by other symptoms. Nervousness can emerge as the sine qua non of mental dysfunction, especially in times of rapid social change, only to be cast aside in favor of other symptoms or disorders. The idea of a nervous breakdown can gain widespread cultural resonance, only to fall out of favor and be replaced by major depression as new treatments for mood disorders emerge. Anxiety can be regarded as especially destructive of emotional well-being, even as it is understood as necessary for a well-functioning person.

The liminal status of anxiety is at least partly attributable to the fact that anxiety is, in fact, closely related to other symptoms. The transition from talking about a nervous breakdown to talking about major depression was facilitated, in part, by the strong correlation between depression and anxiety. To a fault, Beard's concept of neurasthenia included a wide variety of symptoms, but in fact, the more modern concept of psychological distress is broad as well and involves multiple systems and symptoms, almost always including both depression and anxiety.

Up to this point, I have mostly discussed the *concept* of anxiety relative to other symptoms, though there is now a strong empirical science surrounding anxiety, fear, and worry. Understanding anxiety in the twenty-first century requires understanding how science has approached the difference between anxiety and other symptoms, the ways in which it has occasionally obliterated the distinction, and the ways in which it is now providing an empirical and conceptual foundation for appreciating anxiety as important in its own right. This foundation is important for, among other things, thinking about how anxiety is treated in clinical settings. Although the ascent of major depression as a disorder was facilitated by the ability of the category to absorb people suffering from a variety of other problems, there is abundant evidence that anxiety and depression differ in ways that are important, whether with respect to their phenomenology, their evolutionary origins, their determinants, or their consequences. A review of the contemporary science of psychiatric disorders—in which anxiety can be measured, cases counted, and causes evaluated—helps to illustrate why anxiety is now seen as unique. With a firmer scientific understanding of anxiety, contemporary wrangling over the distinction between anxiety and depression is different from the kind of discussions that surrounded neurasthenia, nervous breakdowns, and the nature of mood and anxiety disorders in *DSM-III*. And it provides a basis for thinking of anxiety as an especially significant disorder in the twenty-first century.

INTERPRETING COMORBIDITY BETWEEN ANXIETY AND DEPRESSION

Anxiety and depression are highly comorbid: a case of one disorder is likely to involve a case of the other. More than 50 percent of those who report a lifetime major depressive disorder have also experienced a lifetime anxiety disorder.[1] The converse is true as well: among those with generalized anxiety disorder, for instance, between 58 percent and 70 percent have also experienced a major depressive disorder.[2] The overlap at the level of symptoms is higher still: among patients with either major or bipolar depression, the vast majority also report some worry, even if few report worry sufficient to meet the diagnostic threshold for a phobia.[3] The connection between anxiety and depression is even deeper from the standpoint of timing: about a third of all lifetime co-occurring episodes of major depression and generalized anxiety disorder occur among those for whom the disorders started in the same year.[4] In most cases where the two disorders are present simultaneously, the anxiety disorder comes first.

The basic facts of comorbidity between anxiety and depression are well established, but how one interprets them is more controversial. The push and pull between different interpretations—whether to regard the two disorders as entirely separate, or whether to regard one as the primary disorder, or whether to create an entirely new disorder based on the presence of both—provides the crux for understanding how the scientific appreciation of anxiety has evolved. One way to interpret comorbidity is that it is false, in the sense that the two disorders are essentially the same and therefore do not represent the presence of two unique disorders.[5] Anxiety and mood disorders do, in fact, share some symptoms, including sleep disturbance, fatigue, and difficulty concentrating.[6] This alone will increase comorbidity. Furthermore, when psychiatric disorders are relatively mild, anxiety and depression are difficult to disentangle, because they present themselves in similar ways, a fact that has bedeviled disorders like neurasthenia.[7] But the concept of comorbidity presupposes a distinction. The *DSM* itself encourages a distinction by creating separate disorders—with a description of a "mixed" episode relegated to an appendix—though the *DSM* hardly does all the work in this regard.[8] The distinction between the two has some simple face validity. Anxiety and depression are different emotions, and they certainly feel different to those who experience them, in a way that is not the same for, say, depression and melancholia.

Psychiatrists, too, appreciate the difference between anxiety and depression, though in clinical practice the relationship between the two is occasionally obviated by interpreting anxiety as inferior. There are, in fact, clinically valid reasons to emphasize one disorder over the other. For one, anxiety tends to be less disabling than depression. Psychiatric researchers routinely divide psychiatric disorders into three categories—serious, moderate, and mild—based on a disorder's consequences. For instance, serious disorders involve, among other things, a suicide attempt and serious work impairment. Moderate disorders, by contrast, involve suicide ideation without an attempt and milder forms of work impairment. Divided in this

fashion, anxiety disorders are still the most prevalent category of psychiatric disorders, though as a category they are also mild: 44 percent of anxiety
disorders are considered mild and only 23 percent are considered serious.[9]
Among mood disorders, this ratio is very different: 45 percent are considered serious and only 15 percent are considered mild. Furthermore, some
of the most common anxiety disorders are especially mild. The single most
prevalent anxiety disorder is specific phobia, but nearly half of all cases
of specific phobia are mild. There are a variety of ways to account for the
relatively mild severity of anxiety disorders, but a likely explanation is the
ease with which worry can be averted. In the case of specific phobias, for
instance, people may be able to prevent the most severe consequences of
the disorder simply by avoiding the thing they fear the most.[10] Recognizing that anxiety disorders are milder than mood disorders has implications
for treatment. In particular, the idea can lead clinicians to treat depression first when treating comorbid cases, under the assumption that treating
depression will resolve most of the disability a patient is experiencing. The
instinct to treat depression is made even stronger when there is a well-
established and popular pharmaceutical treatment for the disorder, as in
the case of SSRIs like Prozac.

If anxiety is not subsumed outright, it is often interpreted merely as a
marker for the severity of depression and is therefore seen as a diagnostic
modifier but not a diagnosis in its own right. Along these lines, a long-
standing proposal is to consider *anxious depression* as a different kind of
depression, if not a different kind of anxiety.[11] As the concept is usually articulated, anxious depression is a form of depression that includes symptoms
associated with anxiety, such as agitation, obsessive-compulsive behavior,
and gastrointestinal distress. Here, too, depression is assigned greater significance. When specific diagnostic criteria for anxious depression have
been proposed, they usually require the presence of major depression but
not the presence of an anxiety disorder. Anxious depression remains, then,
a type of depression.

Another way to interpret comorbidity is to use it as a mandate to con-
struct a new kind of disorder altogether. The premise of such proposals
is that the combination of anxiety and depression is qualitatively different from either of its components. Peter Tyrer, for instance, has proposed
cothymia as a single diagnosis for mixed anxiety and depression.[12] This
disorder, in effect, would obliterate the distinction between the two but

recognize that the combination of anxiety and depression is more than the sum of its parts. There is some evidence in support of cothymia as a valid diagnosis, including evidence that it involves a unique combination of genetic risk factors not characteristic of anxiety or depression and, potentially, strong correlations with some dimensions of personality, such as neuroticism.[13] Furthermore, the co-occurrence of anxiety and depression tends to lead to significantly worse outcomes than either anxiety or depression on its own, including more persistent cases.[14]

Cothymia is not the only proposal to blend the two. A related proposal posits *mixed anxiety and depression*, wherein a patient does not meet the diagnostic criteria for either specific disorder but has the presence of both kinds of symptoms at a subclinical level.[15] Of all the proposed diagnoses blending anxiety and depression, mixed anxiety and depression has perhaps been the most successful, at least in attracting serious consideration. Yet the success of the proposal has also revealed exactly how hesitant researchers are to blend anxiety and depression. The *ICD*, for instance, includes language for identifying a "mixed" episode, but is not forthright about the matter.[16] It does include specific diagnostic criteria for a mixed episode, but the text ultimately falls back on considering the two disorders separately. In particular, the *ICD* stipulates that a mixed episode can be used "when symptoms of anxiety and depression are both present, but neither is clearly predominant, and neither type of symptom is present to the extent that justifies a diagnosis if considered separately."[17] The *ICD* also stipulates that if both disorders are present and severe enough on their own, then both diagnoses should be used.

In fact, uncertainty surrounding the concept of mixed anxiety and depression remains, in large part because of the implication that anxiety is less than depression. The most recent revision of the *DSM*—moving from *DSM-IV* to *DSM-5*—provided a clarifying moment. The *DSM-IV* contained diagnostic criteria for a mixed anxiety-depressive disorder, though the criteria were presented in an appendix and largely overlooked.[18] *DSM-5* provided an opportunity to revisit the concept and perhaps to promote a mixed diagnosis to the main part of the manual. Neeltje Batelaan and colleagues argued against the inclusion of mixed anxiety-depression.[19] Their skepticism was premised both on the existing empirical evidence regarding the disorder and on concerns about admitting a new diagnostic entity that was very different from those already enshrined in the *DSM*. For one, they argued there was little research on mixed anxiety-depression that clearly established its characteristics and boundaries. Furthermore, they argued that, to the extent that mixed anxiety-depression existed at all, it did not provide much clinical value relative to those disorders that were already included in the *DSM*. Mixed anxiety-depression looked, for instance, much like subthreshold anxiety or subthreshold depression, and these disorders could easily be incorporated into *DSM-5* without having to craft something entirely new. Batelaan and colleagues further questioned the stability of mixed anxiety-depression. In general, the *DSM* prefers to identify chronic disorders rather than transitory states. It is debatable whether the *DSM* succeeds at this task over all its many disorders, though mixed anxiety-depression would seem to be uniquely problematic in this regard. Within a year, about half of patients diagnosed with mixed anxiety-depression go on to develop another disorder, one already formally classified in the *DSM*.[20] Although this observation could be used as an argument for *including* mixed anxiety-depression in *DSM-5* insofar as it suggests some predictive validity for the disorder, its value is undercut by the fact that it does not predict later disorders in a specific fashion. The list of disorders predicted by mixed anxiety-depression is long and disjointed. It includes mood and anxiety disorders, such as major depressive disorder and agoraphobia, but it also includes disorders further afield, such as somatization disorder, hypochondriasis, and alcohol abuse. Furthermore, there is little evidence that mixed anxiety-depression even predicts its own recurrence, something that is true for most other disorders. Among those who test positive for mixed anxiety-depression at one point in time, few test positive for the disorder later on.[21]

THE PHENOMENOLOGY OF ANXIETY AND DEPRESSION

When scientists debate how comorbidity should be interpreted, they are in part debating what they think psychiatric disorders are or ought to be. To insist on chronic disorders, for instance, is to dismiss those that are circumstantial. To regard depression as more significant than anxiety because it is more disabling is to assert that impairment is tantamount to validity. Still, all this scientific and conceptual wrangling begs more elementary questions. How do depression and anxiety differ? And why might these differences be important? On this point, the science is a bit clearer, in part because research regarding fear, anxiety, and worry has developed, in many cases, independent of the *DSM* and all its controversies. Scientists who study worry, for instance, can study worry independent of its relationship with generalized anxiety disorder. By the same token, scientists can study fear apart from its association with specific phobias. Studies focused on emotions provide clear evidence for a distinction between anxiety and depression, not just as different disorders, but as different states, evolved from different mechanisms, represented in different parts of the brain, and entailing different thoughts. The science of emotions has revealed real distinctions between anxiety and depression.

For one, anxiety and depression have different characteristic features.[22] Although it is common to regard the separation of anxiety and mood disorders as artificial from the standpoint of comorbidity, it is not at all unusual to regard them as different from the standpoint of emotions. Fear about the future is different from regret about the past. Worrying about finances feels different from the sense of loss over a layoff, though the two are obviously related. Both anxiety and depression involve negative affect, but those with anxiety and depression attend to different things. Those with anxiety direct their attention toward potential threats, whereas those with depression direct their attention toward negativity.[23] In this vein, Daniel Nettle and Melissa Bateson position anxious and depressed moods on orthogonal dimensions, based on their relationships with reward and punishment.[24] Anxious mood corresponds to a low threshold for responding to punishment—that is, people who are anxious change their focus in the presence of potential threats. Associated with this position is hyperarousal and vigilance. Depressed mood, on the other hand, corresponds to a high threshold for responding to rewards—that is, depressed people are reluctant to engage in potentially rewarding behavior. Associated with this position are pessimism and fatigue. Depression and anxiety can co-occur in this model, though in representing them on different dimensions, Nettle and Bateson argue that they serve different functions and have different levels at which they become problematic.

In a related way, depression and anxiety differ in terms of their cognitive biases. Moods can distort thought, often in powerful ways. Those who suffer from depression, for instance, systematically recall more negative life events. Anxiety involves biases, too, but different ones. Moreover, some evidence indicates that the biases associated with anxiety are simply much stronger than those associated with depression. Those who suffer from anxiety process threats differently from those who do not.[25] The strongest evidence for such a difference between anxiety and depression comes from studies measuring the amount of mental processing individuals devote to certain concepts. Studies of this sort allow for useful precision. They allow scientists to test whether the anxious attend to threats more than the depressed attend to negativity. Various tools for measuring mental processing exist.[26] In the Stroop test, for instance, participants are shown words written in different colors and are asked to name the color while disregarding the word. The speed with which this is done is thought to reflect the amount of cognitive resources allocated to the word. If the word is not significant to the participant, the task is easier, because the word can be readily separated from the color. This test is valuable in part because it is flexible—it can be used to explore a variety of attention-related biases. In the case of psychiatric disorders, the test can be used to explore the biases associated with anxiety and depression separately, because the two disorders are presumed to involve attention to distinct concepts. In the case of anxiety, a bias is indicated by the extent to which those with an anxiety disorder take longer to name the colors of threatening words such as *die*, *fear*, or *infect*. The assumption is that anxious people focus more on threatening words than do non-anxious people. In the case of depression, the stimuli words are different. They are negative but not explicitly threatening, including words such as *rain*, *accident*, or *pain*.[27] In this case, the assumption is that depressed people focus on negative things more than non-depressed people do. Similar tests are available with different tasks and stimuli. In a visual probe task, for instance, participants are presented with two words, one threat related (in the case of an anxiety stimulus) and the other neutral.[28] The words are presented briefly and once they disappear, a dot (or some other object) appears behind one of the words. Participants are then asked to identify the location of the dot as quickly as possible. As with the Stroop test, the assumption is that participants will respond faster when the dot is presented behind a word they attended to more.

Studies of this sort provide evidence that the biases anxious people show toward threatening words are much stronger than the biases depressed people show toward negative words. Part of this imbalance stems from the breadth of the attention processes involved. Whereas anxious people attend to *any* potentially threatening material, and therefore attend to virtually all threatening words, depressed people only attend to negative words that have personal associations.[29] Depression seeks signals that are relevant to the individual, whereas anxiety seeks anything that might be threatening, whether the person has been threatened by it in the past or not. In other words, anxiety is more broadly active in the minds of the anxious than depression is in the minds of the depressed, and as a result, anxious people attend to their environments in ways that tend to confirm that the environment is threatening.[30]

A different sort of bias pertains not to how much anxious people attend to threatening words but to how they interpret other words. The stimuli words used in most experiments are threatening by design: as stimuli they clearly invoke fear, as in the word *die*. Yet anxious people also interpret *ambiguous* stimuli as threatening, perhaps a more significant cognitive bias, as it suggests that people can construe the environment in ways that enhance fear. In one study, participants were asked to respond to sentences that could be interpreted in several ways, depending on the referent.[31] Participants in one version of the study were presented with three related sentences of varying degrees of specificity: "They discussed the priest's convictions" (an ambiguous sentence); "They talked about the clergyman's criminal record" (a disambiguated threatening sentence); or "They talked about the clergyman's strong beliefs" (a disambiguated nonthreatening sentence).[32] Relative to non-anxious participants, anxious participants were much more likely to interpret the first sentence as threatening, because they saw *convictions* in terms of guilt rather than a firm belief.

Processing biases of this sort are sufficiently large that they can skirt conscious awareness and efforts to overcome them.[33] Those whose perceptions are tainted by the bias of anxiety are often unaware of the bias, and even when they are, the bias is difficult to defeat, because it smuggles with it the appearance of reality. Much of what we know about anxiety disorders is premised on what individuals can actively report to a researcher or clinician—that is, reports of anxiety pertain to what individuals are consciously aware of. In studies of specific anxiety disorders, for instance, participants tell a researcher what they worry about most and how worried they are about that topic on average. People know what they fear most. Yet it is increasingly clear that anxious people direct their attention toward threatening information in a rapid, widespread, and automatic fashion, apart from any strategic decision to attend to one risk or another.[34] In other words, anxious people focus on threats before they realize they are doing so. This is important, because it provides evidence that anxiety can affect cognition apart from the conscious experience of anxiety. It also suggests that many environments can appear threating to anxious people, because they find it difficult to envision nonthreatening situations. Furthermore, these biases are not limited to those suffering from anxiety *disorders*. The diagnostic criteria for anxiety disorders are set at a level regarded as clinically significant, though the underlying symptoms of anxiety disorders exist on a spectrum. It is perhaps reasonable to assume that only those who are clinically anxious are subject to a significant bias—that is, their perceptions might be regarded as fully distorted rather than merely tainted—but this is not the case. Milder forms of anxiety can be sufficient to trigger a bias that is not unlike the bias found among those with anxiety disorders.[35] Furthermore, the specific type of anxiety disorder, including the source of the anxiety, plays little role in the strength of the bias. The same sorts of biases are apparent in generalized anxiety disorder, panic disorder, social phobia, and simple phobia. It is also clear that different kinds of stimuli can trigger anxiety. Stroop tests focus on threatening words, but studies employing other stimuli generally find that visual stimuli of natural threats, like pictures of spiders, are generally no more potent than words.

The cognitive nature of anxiety is one reason behavioral therapy can be more effective for anxiety disorders than depression.[36] Although the biases associated with anxiety are automatic and powerful, the cognitive processes associated with anxiety also imply more places to intervene. Whereas depression involves cognitive biases limited mostly to later stages of attention—when individuals construe the information they have—anxiety involves biases in both attention and information processing, including how quickly people attend to threats.[37] Techniques for modifying cognitive biases may work better for anxiety than depression, insofar as preventing anxious people from focusing on threats in the first place effectively prevents a cascade of biases later on. A related explanation for the divergence between anxiety and depression pertains to the motivational dimensions of anxiety. Both anxiety and depression can spur behavior, although anxiety is more powerful in this regard, as it involves more focused attention. Anxiety does two things at once: it leads anxious people to evaluate things as threatening, and it encourages heightened attention to those threatening things. Depression, by contrast, is more imbalanced: it leads depressed people to evaluate things as negative, but it does not lead to more attention being directed toward those negative things. In short, anxious people devote more mental processing to their fears than depressed people devote to the sources of their unhappiness.[38]

THE EVOLUTIONARY FOUNDATIONS OF DEPRESSION AND ANXIETY

A more elementary way to think about the differences between anxiety and depression is to consider the evolutionary forces that shaped them. There is little doubt that both depression and anxiety are at least partly genetic. Twin studies indicate that a significant amount of the variation in depression and anxiety comes from genetic variation in the population.[39] Research has also gone a step further and identified a specific set of genes related to both anxiety and depression.[40] Anxiety and depression clearly have a genetic component.

Yet the evolutionary origins of anxiety and depression are nonetheless puzzling.[41] For one, given the disability associated with psychiatric disorders, it is unclear why any disorder would be conserved over evolutionary history. This is true for anxiety and mood disorders as well, though the two are not exactly equivalent in this regard. An evolutionary case for depression is more complex than for anxiety. Depression would seem to pervasively undermine fitness. Depression is strongly related to disability: it reduces productivity, increases unemployment, and elevates the risk of divorce. Moreover, depression is associated with lower fertility and an increased risk of mortality, which are even more directly related to the evolutionary concept of fitness.[42] To be sure, anxiety involves disability, too, along with a host of biases that reduce fitness by distorting the ability to accurately perceive the environment. Yet there are good reasons evolution should preserve fear and the capacity to identify threats, even when that capacity is faulty. The evolutionary differences between anxiety and depression are important to consider in some detail for at least two reasons. First, differences in their evolutionary dimensions have been an undercurrent to the argument that anxiety is much less significant than depression, especially among those who argue that the *DSM* mislabels otherwise adaptive levels of anxiety as disordered.[43] The idea that anxiety is natural has historically encouraged its secondary status as a symptom. Second, viewing anxiety through an evolutionary lens provides a way for thinking about why the risk for an anxiety disorder might be more widespread than the risk for major depression. Evolution might be one reason humans are more prone to *dysfunctional* anxiety than *dysfunctional* sadness.

The Evolutionary Origins of Depression

One way to understand the adaptive value of depression is to consider the role of emotions as signals for apprehending the environment. Depression involves a lack of motivation and feelings of diminished self-worth, traits that should not be adaptive from the standpoint of procreation or longevity. Indeed, such traits might have been especially disadvantageous when our ancestors had to routinely contend with grave threats in the environment and assert physical dominance in the face of conflict. But another way to understand depression is to consider how it *suppresses* behavior rather than motivates it. Under some circumstances persistence can decrease fitness, as when expending additional energy risks starvation, when further effort on a hopeless task might be better spent on other projects, or when aggressive behavior exposes the individual to even more risk.[44] If depression encourages passivity when it is wise to do so, it could aid fitness. A similar idea applies to the role of depression in social situations. There is value to yielding to others in competitive situations, especially when the competition is likely to be superior.[45] If depression prevents aggression against a likely vanquisher, it can prevent harm. Similarly, if depression signals to others that someone presents no real threat, as when a person cowers in the face of antagonism, it can forestall predation.

Still another evolutionary account of depression focuses on avoiding infection.[46] Accounts of this sort are especially compelling, as they provide an explanation for the full assortment of symptoms associated with depression, something other accounts emphasize as well. For much of human evolution, infectious disease was the leading cause of death. Under these conditions, depression might improve fitness both by preventing infection and by helping the individual fight infection when it occurred. In this regard, the symptoms of depression match the strategy well. Because it diminishes motivation, for instance, depression can lead to the conservation of energy, which helps immune function. Depression also increases isolation, which minimizes social contacts and, therefore, can decrease the risk of infection. And depression decreases sexual activity, which can reduce the risk of contracting a sexually transmitted disease.

Other evolutionary accounts of depression focus less on the disorder's behavioral implications than its cognitive ones. Depression often involves rumination, or focusing on the source, experience, or consequences of one's sadness. Ordinarily rumination leads to further suffering, as people remain focused on the sources of their stress—depressed people do not ruminate on the positive aspects of their lives. The upside of rumination, however, is that it can force the sufferer to actively analyze a complex problem.[47] Solving some problems—especially social ones—requires the sort of sustained and slow cognitive processing that individuals routinely avoid. Depression encourage productive problem solving in at least three ways. It prioritizes the problem over other things the person could attend to (even to the point of obsession); it reduces the attraction of engaging in other activities by, in effect, reducing the amount of pleasure an individual can derive from those activities (as in the case of anhedonia, the inability to experience pleasure); and it diminishes other distractions by inducing lethargy (as in the case of psychomotor retardation).[48]

The Evolutionary Origins of Anxiety

Although a case for the evolutionary origins of depression can be made, the evolutionary case for anxiety is perhaps more straightforward, a fact appreciated by Darwin himself. Darwin argued that fear was likely the oldest emotion and, further, that fear has probably maintained the same character over time.[49] The evolutionary case for anxiety is compelling for at least three reasons: because anxiety has plain fitness implications, because its behavioral consequences are more tailored to the threat, and because parallels to anxiety have been found in many other species, as would be expected if anxiety were advantageous in any animal that takes defensive action.[50]

Our evolutionary ancestors had much to fear. Indeed, they had every reason to worry about things that generally do not concern us today. Some predators were a threat to life. Infectious disease was common. Food could not be easily preserved and had to be guarded assiduously to avoid starvation. Other people, too, were a risk and not always a source of comfort. In such an environment, anxiety, fear, and social unease were useful and, indeed, there is apparent overlap between these evolutionary considerations and the specific types of anxiety disorders diagnosed today.[51] If a fear of animals leads to a swift retreat from a predator, a specific phobia can improve fitness. If other people are threatening to life or reputation, social anxiety can increase fitness by leading people to avoid others. Even in the case of generalized anxiety disorder, with anxiety cutting across two or more concerns in a somewhat indiscriminate way, the function of the disorder can be understood in a parsimonious fashion: trepidation in the face of numerous undefined threats parallels the more or less uniform response of a healthy immune system to a variety of foreign materials.[52] Some evidence is consistent with the fitness value of at least some level of anxiety. Whereas depression increases mortality in a continuous fashion, low levels of anxiety are associated with higher mortality.[53]

Beyond their intuitive appeal, evolutionary accounts of anxiety are further supported by the specificity of the behavioral response. In general, the motivating force of anxiety is more precise than that of depression. For instance, a fear of heights evokes freezing, thereby preventing a fall and allowing the individual to locate the danger. Social anxiety evokes avoidance and submissive behavior, thereby preventing conflict, whether the threat is from within one's social group (where submission is effective) or from the outside (where avoidance is effective). A fear of animals evokes retreat, removing the person from the source of the harm. Even symptoms that are shared across different anxiety disorders are potent and useful. Across all types of fear, for instance, anxiety heightens attention and elevates the heart rate, preparing the individual for action. These responses are found in other species, too. Humans startle at the sound of an unexpected noise, rapidly increasing their attention, but deer, too, show a startle response, especially at the sound of breaking branches. Many humans fear heights, especially being in tall buildings, but this fear is, in fact, widespread in the animal kingdom. Land-dwelling animals generally withdraw from cliffs. Even the expression of fear on the face tends to be similar between species.[54] Fear usually involves wide-open eyes and mouth, conveying shock.[55] Fear also involves a lowered brow and stretched lips, which help to distinguish the appearance of fear from the otherwise similar appearance of surprise.

Other aspects of anxiety map well onto an evolutionary account as well, including the ages at which fears tend to emerge. In humans, specific fears tend to emerge at the age when that fear becomes adaptive.[56] Infants, for instance, first show fear when they are able to crawl, developing a fear of strangers, animals, and heights.[57] Some of these fears are particularly well balanced with respect to the infant's growing abilities. A fear of strangers, for instance, tends to peak around fifteen months and then begins to subside as the infant's skill in ambulation progresses into a capacity to flee.[58] As infants begin to move, parents must still prevent toddlers from, for instance, touching a hot stove or sticking their fingers into an electrical outlet. But infants instinctively fear those things that our forebears would have feared.

If the evolutionary case for anxiety is strong, it nonetheless complicates arguments regarding when to consider anxiety clinically significant. In particular, the evolutionary origins of anxiety make it difficult to determine precisely when anxiety is abnormal, and they certainly impede regarding anxiety as inherently disordered. Some critics of the *DSM* have targeted anxiety disorders precisely on this point. Allan Horwitz and Jerome Wakefield have been especially strong supporters of the idea that psychiatric disorders are overdiagnosed and that the *DSM* wrongly categorizes a variety of normal and appropriate responses as psychiatric disorders.[59] Following a framework developed by Wakefield, they advance an alternative framework for thinking about true mental disorders as those involving harmful dysfunctions. According to this idea, anxiety per se is not a problem and, indeed, can be entirely functional, but anxiety that is out of proportion to the actual threat represents a dysfunction. Disproportionate anxiety is the failure of an otherwise adaptive psychological mechanism and, therefore, can be regarded as a true disorder, much like an autoimmune disease represents the overactivation of an otherwise beneficial system. Because the *DSM* makes no allowance for this, they argue, it conflates normal fears with pathology and, according to their framework, yields a large number of false positives.

The harmful dysfunction framework is broadly applicable. Horwitz and Wakefield have applied it effectively to a variety of other psychiatric disorders, including mood disorders.[60] Yet their case against anxiety disorders is perhaps especially compelling, for at least two reasons. First, there are many instances in which an anxiety disorder is not harmful because the source of the fear can be readily avoided or the anxiety is relatively mild. A fear of public speaking might limit some career opportunities, for instance, but there are still many occupations that do not require speaking to large crowds. Second, the dysfunction of anxiety, as depicted in Horwitz and

Wakefield's framework, is not well represented in the *DSM*. The usefulness of anxiety implies that too *little* anxiety can sometimes be a problem, something rarely relevant for other psychiatric symptoms. Someone with no fear of heights risks a fall, for instance, just as someone with no social anxiety risks being ostracized. By Horwitz and Wakefield's account, anxiety is not only natural but sometimes even desirable, something the *DSM* does not explicitly consider.

The Evolutionary Case for Anxiety Disorders

Virtually everyone would agree that there is a distinction between anxiety and anxiety *disorders*, just as there is a distinction between depression and *major* depression. The evolutionary account of anxiety and fear has mostly developed around the traits of anxiety and fear and not necessarily any disordered versions of those traits. The fitness value of a startle response, for instance, is probably much higher than the fitness value of a full-scale panic. Indeed, Horwitz and Wakefield employ the idea of a spectrum in arguing that anxiety disorders exist precisely when the anxiety is inconsistent with the level of anxiety that evolution ought to promote.

Yet the evolutionary approach to the *spectrum* of anxiety can be extended to anxiety *disorders* as well. There are reasons to suspect that evolution has left humans vulnerable to anxiety disorders in much the same way that it has preserved anxiety as a useful emotion, and that even normal anxiety can be susceptible to dysregulation. There are at least two ways to understand the evolution of anxiety disorders. The first is the so-called smoke detector principle.[61] This perspective begins with the widely accepted idea that anxiety is a signal, much like the alarm of a smoke detector, that alerts the individual to potential danger. The smoke detector principle goes a step further, however, to highlight the asymmetry between the high costs of failing to detect a true threat (e.g., your alarm does not go off and your house burns down) relative to the low costs of a false alarm (e.g., you must silence your smoke detector when you burn something in the oven). Given this asymmetry, an optimal fire detector—accepting that no fire detector is perfect—is one that produces far more false positives than false negatives, given that an alarm can be silenced. By extension, the optimal level of anxiety—accepting that it is a useful signal—is one that produces fewer false negatives than false positives, which can presumably be corrected once the individual realizes there is no threat.[62] The value of a false positive is further enhanced by the speed in which the alarm sounds. An alarm that is too sensitive can be irritating, but by rapidly motivating a response—including the response merely to stop the klaxon—a sensitive alarm can improve fitness in environments where a quick response is essential.

Frazer Meacham and Carl Bergstrom develop a different approach to anxiety disorders premised on some of the same ideas.[63] Like the smoke detector approach, their approach is based on the idea of anxiety as a signal, but in explaining the frequency of dysfunctions, they emphasize an iterative process of choices and outcomes. They further argue that the social environment itself produces an asymmetry in how frequently the extremes of anxiety will emerge. By their logic, disorders of excess anxiety will be common, but disorders of insufficient anxiety will be rare. The key to understanding this process is twofold: one, consider feedback between choices and environments and, two, consider differences in the amount of information gained from being either too prudent or too rash. In their model, people are provided with opportunities. Some of these opportunities involve risk, but some also involve reward. Before deciding whether to pursue an opportunity, individuals evaluate how threatening that opportunity is by relying, in part, on emotional signals such as fear and anxiety. People who are excessively anxious will be cautious and deferring, whereas people who are insufficiently anxious will be impulsive and rash. In this regard, the Meacham and Bergstrom approach is similar to other evolutionary accounts premised on the idea that anxiety is a signal and impetus for caution. What happens next in their model, though, provides the mechanism for making excess anxiety common. Only when people pursue an opportunity are they able to observe the correspondence between their fear and the actual threat the opportunity entailed. If they decide not to pursue the opportunity, they get no information and, therefore, no data to test the accuracy of the assessment or the value of their fear as a signal. On average, there may be an optimal level of anxiety sensitivity in a given environment, a level that allows people with an ordinary level of fear to pursue the kinds of opportunities that will prove valuable more often than not. But an iterative process of opportunities and choices that yields information only following one kind of choice produces a great many people who are overly anxious and cautious and, so, produces people who are provided with few opportunities to correct their misconceptions.

The Meacham and Bergstrom approach is a theory, but it also helps to explain several facts. For one, their approach is fundamentally iterative, implying that individuals who are anxious at one time should also be anxious later on, a prediction that dovetails with the chronicity of anxiety disorders. Furthermore, their approach helps to explain the apparent effectiveness of exposure therapy, wherein anxious individuals are safely exposed to the thing they fear to demonstrate their fear was unfounded. Their approach also helps to explain why anxiety disorders can emerge even under seemingly favorable circumstances. If the environment is uniformly risky, then high anxiety will quickly emerge as the optimal strategy, and anxiety disorders will be common. Early evolutionary conditions likely matched this description. But even in a low-risk environment, where many opportunities are likely to bear fruit, anxiety disorders can be common. This happens because no environment is entirely free of risk. Under favorable and low-risk conditions, enough people will encounter real threats early on that a subset of people will incorrectly infer that most subsequent opportunities are threatening. The Meacham and Bergstrom approach, then, has the additional benefit of keeping anxiety—and even anxiety disorders—well within the confines of the rational and judicious. In both good and bad environments, anxiety is sensible, in the sense that it is premised on responding to the actual environment as it presents itself. The self-perpetuating pessimism of those who encounter threats early on is not born from a lack of judgment or poor intuition. Indeed, no less than anxiety in a bad environment, anxiety in a good environment can reflect an optimal learning strategy insofar as it is present in an environment with at least some risks. For the same reason, a good environment will produce far more people with unusually high levels of anxiety (as in too pessimistic) than people with unusually low levels of anxiety (as in too optimistic). For a variety of reasons, then, evolution might not only preserve anxiety as a trait, but also preserve seemingly harmful levels of anxiety to the point of a disorder.

THE GROWING SCIENTIFIC APPRECIATION OF ANXIETY

An evolutionary approach to psychiatric disorders highlights distinctions between anxiety and depression. Yet beyond theories suggesting different pathways to anxiety and mood disorders, the science of anxiety has developed in ways that have allowed scientists to better appreciate distinctions and to highlight the unique nature of anxiety. Anxiety is a more scientifically engaging object of study, in part because the study of anxiety is occurring outside the muddled confines of the *DSM*.

In recent years, the National Institute of Mental Health has made an effort to foster "precision medicine"—a theme guiding medical practice more generally—within psychiatry.[64] The principle activity in this effort has been the creation of Research Domain Criteria (RDoC), a framework that encourages researchers to study the more elementary dimensions of mental illness. Rather than focusing on the psychiatric disorders included in the *DSM*, RDoC proposes focusing on a variety of dimensions of mental and behavioral functioning, referred to as "constructs" to reflect their abstract and provisional nature. RDoC includes, for instance, basic cognitive and motivational systems such as attention, habit, and perception. Furthermore, RDoC includes both positively and negatively valenced systems, such as how much individuals respond to reward and how frustrated they are with nonreward. Constructs of this sort are, to be sure, related to the disorders that appear in the *DSM*. Indeed, in some cases, the constructs are fundamental to how the *DSM* defines the disorder. Depression, for instance, involves individuals failing to respond to reward. Yet these constructs are not tantamount to psychiatric disorders, and RDoC stipulates that most of the constructs should be considered dimensions for which no level can be regarded a priori as dysfunctional. In this sense—and others—RDoC is a radical departure from the *DSM*.

RDoC rests on several guiding concepts and ideals, including that RDoC might eventually provide a better and more useful framework for diagnosing psychiatric disorders.[65] For one, RDoC conceptualizes psychiatric disorders as problems of the brain.[66] From the start, the creators of RDoC have been clear in emphasizing the brain, noting, "The primary focus for RDoC is on neural circuitry, with levels of analysis progressing in one of two directions: upwards from measures of circuitry function to clinically relevant variation, or downwards to the genetic and molecular/cellular factors that ultimately influence such function."[67] The hope is that brain–behavior linkages will not only provide science with a better understanding of behavior, but will also supply clinicians with better tools for diagnosis, including more reliable information on symptoms. Rather than relying on behavioral observations or self-reports, as is the case in the *DSM*, a diagnostic system premised on RDoC would allow clinicians to render diagnoses on the basis of dysfunctional neural circuits or, short of that, other biological signatures of dysfunction. RDoC already allows scientists to study a variety of dimensions of psychological functioning and not just the symptoms that align neatly with the *DSM*. To date, RDoC may not have produced breakthrough treatments, though in the words of Insel, "RDoC is already freeing investigators from the rigid boundaries of symptom-based categories."[68]

Whatever its scientific or clinical merits, the ascent of RDoC has implications for thinking about anxiety disorders in particular, especially given the ambiguous place of anxiety in the *DSM*. Indeed, the ambitions of RDoC might be realized first in how it deals with anxiety and fear. If RDoC is pushing a new approach to studying mental health, it is perhaps pushing most strongly with respect to anxiety. In an interview with Scott Stossel, Insel noted the ease with which anxiety can be mapped onto the kinds of neural systems RDoC emphasizes. For Insel, anxiety disorders are "one of the places where we can begin to make the transition between understanding the molecules, the cells, and the system right to the emotion and behavior."[69] The most recent version of RDoC provides clues that it is moving in this direction.[70] Anxiety is, in general, already well represented across the domains and systems of RDoC. Three of the five so-called negative valence systems (one of its core dimensions) are directly related to anxiety, including acute threat (fear), potential threat (anxiety), and sustained threat. Other aspects of anxiety are represented in other domains, including arousal, which includes, among other things, the startle response.

The elements of anxiety disorders are well represented in RDoC, in part because much of the research on anxiety and fear has already focused on the brain-to-behavior linkages RDoC seeks. Fear circuitry in the brain is well established, for instance, in neuroimaging research. In addition, neuroscience has already identified ways to study phobias without relying on self-reports. Fear-potentiated startle responses, for instance, have strong linkages with brain circuitry and, as behaviors, require no subjective reporting.[71] In addition, studies have demonstrated commonalities across anxiety disorders at the level of RDoC constructs, a development that could promote a more cohesive research agenda for the study of anxiety relative to other categories of disorder. For instance, Lisa McTeague and Peter Lang studied patients diagnosed with *DSM*-based anxiety disorders, including specific phobia, social phobia, panic disorder, obsessive-compulsive disorder, generalized anxiety disorder, and post-traumatic stress disorder.[72] From the standpoint of the *DSM*, these disorders look very different from one another, and the *DSM* would, of course, insist that they are distinct. Yet McTeague and Lang show how anxiety disorders might be related through dimensions not apparent in the *DSM* but easily slotted into RDoC. In particular, they show that disorders involving fear and impairment, such as a specific phobia, differ from disorders involving apprehension and avoidance, such as generalized anxiety disorder. In their study, patients were asked to imagine a threatening situation. After doing so, patients with a fear-based disorder exhibited a heightened startle response, whereas patients with an apprehension-based disorder exhibited a diminished startle response. These patterns might reflect what the authors refer to as a "defensive physiological gradient" linked to deficient amygdala activation. It is not hard to imagine deficient amygdala activation as a disorder of its own.

RDoC has also illuminated new pathways for treating anxiety.[73] Insofar as the apprehension of a disorder is driven in part by the ability to treat it, these pathways point to a rising profile for anxiety. Despite the diversity of anxiety disorders in terms of the fears they represent, most anxiety disorders share the characteristic of an inability to extinguish a maladaptive fear response—in other words, those with an anxiety disorder have difficulty controlling their fear. Such a maladaptive response has been recognized by scientists for a long time, though the idea has attracted more attention in recent years as scientists have begun to map where the response is located in the brain. And with knowledge of these locations, scientists have identified more precise pharmacological treatments for anxiety. Glutamate transmission is especially important in the fear response, perhaps more so than serotonin is in major depression.[74] In contrast to other psychiatric disorders whose symptoms do not align as cleanly with RDoC, anxiety disorders provide an especially coherent and useful proof of concept for RDoC.

ANXIETY AND FEAR IN MODEL ORGANISMS

Other developments have further drawn scientific attention to anxiety and, as with RDoC, have helped to cast anxiety as unique. As a state, anxiety can be studied intensively using the tools of model organisms and classical conditioning.[75] Fear can be induced in nonhuman animals in direct ways.

Rats, for instance, can be taught to fear a noise that is accompanied by a shock and, in turn, scientists can study the behaviors that accompany that fear. Scientists can study depression in nonhuman animals as well, though major depression involves symptoms that do not lend themselves as well to model organisms. Mouse models of depression, for instance, rely on exposing the animal to a stressful and uncontrollable situation and then monitoring the animal for learned helplessness. Learned helplessness is indicated by behaviors such as failing to avoid harmful stimuli and, in this sense, can be readily observed. Learned helplessness is not, however, tantamount to a major depressive episode, at least as articulated in the *DSM*. Other symptoms common to depression, including anhedonia, recurrent thoughts of death or suicide, and feelings of worthlessness or inappropriate guilt, have no clear behavioral signatures in mice.[76] To the extent that animal models lend themselves to the study of depression at all, they allow scientists only to study a particular kind of depression, one that may not be representative of the disorder. In some animal studies, for instance, depression is at least implicitly conceptualized as the inability to cope with stress, as when mice are forced to swim and "depressed" mice are reluctant to maintain effort, a putative corollary of psychosocial impairment in humans.[77]

Animal models of anxiety are more straightforwardly useful and provide a more direct analog of anxiety in humans. Classic Pavlovian conditioning can be used to study the development, consequences, and extinction of fears. Animals can be startled, and a stronger startle response can be interpreted as greater vigilance. To be sure, not all the relevant symptoms of anxiety can be studied effectively. Some anxiety disorders involve a fear of losing control or a sense of a foreshortened future, neither of which can be well approximated in nonhuman animals.[78] In addition, anxiety disorders are maintained by cognitive processes that are probably unique to humans.[79] Nonetheless, many other aspects of anxiety in humans can be studied precisely in nonhuman animals. Animals freeze in the face of fear and run in the opposite direction when presented with a threat, things humans do as well. Indeed, the overlap between the behavior of humans and nonhuman animals is sufficiently strong that animal models can be used to study specific types of anxiety. Agoraphobia, for instance, is characterized by a fear of places where escape is difficult and detection is easy. Such a fear can be modeled in mice by monitoring the degree to which they avoid well-lit areas. In a so-called open field test, the animal is placed in a box and the amount of reluctance to enter the center of the box, where an animal would ordinarily be most prone to predation, is interpreted as akin to agoraphobia. By the same token, generalized anxiety disorder is characterized by difficulty in concentrating, which can be assessed in mice by monitoring their ability to sustain attention on a task. Animal models even allow scientists to separate fear from anxiety to the extent that fear involves a specific object that can be situated in a conditioning experiment. In the case of anxiety, a mouse avoids *cues* related to some specific fear, such as a sound, whereas in the case of fear, a mouse responds to exposure to the actual thing that is feared, such as a cat.[80] Even the physiological response of fear in mice overlaps with the physiological response in humans, including autonomic arousal indicated by an increased heart rate, hyperthermia, and sleep impairment. These aspects of fear have allowed scientists to study something like panic attacks in nonhuman animals.[81]

The value of animal models for anxiety stretches well beyond the ability to simulate analogs of anxiety in a credible fashion. Animal models provide scientists with tools to study how fear and anxiety appear in the brain in ways that are not possible with humans.[82] For instance, they allow scientists to study the effects of genetic modifications on brain development.[83] They also allow for an unusual degree of control over environmental conditions in ways that studies of humans cannot. This is especially true in studies that employ rodents, whose small size facilitates a range of environmental experiments in limited spaces.[84] A rodent maze, for instance, requires very little space, though that space is more than sufficient to simulate a complex geospatial puzzle. Similarly, the short life span of most rodents permits scaling not possible in animals with greater longevity. In particular, this short life span allows scientists to study life-course development over months rather than decades, linking the lingering effects of "childhood" exposures, such as maternal separation, to "late life" anxiety behavior, even though the actual time span between those two periods is two years or less.[85] Animal models also allow scientists to simulate stress of varying durations and intensities, approximating the distinction between a stressful event and ongoing stressful circumstances. Chronic mild stress, for instance, can be modeled by exposing the rodent to a tilted cage over a series of weeks, while eventful stress can be modeled using a short shock.[86] These designs, in turn, allow scientists to study differences between episodic panics and more chronic anxiety.

Animal models are far from perfect. Scientists who employ model organisms, for instance, have not neglected the unusually rational nature of the anxiety they study. In many instances, the anxiety a rodent learns is appropriate in the sense that the sound they have been taught to fear warns the rodent of an impending shock with reasonable certainty. Scientists also employ ethologically appropriate designs, which might diminish the relevance of animal experiments for humans, though is entirely appropriate when studying nonhuman animals. Scientists use the sort of "normal" fears mice are likely to encounter in their environments, such as cats, further separating the fear used in rodent studies from the sort of exposures of interest to psychiatrists. For some critics, then, animal "models" are better described as animal "assays," lest scientists engage in the sort of over-interpretation that renders anxiety-like behaviors tantamount to anxiety or regards the pathophysiology of anxiety-like behaviors in rodents as representative of the pathophysiology of anxiety disorders in humans.[87]

Nonetheless, the appeal of animal models has important implications for how scientists regard anxiety as a phenotype. In particular, the widespread use of animal models has further split anxiety and depression and lent credibility to treatments focused on anxiety specifically. Animal models have solidified the evidence base surrounding anxiety in a way that has not been possible for depression. Furthermore, animal models have lent themselves to important clinical applications. Animal models were, in fact, developed in response to the observation of anxiety in humans. In particular, animal models rose to prominence in the early 1960s to address the apparent effectiveness of benzodiazepines in the treatment of anxiety.[88] Early animal models involving mazes and electrocharged plates were used to study why benzodiazepines had anxiolytic effects. Although animal models have generally been used to show why existing medications work (more than they have been used to develop entirely new medications), animal models have played an important role in encouraging the view that anxiety, whether chronic or episodic, can be effectively treated by drugs.[89]

The scientific approach to the study of anxiety has evolved in remarkable ways. As medicine has shifted toward a more precise focus on the brain, and science has sought to study psychiatric disorders using animal models, the prominence of anxiety as a phenotype has risen. Whereas the *DSM* provides a loose set of heterogeneous anxiety disorders that are often difficult to study empirically, RDoC valorizes the study of the more elemental dimensions of anxiety and fear. All this has implications for thinking about anxiety as a language of psychological suffering. Among other things, the ability to map anxiety and fear to specific neural circuits has promoted the idea that excess anxiety can be treated. In chapter 9, I discuss trends in the treatment of anxiety and its rise as a target in medical care. In the next few chapters, though, I begin to unpack the causes of anxiety and some of the environmental conditions that have helped to increase its prevalence between cohorts.

Chapter Four

ANXIETY DISORDERS IN THE UNITED STATES

In the next four chapters, I explore the social determinants of anxiety. Much of this discussion is thematic and piecemeal, focusing in successive chapters on the role of changes in the family, changes in religious participation, changes in social support, and changes in socioeconomic status. I intend to show that the rise of anxiety reflects a confluence of trends that have increased the prevalence of anxiety without, in most cases, a parallel increase in depression. Relative to depression, anxiety absorbs social change more rapidly and has a higher baseline risk. Before proceeding, though, it is important to outline a general model for understanding the determinants of anxiety. Various models exist, including models focused on biological and neurological determinants, but in the context of the arguments made in this book, I will develop a model that focuses on the elements of the social environment that matter most.

UNDERSTANDING THE ENVIRONMENTAL DETERMINANTS OF ANXIETY

The general case for the social determinants of anxiety disorders is very compelling, even with a strong genetic component. David Barlow has outlined a three-part division among the causes of anxiety disorders, illustrating the space for social influences.[1] In this division, genes account for a relatively small amount of the variation in anxiety, at least relative to the contributions of genes to other disorders.[2] The heritability of anxiety ranges from 30 percent to 40 percent, with variation among specific anxiety disorders. The heritability of panic disorder, for instance, is generally higher than that for generalized anxiety disorder.[3] The heritability among specific phobias varies as well. While general phobias have a heritability of 43 percent, the heritability of agoraphobia is 67 percent; of a fear of blood, 59 percent; and of social phobia, 51 percent.[4] Overall, though, other determinants are as or more important than genes. Barlow divides the remaining causes of anxiety into learned experiences, which account for about 30 percent of the variation, and general psychological factors, which account for another 30 percent. These divisions are not crisp, and their organization would seem to underplay the contributions of the environment, a point Barlow himself makes. Gene by environment interactions, for instance, complicate any neat division between genes and any other contribution that is not strictly genetic. Furthermore, general psychological factors, such as a tendency to view a situation as uncontrollable, can be learned based on experience, suggesting interactions between the two nongenetic categories. Nonetheless, this three-part division summarizes some key facets of anxiety. Anxiety is not entirely a matter of genetic or biological determinism, and there are no necessary and sufficient determinants. There are no genes that will, under all circumstances, produce anxiety. In addition, much about anxiety is learned and reinforced. Experiences can have a lasting impact on how individuals interpret the world and, thus, can influence the risk for developing an anxiety disorder or having a repeat episode.

At an abstract level, the primary social determinants of anxiety are experiences that either increase uncertainty, diminish one's sense of control, or introduce a potential threat. Although there are important differences in the determinants of anxiety between children and adults, the experiences that increase the risk of anxiety are similar in their meaning. Experiences that are threatening increase anxiety, whether with respect to threatening a child's growing sense of the world or an adult's more settled one. For this reason, there are important thematic continuities between childhood and adulthood, even if the sources of worry are decidedly different. Generalized anxiety disorder among adults, for instance, is associated with the same sorts of family background factors that are associated with phobias in children.[5]

A related point pertains to the *multifinality* of social causes. Multifinality refers to when risk factors affect multiple disorders.[6] This can occur across disorder types, but also within them. There are few risk factors related to one anxiety disorder that are not also related to another anxiety disorder. Abuse, for instance, can increase the risk of generalized anxiety disorder, but also the risk of specific and social phobias. Social conditions are especially likely to involve multifinality, because they are distal. Proximate mechanisms, like biological factors, are more likely to be related to a specific disorder, though even these factors can span disorder types.[7]

Some of the strongest distal causes of anxiety pertain to interpersonal relationships.[8] Friendships are ordinarily a source of stability and support, but their frustration or absence can be a source of distress. Anxiety is associated with having too few social ties, with inadequate support from friends, and with social conflict. Marital distress has a particularly strong relationship with anxiety disorders, both increasing the risk of a new anxiety disorder and the likelihood that an existing anxiety disorder will persist.[9] Evidence that interpersonal problems play a significant role in anxiety is also apparent in what anxious people worry about. By definition, people with generalized anxiety disorder worry about several things. Yet, of all the things they worry about, those with the disorder worry the most about family and interpersonal issues.[10] The relevance of social relationships in anxiety is not entirely unexpected. It is consistent with the strong role of social relationships in health overall.[11] Nonetheless, relationships appear to play an especially powerful role in allaying fear, decreasing worry, and instilling confidence.

Children, too, are affected by the quality of their relationships. Abuse is strongly associated with anxiety, as is conflict between parents.[12] Some particular forms of abuse are especially potent. Childhood sexual abuse, for instance, affects a wider variety of anxiety disorders than does physical abuse, though both are significant.[13] In particular, sexual abuse is related to social anxiety disorder, panic disorder, generalized anxiety disorder, and post-traumatic stress disorder (PTSD), whereas physical abuse is associated with PTSD and specific phobia. Although abuse is a powerful risk factor, it is not the only risk factor for children, and indeed, anxiety can be increased by behaviors that some parents might regard as beneficial. Generalized anxiety disorder, for instance, is associated with parental overprotection and pressure.[14] Especially anxious children may experience both more shielding and harsher discipline when they break the rules. In the same vein, children whose parents are more rejecting report more worry, indicated by endorsing questions such as "your parents wish that you were like someone else" or "your parents are scared when you do something on your own."[15] In contrast, children whose parents provide them with opportunities to learn they have control over their environment tend to have less risk for an anxiety disorder.[16]

Because anxiety involves learning about the environment and making inferences about its stability, any model of the social determinants of anxiety must also be sensitive to its life-course dimensions. Often the lessons of anxiety are learned early and retained over a lifetime. Anxiety disorders have a relatively early age of onset. On average they emerge about a decade before mood disorders.[17] There are a variety of ways to think about the connection between childhood environments and adult environments, though a complete accounting of anxiety in adults must still explain what childhood circumstances lead to the initial onset of an anxiety disorder in childhood. Anxiety in an adult is often the continuation or recurrence of a disorder that started much earlier. A full accounting of anxiety must also recognize that, if anxiety shapes how the environment is interpreted, then early-onset anxiety affects the recurrence of anxiety by shaping sensitivity to stress. Anxious people attend to their environments in ways that accentuate threats.

THE DETERMINANTS OF ANXIETY AND DEPRESSION

Any argument regarding the ascent of anxiety must also contend with the idea that the same environmental conditions that increase anxiety might also increase depression. To argue that we are entering an age of anxiety is to argue, at least implicitly, that we are not also entering an age of depression, that the same conditions that make us more anxious do not also make us more depressed. In discriminating between the causes of anxiety and depression, two general concepts are important. First, the risk for anxiety is probably more prevalent than the risk for depression, a point I return to later. One upshot of the evolutionary approach to psychiatric disorders is that the capacity to feel fear—even dysfunctional fear—should be preserved in most species. For this reason, there are probably more people at risk for an anxiety disorder than are at risk for major depression. Second, anxiety ought to be more sensitive to environmental conditions than depression, especially if anxiety represents a signal of potential threats. Virtually all evolutionary accounts of anxiety begin with the idea that anxiety helps people avoid risks by providing information about the environment. For anxiety to function properly in this respect, it should at least encourage vigilance, even when potential threats are minimal, and it should respond rapidly to environmental change. In evolutionary accounts, depression serves a purpose, too, though a different one. It usually serves as a lagging indicator of a behavioral strategy that needs reconsideration, as a prompt for more complex problem solving. One implication of these accounts is that many environmental risk factors should have a stronger relationship with anxiety than depression.

There is already research that directly explores similarities and differences in the determinants of anxiety and depression. Among other things, this research indicates that the environment can play a critical role in separating the two. Evidence drawn from twin studies, for instance, indicates that anxiety and depression are likely influenced by a similar set of genes.[18] But the same evidence indicates that anxiety and depression are influenced by different environments—that is, there are environmental experiences that affect depression without affecting anxiety, just as there are environmental experiences that affect anxiety without affecting depression. This idea can be put even more sharply. According to this evidence, the *only* reason a vulnerable person would suffer from one disorder rather than the other is because of environmental factors.[19]

Twin studies of this sort leave open what specific environmental influences matter, but other research has filled the gap. Stressful life events are detrimental to mental health in general, though different types of events matter more for some disorders than others. Stressful life events can be characterized by their existential dimensions, as involving danger, loss, or humiliation, and studies of these dimensions find differences in their consequences.[20] One study found remarkable specificity in the effects of events. Loss-related events were associated with the onset of depression, danger-related events were associated with the onset of anxiety, and experiencing *both* loss- and danger-related events was associated with the onset of a mixed anxiety/depression disorder.[21] A different study found similar specificity in outcomes, though it was conducted among older people and explored different kinds of losses.[22] In this context, a death in the family was associated with depression, whereas a major illness in a partner was associated with anxiety. Other losses mattered as well. The development of functional limitations increased the risk of depression, though it did not affect the risk of anxiety. Events involving humiliation, such as a divorce initiated by a spouse or a public put-down from a person of authority, were especially potent determinants of depression, but again, not anxiety.[23]

Another strategy for uncovering differences between anxiety and depression is to consider not just the type of event but when the event occurred. Here, too, there are important differences. In general, early-life adversity might be more strongly predictive of anxiety.[24] For instance, pure generalized anxiety disorder (not accompanied by major depression) is strongly associated with low socioeconomic status and maltreatment, whereas pure major depression (not accompanied by generalized anxiety disorder) is strongly associated with a family history of depression.[25] More generally, adolescents who develop anxiety are more likely to have experienced a wider variety of adverse conditions than those who develop depression. Studies have found, for instance, that early anxiety is associated with low socioeconomic status, maltreatment, an inhibited temperament, conduct problems, and maternal internalizing symptoms, whereas depression is associated with a much narrower set of risks.[26] The type of risk matters as well. Whereas depression is linked to loss and insufficient social support in adulthood, anxiety is related primarily to exposure to danger-related events in childhood.[27]

A more abstract way to think about the kinds of environments that produce depression and anxiety is in terms of the length of the path to each disorder. George Brown and colleagues provide a model wherein the path to depression involves more steps than the path to anxiety.[28] Because the path to depression is longer, the development of depression in adulthood is contingent on more factors. Earlier adverse experiences increase the risk of depression in adults, but only when the current environment is also stressful. In addition, while both anxiety and depression involve early adversity, depression also tends to involve a major adult loss (whereas anxiety does not), followed by deficiencies in social support (not a factor in anxiety). In the case of anxiety, the relationship between early adversity and adult anxiety is more direct, because the risk that adversity sparks is more enduring. Once anxiety begins, according to this model, it tends to stay, whereas the continuation of depression depends on ongoing environmental strains. Anxiety sustains itself, whereas depression requires more fuel.

UNDERSTANDING CHANGE IN ANXIETY
OVER COHORTS AND TIME

Trends in anxiety can be understood in diverse ways. In studying how populations change, social scientists draw a distinction between age, period, and cohort effects, with the latter two generally being most relevant for understanding trends over time. Anxiety can increase in several ways. It can increase as a period-based process, wherein some set of influences affects all age groups at a particular point in time. Those who argue for an age of anxiety are, in effect, arguing that social and cultural conditions present during a certain period increase anxiety. If these influences grow stronger over time, anxiety can increase over time, too, consistent with a period-based process. Anxiety can also increase as a function of cohort-specific changes. A cohort-based process pertains to a set of influences that are unique to a birth cohort. Anxiety can increase over time as a cohort-based process if each subsequent cohort is exposed to more anxiety-provoking conditions. A cohort-based process is especially compelling when conditions experienced early in life exert a lasting influence into adulthood, thereby inducing sharp differences between cohorts that do not recede with age. An age-based process is linked to influences that are particular to aging. Age-based processes are frequently biological or developmental in nature—that is, they have well-established correlations with age-based or known features of aging. The risks of cardiovascular disease and cancer, for instance, generally increase with age for all individuals. To the extent that age processes are shared by cohorts, they will not contribute to trends in anxiety.

Distinguishing between age, period, and cohort effects is difficult, because the three have exact linear dependencies among them. If we know the current year and someone's age, we know the year they were born and their cohort. Unless the properties of one component are sufficiently well characterized to identify the remaining two, it is difficult to recover age, period, and cohort effects simultaneously. These difficulties are accentuated in the case of psychiatric disorders because of how they are measured and manifest over the life course. At least three kinds of influences could produce differences between age groups (e.g., a prevalence higher among those aged eighteen to twenty-nine than among those sixty and over) that risk being wrongly interpreted as differences between cohorts. First, when asked to reflect on their history, older persons might be more prone to forgetting a lifetime episode of depression or anxiety, whereas younger people might not, especially because psychiatric disorders tend to first occur in adolescence or early adulthood. When reflecting on their first episode of a disorder, older people are likely recalling much more distant events than are younger people. Most of the data used to estimate prevalence, including data used in this book, are based on retrospective accounts of psychiatric symptoms. Second, social desirability bias—an interest in making a favorable impression—could lead some people to suppress reporting depression or anxiety in a survey interview. This, too, complicates cohort differences. If attitudes toward mental illness are shifting, social desirability bias might be weaker among younger people, meaning older persons might appear less depressed but in fact be just as depressed as younger persons. Third, setting aside social desirability per se, older persons might be less familiar with the formal labels of psychiatric disorders, leading to an underreporting of symptoms because those symptoms are not as well appreciated and, therefore, are reported with greater error.

Although there is some support for all three kinds of influences, there is considerable evidence that apparent age differences in the prevalence of psychiatric disorders likely reflect cohort patterns instead, and, further, that the prevalence of psychiatric disorders is increasing over cohorts (a point I return to shortly). For instance, evidence suggests that the *lifetime* risk of a psychiatric disorder—that is, the risk a person will develop a psychiatric disorder at some point in his or her lifetime—has been increasing between cohorts.[29] Furthermore, even closely spaced cohorts—such as the difference between those born between 1968 and 1971 and those born between 1972 and 1974—are significantly different from each other, with more recent cohorts showing a higher risk.[30] Although older persons are more prone to social desirability bias in surveys, social desirability is not correlated with the reported number of psychiatric disorders.[31] And although some people are more likely to identify themselves as anxious or depressed at a given level of symptoms, labeling processes of this sort do not explain cohort differences.[32] Cohort differences are pronounced in part because psychiatric disorders tend to recur. Even if a birth cohort has yet to reach the age of thirty, their elevated risk for a psychiatric disorder is likely to remain elevated for their entire life span because the risk does not recede as they get older.

These sorts of differences have implications for many of the analyses presented in this book. Much of the book is based on cross-sectional data—that is, data collected at one point in time and not following individuals over time. In such data, we know the years respondents were interviewed and their ages, and we therefore know the cohorts in which they were born. But in such data it is still impossible to distinguish whether any difference between age groups is a function of age or cohort, because we do not follow these individuals over time. The analyses presented in this book deal with these difficulties on a case-by-case basis, depending on the social trend or risk factor under consideration, though three assumptions and strategies inform my emphasis on cohort rather than age.

For one, most of the analyses allow for a distinction between lifetime disorders and current disorders. In cross-sectional data, individuals are essentially asked questions regarding whether they ever experienced a psychiatric disorder (a lifetime disorder) and whether they currently are experiencing a psychiatric disorder (often framed within the last twelve months). It is tempting to infer that the total lifetime prevalence of a disorder corresponds to the percentage of Americans who will ever develop a psychiatric disorder in their lifetime, but this is incorrect without some additional assumptions. In cross-sectional data, the lifetime prevalence is the percentage of Americans who have experienced a psychiatric disorder *to that point in their lifetime*. Nationally representative surveys of adults will include a representative cross section of age groups. The lifetime prevalence reported by a twenty-year-old corresponds only to whether he or she has experienced a disorder to that point. The lifetime prevalence reported by an eighty-year-old is also the prevalence to that point. The latter is closer to the expected lifetime risk of a disorder, but in a cross section of age groups, the lifetime risk will depart from the expected lifetime risk, especially for younger cohorts.

It is possible to estimate the expected lifetime prevalence by considering information on the age distribution of initial onset for disorders and then projecting forward over age groups. Thus, for instance, we might expect that some twenty-year-olds who have not yet reported major depression will report it at some point in the next two decades, given what we observe among those aged forty and over. Studies that do this, however, generally find small differences between the cross-sectional lifetime prevalence and the projected lifetime risk.[33] For instance, in the National Comorbidity

Survey Replication, one of the data sets used in this book, the observed cross-sectional lifetime prevalence is 46.4 percent, whereas the projected lifetime risk to age seventy-five is 50.8 percent.[34] The reason for this similarity is simply that the age of onset for the most common psychiatric disorders is quite young, meaning even among younger survey respondents most of the people who will ever develop a psychiatric disorder have developed at least one by the age of twenty.

These empirical exercises have direct implications for cohort differences. It is entirely possible that apparent cohort differences in psychiatric disorders—which are seen in a wide variety of data sets—are actually age differences. This could occur if there were differences in the age-of-onset distribution over cohorts but the same lifetime risk. Age-of-onset differences could occur either because the onset of psychiatric disorders is happening at younger ages in more recent cohorts or because differences in mortality, which is naturally higher in older ages, has produced a psychologically healthier sample of older survivors. To test for this possibility, studies using the same projection method have explored whether the effects of cohort decrease with age and have found no evidence for such a decrease for anxiety or mood disorders in particular.[35] If some younger people report no disorder but in fact will go on to experience a disorder later on, this renders estimates of the lifetime prevalence of disorders in younger cohorts conservative.

The second strategy that informs my emphasis on cohort rather than age is one that relies on what previous studies have identified as the significant sources of social change. Much of the latter part of this book is focused on the extent to which particular kinds of risk factors explain the higher risk for anxiety among more recent cohorts. These analyses, too, are usually cross-sectional, though they draw upon different information concerning how certain risk factors have changed over the course of the twentieth and twenty-first centuries. In these instances, there is sometimes good evidence from other sources to adjudicate age, period, and cohort effects. In the case of family change, for instance, there is evidence from ongoing demographic surveys regarding trends in divorce, family formation, and fertility. This information can be applied to understanding how cohorts differ in the likelihood of being raised in a single-parent household, as a function of being raised in different periods. By the same token, there is evidence from studies of college students collected over multiple eras that can be used to understand how attachment styles have changed among young people. In these instances, the data can be combined to explore whether the prevalence of a secure attachment, for instance, has declined among those age eighteen to twenty-two over the last fifty years. In each period, the age group under consideration is the same, so the trends detected in such a study cannot be attributed to aging. My strategy, then, is to use cross-sectional analyses, to assume that cohort differences in anxiety reflect cohort rather than age, and to evaluate whether certain risk factors explain these differences based on information that confirms that these risk factors follow cohort patterns rather than age. This strategy of borrowing and applying evidence from other studies has a secondary implication. For those who fear that apparent cohort differences reflect methodological artifacts rather than substantive differences, evidence that family background partly explains cohort differences in the risk of anxiety, for instance, provides further evidence that cohort differences are real.

Third, and finally, I do at times explore repeated cross-sectional data. I begin my empirical analysis of historical trends using Americans View Their Mental Health (AVMH), which was collected twice over a long and historically significant interval, 1957 and 1976. Although the survey was not conducted among the same respondents, making it impossible to evaluate change within individuals, it is possible to study synthetic cohorts in repeated cross sections and to distinguish the magnitude of intracohort versus intercohort change.[36] A synthetic cohort refers to a cohort of people of a given age in the first period studied as the same cohort in the second. In my analyses, I explore what happened to anxiety in the cohort of twenty- to twenty-four-year-olds as they became forty- to forty-four-year-olds approximately twenty years later. In a synthetic cohort analysis, two specific trends can be compared: differences in the level of anxiety among twenty- to twenty-four-year-olds in 1957 relative to anxiety among twenty- to twenty-four-year-olds in 1976, referred to as intercohort differences, and differences in the level of anxiety among twenty- to twenty-four-year-olds in 1957 relative to the forty- to forty-four-year-olds they are twenty years later, referred to as intracohort differences. In intercohort differences, age is constant, though historical experiences are, of course, different. In intracohort differences, historical experiences are shared, though the age of the cohort members is advanced. Comparing these two quantities can help to identify potential sources of change and to evaluate their relative contributions.

AN EMPIRICAL PORTRAIT OF ANXIETY IN THE UNITED STATES

With the above as background, the remainder of this chapter presents descriptive information on anxiety in the United States, providing the foundation for later chapters. Several themes are important to establish upfront. For one, it is useful to consider anxiety relative to other symptoms, including the broader symptom pool that constitutes psychological distress. Furthermore, it is useful to evaluate the relative prevalence of mood and anxiety disorders. And across all these comparisons and empirical exposition, it is useful to consider trends, either over time or by cohort.

Anxiety in the Symptom Pool of Midcentury America

Before moving to a discussion of anxiety in the late twentieth and early twenty-first centuries, it is important to take a step back and explore anxiety and depression in the 1950s and 1970s. An important data source in the regard is the nationally representative AVMH survey, conducted initially in 1957 and replicated in 1976.[37] For at least two reasons, this period of time is especially valuable. For one, the period reflects an important transition, when the language of anxiety was shifting from one concept to another. The period saw the ascent of nerves, along with the early development of more formal psychiatric nomenclature for anxiety disorders, as eventually codified in *DSM-III*. Although AVMH survey did not use the formal language of psychiatry, it did ask participants questions about their mental health in a fashion that was resonant at the time. The survey asked respondents, for instance, if they ever felt like they had a nervous breakdown, as well as simply whether they were happy and whether they worried a lot about things. The period covered by AVMH is also useful, because it reflects the start of the midcentury age of anxiety and the rise in the pharmaceutical treatment of nerves. As much as anything, the pharmaceutical treatment of nervous breakdowns likely affected how Americans conceptualize anxiety and their mental health. Andrea Tone, for instance, argues that the widespread use of tranquilizer drugs set the stage for how successive generations of Americans have interpreted anxiety.[38]

An analysis of AVMH reveals evidence for a changing language of mental health, both on the surface of what Americans report and in the experiential basis for those reports. Table 4.1 begins with a basic description of

TABLE 4.1
Worry and sadness in midcentury America, 1957 to 1976

	1957	1976
Ever had a nervous breakdown (%)	18.9	20.9
Age 21 to 29	17.4	23.2*
Age 30 to 44	21.3	24.5
Age 45 to 59	20.2	18.9
Age 60 and over	14.4	16.2
Worry a lot (%)	33.8	44.8***
Age 21 to 29	32.4	51.0***
Age 30 to 44	33.1	52.6***
Age 45 to 59	34.8	40.1
Age 60 and over	35.0	33.8
Not happy (%)	11.2	10.9
Age 21 to 29	5.1	10.1**
Age 30 to 44	8.5	9.6
Age 45 to 59	12.9	9.4
Age 60 and over	19.3	14.6*
Frequency of symptoms (0 to 6)		
Physical symptoms of anxiety	1.22	1.42***
Age 21 to 29	.90	.97
Age 30 to 44	1.00	1.19**
Age 45 to 59	1.34	1.58*
Age 60 and over	1.71	2.01*
Psychological symptoms of anxiety	2.02	2.28***
Age 21 to 29	1.81	2.14***
Age 30 to 44	1.95	2.17**
Age 45 to 59	2.07	2.33**
Age 60 and over	2.26	2.51*

* $p < .05$, ** $p < .01$, *** $p < .001$ (for test of significant between-period differences).
Source: Joseph Veroff, Elizabeth Douvan, and Richard Kulka, Americans View Their Mental Health, 1957 and 1976: Selected Variable (Ann Arbor, Mich.: Inter-university Consortium for Political and Social Research, 2005) ($N = 4,676$).

Americans' mental health during these two periods. Three basic outcomes are presented: the percentage reporting they ever had a nervous break-down, the percentage reporting that they were not happy (or, specifically, reported being "not too happy" when asked about happiness in the context of "taking things all together"), and the percentage reporting that they worry "a lot." Although these reports are all correlated, the only statistically significant change over the period was an increase in worry. The percentage of Americans reporting that they worry a lot increased from 34 percent to 45 percent. There was no significant increase in the percentage reporting that they had ever experienced a nervous breakdown or the percentage reporting that they were unhappy.

Table 4.1 also presents the same trends broken down by cohort. Echoing a theme that will emerge in later chapters, the increase in anxiety was considerably more pronounced among younger cohorts. Indeed, by 1976, most adults under the age of forty-five reported worrying a lot. Among those aged twenty-one to twenty-nine, the percentage reporting being unhappy increased significantly, too, though the percentage reporting worrying a lot was 51 percent, whereas the percentage reporting being unhappy was a mere 10 percent. Although the difference with the youngest cohort is small, the cohort with the most worry in 1976 was the cohort of those between the ages of thirty and forty-four. Anxiety certainly was not limited to those in their twenties.

There are, of course, other ways to assess mental health. And it is important to know what precisely Americans are thinking about when they report more worry. The next set of rows explores two separate dimensions of anxiety. The first represents the physical symptoms of anxiety and the second represents the psychological symptoms. The former is assessed by the frequency of shortness of breath and a racing heart, in both cases with responses of "never or hardly ever," "sometimes," or "many times." The numerical values represented in the table correspond to the sum of the two items, ranging from zero (never experiencing either symptom) to six (experiencing both symptoms many times). The psychological symptoms of anxiety, meanwhile, represent the sum of sleep problems, either going to sleep or staying asleep, and the extent of "nervousness, feeling fidgety and tense." Previous research has shown these two kinds of symptoms reflect underlying concepts of physical and psychological symptoms, respectively, and have divided them in this fashion.[39] Consistent with a general increase in worry, both kinds of symptoms increased over time. Americans reported that they worried more and experienced more of the symptoms of anxiety, too, even as reports of a full-scale nervous breakdown remained about the same. Furthermore, the shift in the symptoms

TABLE 4.2
Trends in worry and sadness, inter- and intracohort change, 1957 to 1976

	Ever had a nervous breakdown	Worry a lot	Not happy
Age 21 to 24			
Intercohort change	+4.9	+14.1**	+6.5*
Intracohort change	+10.8*	+17.3**	+7.2*
Age 25 to 29			
Intercohort change	+7.2*	+21.8***	+4.0
Intracohort change	+1.4	+10.8*	+.6
Age 30 to 34			
Intercohort change	+5.6	+24.1***	+2.5
Intracohort change	+1.0	+9.6*	+5.8*
Age 35 to 39			
Intercohort change	+1.2	+16.1***	+.2
Intracohort change	+7.2	+3.8	+.6
Age 40 to 44			
Intercohort change	+2.7	+16.9***	+1.6
Intracohort change	+1.3	+8.1	+4.9

* $p < .05$, ** $p < .01$, *** $p < .001$ (for test of significant between-period differences).
Source: Joseph Veroff, Elizabeth Douvan, and Richard Kulka, Americans View Their Mental Health, 1957 and 1976: Selected Variable (Ann Arbor, Mich.: Inter-university Consortium for Political and Social Research, 2005) ($N = 2,512$).

of anxiety was more consistent over cohorts than reports of worry. Even among those forty-five and over the symptoms of anxiety—if not reporting significant worry—increased over time. The way anxiety was coded might have been changing during this time, but the experience of anxiety was only growing more acute.

Table 4.2 turns to a synthetic cohort analysis. Because not all cohorts can be studied in this way over the period of observation, the table presents cohorts over a narrower age range. For each cohort, two quantities are presented, the intracohort change (that is, change among 20-year-olds as they age between 1957 and 1976) and the intercohort change (that is, change between 20-year-olds in 1957 and 20-year-olds in 1976). The table shows, again, the remarkable increase in worry over this period. Between 1957 and 1976, the percentage who worry a lot increased 24.1 percentage points among those ages thirty to thirty-four and 21.8 percentage points among those twenty-six to twenty-nine. Moreover, table 4.2 reveals that the increase between cohorts, in most cases, exceeded that within cohorts. With respect to trends in worry, the intercohort change is at least twice as large as the intracohort change for all but the twenty-one to twenty-four-year-old cohort. This ratio is especially pronounced for worry. With respect to happiness, by contrast, four of the five cohorts show larger changes within cohorts than between, suggesting a stronger aging effect.

In addition, the sources of worry shifted in ways that are likely relevant for thinking about anxiety in the twenty-first century. Americans were not only worrying more. They were expanding the scope of their worries, as shown in table 4.3. In an open-ended fashion, the AVMH survey asked respondents to report what kinds of things they worried about most. The question was asked of everyone in the survey, including those who reported that they did not worry much. Respondents were allowed to list four things, which were then coded and consolidated according to their thematic content. There are a variety of ways to characterize the sources of worry, but for understanding trends, it is particularly informative to explore trends in the scope of worry. The potential for worry is stronger when it is based on things that have yet to materialize relative to things that have already occurred. Table 4.3 presents summary statistics across four thematic categories. The first corresponds to those who worry only about things that have no obvious time frame, such as "I worry about lots of little things" or "I worry about many things"; followed by those who worry only about current circumstances, such as paying bills or supporting a family; followed by those who worry only about future possibilities, such as economic or job security; and followed finally by those who report a mix of both current and future worries. Between 1957 and 1976 the distribution of worry is similar for most categories, with the exception of those who worry exclusively about future considerations, which increased from about 14 percent to around 19 percent, while the percentage worrying only about current circumstances declined somewhat. The distribution of worries among those who worry a lot also differed between the two periods, though in more pronounced ways. In 1957, about 32 percent of those who worried a lot worried only about current circumstances. By 1976, this percentage had declined to 22 percent, while the percentage worrying only about future circumstances increased from 10 percent to 17 percent. Table 4.3 also presents the

TABLE 4.3
Trends in the sources of worry, 1957 to 1976

	1957		1976	
	Among all adults (%)	Among those who worry a lot (%)	Among all adults (%)	Among those who worry a lot (%)
Theme of worry				
Undefined or general circumstances	21.8	13.0	22.7***	15.7***
Current problems only	24.8	32.3	21.9***	21.8***
Future or potential problems only	13.9	10.1	18.8***	17.2***
Both current and future problems	39.4	44.6	36.7***	45.4***
Topic of worry				
General worry	2.1	2.3	4.7***	5.3**
Economic worry	39.8	41.5	35.2***	43.0
Job worry	13.2	14.4	16.8***	18.9*
Family worry	39.4	27.2	41.3	34.7***
Health worry	28.1	33.7	25.8	25.8***
Other personal worry	6.7	9.1	8.2	7.9
Non-personal worry	13.0	13.5	21.6***	20.1***

* $p < .05$, ** $p < .01$, *** $p < .001$ (for test of significant between-period differences).
Source: Joseph Veroff, Elizabeth Douvan, and Richard Kulka, Americans View Their Mental Health, 1957 and 1976: Selected Variable (Ann Arbor, Mich.: Inter-university Consortium for Political and Social Research, 2005) ($N = 4,676$).
Note: Theme of worry categories are exclusive and sum to 100% (with rounding).

specific topics of worry, again among all Americans and among those who worry a lot. Worry increased across a range of topics. Although health and economic worry declined somewhat, other sources of worry increased. Among those who worry a lot, general worry increased, as did job worry, family worry, and worry about nonpersonal situations.

In short, worry assumed a more forward-looking and balanced character over time. Worrying more turned into worrying about both what is happening now and what might happen in the future. This rebalancing also provides a partial explanation for why worry has increased over time. In many ways, the economic circumstances of Americans improved over this interval. Unemployment was somewhat lower in 1976 and educational attainment had increased. Economic worry is the most common source of worry overall but was somewhat less common in 1976 than 1957. In 1957, the second most common source of worry pertained to health. This, too, changed. Life expectancy continued to improve during this time and health worry declined in tandem. Yet overall worry increased, and the scope of worry appears to have shifted, making up for the difference. If Americans are increasingly focused on future risks, the sources of worry are less tethered to present comforts, including regarding things that ordinarily are quite important.[40] Although there is no direct evidence that this trend has continued—the AVMH survey was particular to its time and it has not been replicated since 1976—there is certainly evidence that many Americans suffer from significant anxiety and, further, that people under the age of sixty are especially affected.

Anxiety and Anxiety Disorders in the Twenty-First Century

The remaining tables turn to data from the twenty-first century. One reason it is difficult to study long-term trends in anxiety is that the terms themselves have shifted. For instance, no study has consistently asked about a nervous breakdown, because the concept itself has been more or less retired from the social sciences. More research has explored anxiety disorders, but here, too, the formal nomenclature has shifted with periodic revisions of the *DSM*, making a clean analysis of trends difficult. There are, however, some empirical tools for assessing change more precisely and at least considering what anxiety looks like in the twenty-first century. I will begin by discussing the symptoms of anxiety, followed by a discussion of formal anxiety disorders.

Figure 4.1 presents trends in anxiety and depression symptoms between 1997 and 2018. Data are taken from the National Health Interview Survey, an ongoing survey of health and health care.[41] Since 1997 the survey has included a measure of nonspecific psychological distress, referred to as the K6 (in reference to creator of the six-item scale, Ronald Kessler).[42] The concept of nonspecific psychological distress refers to overall psychological well-being and symptoms that are not specific to any one disorder. Instead, the K6 reflects a set of symptoms that are prominent dimensions of emotional well-being. Not surprisingly this set includes a mix of anxiety and depression symptoms. In the K6, respondents are asked how often in the last thirty days they felt, "so sad that nothing could cheer you up; hopeless; that everything was an effort; nervous; and restless and fidgety." Respondents are provided with five response categories to

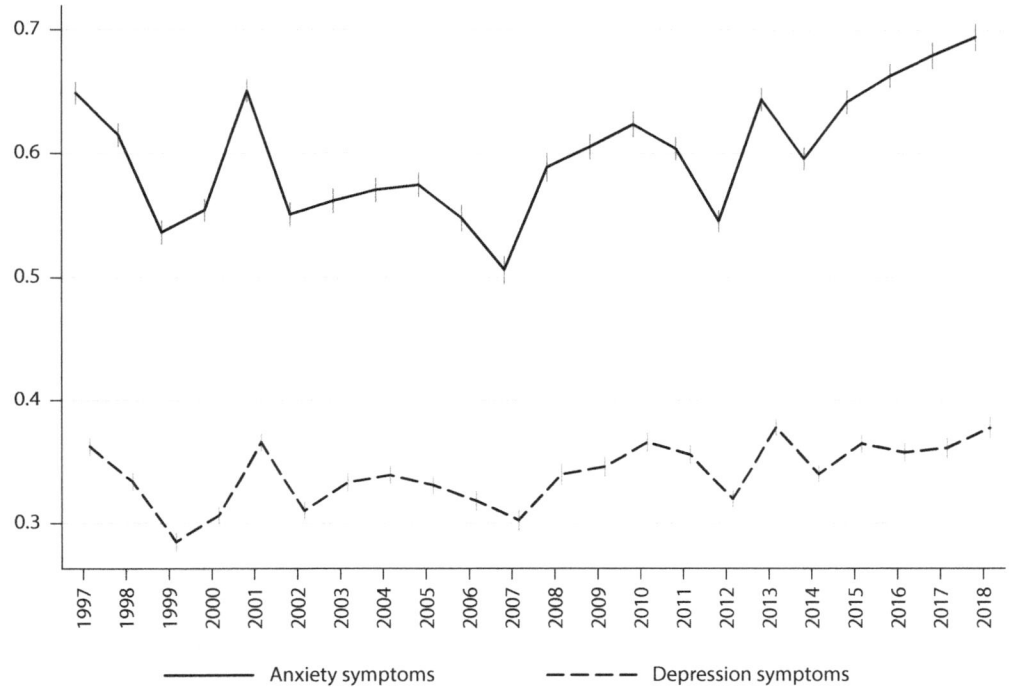

FIGURE 4.1. Anxiety and depression symptoms over two decades
National Health Interview Survey, N = 659,633

each of these questions, ranging from "none of the time" to "all of time," scored zero to four. Although the K6 is conventionally summed to create a continuous measure of distress, ranging from zero to twenty-four, two separate dimensions of distress can be created, the first corresponding to depression, and consisting of the first four symptoms listed, and the second corresponding to anxiety, and consisting of the last two symptoms. Figure 4.1 presents the mean response to each of the two dimensions over time. Each category of symptoms has increased over time, though the trends can effectively be separated into two components, the first corresponding to the trend from 1997 to 2007 and the second corresponding to the trend from 2007 to 2018. Before 2007 both depression and anxiety were decreasing somewhat. But after 2007 both began to increase, with the increase in anxiety exceeding that for depression (a change likely

TABLE 4.4
Trends in anxiety and depression symptoms, 1997 to 2018

	Anxiety	Depression
1997 to 2007 trend (expected yearly change)	−.004***	.000
2007 to 2018 trend (expected yearly change)	.011***	.005***
Age-specific trends		
1997 to 2007 trend (expected yearly change)		
18 to 29	−.004**	−.003***
30 to 44	−.005***	.000
45 to 59	−.002*	.003***
60 and over	−.007***	−.001
2007 to 2018 trend (expected yearly change)		
18 to 29	.016***	.007***
30 to 44	.015***	.005***
45 to 59	.012***	.005***
60 and over	.006***	.003***

* $p < .05$, ** $p < .01$, *** $p < .001$.
Source: Lynn A. Blewett, Julia A. Rivera Drew, Miriam L. King, and Kari C.W. Williams, IPUMS Health Surveys: National Health Interview Survey, Version 6.4 [data set] (Minneapolis, Minn.: IPUMS, 2019), https://doi.org/10.18128/D070.V6.4 ($N = 659,633$).

attributable to the economic recession). In every year, the average for anxiety exceeded that for depression, a point echoed in formal psychiatric disorders as well (as discussed shortly).

Table 4.4 presents estimates of the per-year change in depression and anxiety over these two periods, based on coefficients from regression models. Before 2007, anxiety was declining somewhat, while depression remained the same. Since 2007, however, anxiety has increased, and it has increased faster than depression. The strength of these trends varies by age, not unlike what was seen between 1957 and 1976. Although all age groups experienced a statistically significant increase in anxiety, the increase was much stronger among younger cohorts. Each progressively younger cohort experienced a sharper increase in anxiety, with the youngest group experiencing per-year increases in anxiety that were more than three times larger than for the oldest group. A similar pattern is apparent for depression as well, though the increase in depression was much weaker overall. Across all cohorts, the per-year increase in anxiety has exceeded that for depression by at least two to one. Anxiety and depression are moving further apart, especially among young people.

THE PREVALENCE OF ANXIETY AND MOOD DISORDERS

Table 4.5 shifts the focus and presents basic descriptive information regarding the prevalence of mood and anxiety disorders drawn from an especially large data source, the Collaborative Psychiatric Epidemiological Surveys, a composite of three surveys, each focused on a different population segment.[43] Together, these surveys represent nationally representative data on psychiatric disorders in the United States, the highest-quality and most comprehensive data set of its kind. Two types of prevalence are presented, the first corresponding to the lifetime prevalence of the disorder, referring to the percentage of adults in the United States who ever experienced a given disorder, and the second corresponding to the twelve-month or current prevalence, referring to the percentage who experienced the disorder in the preceding twelve months. The table focuses on mood and anxiety disorders. When the two disorders are compared, the prevalence of anxiety disorders is considerably higher. The lifetime prevalence of any anxiety disorder is 26 percent, whereas the lifetime prevalence for mood disorders is 19 percent. The single most prevalent lifetime disorder is major depression, though both specific phobia and social phobia are close, at 12 percent. The twelve-month prevalence patterns are similar to those for lifetime prevalence, although the discontinuities between anxiety and mood disorders are, if anything, sharper for more current disorders. The single most common twelve-month disorder is a specific phobia. As with lifetime disorders, the most common twelve-month disorders are anxiety disorders, but in the case of twelve-month disorders, the overall prevalence of anxiety disorders is about twice that of mood disorders.

Another way to look at differences between mood and anxiety disorders is to think of comorbidity between the two. Table 4.5 presents the prevalence of pure anxiety disorders, or anxiety disorders not accompanied by a mood disorder, and pure mood disorders, reflecting the converse, as well as the prevalence of both disorders together. The table shows that pure anxiety disorders are far more common than pure mood disorders. Indeed, pure anxiety disorders far exceed even comorbid mood and anxiety disorders. This is especially apparent for twelve-month disorders, for which the

TABLE 4.5
Lifetime prevalence of mood and anxiety disorders, 2001–2003

	Lifetime prevalence	12-month prevalence
Any anxiety disorder	25.6%	16.4%
Panic disorder	4.7%	2.7%
Agoraphobia	2.4%	1.4%
Specific phobia	12.5%	8.7%
Social phobia	12.1%	6.8%
Generalized anxiety disorder	7.8%	4.0%
Any mood disorder	19.0%	8.3%
Major depression	16.6%	6.7%
Dysthymia	2.5%	1.5%
Bipolar disorder	2.1%	1.4%
Mood and anxiety disorders		
Neither disorder	66.3%	80.0%
Mood but not anxiety	8.1%	3.6%
Anxiety but not mood	14.7%	11.7%
Both mood and anxiety	10.9%	4.7%

Source: Margarita Alegria, James S. (James Sidney) Jackson, Ronald C. Kessler, and David Takeuchi, Collaborative Psychiatric Epidemiology Surveys (CPES), 2001–2003 [United States] (Ann Arbor, Mich.: Inter-university Consortium for Political and Social Research [distributor], 2016), https://doi.org/10.3886/ICPSR20240.v8 (primary survey: National Comorbidity Survey Replication, $N = 9,282$).

prevalence of pure anxiety disorders exceeds that of comorbid disorders by more than two to one. If individuals suffer from a single disorder, it is far more likely to be an anxiety disorder than a mood disorder. Pure anxiety disorders exceed pure mood disorders by more than three to one.

Table 4.6 further unpacks the life-course dimensions of psychiatric disorders. The discontinuity between lifetime and twelve-month disorders reflects, in part, the remission of disorders. Because some earlier disorders remit, the twelve-month prevalence is consistently lower than the lifetime prevalence. Beyond this fact, though, it is useful to consider the ratio of twelve-month to lifetime disorders. If a disorder is chronic in every case, the ratio will be one: every lifetime disorder will also be a current disorder, because no lifetime disorder remits. As the ratio approaches zero, it indicates that every case of a disorder eventually remits. Table 4.6 presents the mean of this ratio over the sample. No ratio equals one, although the

TABLE 4.6
Life-course dimensions of mood and anxiety disorders

	12-month/lifetime ratio	Mean age of onset
Any anxiety disorder	.639	13.13
Panic disorder	.579	23.49
Agoraphobia	.593	18.32
Specific phobia	.699	8.77
Social phobia	.563	11.69
Generalized anxiety disorder	.521	26.97
Any mood disorder	.438	25.97
Major depression	.405	26.77
Dysthymia	.589	25.18
Bipolar disorder	.686	23.44

Source: Margarita Alegria, James S. (James Sidney) Jackson, Ronald C. Kessler, and David Takeuchi, Collaborative Psychiatric Epidemiology Surveys (CPES), 2001–2003 [United States] (Ann Arbor, Mich.: Inter-university Consortium for Political and Social Research [distributor], 2016), https://doi.org/10.3886/ICPSR20240.v8 (primary survey: National Comorbidity Survey Replication, N = 206 to 2,434).

ratio for anxiety disorders as a category is considerably higher than for mood disorders. Anxiety disorders tend to be more chronic. The single most chronic disorder is a specific phobia, followed closely by bipolar disorder. The lowest ratio is for major depression. One way to interpret these differences is to think of mood disorders as episodic and anxiety disorders as dispositional. For instance, those who fear enclosed spaces tend to fear enclosed spaces consistently, whereas major depressive episodes can come and go. The table also presents the mean age of onset in reference to the age at which a disorder first emerges. The age of onset for the category of mood and anxiety disorders refers to the onset of the earliest anxiety or mood disorder. The average age of onset for anxiety disorders is more than a decade earlier than for mood disorders. The average anxiety disorder begins in a person's teens, whereas the average mood disorder begins in a person's midtwenties. In other words, anxiety disorders tend to start early in life and persist.

Anxiety is both more common and chronic than depression, but it is also useful to think of the percentage of people who are simply at risk for a mood or anxiety disorder, that is, those who at least have symptoms consistent with the disorder if not a full-blown case. One way to think about this is to estimate the percentage of the population who are at risk for an anxiety disorder because they experienced one of its essential symptoms, such as excessive worry, and to compare it with the percentage of the population who are at risk for a mood disorder because they experienced one of its essential symptoms, such as persistent depressed mood. Each of the mood and anxiety disorders discussed thus far has such a symptom (or set of symptoms), referred to as a screen-positive symptom. Although each of the specific anxiety disorders involves a different set of screen-positive symptoms, all the mood disorders involve a set of three such symptoms: Have you ever in your life had a period of time lasting several days or longer when "most of the day you felt sad, empty or depressed?," when "most of the day you were very discouraged about how things were going in your life?," or when "you lost interest in most things you usually enjoy, like work, hobbies, and personal relationships?" Answering affirmatively to any question qualifies as screening positive. Table 4.7 presents the prevalence of these screen-positive symptoms. Overall, the risk for an anxiety disorder is much higher than the risk for a mood disorder. Whereas 62 percent of Americans have at least experienced the primary symptom(s)

TABLE 4.7
Screen positive lifetime prevalence for anxiety and mood disorders

Any anxiety disorder screen	87.3%
Any panic screen	50.9%
Any worry screen (for GAD)	50.5%
Any fear screen	66.2%
Any specific phobia screen	55.8%
Any social phobia screen	59.3%
Any agoraphobia screen	20.8%
Any mood disorder screen	62.0%
Anxiety and mood disorder screen	
Screen for neither	10.4%
Mood only	2.3%
Anxiety only	27.5%
Mood and anxiety	59.7%

Source: Margarita Alegria, James S. (James Sidney) Jackson, Ronald C. Kessler, and David Takeuchi, Collaborative Psychiatric Epidemiology Surveys (CPES), 2001–2003 [United States] (Ann Arbor, Mich.: Inter-university Consortium for Political and Social Research [distributor], 2016), https://doi.org/10.3886/ICPSR20240.v8 (primary survey: National Comorbidity Survey Replication, N = 9,277).

of a mood disorder, nearly 90 percent of Americans have experienced the primary symptom(s) of at least one anxiety disorder. Put differently, nearly 40 percent of Americans appear to have no real risk for a mood disorder (at least to this point in their lifetime), whereas only 10 percent of Americans have never experienced significant anxiety. Some especially common experiences pertain to phobias and general fear. Table 4.7 also presents combined screening for mood and anxiety disorders. Only about 10 percent of Americans have never experienced either symptom type. More than half have experienced both. Among those who experienced either one or the other, far more have experienced anxiety symptoms than mood symptoms, with anxiety affecting more than one in four Americans. Screening positive for a potential anxiety disorder without a mood disorder is more than eleven times more common than screening for a potential mood disorder alone.

Cohort Differences in Anxiety

There are many ways to consider how the prevalence of anxiety disorders has changed over time, but an especially important one is differences between cohorts. Table 4.8 presents prevalence estimates for anxiety disorders over four cohorts. All else being equal, the lifetime prevalence of anxiety disorders should be higher among older cohorts, as lifetime prevalence corresponds to the proportion ever experiencing a disorder to that point. Yet the lifetime prevalence of anxiety (and mood) disorders is much higher among younger cohorts than in the oldest cohort, a result consistent with midcentury trends in worry documented earlier. The lifetime prevalence of any anxiety disorder among those eighteen to twenty-nine is 26 percent, whereas the lifetime prevalence among those sixty and over is 16 percent. The twelve-month prevalence mirrors these differences and is, if anything, larger. Among the two youngest cohorts, the twelve-month prevalence of any anxiety is nearly one in five, whereas among those sixty and older it falls to just under one in ten. The high prevalence of anxiety disorders is not limited to the youngest cohort. Indeed, the highest overall prevalence is found among those thirty to forty-four, another pattern consistent with those found in 1976 with respect to worry. A comparable cohort gradient is apparent for mood disorders as well, though the prevalence of mood disorders is much lower.

TABLE 4.8
Cohort differences in the prevalence of mood and anxiety disorders

	Cohort							
	18 to 29		30 to 44		45 to 59		60 and Over	
	12 month	Lifetime	12 month	Lifetime	12 month	Lifetime	12 month	Lifetime
Any anxiety disorder	18.5%	26.0%	19.2%	29.3%	17.5%	28.8%	8.7%	16.2%
Panic disorder	2.8%	4.2%	3.7%	5.9%	3.1%	5.9%	.8%	2.1%
Agoraphobia	1.5%	2.1%	1.6%	2.8%	1.9%	3.1%	.5%	1.2%
Specific phobia	10.1%	13.0%	9.4%	13.9%	9.7%	14.4%	5.2%	7.7%
Social phobia	8.9%	13.3%	8.3%	14.5%	6.5%	12.6%	2.8%	6.8%
Generalized anxiety disorder	3.3%	5.5%	5.1%	9.1%	5.2%	10.4%	1.9%	5.3%
Any mood disorder	10.1%	18.4%	10.3%	21.9%	8.6%	22.5%	3.2%	11.4%
Major depression	8.1%	15.5%	8.2%	18.9%	6.9%	19.8%	2.9%	10.6%
Dysthymia	1.1%	1.8%	1.7%	2.8%	2.3%	3.7%	.5%	1.3%
Bipolar disorder	2.0%	2.8%	1.8%	2.7%	1.4%	2.1%	.3%	.5%
Mood and anxiety disorders								
Neither disorder	76.8%	66.7%	76.7%	61.9%	78.7%	61.4%	89.7%	77.9%
Mood but not anxiety	4.7%	7.3%	4.1%	8.8%	3.8%	9.8%	1.5%	5.9%
Anxiety but not mood	13.1%	14.9%	13.0%	16.2%	12.7%	16.1%	7.0%	10.7%
Both mood and anxiety	5.4%	11.1%	6.2%	13.1%	4.8%	12.7%	1.7%	5.5%

Source: Margarita Alegria, James S. (James Sidney) Jackson, Ronald C. Kessler, and David Takeuchi, Collaborative Psychiatric Epidemiology Surveys (CPES), 2001–2003 [United States] [Ann Arbor, Mich.: Inter-university Consortium for Political and Social Research [distributor], 2016), https://doi.org/10.3886/ICPSR20240.v8 (primary survey: National Comorbidity Survey Replication, *N* = 9,277).

In addition to a higher prevalence of anxiety among younger cohorts, the average age of initial onset has been decreasing. Table 4.9 presents the average age of onset across cohorts for each of the specific disorders. For every disorder, the age of onset is earlier for more recent cohorts. Some of this difference is almost certainly attributable to retrospection: people may remember their most recent episode of a disorder more than their first episode, which for older cohorts could be decades prior. Of note, though, the average age of onset is very early, even for cohorts in middle age and older. This is especially true for anxiety disorders. In the oldest cohort, as in the youngest cohort, the average age of onset remains in the teens. For specific phobia, even the oldest cohort reports a mean age of onset under the age of twelve. Mood disorders have a very different character. Among the oldest cohort, the average age of onset for the first mood disorder is nearly twenty years later than for the first anxiety disorder. The progressively younger age of onset for anxiety disorders across cohorts is unlikely to be entirely attributable to a retrospection bias.

Table 4.10 presents cohort differences in the screen-positive prevalence. Here, too, there are strong cohort differences, though the cohort differences are notably less sharp than they are for formal psychiatric disorders. The

TABLE 4.9
Mean age of onset by cohort

	Cohort			
	18 to 29	30 to 44	45 to 59	60 and Over
Any anxiety disorder	9.2	12.5	14.6	18.6
Panic disorder	14.5	22.2	27.3	35.3
Agoraphobia	14.0	17.1	22.2	18.3
Specific phobia	6.8	8.4	9.5	12.0
Social phobia	10.6	11.5	12.1	13.7
Generalized anxiety disorder	15.8	23.8	29.6	41.0
Any mood disorder	16.5	23.3	30.4	39.5
Major depression	16.6	24.0	31.0	40.5
Dysthymia	14.3	22.2	29.1	37.8
Bipolar disorder	17.1	22.1	31.2	32.2

Source: Margarita Alegria, James S. (James Sidney) Jackson, Ronald C. Kessler, and David Takeuchi, Collaborative Psychiatric Epidemiology Surveys (CPES), 2001–2003 [United States] (Ann Arbor, Mich.: Inter-university Consortium for Political and Social Research [distributor], 2016), https://doi.org/10.3886/ICPSR20240.v8 (primary survey: National Comorbidity Survey Replication, N = 9,277).

TABLE 4.10
Lifetime screen positive prevalence for anxiety and mood disorder

	Cohort			
	18 to 29	**30 to 44**	**45 to 59**	**60 and Over**
Any anxiety disorder screen	90.1%	88.0%	88.8%	81.1%
Any panic screen	54.4%	51.9%	55.2%	40.4%
Any worry screen (for GAD)	55.2%	53.2%	51.5%	40.4%
Any fear screen	70.7%	65.6%	66.0%	62.0%
Any specific phobia screen	61.3%	56.3%	56.9%	47.9%
Any social phobia screen	62.7%	62.5%	61.5%	48.2%
Any agoraphobia screen	23.0%	22.7%	20.9%	15.3%
Any mood disorder screen	66.3%	64.3%	64.7%	50.8%
Anxiety and depression screen				
Screen for neither	8.2%	10.0%	8.4%	16.0%
Depression only	1.7%	2.0%	2.8%	2.9%
Anxiety only	25.5%	25.7%	26.9%	33.3%
Depression and anxiety	64.6%	62.4%	61.9%	47.8%

Source: Margarita Alegria, James S. (James Sidney) Jackson, Ronald C. Kessler, and David Takeuchi, Collaborative Psychiatric Epidemiology Surveys (CPES), 2001–2003 [United States] (Ann Arbor, Mich.: Inter-university
Consortium for Political and Social Research [distributor], 2016), https://doi.org/10.3886/ICPSR20240.v8 (primary survey: National Comorbidity Survey Replication, $N = 9,277$).

vast majority of Americans report at least some anxiety symptoms, irrespective of cohort. Among those eighteen to twenty-nine, about 90 percent
report an anxiety screen-positive symptom, whereas among those sixty and
over, about 81 percent do. More than half also report at least one of the
primary symptoms of a mood disorder. In addition, for all cohorts, the
likelihood of a positive screen for an anxiety disorder alone is much higher
than that for a mood disorder alone. In this case, the screen-positive prevalence for a pure anxiety disorder is actually highest in the oldest cohort. The
latent risk for an anxiety disorder has perhaps been increasing over time,
but not as fast as the actual realization of an anxiety disorder.

Anxiety is common. Across the twentieth century, anxiety grew increasingly prevalent, even as depression stalled or grew at a slower pace. Virtually every American has some real risk of developing an anxiety disorder,
whereas nearly 40 percent have never experienced the primary symptom

of a mood disorder and, by the criteria in the *DSM*, cannot develop major depression. In addition, far more people experience an anxiety disorder without an accompanying mood disorder than experience a mood disorder without an accompanying anxiety disorder. Although comorbid mood and anxiety disorders are common, anxiety can and does emerge on its own. Since 2007, trends in anxiety and depression symptoms have diverged further, accelerating a distinction that was already apparent in the middle of the twentieth century. In addition, there are pronounced differences between cohorts. Although anxiety is not uncommon among those sixty and over—especially the general experience of having significant fears and phobias—anxiety disorders are especially common among younger cohorts. Furthermore, anxiety disorders are starting at an earlier age, even as they remain persistent over the life course. The next chapter addresses the social conditions responsible for these differences, focusing, at least initially, on early life conditions and family change.

Chapter Five

FAMILY CHANGE AND COHORT DIFFERENCES
IN ANXIETY

Younger people have a much higher lifetime prevalence of anxiety disorders than do older people. There are diverse ways to account for this difference, though early-life conditions are almost certainly important, given the average age at which anxiety disorders emerge. Among adults, anxiety disorders are rarely new or first-onset: they reflect the recurrence or persistence of disorders that started much earlier. For this reason, it is critical to explore the role of early-life experiences and how those experiences have changed between cohorts. In this chapter, I explore cohort differences relative to changes that occurred across the twentieth century, especially with respect to the family. There is little doubt that there have been significant changes in family formation. Indeed, demographers have characterized some of these changes as seismic in nature. Certainly, too, some social scientists have argued that the current mental health crisis reflects the deterioration of the traditional family. Yet trends in the family are more complex than is often appreciated, especially with respect to their implications for child well-being.[1] Even accepting that significant change has taken place in child raising patterns, it is unclear what experiences might be implicated in anxiety and whether any trends in the family are sufficiently powerful to explain cohort differences.

Considering the long history of speculation about the causes of anxiety disorders, it is certainly *not* the case that scientists interested in anxiety have neglected family conditions altogether. Indeed, interest in anxiety was sparked, at least in part, by Freud, who famously emphasized early-life family dynamics. By the same token, the twentieth century is replete with examples of speculation regarding what changing family dynamics were doing to the well-being of children. Anxiety and depression have been prominent in virtually all these accounts, not least because most people instinctively regard parental behavior as critical to mental health. Historically, the scientific study of the role of the family has been complicated by a shifting focus across a particular set of topics and a general neglect of the bigger demographic picture. Over time, what has concerned observers has shifted as well, often dramatically and sometimes inconsistently. In the middle of the twentieth century, for instance, scholars were concerned about the consequences of smaller families and, related to this, a decline in the number of households that included grandparents. In the late twentieth century, concern shifted to the consequences of being raised in a single-parent household and the growing number of children being raised in households with stepparents.[2] Meanwhile, much of the literature settled on the specific topic of the consequences of divorce, perhaps recognizing divorce as the sharpest edge of family change. Yet here, too, research has often employed a narrow scope and failed to grasp the big picture, one that involves more countervailing influences than critics seem willing to acknowledge.[3] Research on divorce evolved in such a way as to put forward widely divergent views of its effects, creating little space for a middle ground or a more temperate approach. Influential scholars advocated from the poles of a debate. Judith Wallerstein was instrumental in arguing that divorce exerted a profoundly negative impact on the well-being of children, assuming the significance of parental behavior, whereas Judith Rich Harris was instrumental in arguing that divorce played a minor role in child well-being, assuming instead that nature was much more significant than nurture.[4] How divorce was framed varied along similar lines, with some depicting divorce as the liberation of women from traditional forms of authority and others framing divorce more squarely in terms of the destruction of a once-whole family. The extremes of the debate often failed to consider the reasons a couple might separate, factors of particular relevance for understanding the effects of divorce on the mental health of children. The end of a conflictual marriage is good for children, to be sure, though there are certainly other antecedents of divorce that are correlated with child well-being. For instance, studies claiming that divorce hurts well-being often do not consider the mental health of parents, which is strongly related to divorce and, moreover, can affect the well-being of children in both direct and indirect ways. An important upshot of research on family change is that those who are interested in the effects of the family must consider an array of potential influences simultaneously, not simply those they presume to be most important.

FAMILY CHANGE ACROSS THE TWENTIETH CENTURY

Many significant social transformations occurred across the twentieth century, but changes in the family were among the most important. Demographers routinely refer to the "earthquake" that began in the 1960s and continues to reverberate through the American family.[5] Perhaps the signature change during this time was the increasing risk of divorce. In the 1990s, demographers estimated that about half of all marriages would end in divorce, though the 1990s were hardly an aberration in this regard.[6] In fact, many important family trends have much deeper historical roots, belying the idea that there is anything particularly unusual or unprecedented about the last fifty years. Divorce, for instance, has been steadily increasing since the Civil War.[7] The divorce rate tended to increase for each successive generation in the twentieth century in comparison with the divorce rate of the preceding generation.[8] To be sure, there have been some abrupt shifts, associated with major events, as well as some significant reversals. For instance, divorce increased sharply after World War II. Furthermore, the number of divorces per one thousand married women—an indicator of remarriage—leveled off somewhat in the 1980s.[9] Nonetheless, the divorce rate has continued to increase in the last three decades.

Given the overlay of trends in time and over cohorts, the increase in divorce implies that recent cohorts are more likely to have experienced parental divorce themselves. Children are increasingly less likely to live with both their biological parents. Furthermore, if the experience of divorce is traumatic, trends in divorce might affect the anxiety of adults. Divorce is often adversarial, and joint custody arrangements are rarely smooth. Children may be affected by a divorce even if their parents remarry and enter a stable union later on. Nonetheless, it is important to understand what else is at stake in divorce and remarriage and the deeper currents that have shaped these trends.

Increases in divorce have been driven largely by changes in the relative economic fortunes of men and women, combined with attitude changes that have made divorce and remaining unmarried more socially acceptable.[10] For much of the early twentieth century, the male-breadwinner model prevailed in American families, characterized by the greater economic power of men over women. Indeed, the breadwinner model prevailed even as women slowly gained more independence. In the early twentieth century, women had few economic opportunities outside the home, limiting their capacity to delay marriage or live alone. Although women gained the right to vote in 1920, their political power was limited, slowing the chance for progress. Among men the situation was very different. Stable job opportunities were abundant, offering salaries sufficient to support a family over a long tenure. The situation began to change in the middle of the century, especially with respect to women's labor force participation. In the 1960s more women began to enter the labor force and across a widening range of occupations, from sales to management. This, in turn, increased their power within and outside the home. Women were able to delay marriage, resulting in a steady increase in the age at first marriage, if not forgoing of marriage altogether. Women were also able to seek divorce in greater numbers, confident in their ability to maintain a household on their own. Geographic data are consistent with this idea. In locations where more women held jobs, the prevalence of separation and divorce increased.[11] Somewhat later, the relative empowerment of women improved even more because of declining opportunities among men.[12] Whereas the middle of the twentieth century was characterized by growing wages and intergenerational mobility among men—men could feel confident that they would do better than their fathers and better over time—the late 1980s were characterized by young men making much less progress. Indeed, relative income between generations—a measure of intergenerational prosperity—has dropped 80 percent since its peak in 1958.[13] Women's wage labor has declined as well, though starting at a later point and deteriorating at a slower rate.

Attitudes have changed as well, as American culture has evolved in parallel with progress in women's opportunities. To be sure, cultural change happened slowly and changing attitudes have not been the whole story with respect to family change. It is unlikely, for instance, that more progressive attitudes regarding women's capabilities wholly produced more economic opportunities for them. Employers did not suddenly realize the value of women and start hiring more women, nor did women abruptly appreciate their own skills and suddenly start advocating on their own behalf. Nonetheless, a more progressive mindset likely did reduce some of the headwinds against economic advancement, especially in the late twentieth century. Starting in the 1970s, the percentage of married women who disagreed that women should stay at home increased precipitously, growing from a solid minority, around 20 percent, to the clear majority, over 70 percent, in just over a decade.[14] Over approximately the same period of time, attitudes regarding divorce began to shift as well, reducing the stigma surrounding a once highly stigmatized decision. Here, too, attitudes about divorce almost certainly helped to shift behavior, even if the appeal of divorce among women also required more economic security. As attitudes surrounding divorce changed, more people felt enabled to pursue a divorce.[15] Other changes further entrenched the increase in divorce. Women's educational attainment rose, as did their control over their fertility, leading to a further increase in the age of first marriage. Age of first marriage has increased more or less steadily since 1960 and is, at present, the highest it has ever been, especially among women with a college degree.[16]

Fertility also changed over this period, though in complex ways. To understand the implications of family change for anxiety, it is important to understand the actual production of cohorts through births, as well as the kinds of family backgrounds that cohorts experience. In this regard, the situation with respect to the average fertility of *women* is not the same as the situation with respect to the average situation of *households*.[17] Over the course of the twentieth century, total fertility—the total number of children a woman will have in her lifetime—declined from around four to two, with some fluctuation, including an increase from just over two children to just over three between 1940 and 1965. Yet *variation* in family size is just as important as the central tendency for understanding trends in the circumstances in which children are raised. On this score, changes across the twentieth century are even sharper and more consequential. The frequency of especially large families has declined. In the early twentieth century, more than 20 percent of women bore seven or more children.[18] By 1939, this percentage had dropped to around 5 percent, and by 1989, it had dropped further to under 2 percent. The overall trend in family size can be characterized by growing compression around the average of two children. The range between a woman at the 20th percentile of total fertility and a woman at the 80th percentile has collapsed from around six births to just over two.[19]

FAMILY CHANGE AND ANXIETY

Trends in marriage and fertility have implications for how generations of children have experienced their upbringing, perhaps the critical piece for understanding anxiety. Many of the previously noted trends are slow and steady, realized across a century of larger structural and cultural change. The economic opportunities available to women, for instance, have improved steadily, and the culture surrounding gender has evolved slowly in tandem. Yet from the standpoint of cohorts of children—that is, from the standpoint of what children experience—these trends are more sweeping in their significance. The percentage of children living with both parents in a first marriage decreased from 73 percent in 1960 to 46 percent in 2014.[20] Over the same period of time, the percentage living with a single parent increased from 9 percent to 26 percent. If one considers whether children ever spent time in a single-parent household—something that may happen for only a short period of time given remarriage—the percentage is even higher. About 50 percent of children spend at least some time in a single-parent household.[21] In addition, about 16 percent of children are living in blended families involving a household with a stepparent and a step- or half-sibling. This percentage has remained stable since the early 1990s but increased in the decades prior. Furthermore, children who have half-siblings from one side of the family are also more likely to have half-siblings from the other, further increasing family complexity.[22] Of course, fertility trends also imply that a growing number of children have no siblings. In 1964, just under 10 percent of women bore only one child in their lifetimes, whereas by 1989 this had increased to just under 20 percent. The percentage of adults who have grown up with a biological sibling is decreasing, which likely has implications for feelings of support.[23] All told, the experiences of children have changed dramatically: a minority of children spend their entire childhoods with both biological parents and about 30 percent spend at least some time with a stepfamily.[24]

These trends are likely relevant to anxiety, though the implications are unclear. There is little doubt that some of these trends are beneficial to children's development and mental health, especially when considered in the context of other improvements. The increase in women's employment prospects has not only increased their economic opportunities but provided women with skills they can potentially pass on to their children, including a more positive mindset. Furthermore, other institutions have changed alongside the family in ways that might cushion any adverse effects of growing family complexity. For instance, as divorce has risen, the obligation to pay child support has been taken more seriously by the courts, increasing the economic security of children following divorce.[25] Moreover, despite significant increases in family instability, actual parenting behaviors have changed less than expected. Although parents spend more time out of the home than they did in the past, they still spend time with their children after work and appear to monitor their behavior just as much as before.[26] Indeed, despite rising participation in the labor force among women, the time mothers spend with their children has remained quite stable or even increased.[27] More detailed explorations of *how* parents spend their time with children—not just the amount of time—is even more encouraging.[28] Mothers and fathers spent more time in childcare activities in the 1990s than they did in the 1960s, despite the earlier period being characterized as the more "family-friendly" era. Even when mothers and fathers are not spending time with their children, they are making other investments in their children's development. The amount spent on childcare has increased over time, as has the percentage of children enrolled in preschool.[29] Other trends in the behavior of parents are also favorable. Data based on substantiated cases of child maltreatment indicate that both physical and sexual abuse have declined.[30] Between 1990 and 2010, physical abuse declined 56 percent, while sexual abuse declined 62 percent.[31] To be sure, not all of these trends are rooted in better parental behavior. For instance, one reason for the decline in abuse is the increased effort of organizations to protect children, as well as the greater involvement of the criminal justice system in incarcerating abusive parents.[32] Nonetheless, these trends are also driven by a growing capacity of families to encourage better behavior. Evidence from Sweden, for instance, indicates that recent cohorts of adults report parents who were less authoritative in their parenting styles, encouraging them, for instance, to express their anger more freely.[33]

Some other trends are likely to increase anxiety. Parental divorce will not necessarily undermine a child's well-being, but there is no doubt that divorce is at least disruptive, involving a drop in the amount of time spent with both parents, often a move, and on average, a decline in economic well-being.[34] Furthermore, even if divorce per se is not harmful, it is often preceded by events that are. Witnessing domestic violence has increased over time.[35] There is also evidence that families based on remarriage can have distinctive problems that affect children in adverse ways.[36] For one, parents in families with biological and stepchildren must allocate resources among a diverse set of children with whom parents have relationships of varying depth. Among the resources to be allocated is time. Although there may be no decline in the total amount of time spent with children, there could be an increase in inequality among siblings, especially in complex families. Some evidence indicates that children raised by stepmothers obtain significantly less education—about one year less—than do the birth children of the same mothers.[37]

Relationships among siblings can accentuate these risks and are an important, if neglected, aspect of family change. By one count, references in the scientific literature to parents or parenting exceed references to siblings or sibling relationships by more than forty-five to one.[38] Yet sibling relationship are important to well-being, perhaps even more so than parental behavior. Sibling relationships may be especially important because they are critical to learning about social relationships generally. Siblings provide a ready opportunity for emotional understanding, negotiation, taking the perspective of another, and joint problem solving, even in the context of pretend activities for which the stakes would seem to be low.[39] All of these lessons can carry over to adult relationships.[40] Furthermore, the character of sibling relationships is unique, as they involve two things at once: the kind of support typical of parent–child relationships and the kind of reciprocity typical of peer relationships. Children who are close to their siblings often have an enhanced sense of security they carry into adult friendships, whereas children who do not have secure sibling relationships are often more aggressive as adults.[41] Some evidence links sibling relationships more directly to adult mental health. Children who experienced warm relationships with their siblings while growing up have fewer psychological symptoms as adults, even controlling for the quality of their relationships with their parents.[42]

Complex families may blunt some of the emotional benefits of close siblings. In complex families, the distribution of time and affection is more fraught, and distinctions between how siblings are treated are more readily apparent.[43] Some evidence is consistent with this idea. Although parents overwhelmingly profess to have no favorites, evidence indicates that most parents do in fact treat their children differently and, further, that children attend to such differences at an early age.[44] Differential treatment is not always a result of favoritism—parents can treat children differently based on their needs and behavior. Nonetheless, there is evidence that differential treatment, even when not invidious, can be detrimental. In general, comparisons by parents can lead to personal feelings of insecurity and anxiety among siblings, irrespective of whether one child is treated better or worse than the other.[45] Frequent arguments among siblings have been linked to subsequent increases in depression and anxiety. And different kinds of arguments have different kinds of associations. Arguments regarding personal space or possessions (e.g., borrowing something without permission) are associated with higher anxiety, whereas arguments regarding equality and fairness (e.g., the equal division of time spent with a family computer) are associated with higher depression.[46] Furthermore, differential treatment is more consequential among young children than adolescents, perhaps because adolescents draw social comparisons among their peers more than among their siblings.[47] More generally, evidence indicates that the presence of step- or half-siblings increases aggressive behavior in children, even controlling for other characteristics associated with living in a complex family.[48]

Apart from trends in family formation and composition, some parenting strategies have changed in ways that undermine mental health. One argument for why time spent with children has increased even as outside demands have grown is that expectations regarding appropriate parenting have changed. Investments in children increasingly involve the expectation of significant oversight. Children across different generations report somewhat different parenting styles. Approximately 68 percent of millennials (those ages eighteen to thirty-four) report that their parents were overprotective, but among Generation X (those ages thirty-five to fifty) this drops to 60 percent, and among baby boomers (those ages fifty-one to sixty-nine) it drops further still to 54 percent.[49] Overbearing parenting is often used to explain differences between cohorts, although it is not clear whether it is particularly relevant compared with other influences. To be sure, there is evidence that children whose parents routinely intervene to stop them from exploratory activities are more anxious and, further, that the effects of overinvolvement are stronger for anxiety than depression, though the effects are not especially large.[50] As with much else when it comes to early life influences, the scientific literature is more nuanced than the intuitions surrounding it.

FAMILY BACKGROUND AND EARLY-ONSET ANXIETY

I now turn to data on family background and early-onset anxiety disorders. Table 5.1 starts with the prevalence of childhood experiences associated with anxiety, arrayed over cohorts. Data are drawn from the Collaborative Psychiatric Epidemiology Surveys (CPES). Respondents were asked a variety of questions about their experiences. In these items, as in other data discussed to this point, there are significant cohort differences. In general, the percentage reporting their mother likely had any of three psychiatric disorders (based on reports of symptoms) has increased. The lowest level of maternal psychiatric disorders is among those sixty years of age and older. There are few major between-cohort differences in abuse and neglect. And even the percentage reporting that their mother frequently stopped them from doing things does not vary much between cohorts.

Among the most significant cohort differences pertain to family. The percentage reporting no biological siblings, for instance, has dropped precipitously between cohorts. Although most people report having a sibling, the percentage reporting a biological sibling has declined from 77 percent in the oldest cohort to 54 percent in the youngest. Conversely the percentage reporting either both biological and other siblings and the percentage reporting only nonbiological siblings has increased, from 13 percent to 27 percent for the former and from 4 percent to 15 percent for the latter. Other changes are also significant. The percentage reporting frequent moves to a new neighborhood while growing up (six or more moves) has increased. The percentage not growing up with both biological parents has also increased, from 23 percent among those sixty and over to 41 percent among those eighteen to twenty-nine. Table 5.1 presents a summary

TABLE 5.1
Means of early childhood adversity by cohort

	Cohort			
	18 to 29	30 to 44	45 to 59	60 and Over
Mother anxious	8.4%	10.4%	10.0%	5.6%
Mother depressed	6.0%	6.1%	6.2%	3.3%
Mother drank frequently	3.7%	3.2%	3.5%	.9%
Abuse	4.7%	7.8%	7.3%	4.1%
Neglect	3.5%	4.7%	4.9%	3.8%
Mother intervened frequently	27.2%	25.7%	27.9%	28.0%
Frequent residential moves	12.1%	9.8%	10.0%	8.0%
Did not live with both biological parents at age 16	41.0%	32.6%	21.9%	23.3%
Siblings				
No siblings	4.3%	3.2%	4.0%	5.7%
Only biological Siblings	53.9%	61.7%	72.4%	77.2%
Only stepsiblings	14.8%	7.0%	5.6%	4.4%
Both biological and stepsiblings	27.1%	28.1%	18.0%	12.7%
Total number of risks	1.253	1.105	1.012	.873
Any adversity	65.6%	61.4%	57.2%	56.1%

Source: Margarita Alegria, James S. (James Sidney) Jackson, Ronald C. Kessler, and David Takeuchi, Collabora-tive Psychiatric Epidemiology Surveys (CPES), 2001–2003 [United States] (Ann Arbor, Mich.: Inter-university Consortium for Political and Social Research [distributor], 2016), https://doi.org/10.3886/ICPSR20240.v8 ($N = 5,528$).

measure, counting the total number of risk factors (and counting no bio-logical siblings as one).[51] The total number of risks varies between cohorts in a monotonic fashion. The youngest cohort experiences the most total risk, with 66 percent experiencing at least one risk, relative to 56 percent among those sixty and over.

Many of these experiences are related to the risk of developing an anxi-ety disorder. Table 5.2 presents results from three models, the first two pre-dicting the risk of a current anxiety disorder and the last predicting the risk of an early-onset anxiety disorder (onset before the age of eighteen). In all cases, the coefficients can be interpreted in terms of the expected change in the probability of an anxiety disorder given the presence of the risk factor. Among the strongest predictors are the presence of a mental

TABLE 5.2
Linear probability regression models of anxiety disorders with early childhood adversity

	Model 1	Model 2	Model 3
	Any current anxiety disorder	Any current anxiety disorder	Any early anxiety disorder
Mother anxious	.085***	.023	.100***
	(.019)	(.018)	(.021)
Mother depressed	.081*	.034	.076*
	(.030)	(.021)	(.031)
Mother drank frequently	.072*	.052*	.032
	(.028)	(.022)	(.045)
Abuse	.127***	.054**	.117**
	(.030)	(.016)	(.034)
Neglect	.072	.006	.107***
	(.038)	(.033)	(.028)
Mother intervened frequently	.036**	.021**	.024
	(.011)	(.007)	(.013)
Frequent residential moves	−.008	−.019	.017
	(.019)	(.012)	(.016)
Did not live with both biological parents at age 16	−.015	−.003	−.020
	(.012)	(.006)	(.015)
Siblings (versus none)			
Only biological siblings	−.065*	−.020	−.073*
	(.026)	(.014)	(.029)
Only stepsiblings	−.054	−.031	−.037
	(.032)	(.019)	(.033)
Both biological and stepsiblings	−.025	−.009	−.025
	(.024)	(.015)	(.028)
Any early anxiety disorder		.619***	
		(.015)	

* $p < .05$, ** $p < .01$, *** $p < .001$ (standard errors in parentheses).

Source: Margarita Alegria, James S. (James Sidney) Jackson, Ronald C. Kessler, and David Takeuchi, Collaborative Psychiatric Epidemiology Surveys (CPES), 2001–2003 [United States] (Ann Arbor, Mich.: Inter-university Consortium for Political and Social Research [distributor], 2016), https://doi.org/10.3886/ICPSR20240.v8 (N = 5,528).

Note: All models also include coefficients for age, sex, and race/ethnicity (results not shown).

illness in the mother and abuse. Physical and/or sexual abuse increases the risk of a current anxiety disorder by 12.7 percentage points. An anxious mother increases the risk by 8.5 points. A strict mother also increases the risk, though by a much smaller amount, 3.6 points. The presence of siblings generally reduces the risk of an anxiety disorder, though the only significant negative association is for the presence of biological siblings. Neither frequent moves nor living with both parents is significantly related to an anxiety disorder in adulthood.

Many of these associations are mediated through an early-onset anxiety disorder: that is, these early experiences increase the risk of an anxiety disorder in childhood or adolescence that persists into adulthood. The second model presented in the table adjusts for any early-onset anxiety disorder and in effect reduces or eliminates many of the significant associations. The third model puts these two pieces together and explores the relationship between the same childhood experiences and an early-onset disorder. Once again abuse is strongly related to an early-onset anxiety disorder, as is an anxious mother. In this case, neglect also increases the risk of an early-onset disorder. But as before, neither frequent moves nor living with both biological parents is significantly related to the risk of an early-onset anxiety disorder. In short, some of the most significant changes between cohorts with respect to family background have among the weakest relationships with the onset of anxiety.

One implication of the earlier discussion of mood and anxiety disorders is that anxiety disorders should be more strongly associated with environmental factors than mood disorders. In the presence of a stressful environment, the risk for anxiety in children should be stronger than the risk for depression. Figure 5.1 presents expected values from a model predicting an early-onset anxiety disorder (with no co-occurring mood disorder, for which the cases were dropped) and another model predicting an early-onset mood disorder (with no co-occurring anxiety disorder). The model includes the total sum of all risk factors rather than each risk factor individually. The relationship between this count and the risk of an early-onset psychiatric disorder is more than three times stronger for anxiety ($b = .039$) than for mood disorders ($b = .011$, each coefficient significant at $p < .001$ and the difference between them also significant at $p < .001$). Table 5.3 presents coefficients summarizing the childhood experiences over three dimensions and their relationships with early-onset mood and anxiety

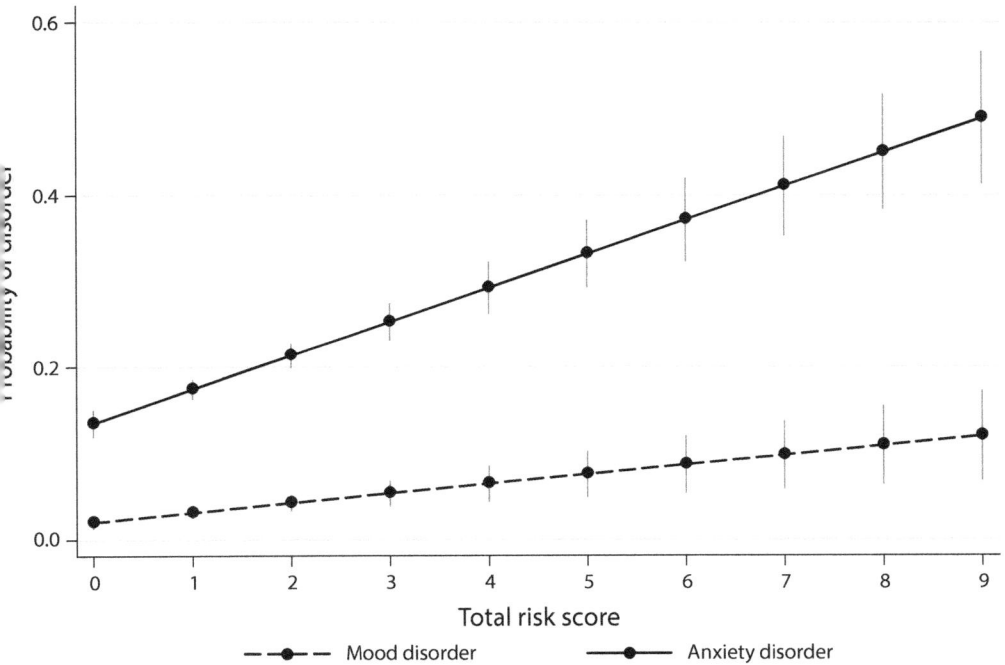

FIGURE 5.1. Predicted probability of any early anxiety or mood disorder based on total risk
Source: Collaborative Psychiatric Epidemiological Surveys (Primary Survey, National Comorbidity Survey Replication, *N* = 5,528). Based on models presented in table 5.2.

disorders. Each of the three dimensions is the count of the specific type of childhood experience within each dimension. Maternal mental illness has the strongest relationship in both cases, followed by abuse and neglect. In both cases the relationship of these influences with anxiety is much stronger than the relationship with mood disorders. In neither case is the total of other family-related risk factors significantly related to the risk of an early-onset disorder.

Table 5.4 returns to the question of how much these risk factors, as a set, explain differences between cohorts. The table presents summaries of four models, two for current anxiety and two for early-onset anxiety. In all cases, the models focus on differences between cohorts. The first model presents a basic unadjusted model, in which the coefficients represent the expected increase in anxiety relative to the oldest cohort. The

TABLE 5.3
Linear probability regression models of early-onset anxiety and mood disorders on early childhood adversity

	Early-onset mood disorder	Early-onset anxiety disorder
Total mother mental illness	.024***+	.074****+
	(.008)	(.013)
Total abuse and neglect	.010+	.053***+
	(.006)	(.012)
Total family experience risk	.006	.010
	(.004)	(.006)

* $p < .05$, ** $p < .01$, *** $p < .001$ (standard errors in parentheses). + $p < .001$ (for test of difference between coefficients)
Source: Margarita Alegria, James S. (James Sidney) Jackson, Ronald C. Kessler, and David Takeuchi, Collaborative Psychiatric Epidemiology Surveys (CPES), 2001–2003 [United States] (Ann Arbor, Mich.: Inter-university Consortium for Political and Social Research [distributor], 2016), https://doi.org/10.3886/ICPSR20240.v8 ($N = 3,856$ for mood disorders, $N = 5,093$ for anxiety disorders).
Note: All models also include coefficients for age, sex, and race/ethnicity (coefficients not shown).

second model adjusts for family background factors. Differences between the models are informative with respect to how much family change explains cohort differences. The results indicate that family background explains no more than 15 percent of the between-cohort differences and generally more of the difference between the middle-aged (forty-five to fifty-nine) and oldest (those sixty and over) cohorts than between the youngest and oldest cohorts. Among those eighteen to twenty-nine, about 10 percent of the cohort's excess anxiety can be explained by family background. Among those forty-five to fifty-nine, the explanatory power of family background rises to only 13 percent. The relatively small role of family background is mostly attributable to a discontinuity: the experiences that most divide cohorts have the weakest relationships with anxiety. For instance, younger cohorts are far less likely to live with both parents at the age of sixteen, but this experience is largely unrelated to anxiety disorders. Younger cohorts are also much less likely to have a biological sibling, though the relationship between having no biological siblings and anxiety is not especially strong. Abuse and neglect remain powerful predictors of anxiety, as does a mother who suffers from some

TABLE 5.4
Cohort differences in anxiety disorders with and without adjustment for early childhood adversity

	Model 1	Model 2	Model 3	Model 4
	Any current anxiety disorder	Any current anxiety disorder	Any early anxiety disorder	Any early anxiety disorder
Cohort (relative to 60 and over)				
18 to 29	.111***	.100***	.138***	.124***
	(.009)	(.010)	(.015)	(.017)
30 to 44	.127***	.111***	.133***	.115***
	(.011)	(.011)	(.017)	(.018)
45 to 59	.099***	.084***	.113***	.098***
	(.019)	(.019)	(.018)	(.020)
Including early childhood adversity	No	Yes	No	Yes

* $p < .05$, ** $p < .01$, *** $p < .001$ (standard errors in parentheses).
Source: Margarita Alegria, James S. (James Sidney) Jackson, Ronald C. Kessler, and David Takeuchi, Collaborative Psychiatric Epidemiology Surveys (CPES), 2001–2003 [United States] (Ann Arbor, Mich.: Inter-university Consortium for Political and Social Research [distributor], 2016), https://doi.org/10.3886/ICPSR20240.v8 (N = 5,528).
Note: All models also include coefficients for age, sex, and race/ethnicity (results not shown).

form of mental illness. But the differences between cohorts in these experiences are relatively small.

Anxiety has increased between cohorts, just as many experiences with family background have changed. Yet when it comes to the major family-related determinants of anxiety, cohorts are more similar than different. In the twenty-first century, there is considerably more family complexity, but family complexity alone does little to increase anxiety. Similarly, parents who intervene to prevent their children from doing things that other children are doing might produce somewhat more anxious children, but this effect is not terribly strong. Furthermore, strict parents are no more common today than they were in the past. The mediating effects shown in this chapter are, to be sure, not unimportant. Explaining even 10 percent of a cohort difference moves us closer to an explanation. Furthermore, it is not wrong to assert that family background, in general, matters for anxiety. But there are other factors in play, and a comprehensive understanding requires other considerations.

The next chapter explores cohort differences in religious participation. Here, too, the potential relevance of religion is high. Religious participation is declining. Religious beliefs from a variety of traditions often focus on allaying anxiety specifically. And there are important continuities between religious experiences in childhood and religious practices in adulthood, making religion relevant for early-onset anxiety as much as adult anxiety. The argument that our age of anxiety reflects a crisis of meaning, or a decline in existential security, or even an explicit crisis of faith is a recurrent theme in the literature. Religious participation has certainly declined between cohorts, but it is once again important to consider the larger context in which this decline has occurred, as well as the specific dimensions of religious belief and practice that have been affected. The modern crisis of faith, such as it is, might be slow moving and, in the end, perhaps only one of many gradual transformations.

Chapter Six

THE DECLINE IN RELIGIOUS PARTICIPATION

In any account of anxiety, religion deserves special attention. The modern history of anxiety is tightly intertwined with the history of religious involvement. Religious participation is declining, just as anxiety seems more common, and some observers attribute the latter to the former.[1] Some go even further and argue that the decline in religion provides an explanation for a range of social problems, including growing moral drift, an increasing sense of purposelessness, and a rise in social isolation. Writing in *National Review*, Paul Vitz and Bruce Buff make an especially forceful case along these lines, arguing that the decline in religion is the primary explanation for the rise in anxiety, among many other problems.[2] For them, the issue is not only that the influence of religion has waned, but that the cultural vacuum its loss has created has been filled by mindsets that fail to provide a proper equivalent. Although other critics might put forward different influences to fill the putative vacuum, Vitz and Buff argue that postmodern nihilism is to blame, characterized by the deconstruction of shared understandings that ordinarily provide a ballast in difficult times. For Vitz and Buff, standards for truth and goodness have been eroded in a wholesale fashion. Young people now live in a "world without any real meaning" and so turn to external sources of validation, none of which can provide an adequate substitute.

Even without the severe and moral tone, other critics have at least made similar arguments, assuming there is little in the broader culture to deliver guidance now that transcendental authority has waned. Writing in *The Atlantic*, Emma Green argues that the decline in religious involvement is a significant crisis in American culture.[3] She maintains more optimism than Vitz and Buff, pointing to the proliferation of spiritual and religious choices, an opportunity, as she sees it, to assemble a spiritual life from fragments if one has not acquired a formal religious doctrine from scripture. In this climate, she argues, it is still possible to create new kinds of spirituality, well before a full embrace of atheism. Others, too, have pointed out that while the number of Americans reporting no religious affiliation has increased, the percentage of Americans believing in God has hardly changed at all.[4]

The line between religious and atheist is perhaps too crude to characterize the modern mindset, but it remains to be seen whether the decline in formal religious participation is a cause of rising anxiety. Indeed, for all the potential power of religion, it is easy to imagine a secular mindset that provides comfort even if fails to provide an entire theology.[5] For one, there is no obvious relationship between atheism and nihilism. If there is a path between the two, it is a long one. Atheists, after all, can have convictions that inform their choices, projects that guide their behavior, and ideals they can live up to. Most people strive toward moral behavior, and the capacity to judge values does not depend on belief in a god. Atheists can wonder at the seemingly miraculous without resorting to an explanation beyond the material. The religious might see signs of divine intervention in everyday events, but atheists, too, can derive satisfaction from a problem solved or troubles averted. A belief in simple fate—where events are destined to happen irrespective of individual action—is not so far removed from a belief in divine providence. And appreciating the transcendental—or something that surpasses our individual lives—does not necessitate a belief in the supernatural. In short, it is a mistake to believe religion per se is the only framework for providing meaning. At an even more fundamental level, it is useful to unpack what is meant by the term "religious," given that most claims about the importance of a spiritual life for well-being are cast using this term. The empirical literature on religion and well-being provides at least some clues about what religion does and does not do.

RELIGION AND WELL-BEING

The case for a role for religion in reducing anxiety would seem to be, on its face, very strong. Religious faith is replete with emotional elements. Individuals *feel* their faith as much as they reflect on it. Articles of faith are replete with beliefs meant to ease a fearful mind. Religion might be especially powerful in the prevention of anxiety for at least three reasons.[6] First, religious teachings often focus directly on the kinds of cognitive tools meant to reduce anxiety, including coping with fear, reducing uncertainty, and reinterpreting the past. Perhaps the most prominent existential fear is the fear of death, and religions speak frequently to that particular concern. Yet religious teachings are as farsighted in life as they are in death, speaking to everyday worries and concerns. Moreover, religious individuals gravitate toward these teachings, as is reflected in their behavior. When individuals pray, for instance, they often pray for guidance about what comes next in life, not just for assurance of an afterlife. At the same time, religion provides a framework for how to interpret the past. To be sure, religious beliefs often center on miracles. And religion may be comforting precisely because it dwells on the extraordinary. Yet religion also sheds light on the quotidian and mundane. In fact, most religious people see the workings of divinity in their daily lives and routine events, including whether certain things happen at all, the timing of those experiences, and the meaning of those experiences after they occur.[7] In addition, religious beliefs are sufficiently flexible to allow individuals to interpret good events as answers to prayers or bad events as unexpected opportunities. Even short of religion's explanatory power, religion generally encourages behaviors that can be conducive to mental health, especially through its emphasis on values. Although they might frame their advice in a very different fashion, professional counselors often encourage the kind of mindsets that are fostered by religion, including maintaining a sense of purpose, forgiving others for transgressions, and being faithful in marriage.[8] Religion provides a moral order that is readily internalized and resistant to competing messages.[9] Ultimately, the effects of religious faith on well-being are not contingent on demonstrating that religious beliefs are accurate. In this sense, the effects of religion on well-being could be likened to a placebo effect—a treatment with no active ingredient that nonetheless has a therapeutic effect—but if so, this interpretation is hardly cynical. It does not invalidate the effects of religion any more than it invalidates those of a placebo.[10] Expectations can strongly affect well-being, and the expectations surrounding religious faith—that God provides for the faithful—are probably stronger than the positive expectations surrounding pharmaceutical treatment, which people are well aware have side effects.

Second, religion has a potentially powerful effect on well-being because it involves mechanisms that operate at multiple levels.[11] Religion certainly affects the beliefs and behaviors of adherents. Yet beyond its prescriptive teachings, organized religion provides individuals with a community of like-minded others, involving relationships of trust, commitment, and reciprocity.[12] Religious people are perceived as nicer and more cooperative by other people.[13] In addition, the social dimensions of religion are strongly reflected in the practices of adherents. Religious services provide a routine mechanism for support, comfort, and instrumental assistance. As discussed in more detail in a later chapter, social support exerts a powerful effect on emotional well-being. And religious networks are generally stronger relative to other sources of affiliation. Congregants often turn to fellow congregants for assistance, and religion's emphasis on community encourages assistance in turn. Even private religious practices have a social quality. When Americans pray, for instance, they are more likely to pray about the concerns of family and friends than personal matters.[14] If anything, the social value of religion has increased over time as proselytizing denominations have promoted a more welcoming environment to attract adherents. Across the twentieth century, religious views, especially among Protestants, shifted from a focus on God's wrath, emphasizing obedience and behavioral strictures, to a more benign and welcoming view, emphasizing love, comfort, and fellowship.[15]

Third, the influence of religion is apparent across the life course. Anxiety disorders tend to start at a young age, and religious practices, too, tend to begin early. Many things change over a life span, including habits, attitudes, and preferences, but relative to these characteristics, religious orientations are more consistent. Most people raised in a tradition tend to claim that tradition as an adult (or a closely related one, as in switching among Protestant denominations).[16] Religious practices are nearly as stable as religious identities. Those reporting attending religious services routinely in one year tend to report the same thing the following year.[17] Such stability might be especially consequential for the lives of children. Being raised in a family where religious involvement is important could provide stability that reduces the risk of anxiety. Religious compatibility between spouses, for instance, tends to decrease the risk of divorce.[18] Furthermore, religious families may invest in their children in ways that promote well-being. Religious families tend to be more generous with their time and money, including volunteering more in schools and youth groups.[19]

Yet there is much more nuance to the idea that religion assuages fear. For every claim of religion's role in reducing anxiety, there is an equally strong claim to the contrary. This tension is hardly new and, indeed, is apparent in virtually every major statement on anxiety written over the last century. In *The Future of an Illusion*, for instance, Freud directly aligned religion and anxiety, but in an ironic fashion, drawing a parallel between the obsessions of the anxious with the beliefs of religious adherents.[20] For Freud, both were a form of fanaticism rooted in irrationality—they involved a degree of inflexibility, resignation, and deference that was anathema to emotional maturity. In the middle of the twentieth century, the discussion surrounding anxiety assumed a decidedly more existential cast. Atheism per se was not advanced as a cause of any crisis, but scholarly ambivalence toward religion was nonetheless apparent.[21] For Rollo May and Paul Tillich, religion provided a means for coming to terms with the freedom of life and, thereby, a way to resolve existential terror. Yet they also thought that many other philosophical frameworks provided the same.[22] In an earlier era, William James split the difference on the psychological value of religion by emphasizing what individuals did with their religion rather than whether they were religious at all.[23] For James, there were both healthy and unhealthy forms of religious involvement, and the many different kinds of religious participation he cataloged belied any claim about the general value of religious practice.

At the root of most skepticism surrounding the role of religion in well-being are two arguments. The first is that religion involves a mix of beliefs and behaviors, only some of which are conducive to mental health. Religion, in this framing, involves a set of bargains. In surrendering to religious authority, for instance, individuals cede some of their own agency. And in accepting guidance regarding proper behavior, individuals tempt wrath if they fail to measure up. The second argument pertains to what religion is set against. When scholars argue that the retreat from religion is responsible for the rise in anxiety, they imply that a commitment to religion cannot be replaced by something else, that atheism takes the place of religion and cannot provide an alternative vision of salvation. It is entirely possible, though, that a more secular era can encourage mindsets that are more suitable to emotional well-being or, short of that, that an idiosyncratic spirituality can do just as well as orthodox religion. The idea that a decline in religious affiliation has produced a void in meaning also rests on the notion that a retreat from religion is a retreat from *belief* as much as *practice*. At times arguments regarding growing secularization and its role in deteriorating mental health involve an elision, that an increase in the percentage of Americans who profess no religious affiliation is a full-scale retreat from religion. But it is not entirely clear that this is what has occurred.

To better understand the role of religion in anxiety, a precise understanding of trends in twentieth-century religious participation is necessary. A close examination reveals both consistency and change. By some measures, Americans are less religious than they used to be, though it is unclear whether religion truly plays less of a role than it used to in, for instance, maintaining an individual's moral framework. It is also unclear whether a decline in religious participation truly reflects a rise in secularism. Although one interpretation of recent trends is that secular liberalism has slowly triumphed over religion, survey data are more consistent with the idea that secular liberalism has pushed religion further into the private sphere but has not eliminated it. These deeper currents in the political and the personal are important. Understanding the role of religion in anxiety depends a great deal on the source of religion's comforts, as well as understanding how religious change, such as it is, fits within the context of other cultural changes.

RELIGIOUS CHANGE AND SOCIAL UPHEAVAL
IN MIDCENTURY AMERICA

Dating the precise moment when religious participation began to change in the United States is difficult, though Robert Putnam and David Campbell locate an especially pivotal moment in the 1960s.[24] The period witnessed a number of simultaneous cultural and social revolutions, including a growing acceptance of premarital sex, the rise of antiwar sentiment, and the ascendance of the civil rights movement. During the same period, Americans began to lose confidence in many institutions and traditional sources of authority. Although, in this sense, the loss of confidence in religious organizations was simply one facet of a much broader movement, there was still something remarkable about America's turn from religion. Up to that point, organized religion had enjoyed remarkable influence and broad support, seemingly removed from the fray of 1960s counterculture. Indeed, as late as the 1950s, religious organizations appeared to be at the height of their power, holding considerable sway over adherents' beliefs, conduct, and politics.[25] Nonetheless, after the 1960s, religious institutions suffered a dramatic decline. Survey data from the period point to significant changes in religious beliefs and affiliations. The percentage of Americans who reported that religion was "very important" in their lives declined from 75 percent in 1952 to 52 percent in 1978.[26] Americans' confidence in the teachings of religion also declined. The percentage reporting that religion "can answer today's problems" dropped from 82 percent in 1957 to 51 percent in 2015, an all-time low.[27] In addition, the percentage of Americans endorsing the idea that the Bible is the "actual word of God" declined by more than half.[28] In the early 1960s, about 65 percent of Americans believed the Bible was the word of God, but by 2010 this percentage had dropped to around 30 percent.[29]

An even more significant trend is the percentage of Americans professing no religious affiliation. In 1987, only one in fourteen Americans reported no affiliation, but by 2012 this had increased to one in five.[30] Although this situation has been realized over time, it has a strong cohort component, given how religious affiliation tends to remain consistent over the life course. Americans born between the years 1900 and 1925 were probably more religious than those born either before or since. Moreover, their religiosity was comprehensive: they believed in God, they attended religious services regularly, and they raised their children squarely within their religious traditions. Survey data from adults in midcentury America reflected this pattern (as well as its subsequent decline). At the time, 99 percent of adults professed a belief in God, but by 2000 this had fallen by 6 percentage points to 93 percent.[31] To be sure, this means more than 90 percent of Americans still profess a belief in God, which reflects a remarkable degree of consistency. Nonetheless, a detailed look at this belief reveals more doubt just beneath the surface. When Americans are provided with a range of responses regarding their belief in God, including "I have doubts," and not just "yes" or "no," only 65 percent report no doubt.

One of the most prominent theories for understanding the decline of religious participation is secularization theory, an idea that at least implicitly informs the idea that the retreat from religion has been detrimental to mental health.[32] The theory is counterposed: it posits a decline of religion and faith in direct response to an ascent of science and rationality. In this theory, religion as a form of traditional belief is replaced by a more modern mindset and, in the process, religion loses its hold. The theory has much to recommend it and coheres with some of the facts surrounding religious decline, as well as some of the facts in the rise of a more rational mindset. The decline in religious affiliation has, in fact, occurred at the same time as a rise in educational attainment. Furthermore, there are now many scientific tools to address problems that were once seen as almost entirely religious, especially with respect to health. Where the sick once looked for miracles, they now find medical cures. Yet secularization theory makes predictions that are too broad to encompass all the facets of religious change. In its essence, secularization theory argues for the growing *irrelevance* of religion, but as critics of the theory have pointed out, the decline in religious affiliation at the individual level has occurred despite the continued prominence of religious institutions at the cultural level, as has the persistence of many religious beliefs despite a decline in denominational identification. Those who report having no religion are not necessarily claiming to be atheists. And religious groups remain formidable in American politics, even if the number of evangelicals, for instance, is declining.

An especially persuasive critique of secularization theory inverts the logic of the theory to argue that the rise of those with no religion has been *caused by* the prominence of religion. According to this argument, the rise in the percentage of those with no religion reflects a backlash to how religious organizations have aligned themselves with divisive political issues. As religious organizations became more politically forthright in the late twentieth century, they lost adherents who did not share their political leanings. In support of this dynamic, critics point to especially sharp generational differences in religious involvement and political beliefs. Younger generations are increasingly supportive of issues that many churches have taken a strong stance against, including gay marriage, the legalization of marijuana, and premarital sex. In effect, Americans have grown increasingly uneasy with mixing religion and politics, and young people in particular have decided to sever their formal ties, even as they maintain at least some openness to spirituality. There are considerable data to support this idea. For one, most people who profess no religious preference still hold conventional religious beliefs—they may be skeptical about certain articles of faith but still believe, for instance, in life after death.[33] From the 1940s to the 1990s, about 72 percent of Americans believed in an afterlife.[34] In the late 1990s, this percentage increased slightly to about 77 percent. Belief in an afterlife is largely unrelated to political beliefs. Furthermore, surveys indicate that the increase in the percentage of Americans professing no religious preference does, in fact, have a political dimension. Among self-identified liberals, for example, the percentage professing no religious affiliation increased precipitously between 1974 and 2012, from just under 20 percent to around 38 percent, whereas among conservatives the percentage increased by only 3 percentage points.[35] In addition, evidence from surveys that follow people over time shows evidence for personal change (and not just change in a population average): political beliefs at one point in time are strongly predictive of moving from some religious affiliation to none.[36]

Critics of secularization theory also point to specific events that have split generations, further elevating the relevance of politics rather than the slow ascent of a more rational culture.[37] Over the course of the twentieth century, the decline in religious affiliation was in part driven by cohort replacement. Cohort replacement is a slow process. And, in general, the most religious cohorts have been gradually replaced by cohorts with no religious affiliation. Yet the 1960s were an especially critical period in accelerating the decline, and subsequent cohorts have been increasingly receptive to apostasy. The 1960s were, in fact, different. Those who were teenagers during the 1960s value autonomy and mistrust authority much more than those born before.[38] Analyses of repeated cross sections of data make the cohort component of religious change even clearer. Between 1987 and 2012, the percentage of Americans professing no religious affiliation increased around 13 percentage points, though within each cohort the increase was only around 4 percentage points.[39] This implies substantial cohort differences, which were, indeed, apparent. Among those born after 1975, about 25 to 30 percent report no religious preference, whereas among those born between 1946 and 1965, about 13 to 15 percent report no preference. Furthermore, there is little evidence for any retrenchment in these trends, as might occur if people raised in a household with no religion later adopted a religion. Among those born in the 1980s and raised with no religion, about 80 percent maintained no religious affiliation as adults.[40] Even this kind of intergenerational persistence has a cohort component. Earlier generations raised with no religion at least remained open to the possibility of adopting a religion as adults. For instance, among those born in the 1930s and raised with no religion, only 24 percent maintained no religious affiliation as adults.[41] Although these patterns might suggest that younger generations feel more freedom to choose their religion, consistent with the idea of spiritual freedom, they also suggest that younger cohorts have the freedom to turn their back on a religious upbringing. Among those born in the 1980s and raised with some religion, 22 percent professed no religion as adults, whereas the parallel figure among those born in the 1930s was only 4 percent.[42] Expressed in terms of religious service attendance rather than religious affiliation, the patterns are just as stark. Compared with their parents, baby boomers attend religious services 25 to 30 percent less frequently.[43]

ASSESSING THE IMPACT OF RELIGIOUS CHANGE ON ANXIETY

Cohorts differ in their religious identification and participation, but the implications of these differences for anxiety are nonetheless unclear. They are unclear in several respects. For one, it is unclear whether religion plays much of a role in the prevention of anxiety disorders. Very few studies regarding religion and mental health have focused on formal psychiatric disorders. Research has largely focused on variation in nonspecific psychological distress and, at that, has rarely tackled anxiety specifically. Despite the potential for an especially powerful role for religion in assuaging fear, research has mostly blended the symptoms of anxiety and depression, and interpreted the effects of religion in broad strokes consistent with the terms set by religion itself, as akin to comfort, ease, or grace. Religion surely provides relief and consolation, but it might be unable to prevent clinically significant anxiety. Furthermore, even if religious involvement is sufficiently powerful to prevent psychiatric disorders, it is unclear whether these effects are sufficient to explain cohort differences. In an earlier chapter, I noted that the seeds of anxiety among adults are planted early. To the extent that part of the turn from religion represents *adults* abandoning formal religious affiliation, cohort differences might be tempered by a lingering discontinuity between religious experiences in childhood and adulthood. Increasingly, Americans might not have the latter, but they often had the former, and even apostate adults might have benefited from having been raised in religious households.

Perhaps even more significant, most of the evidence on religious behavior and belief suggests that secularization per se is not occurring. Americans are maintaining their religious beliefs if not their religious affiliations, and this might soften differences between cohorts, depending on what aspect of religious behavior matters most. If, for instance, the psychological benefits of religion stem from confidence in a divine order or faith that God has a plan, the growing reluctance of Americans to affiliate with a religious organization might be largely inconsequential, because most Americans still believe in God. An important consideration in any discussion of the role of religion in anxiety pertains to what particular dimensions of religion are important. It is a mistake to regard religion as one belief rather than a collection of beliefs and behaviors. Indeed, as William James pointed out, Americans have a perhaps unique way of fashioning religion in a way that meets their needs, born of trying to square the authority of religion with the individuality of American culture.[44] It is perhaps not surprising that Americans can be comfortable with the authority of God but embrace a nonrestrictive view of their own practices, effectively claiming to be spiritual but not religious, or practicing but not habitual, or observant but not devout.[45] If cohort trends reflect the emergence of a more eclectic spirituality, the religious practices found among younger cohorts might still provide as much comfort as more traditional forms of participation.

Yet considering all the theory and data, some observers still see a stark deterioration. Christian Smith has studied the lives of young people, and he argues persuasively that their growing lack of religion is one factor contributing to their unhappiness.[46] His approach is multidimensional, focusing on a variety of dimensions of emotional and behavioral health, as well as the broader worldviews of the young.[47] He attributes much of the decline in religion to "bigger issues of cultural vision, historical meaning, and social purpose implicated in the troubling symptoms of emerging adult life."[48] Yet there is no mistaking the centrality of religion to his argument. For Smith, religion is especially conducive to well-being, because it allows young people to articulate a less individualistic version of morality. Smith argues that young people are prone to poor mental health because they no longer endorse values that allow them to transcend a consumerist culture and thus fall prey to influences that undermine their well-being. Through interviews, he explores the moral world views of young adults. About 60 percent of the young adults he interviewed reported a morality based on the priorities of the individual.[49]

They eschewed judging others and preferred letting individuals decide matters on their own. Smith stops short of characterizing these beliefs as nihilism (something other critics have been comfortable pushing forward), though he does highlight how young people are not able to defend strong moral claims.[50] For those who are religious, Smith finds a less individualistic morality that is readily articulated through religious teachings.

Smith brings other evidence to bear on the topic.[51] In some work he documents a near-linear relationship between the amount of religious involvement—spanning, in his words, the *disengaged*, the *sporadic*, the *regular*, and the *devoted*—and indicators of emotional and social well-being.[52] Relative to the other groups, the devoted are more likely to report never feeling depressed or believing life is meaningless, while they also report being accepted and understood by others. They are no less likely to experience traumatic events than are the less religious, though they appear to suffer less as a result. The religious also report more of a sense of purpose, in terms of having a clear set of goals.[53] In addition, the religious are less likely to experience a sharp difference between what they have and what they want. More than 80 percent of religious young adults—significantly more than among young adults who are not religiously engaged—report that they have gotten the most important things out of life thus far, as they understand those things.

RELIGIOUS PARTICIPATION AND ANXIETY DISORDERS

Some of these themes are echoed in nationally representative data on the correlates of anxiety disorders, though certainly not all of them. Table 6.1 begins by presenting various indicators of religious participation, arrayed by cohort. The results reveal, as has been found in other surveys, a decline in religious participation over consecutive cohorts. Most Americans spend at least some time in religious services, though younger cohorts attend less frequently. By the same token, the percentage who pray has declined. Even more remarkable is the shift in the percentage who identify as very religious. Fewer than one in five young people identify as very religious, whereas in the oldest cohort about 41 percent do. Although some of the loss in those identifying as very religious has been made up by those who identify as "spiritual" (asked in a separate question), the percentage identifying as very spiritual has declined as well. Among the youngest cohort, about 30 percent identify as spiritual. In the oldest cohort, the percentage

TABLE 6.1
Religious participation by cohort

	Cohort			
	18 to 29	30 to 44	45 to 59	60 and over
Religious service attendance				
Never or less than once per year	30.8%	20.4%	23.7%	18.8%
A few times per year	22.3%	27.0%	20.9%	16.4%
At least once per month	46.8%	52.6%	55.3%	64.8%
Pray daily	61.9%	71.7%	76.2%	83.9%
Very religious	17.2%	23.1%	27.6%	40.5%
Very spiritual	29.5%	36.7%	43.9%	45.1%
Religious upbringing	53.3%	52.8%	61.4%	70.0%

Source: Margarita Alegria, James S. (James Sidney) Jackson, Ronald C. Kessler, and David Takeuchi, Collaborative Psychiatric Epidemiology Surveys (CPES), 2001–2003 [United States] (Ann Arbor, Mich.: Inter-university
Consortium for Political and Social Research [distributor], 2016), https://doi.org/10.3886/ICPSR20240.v8 (primary survey: National Survey of American Life, N = 5,887).

identifying as spiritual and the percentage identifying as religious are more
aligned (45 percent relative to 41 percent). In the youngest cohort, more
identify as spiritual than religious (30 percent relative to 17 percent). The
percentage reporting a religious upbringing has also declined, from a high
of 70 percent to 53 percent among those under the age of forty-five. At least
among the youngest cohort, more than half report a religious upbringing,
even if fewer than one in five report being very religious as an adult. Figure 6.1 presents the fraction of those with a religious upbringing who are
also very religious as adults, effectively showing the persistence of religion
over the life course. This figure, too, shows a steady decline over cohorts.
Whereas among the oldest cohort nearly 50 percent of those raised in some
religious tradition reported being very religious as an adult, this percentage
is only about 25 percent among the youngest cohort.

Table 6.2 explores the relationship between these measures of participation and the presence of any current anxiety disorder. As a set, the religious
participation variables are significant—a test of their joint significance was
statistically significant at $p < .001$—though this significance is driven primarily by attendance at religious services. Relative to not attending religious services, those who attend services regularly see a reduction in the
risk of an anxiety disorder by 7.2 percentage points, implying about half of

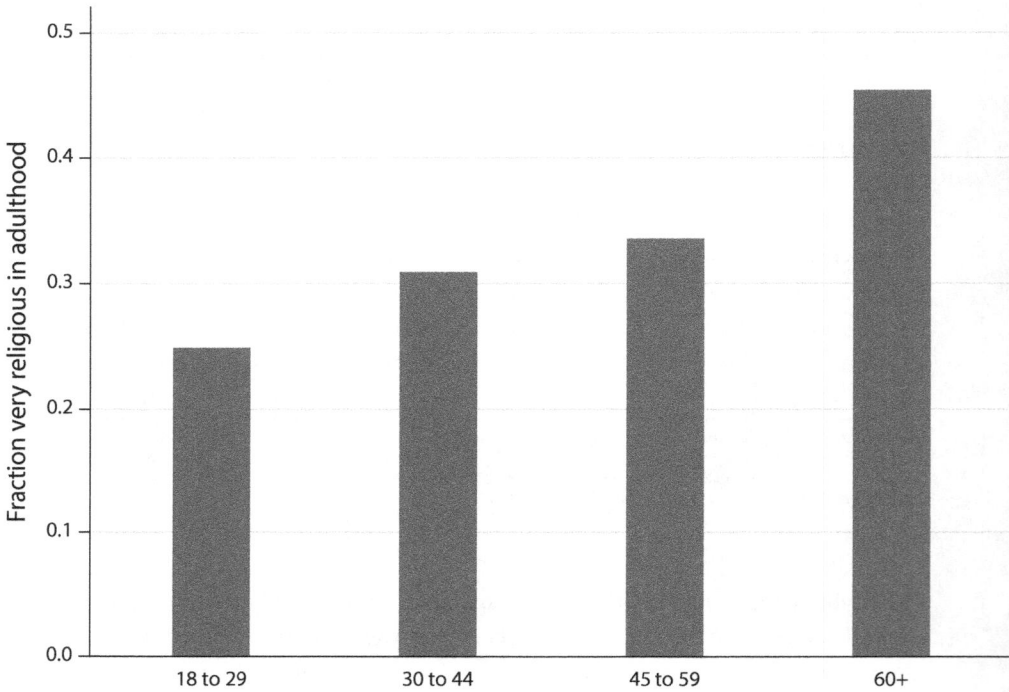

FIGURE 6.1. Fraction of Americans with religious upbringing who are also religious as adults, by cohort
Source: Collaborative Psychiatric Epidemiological Surveys (Primary Survey, National Survey of American Life, *N* = 4,068)

the average prevalence of an anxiety disorder (16.4 percent; see table 4.5). This is a large relationship relative to other risk factors, though it is not emblematic of all forms of religious participation. It is not matched by the other measures of religious identification and participation. Prayer does not have a statistically significant relationship with anxiety. Those who report being very religious are no more or less anxious than those who are not as religious. And spirituality, too, has no relationship with anxiety.

Given the early onset of anxiety disorders and the correlation between early-life religious participation and later-life participation, it is important to explore early-life conditions together with later ones. Model 2 presents the same model but inserts controls for any early-onset anxiety disorder. The relationship between early-onset anxiety and adult anxiety is strong. An early-onset anxiety disorder increases the probability of an adult

TABLE 6.2

Linear probability regression model of any current anxiety disorder with religious participation variables

	Model 1	Model 2
	Any current anxiety disorder	Any current anxiety disorder
Religious service attendance (relative to less than once per year)		
A few times per year	−.024	−.002
	(.018)	(.013)
At least once a month	−.072***	−.038**
	(.017)	(.013)
Pray daily	.026	.014
	(.021)	(.017)
Very religious	−.002	.012
	(.017)	(.014)
Very spiritual	.000	−.025
	(.020)	(.015)
Any early anxiety disorder		.543***
		(.034)

* $p < .05$, ** $p < .01$, *** $p < .001$ (standard errors in parentheses).

Source: Margarita Alegria, James S. (James Sidney) Jackson, Ronald C. Kessler, and David Takeuchi, Collaborative Psychiatric Epidemiology Surveys (CPES), 2001–2003 [United States] (Ann Arbor, Mich.: Inter-university Consortium for Political and Social Research [distributor], 2016), https://doi.org/10.3886/ICPSR20240.v8 (primary survey: National Survey of American Life, $N = 5,887$).

Note: All models also include coefficients for age, sex, and race/ethnicity (results not shown).

anxiety disorder by 54 percentage points. Moreover, the inclusion of early-onset anxiety reduces the relationship between service attendance and adult anxiety by about half, from 7.2 percentage points to 3.8. The apparent relationship between adult service attendance and anxiety may reflect the continuation of religious practices from childhood. Models 3 and 4 in table 6.3—a continuation of table 6.2—explore this idea further. Both models explore early-onset anxiety as the outcome. Model 3 shows a significant

TABLE 6.3
Linear probability regression model of any current anxiety disorder on religious participation variables

	Model 3	Model 4
	Any current anxiety disorder	Any current anxiety disorder
Religious childhood	−.038*	−.023
	(.018)	(.018)
Mother anxious		.065
		(.044)
Mother depressed		.090*
		(.035)
Mother drank frequently		.041
		(.053)
Abuse		.129***
		(.033)
Neglect		.147***
		(.030)
Mother intervened frequently		.027*
		(.013)
No biological siblings		.020
		(.021)
Frequent residential moves		.026
		(.018)
Did not live with both biological parents at age 16		−.002
		(.014)

* $p < .05$, ** $p < .01$, *** $p < .001$ (standard errors in parentheses).
Source: Margarita Alegria, James S. (James Sidney) Jackson, Ronald C. Kessler, and David Takeuchi, Collaborative Psychiatric Epidemiology Surveys (CPES), 2001–2003 [United States] (Ann Arbor, Mich.: Inter-university Consortium for Political and Social Research [distributor], 2016), https://doi.org/10.3886/ICPSR20240.v8 (primary survey: National Comorbidity Survey Replication, $N = 5,219$).
Note: All models also include coefficients for age, sex, and race/ethnicity (results not shown).

TABLE 6.4
Religious upbringing and adult religious participation

	No religious upbringing	Religious upbringing
Religious service attendance		
Never or less than once per year	33.4%	16.1%
A few times per year	25.9%	20.1%
At least once per month	40.7%	63.8%
Pray daily	57.5%	83.8%
Very religious	15.6%	33.5%
Very spiritual	29.4%	44.8%

Source: Margarita Alegria, James S. (James Sidney) Jackson, Ronald C. Kessler, and David Takeuchi, Collaborative Psychiatric Epidemiology Surveys (CPES), 2001–2003 [United States] (Ann Arbor, Mich.: Inter-university Consortium for Political and Social Research [distributor], 2016), https://doi.org/10.3886/ICPSR20240.v8 (primary survey: National Survey of American Life, N = 5,887).
Note: All means significantly different at $p < .05$.

relationship between a religious upbringing and early-onset anxiety. Though the relationship is much smaller than the relationship between service attendance and anxiety among adults, it is still significant. Model 4 adds controls for the childhood risk factors explored in the previous chapter. The inclusion of these controls reduces the relationship between a religious upbringing and early-onset anxiety to statistical insignificance. In other words, a religious upbringing is associated with a reduced risk of an early-onset anxiety disorder primarily because of its negative relationship with adverse childhood experiences.

Tables 6.4 and 6.5 explore these patterns further. Table 6.4 shows the continuity of religious practices over life-course stages. The table presents two columns of summary statistics, the first showing adult religious practices among those not raised in a religious household and the second showing the same statistics for those with a religious upbringing. Among those with a religious upbringing, 64 percent continue to attend services at least a month, whereas among those not raised in a religious household, this statistic is 41 percent. Although the correspondence is by no means perfect, those who are currently religious tend to have been raised in religious households. Table 6.5 presents the means of the adverse childhood experiences, arrayed across the same two groups. Except for those who responded positively to "mother intervened frequently," individuals who grew up in a religious household have a lower level of risk. They are less likely to report growing up

TABLE 6.5
Religious upbringing and early childhood adversity

	No religious upbringing	Religious upbringing
Mother anxious	7.1%	3.9%
Mother depressed	7.6%	4.7%
Mother drank frequently	5.2%	2.1%
Abuse	8.2%	5.4%
Neglect	6.3%	3.4%
Mother intervened frequently	23.6%	28.7%
No biological siblings	15.5%	10.7%
Frequent residential moves	14.7%	8.3%
Did not live with both biological parents at age 16	38.4%	27.0%

Source: Margarita Alegria, James S. (James Sidney) Jackson, Ronald C. Kessler, and David Takeuchi, Collaborative Psychiatric Epidemiology Surveys (CPES), 2001–2003 [United States] (Ann Arbor, Mich.: Inter-university Consortium for Political and Social Research [distributor], 2016), https://doi.org/10.3886/ICPSR20240.v8 (primary survey: National Comorbidity Survey Replication, *N* = 5,219).
Note: All means significantly different between columns at *p* < .05.

with a depressed or anxious mother, they are less likely to have been abused or neglected, and their families were, on average, more stable.

Table 6.6 explores the role of religion in explaining cohort differences in anxiety. The table presents four columns of coefficients, with the numbers corresponding—as before—to the excess anxiety experienced by younger cohorts relative to the oldest cohort. The first two columns correspond to current anxiety disorders and the second two to early-onset ones. For each pair of columns, the first column presents unadjusted differences, while the second adds controls for two things: religious service attendance and whether the respondent was raised in a religious household. For purposes of this exercise, nonsignificant religious influences were removed from the models. The results indicate that religious involvement can explain no more than 12 percent of the difference between cohorts. In general, religious influences do more to explain the excess anxiety found among the youngest cohort than among the older ones, though significant cohort differences remain. In no pairwise comparison is the difference reduced to statistical insignificance.

These analyses point to both the promise and limits of religious explanations for the increase in anxiety. On the one hand, religious participation

TABLE 6.6

Cohort differences in anxiety disorders with and without adjustment for religious service attendance and religious upbringing

	Model 1	Model 2	Model 3	Model 4
	Any current anxiety disorder	Any current anxiety disorder	Any early anxiety disorder	Any early anxiety disorder
Cohort (relative to 60 and over)				
18 to 29	.108***	.095***	.133***	.120***
	(.011)	(.012)	(.017)	(.017)
30 to 44	.128***	.120***	.134***	.126***
	(.011)	(.011)	(.016)	(.016)
45 to 59	.098***	.091***	.111***	.103***
	(.017)	(.017)	(.018)	(.018)
Including religious participation	No	Yes	No	Yes

* $p < .05$, ** $p < .01$, *** $p < .001$ (standard errors in parentheses).
Source: Margarita Alegria, James S. (James Sidney) Jackson, Ronald C. Kessler, and David Takeuchi, Collaborative Psychiatric Epidemiology Surveys (CPES), 2001–2003 [United States] (Ann Arbor, Mich.: Inter-university Consortium for Political and Social Research [distributor], 2016), https://doi.org/10.3886/ICPSR20240.v8 (primary survey: National Comorbidity Survey Replication, $N = 5,332$).

has certainly declined between cohorts, including the frequency of church attendance, prayer, and religious identification. Yet most of these declines are irrelevant to understanding cohort differences in anxiety. The only element of religious participation significantly related to anxiety is service attendance, plainly the most social indicator of religious participation. And much of the association between adult service attendance and anxiety reflects the continuity of religious behavior from childhood to adulthood, especially service attendance. The role of religious participation in anxiety reduction has as much to do with shaping the behavior of parents toward their children as it does the social behavior of adults.

The limited role of religion in explaining cohort differences in anxiety also reflects the precise nature of the change between cohorts. Although there are cohort differences in religious service participation, these differences are muted relative to other dimensions of religiosity. Among young people, nearly half still attend religious services at least once per month, and more report attending at least once a month than report never attending at all. Religion may be less significant to them, but not enough to forgo service attendance. Furthermore, the social dimensions of religious participation are more prominent among young adults than the identity-related dimensions of religion. In particular, more young people attend services at least once a month than identify as either very religious or very spiritual. The salience of religion varies sharply between cohorts. Whereas 40 percent of those sixty and over report being very religious, only 17 percent of young adults report the same. Although religious participation and beliefs have certainly changed between cohorts, many young adults are still benefiting from the dimensions of participation that matter most. At the same time, older adults are not always participating in ways that maximally reduce their anxiety. Among those sixty and over, 35 percent did not report service attendance levels sufficient to reduce anxiety in a significant way.

One interpretation of the limited role of religion in anxiety is simply that the benefits of religious involvement, such as they are, stem almost exclusively from religion's social dimensions. Attendance at religious services provides a network of support, while being raised in a religious household provides a stable family life. In this regard, though, the effects of religion are not unlike those of social support generally, which studies have repeatedly shown is critical to emotional and physical health.[54] Moreover, if this is true, service attendance is only the tip of the iceberg and worth investigating further. A comprehensive understanding of differences in anxiety between cohorts requires understanding trends in social support generally. And, indeed, when individuals are asked to think about the things that provide them with a sense of community, they think of family and friends more than they do religion and spirituality.[55] The next chapter turns to trends in the quality and nature of social support.

Chapter Seven

UNCERTAIN ATTACHMENTS

Social support is essential to health and well-being. It reduces mortality, improves happiness, and boosts the immune system, often in powerful ways. Its effects on mortality, for instance, rival those of smoking.[1] Social support is a capacious concept and can be interpreted in multiple ways. Perhaps the most common connotation of support is to receive something from another person, including emotional support. In this sense, the benefits of friendship might reflect something more specific: friends might be beneficial to health only when they provide something of value, including things directly related to well-being. But this is incorrect. There is no one active ingredient that explains the effects of social support. Support does not improve health only because our friends might, for instance, encourage healthier behaviors. Even crude indicators of social integration are related to better health. Married people, for instance, live longer than people who are not married, even if some marriages are healthier than others. People with more social roles have better health than people with fewer social roles. People who report more people in their lives with whom they can discuss "important matters" tend to report less depression. There are diverse ways to understand these effects, though some argue that the need for social connection is a core aspect of the human experience. People spend much of their lifetime either with other people or thinking about them.[2]

Like religious participation, the social lives of Americans have changed over the last fifty years. At least among some segments of the population, there has been a slow retreat from marriage. Fewer Americans are getting married, and if they get divorced, fewer are remarrying. There are other signs that Americans are committing less to their social activities. In *Bowling Alone*, Robert Putnam famously documented a decline in social capital, including especially a decline in civic organization memberships.[3] Americans are less likely to go on picnics, join clubs, and eat dinner with friends. Furthermore, more Americans are living alone, though often because it is their preference and they have the means to do so.[4] Of course, the ways in which we communicate with our friends have changed, too. And many of these changes complicate any simple claim of growing isolation. Electronic communication has made keeping in touch simple. When asked in 1970 who was in their social network, Americans nominated a small group of people with whom they were very close, but today the connotations of a "social network" are, of course, much closer to the idea of "Facebook friends," and the network is likely to consist of a much larger group. Furthermore, Americans are, if anything, more open to relationships than they were in the past in the sense that extraversion has increased between birth cohorts.[5] Americans are very outward looking.

But therein lies the problem. Americans might have more friends and be less introverted, but few observers are convinced that social integration has improved or that feelings of support are more common. And that feeling of isolation, that feeling that something is amiss, cannot be dismissed out of hand. There is no shortage of commentary purporting to document an increase in social isolation and adumbrating its many adverse consequences. And, like trends in religious participation, the diagnosis of the problem relies on more than a single symptom. The retreat from marriage, for instance, is seen as only one facet of a much deeper problem with social integration. Some point to growing individualism in American culture, as indicated by the frequency of phrases such as "I am unique" or "I am the best" in books, a trend that is not inconsistent with growing extraversion though certainly casts it as far from a selfless interest in others.[6] Trust in other people has declined as well. Since the 1970s, Americans have grown less likely to endorse the idea that people are helpful, that they can be trusted, and that they are fair, even if Americans interact with more people than they did in the past.[7] Others point to deeper structural issues that are driving Americans apart. In the 1970s, a best-selling book cast the United States as *A Nation of Strangers*, fostered by the increasing mobility of families.[8] More recent work has called attention to an "epidemic of loneliness," a claim that is especially provocative given the apparent ease with which we can now communicate.[9] Even if connections with others are easy, social relationships are hardly free of emotional costs. Sociologists have long documented the "cost of caring," in reference to the spillover effects of being aware of other people's stress.[10] When our friends are distressed, we are, too. Some go further and add to all these basic trends the apparent increase in isolation in terms of more insecure social identities.[11] In the twenty-first century, as distrusting as we are of other people, we may be as insecure about ourselves.

It is important, though, to look closely at patterns of social support. Although there is no shortage of claims of growing isolation, much depends on what aspects of social support we regard as most relevant. Some careful analyses of change find little deterioration and a good deal of persistence.[12] Studies also find that the impact of social media use is highly context specific. Research finds, for instance, that overall social media use affects well-being only when it changes the balance of exposure to other kinds of stress.[13] Frequent internet and social media users do not, in fact, report more stress, and some groups, like women, report less stress with more use. A subset of social media users report an increase in stress, but only because their use exposes them to other people's stress.[14] Even where there are significant trends in social integration, much depends on how those trends are interpreted. Although more Americans are living alone, for instance, much of this increase reflects that more Americans have the means to live alone and choose to do so.[15] Loneliness is less common among those who prefer to live alone. Moreover, there is a potentially sharp difference between objective indicators of social connectedness and subjective feelings about relationships, a difference that has perhaps grown stronger over time. Americans may have just as much social support as they did in the past, though the substructure of those relationships—the confidence people feel in those relationships and the sense of security they derive from their friendships—is beginning to deteriorate. This chapter will focus on the relevance of social relationships for anxiety disorders.

FRIENDS AND FRIENDSHIP

Although social isolation is especially harmful to health, there is abundant evidence that the connection between social support and well-being depends on not just the number of relationships, but on their quality as well. Support itself has many facets, and an array of processes link social support to well-being.[16] Support can vary from emotional to instrumental to financial. In addition, support can mean social regulation, including influence over potentially harmful behaviors. Married men, for instance, are less likely to drink heavily than are single men. In many instances, the psychology of support is as critical as the behavior behind it. Indeed, the expectation of support can matter more than the actual receipt of support. One study found that the effect of perceived support on psychological well-being was at least ten times larger than the effect of actual received support, in part because the receipt of support implies the individual is unable to cope on his or her own.[17] Support is beneficial when it leads people to believe that they are cared for, that they are valued, and that they belong to a network of reciprocal exchange and obligation. It is not necessarily beneficial when the person receives something of value from a friend, but it is beneficial to live in an environment where it is possible.[18]

The idea that social support derives its power from perceptions has several implications. For one, it brings to bear other psychological qualities for understanding support and expands the scope of influences beyond supportive behavior. Although friends can provide support in times of stress, those who feel supported might simply be more optimistic and, therefore, cope better irrespective of what their friends might do. In this sense, perceptions of support are premised as much on what happened in the past as what friends provide now. By the same token, perceptions of support likely reflect working models for evaluating other people generally, not just evaluating a particular person, even if friendship is fundamentally premised on a specific relationship.[19] Trends in social connectedness should be evaluated using this framework.

TRENDS IN SOCIAL CONNECTEDNESS

Social connections have certainly changed over time, but whether this change is significant depends on where you look. For many indicators of support, the change is quite small.[20] Part of the explanation for the persistence of social connections is the range of forces in play, whether technological, demographic, or economic. For those who see evidence of rapid change, the obvious place to look is technology. In the early twenty-first century, the rise of social media has certainly been a watershed. Facebook was launched in 2004 and now has over 2 billion users. Of course, other social medial platforms exist, and users are rarely active on only one. The transformation is clear. Yet other significant changes in the technology of social connection have been in place for well over a century. The electric telephone changed the ease with which we could communicate with others. The widespread use of cellular phones made long-distance communication even more routine. Furthermore, how we relate to one another has changed for reasons quite apart from improvements in communication technology. Air travel has become more affordable over time, allowing people to visit friends at much greater distances. Complementing these improvements have been trends in geographic mobility. In the twentieth century, Americans began to move from rural to suburban and urban areas, increasing the number of people they encounter on a daily basis.

Yet technology and mobility are only part of the picture. The demographic characteristics and behavior of Americans have changed as well, including the composition of households. Some of this change reflects trends in marriage. Well-educated Americans are delaying marriage.[21] This might imply growing isolation, but it is only part of the picture. Parallel to these developments has been the increasing employment and educational attainment of women, improving their ability to form relationships outside the family. At the same time, there has been a slow decline in the size of the average household. The average number of Americans living together has dropped somewhat over time, from about 3.1 people in the 1970s to 2.6 in the 1990s and later.[22] During the same period, the percent living in large households—with four or more other people—fell a great deal, from 38 percent to 21 percent.[23]

The United States has also been transformed because of an influx of immigrants. These trends, too, have implications for thinking about community and social support. Although immigration itself can be a daunting experience, immigrants often arrive with their families and choose to live near other immigrants from the same region. Immigration has increased over the last century. Following a decline in the number of legal permanent residents in the United States from the early twentieth century to the 1940s, the number has increased. At present, first- and second-generation immigrants together account for about one in four members of the U.S. population.[24] Trends in immigration have implications for native-born residents as well. Marriages between immigrants and native-born Americans have increased significantly over time.[25]

Depending on what influences one chooses to focus on, the quality of social relationships appears to be changing, too, though the overall picture is far from clear. The term "Facebook friend" has entered the lexicon to distinguish between superficial connections and deeper ones. There is, to be sure, something accurate in the intuition behind this term. Much of the evidence suggests that time spent online is not necessarily conducive to well-being.[26] The more someone uses the internet, the less they feel connected to others, and the less happy they become.[27] More time spent on Facebook is associated with lower life satisfaction, irrespective of the number of friends one interacts with on the platform.[28] More time spent on the internet means less time spent building other relationships. Time on the internet, for instance, is negatively associated with time spent communicating with family members. But the total impact of social media use appears to be quite small, and the overall trend in social relationships is one of remarkable durability. Extreme isolation is rare. A relatively small number of Americans report two or fewer close friends, and this number has remained stable over time.[29] Furthermore, actual contact with friends has been stable or gone up somewhat over time. Well before the launch of Facebook, social contacts were increasing, consistent with the growing extraversion of Americans and improvements in basic technologies. The percent of adults who called or wrote to a friend three times or more a month went up between 1975 and the early 1990s.[30] Furthermore, despite all the high-tech distractions now available to families, the quality of family relationships has, in fact, changed very little. Most families continue to eat dinner together, even if the percent has gone down somewhat since the 1970s.[31] In general, the amount of time Americans socialize with relatives—including siblings—has remained relatively stable.[32]

TRENDS IN THE QUALITY OF SOCIAL RELATIONSHIPS

If Americans are as socially engaged now as they have ever been, where is the sense of isolation coming from? Overall social support networks have not changed in a dramatic fashion in the last thirty years. But from the standpoint of understanding anxiety, as much should be made of feelings of support as the number of potentially supportive people. And on this dimension, the picture looks different. For one, even if Americans report a relatively constant number of friends, some are also reporting more turbulent relationships. Among married people, reports of serious trouble have remained stable, but the percent of unmarried people who experienced a break-up in the past year has increased.[33] Cohabitation is increasingly common, though cohabitating unions are less stable than marriages.[34] In addition, among married Americans, a larger percentage report wanting to spend more time with their family than they actually do.[35] Relationships may be even more fraught outside the context of close friends and family. Trust in other people has declined over time, based on answers to the question, "Generally speaking, would you say that most people can be trusted or that you can't be too careful in life?" In 2012, about 67 percent of Americans reported that most people could not be trusted, whereas in 1988 about 58 percent reported the same.[36] As with many other trends, there is a significant cohort dynamic to this increase. The rise in mistrust is apparent across most age groups, except those over the age of fifty-five, among whom mistrust has not changed and remains low relative to other age groups, around 54 percent. Mistrust is especially high among young people. Among young adults ages eighteen to twenty-five in 2012, over 78 percent report that most people cannot be trusted.[37]

Mistrust can, of course, extend to friends as well as strangers. In general, social support improves mental health, but friendship involves both conflict and support, and much of the evidence indicates that the former is more consequential than the latter. Positive social support—indicated by reporting, for instance, that someone cares for you, understands you, or appreciates you—has a weaker relationship with anxiety than negative social support—indicated by reporting that the same person criticizes you, makes demands on you, or makes you feel tense.[38] Conflict with some people is more consequential than with others. Conflict with a spouse or relative is generally more consequential than conflict with a friend, and in some studies positive support from a spouse has no significant relationship with anxiety.[39] More generally, positive support appears to do little to promote more positive emotions or to prevent negative emotions, though negative social support affects both.[40] Patterns of this sort have implications for thinking about social support in the twenty-first century. Even if technology has done little to change social connectedness, it may have increased the potential for conflict. Relative to disclosing sensitive information to others in person, disclosing information on the internet elicits more negative reactions.[41]

By the same token, social media increases the potential for stress. Much has been made about how social media fosters social comparison and envy. Yet research on social media use shows that the most emotionally damaging information comes from being aware of others' stress, rather than from learning about their accomplishments and triumphs. And social media users hardly announce only good news. A survey found that social media users were aware of both good and bad events in the lives of their friends. In the preceding twelve months, for instance, 50 percent of social media users knew someone who had become engaged, but 31 percent knew someone who had gone through a separation or divorce, and 36 percent knew someone who had experienced the death of a child, partner, or spouse.[42] By the same token, 57 percent knew someone who started a new job, but 42 percent knew someone who had been fired or laid off. The same study found that only negative events were related to self-reported stress.

TRENDS IN ATTACHMENT STYLE

The increasingly fraught nature of social relationships is apparent in trends in attachment style, which is perhaps especially important for understanding anxiety disorders. Rather than the quality of specific relationships, attachment style refers to the motivations behind social relationships in general.[43] The concept is meant to explain enduring differences between individuals in how they relate to other people across a wide set of different kinds of relationships.[44] Attachment styles tend to be consistent among adults and are formed in part through early-life experiences, providing a bridge between early relationships and later ones. Evidence suggests, for instance, that maternal caregiving shapes how comfortable individuals are around other people and how much they rely on them twenty years later, a critical aspect of an attachment style.[45] Although attachment styles can be subdivided into increasingly specific types, the concept generally involves four distinct styles, reflecting the position a person occupies with respect to two dimensions: beliefs about others and beliefs about the self.[46] Secure attachment is characteristic of those who are comfortable both with other people and themselves and do not worry frequently about being abandoned. The remaining three styles can be considered insecure styles, though each with a different flavor of insecurity. Preoccupied attachment is characterized by holding negative views about the self, but positive views about others. Preoccupied people are frequently anxious in their relationships with other people, even if they are generally satisfied with their friendships. Fearful attachment is characterized by both negative views about the self and others. It involves wanting to be close to other people, but having a difficult time trusting or relying on them. Those with a fearful attachment style fear that they will be hurt. A dismissing style is characterized by being comfortable without social relationships and valuing self-sufficiency over dependence. People with a dismissing style can be cold, though they hold positive views about themselves. In general, the largest differences are between those with a secure attachment style and those with any of the insecure styles. Those with an insecure style are generally uncomfortable around other people. They report lower levels of social support, and the support they receive tends to be more fraught and unstable. They are easily upset, for instance, when friendship is not reciprocated and, in general, are more sensitive to the slights of others.[47]

Although dispositional and seemingly obdurate, attachment styles are shifting rapidly between cohorts. Evidence from studies of college students conducted between 1988 and 2011 suggests that, each year, the percent of students reporting a secure style has declined, while the percent reporting an insecure style has increased.[48] In particular, the percent of college students with a secure style has declined from about 49 percent to 42 percent over this period.[49] Another way to think about trends in attachment is to distill them into positive or negative perceptions of the self and others, the core dimensions of an attachment style. Although it is possible that views about others have decreased while confidence in one's self has increased— as one might expect if cohorts are simply more self-interested—this is not what has occurred. The percent of college students who maintain a positive view of others has declined precipitously from 32 percent in 1988 to 10 percent in 2011, with no corresponding increase in positive views about the self (which shifted from 22 percent to 20 percent). Americans do not necessarily feel better about themselves, though they are generally more concerned about others.

The rise of an insecure attachment style is important for understanding anxiety, especially in an environment that is, in many ways, even more social than it was before. On its own, a more insecure attachment style will be positively correlated with the risk for an anxiety disorder, but the structure of modern social connections likely makes the situation worse. Young people are increasingly anxious about their relationships, but they are no less engaged with their networks, especially given their place in the life course. An anxious style does not imply a retreat from social relationships, especially among younger people. Indeed, young people use social media with extraordinary frequency. To be sure, using social media involves a complex mix of motivations, not all of which involve securing support. Among other things, more social media use is positively correlated with narcissism, and people who are high in narcissism tend to use social media platforms for social promotion.[50] Setting this aside, though, there is no evidence that social media use allays social insecurities. To the contrary, social media use can promote anxiety among already anxious people by encouraging more social comparison, by allowing anxious people to read into ambiguous signals, and by encouraging more personal and invidious interactions.

The explanation for growing anxiety between cohorts might lie not in a decline in social connections but rather in its opposite: more or at least persistent social connections in tandem with growing dispositional insecurity about those relationships. This discontinuity might also help to explain the complicated relationship between basic indicators of social support and anxiety. In general, there is abundant evidence linking social support to emotional well-being and health. Yet the evidence linking social support to anxiety is relatively more complex, in part because even our closest relationships are a source of worry. Inadequate social support increases depression, for instance, but may not be related to anxiety.[51] In some studies, certain aspects of social support *increase* anxiety. A set of particularly provocative studies of women living in the Outer Hebrides found that chronic anxiety was especially common among the *most* socially integrated women, including those who attended church and worked with others on small farms, even as depression was especially common among the *least* integrated women.[52] Other studies have produced similar findings. Both depression and anxiety are shaped by stress, but they differ in the context of stress from relationships. The loss of a friendship is strongly related to depression, whereas ongoing relationship difficulties are strongly related to anxiety.[53] If Americans are just as connected as they were in the past, the growing risk is perhaps particular to anxiety rather than depression.

SOCIAL SUPPORT AND ANXIETY IN THE UNITED STATES

Table 7.1 begins by presenting estimates of attachment style in the United States, arrayed by cohort. Four categories are presented: secure, preoccupied, dismissing, and fearful. The most common attachment style is a secure style, apparent in most adults. But the prevalence of a secure style has declined between cohorts. For the youngest cohort, the prevalence of a secure style is 70 percent, whereas it is 81 percent among the oldest cohort. The remaining attachment styles reflect varieties of an insecure style. All three are more common among the youngest cohort relative to the oldest. By far the most common insecure style is a dismissing style, found in about one in five young adults and about 15 percent of older adults. Among the youngest cohort, an additional 4 percent report a preoccupied style, and an additional 5 percent report a fearful style. The parallel figures in the oldest cohort are 2 percent for each style.

Table 7.2 presents pairs of related indicators of the quality of social relationships and social interactions, starting with the frequency of social interaction, indicated by living alone and frequently meeting up with friends. This is followed by negative dimensions of support, indicated by reporting

TABLE 7.1
Attachment style by cohort

Cohort	Secure	Preoccupied	Dismissing	Fearful
18 to 29	70.4%	4.1%	20.0%	5.5%
30 to 44	73.8%	2.6%	17.9%	5.7%
45 to 59	72.1%	2.9%	19.1%	6.0%
60 and over	81.1%	1.8%	14.7%	2.3%

Source: Margarita Alegria, James S. (James Sidney) Jackson, Ronald C. Kessler, and David Takeuchi, Collaborative Psychiatric Epidemiology Surveys (CPES), 2001–2003 [United States] (Ann Arbor, Mich.: Inter-university Consortium for Political and Social Research [distributor], 2016), https://doi.org/10.3886/ICPSR20240.v8 (primary survey: National Comorbidity Survey Replication, N = 5,692).

TABLE 7.2
Indicators of social support by cohort

Cohort	Married	Live alone	Meet friends often	Positive dimensions of friendship		Negative dimensions of friendship		Net friendship score
				Can rely on friends	Can open up with friends	Demanding friends	Often argue with friends	
18 to 29	29.5%	35.4%	70.7%	79.0%	83.2%	17.8%	18.3%	1.261
30 to 44	67.5%	29.2%	51.8%	76.9%	79.0%	13.6%	6.9%	1.355
45 to 59	68.9%	37.9%	45.4%	74.4%	75.9%	11.8%	7.1%	1.315
60 and over	59.9%	49.5%	57.1%	71.5%	66.2%	8.5%	6.1%	1.231

Source: Margarita Alegria, James S. (James Sidney) Jackson, Ronald C. Kessler, and David Takeuchi, Collaborative Psychiatric Epidemiology Surveys (CPES), 2001–2003 [United States] (Ann Arbor, Mich.: Inter-university Consortium for Political and Social Research [distributor], 2016), https://doi.org/10.3886/ICPSR20240.v8 (primary survey: National Comorbidity Survey Replication, $N = 5,692$).
Note: Net friendship score represents the sum of the positive dimensions of friendship minus the sum of the negative dimensions of support.

demanding friends and frequently arguing with them. This is followed by positive dimensions of support, indicated by reporting being able to open up with friends and being able to rely on them. On these dimensions there are stark cohort differences, but they are not uniform by valence: younger people report more of the good *and* bad dimensions of support. On the one hand, the oldest cohort is more likely to live alone and to report infrequently getting together with others. Among the youngest cohort, for instance, 70 percent report frequently meeting with friends, whereas among the oldest cohort only 57 percent report the same. The oldest cohort also reports somewhat less ability to rely on their friends and open up with them. On the other hand, they also report fewer arguments and less-demanding friends. The table also presents a summary measure of net support, equal to the sum of the two positive dimensions of support minus the sum of the two negative dimensions of support. In this respect, the cohort differences are much more muted. All cohorts report a net positive with respect to social support.

Table 7.3 explores the consequences of these reports for anxiety. The table presents the relationship between social support and the presence of any mood or any anxiety disorder (in separate models). To avoid confounding

TABLE 7.3
Linear probability regression models of anxiety and mood disorders with attachment style

	Any current anxiety disorder	Any current mood disorder
Attachment style (relative to secure)		
Preoccupied	.167***	.116***
	(.044)	(.031)
Dismissing	.128***	.082***
	(.014)	(.011)
Fearful	.287***	.183***
	(.046)	(.029)

* $p < .05$, ** $p < .01$, *** $p < .001$ (standard errors in parentheses).
Source: Margarita Alegria, James S. (James Sidney) Jackson, Ronald C. Kessler, and David Takeuchi, Collabora-
tive Psychiatric Epidemiology Surveys (CPES), 2001–2003 [United States] (Ann Arbor, Mich.: Inter-university
Consortium for Political and Social Research [distributor], 2016), https://doi.org/10.3886/ICPSR20240.v8
(primary survey: National Comorbidity Survey Replication, $N = 5,692$).
Note: Models also include controls for gender, race/ethnicity, cohort, education, and early childhood adversity.
The coefficients for both a dismissing and fearful attachment style differ significantly between any current
anxiety disorder and any current mood disorder at $p < .05$.

factors, the models control for early life risk factors (as discussed in an earlier chapter), which are likely to impact the formation of an attachment style and anxiety. Attachment style has an especially powerful relationship with anxiety disorders, far more important than its relationship with mood disorders. The most common insecure style, a dismissing style, is associated with a 13 percentage point increase in the risk of an anxiety disorder. A fearful style is associated with more than twice that risk, an increase of 29 percentage points. Both styles are also associated with mood disorders, though at a much lower magnitude (both differences between anxiety and mood disorders are significant at $p < .01$).

Table 7.4 presents the remaining dimensions of social support, in this case focusing on anxiety. In general, the relationship between the two negative dimensions of support and anxiety is stronger (absolutely) than the relationship with the two positive dimensions of support. In short, when it comes to predicting anxiety, it is much more informative to know how much you argue with your friends than it is to know how well you get along with them. Marriage, too, reduces the risk of an anxiety disorder, as does frequently socializing with friends.

TABLE 7.4
Linear probability regression model of any current anxiety with social support measures

	Any current anxiety
Married	−.055***
	(.013)
Live alone	−.003
	(.014)
Meet friends often	−.031**
	(.011)
Total positive dimensions of support	−.016
	(.009)
Total negative dimensions of support	.042***
	(.011)

* $p < .05$, ** $p < .01$, *** $p < .001$ (standard errors in parentheses).
Source: Margarita Alegria, James S. (James Sidney) Jackson, Ronald C. Kessler, and David Takeuchi, Collaborative Psychiatric Epidemiology Surveys (CPES), 2001–2003 [United States] (Ann Arbor, Mich.: Inter-university Consortium for Political and Social Research [distributor], 2016), https://doi.org/10.3886/ICPSR20240.v8 (primary survey: National Comorbidity Survey Replication, $N = 5,692$).
Note: Models also include controls for gender, race/ethnicity, cohort, education, and early childhood adversity.

To this point, the results suggest a relatively weak role for social support in explaining cohort differences in anxiety. When considering both the positive and negative dimensions of support, the differences between cohorts are too small to account for the large differences in the risk of an anxiety disorder. But the effects of social support must be understood in the context of cohort differences in attachment style, for which cohort differences are much larger. The youngest cohort may be no less likely to receive support than the oldest cohort—indeed, by the measures explored here, the youngest cohort is, if anything, more socially engaged and receives more positive support from friends—but the youngest cohort is also increasingly insecure in these attachments. Table 7.5 presents the intersection of these two patterns. It presents the relationships between the dimensions of social support and anxiety, as before, but among those with secure and insecure attachment styles separately. This allows, for instance, for a test of the effect

TABLE 7.5

Linear probability regression model of any current anxiety with interactions between attachment style and social support measures

	Any current anxiety
Secure attachment style	−.237***
	(.031)
Insecure attachment × Married	−.085**
	(.025)
Secure attachment × Married	−.028
	(.018)
Insecure attachment × Live alone	.001
	(.024)
Secure attachment × Live alone	−.006
	(.014)
Insecure attachment × Meet friends often	−.050*
	(.022)
Secure attachment × Meet friends often	−.007
	(.011)
Insecure attachment × Net friendship score	−.033*
	(.013)
Secure attachment × Net friendship score	−.003
	(.008)

* $p < .05$, ** $p < .01$, *** $p < .001$ (standard errors in parentheses).

Source: Margarita Alegria, James S. (James Sidney) Jackson, Ronald C. Kessler, and David Takeuchi, Collaborative Psychiatric Epidemiology Surveys (CPES), 2001–2003 [United States] (Ann Arbor, Mich.: Inter-university Consortium for Political and Social Research [distributor], 2016), https://doi.org/10.3886/ICPSR20240.v8 (primary survey: National Comorbidity Survey Replication, $N = 5,692$).

Note: Models also include controls for gender, race/ethnicity, cohort, education, and early childhood adversity.

of marriage on anxiety among those with an insecure attachment style and among those with a secure attachment style. The findings suggest that the benefits of social support depend greatly on attachment style. Those with an insecure attachment style are much more sensitive to social support, in both a positive and negative fashion. The gap between the married and the unmarried, for instance, is much larger among those with an insecure style than among those with a secure style. The effects of both net support and socializing are also larger among those with an insecure style. These patterns suggest that, were it not for the fact that their levels of support remain high, the youngest cohort would be at a much higher risk of an anxiety disorder. Relative to other cohorts, they benefit more from support when it is apparent and simultaneously are hurt more when it is not.

The final table, table 7.6, pulls these patterns together, as has been done in the preceding chapters, and shows the impact of social support and attachment style on cohort differences in anxiety. The first model presents cohort differences adjusted for basic demographic characteristics, as well as, in this case, total childhood risk. The second model shows the same differences but after adjusting for social support, attachment style, and their intersection. Within the youngest cohort, differences in social support explain about 22 percent of their elevated risk for an anxiety disorder. The percentage is much lower, however, in the remaining cohorts, suggesting the risks of insecure attachment are particularly pronounced within the youngest cohort.

It is best to regard social support as a portfolio of elements, consisting of experiences with other people and dispositional characteristics that affect how those experiences are interpreted. Although there are some significant cohort differences in the level of social support and conflict, these differences are muted, especially when considering the net difference between positive and negative dimensions of support. The results certainly do not indicate a pervasive decline in the quality of support between cohorts. The percent of Americans who report some degree of social integration—either being married, living with someone else, or meeting regularly with other people—is high, almost irrespective of cohort. Among the youngest cohort, for instance, 94 percent report social integration of some kind, and among the oldest cohort this percentage only falls to 88 percent. By the same token,

TABLE 7.6

Cohort differences in anxiety disorders with and without adjustment for attachment style and social support measures

	Any current anxiety disorder	Any current anxiety disorder
Cohort (relative to 60 and over)		
18 to 29	.113***	.088***
	(.011)	(.011)
30 to 44	.131***	.120***
	(.012)	(.011)
45 to 59	.103***	.088***
	(.018)	(.017)
Attachment style and social support included	No	Yes

* $p < .05$, ** $p < .01$, *** $p < .001$ (standard errors in parentheses).
Source: Margarita Alegria, James S. (James Sidney) Jackson, Ronald C. Kessler, and David Takeuchi, Collaborative Psychiatric Epidemiology Surveys (CPES), 2001–2003 [United States] (Ann Arbor, Mich.: Inter-university Consortium for Political and Social Research [distributor], 2016), https://doi.org/10.3886/ICPSR20240.v8 (primary survey: National Comorbidity Survey Replication, $N = 5,692$).
Note: Models also include controls for gender, race/ethnicity, education, and early childhood adversity.

the percent who report any positive dimension of support—either having friends one can rely on or friends one can open up with—is very high. Among the youngest cohort, 87 percent report positive experiences with support, whereas among the oldest cohort this percentage only falls to 79 percent. Younger cohorts report more negative experiences with support, too, but not at overwhelming levels. Among the youngest cohort, 30 percent report at least one of the two negative dimensions of support, whereas among the oldest cohort this percentage falls to 12 percent.

Far more relevant are cohort differences in attachment style, which strongly condition the impact of social support on anxiety. When it comes to understanding anxiety, it is not simply whether one feels supported now or has the opportunity to interact with others routinely, but the expectation that the support will continue and how unstable even the most supportive relationships might appear. There are large cohort differences in attachment style, with the youngest cohort reporting a more insecure style. And this increase in insecurity appears to taint even the most supportive encounters. Young people report being more uncomfortable around other people, uncertain about their intentions, fearful of being abandoned, and anxious their friendships will not last. Furthermore, attachment style appears to be relatively independent of actual experiences of support. There is little evidence, for instance, that younger people are more insecure only because they are not yet married. Even among married adults, the prevalence of an insecure attachment style is quite high. Among married persons, about 23 percent report an insecure attachment style of some kind. Among those who report a net positive support score—more positive support than negative support—23 percent report an insecure style. Even among people with strong support, cohort differences in an insecure style are still apparent. The percent with an insecure style rises to 28 percent in the youngest cohort and falls to 18 percent in the oldest. Together, attachment style and patterns of social support explain just over a fifth of the excess anxiety found in the youngest cohort. It is not wrong to argue that young people are worried about their friendships or that their relationships are a significant source of anxiety. Indeed, cohorts are increasingly anxious about their social lives. But it is precisely because the young remain socially engaged and can create relationships that are, on average, net positive sources of support that their anxiety remains lower than it could be.

There are other ways, however, to think about interpersonal insecurity. The insecurity of younger cohorts likely stretches beyond social relationships. If the twenty-first century provides ample opportunities for social connection, it also provides abundant opportunities for social comparison. Status anxiety is perhaps more acute. But as with much else discussed in this book, there is a larger context to understanding status anxiety, including growing income inequality. The next chapter turns to the role of status anxiety in understanding anxiety disorders.

Chapter Eight

STATUS ANXIETY AND GROWING INEQUALITY

By many objective measures, the economic well-being of the average American has improved. Over the course of the twentieth century, real income increased even as work hours for individuals declined.[1] Things that were once regarded as luxuries, from color televisions to washing machines, are now commonplace. Most families own a car or truck, and many own more than one. Computers are, of course, more recent, though they diffused vary rapidly. By 2000 most households owned a computer, whereas in 1980 only about 5 percent did.[2] Median net worth increased as well. In 1962, median net worth was about $55,000 (in 2013 dollars), whereas in 2001 it was about $96,700.[3]

During the same period, consumer spending shifted from essentials to leisure. In 1900, almost half of consumer expenditures went to food, but by the end of the century, this figure had dropped to under 20 percent.[4] Spending on recreation, meanwhile, doubled over the same period. Although some people certainly enjoy more income than others, the average American maintains a high standard of living in terms of consumption.[5] More people can participate in a middle-class lifestyle. Add to these positive trends other consequences of a rising standard of living and the picture is even rosier. Life expectancy improved dramatically over the twentieth century, along with other improvements in health.[6] Americans are living longer on average and with greater assurance they will enjoy a long life, filled with opportunities for leisure and entertainment.

Yet some troubling trends have coexisted with these improvements, and it is far from clear whether economic anxiety has abated. For one, income inequality has increased. This is a relatively recent development. For much of the twentieth century, average incomes increased as variation in incomes shrank. The situation of the average household improved especially sharply from 1949 to 1969. After the 1970s, however, income inequality started to increase, driven by especially rapidly growth in the incomes of the highest earners.[7] In 2000, a family at the eightieth percentile of income had about twice the income as a family at the median.[8] Inequality on the basis of wealth is even greater. In 2000 and 2001, the top 1 percent held 20 percent of the total income, but retained a remarkable 33 percent of the total wealth.[9] The top 20 percent, meanwhile, held more than 80 percent of the total wealth.[10] The skewed distribution in wealth implies a sharp difference between mean and median net worth, which has, in fact, materialized. In 1963, mean net worth was more than three times higher than median net worth, but by 2001, it was five times higher.[11] Income inequality among families with children grew twice as fast as income inequality among full-time earners.[12] Some additional trends further highlight the depth of inequality. Among younger cohorts, for instance, a greater share of wealth is attributable to inheritance than savings.[13] Many young people are now effectively shut out of the housing market, ordinarily a critical step in accumulating wealth apart from inheritance.

Coinciding with growing inequality is an increase in debt.[14] Consumer debt increased more than 170 percent from 1999 to 2008, driven largely by an increase in mortgage debt.[15] The average debt-to-income ratio in the United States increased from around 67 in 1983 to 157 in 2007.[16] During the same period, total consumer debt more than doubled. Since the financial crisis of 2008, debt has decreased somewhat, thought it remains much higher than it was in 1999. Of course, the reasons for this decrease are not entirely a matter of chastened consumers or renwed prudence. Consumers are not choosing to reduce their debt, but rather are being met with resistance by lenders in light of their reduced creditworthiness. The highly leveraged situation of the middle-class family helps to explain some of the more devastating economic consequences of the Great Recession. Between

2007 and 2010, median wealth in the United States plunged 44 percent.[17] It is unlikely to rebound soon. The savings rate in the United States has generally declined since the 1970s.[18] If Americans are enjoying a better lifestyle than they did in the past, it has come in no small part from borrowing.

Even setting aside the unusual circumstances of the financial crisis, there are reasons to doubt that the rosy economic picture realized over much of the twentieth century necessarily improved subjective measures like financial satisfaction. Simply because Americans have more does not mean they want less. With rising income inequality, the opportunity to compare oneself with someone who is doing better has become ubiquitous. Status markers are often quite visible, perhaps increasingly so. Although most households own a car or truck, very few own a Ferrari or Tesla. Most people own a cellular phone, but not everyone has the latest iPhone. The average size of homes has increased, but many families are simply priced out of the most expensive real estate markets. All told, one might objectively be of a higher economic status than before, but that improvement might not prevent the nagging suspicion that the good fortune will not last, that someone else will come along who has more, or that one is not of sufficiently high status on all the markers necessary for a respectable middle-class lifestyle. Consistent with the idea that more is demanded of the average consumer, Americans' satisfaction with their incomes has diverged over the latter half of the twentieth century. Whereas financial satisfaction increased among those in the top 20 percent of income, it declined precipitously among those in the bottom 20 percent.[19] These experiences sharply divide cohorts. There is little reason to doubt that inequality will soon start to decline. Unions have historically helped to support middle-class wages, though membership is declining, contributing to a rise in wage inequality, especially among men.[20] As I write, we are entering yet another recession, one likely to linger for years. Ordinarily a recession affects men more than women, but the COVID-19 pandemic has affected employment sectors with high female employment shares.[21] The negative effects of the pandemic on working mothers are likely to linger for a long time, especially as they leave the workforce. In short, inequality has been growing, and continues to grow, in subjective measures as in objective ones. This likely has implications for anxiety, especially because economic anxiety is rarely limited to financial matters.

SOCIAL STATUS AND ANXIETY

Subjective status is important for understanding psychological well-being and may be even more critical for anxiety disorders in particular. After all, the concept of status *anxiety* refers specifically to the uncertainty and fear surrounding one's position in society, not simply satisfaction with what one has achieved or regret over missed opportunities. In addition, the concept of status highlights the fears that can affect even those who appear to have the most and the insecurity that can seize people even in an era of abundance. Social status refers to one's rank or position in society. Analogous concepts are prestige or standing, in the sense that status refers to matters of reputation and, therefore, has a public component. Status is also fundamentally relational. Although status can be evaluated subjectively—concerning where someone thinks he or she ranks within a group—it matters to self-worth in large part because it is known to others. Status is signaled, often strategically so. People go to great lengths to make their standing apparent to others (or to conceal it). Status can be achieved by the individual, to be sure, but it is no less awarded by other people.[22] Status is also complex and dynamic. Although status is related to assets a person holds, both material and immaterial, it is not simply a property of those assets. High status is not granted only or always because one person is richer, bigger, stronger, older, or more aggressive.[23] These things certainly matter in some contexts. Tall people, for instance, do indeed tend to have more status than shorter people. And income is important to how people think about their own status, including whether they are middle class. But status is usually more fluid than any fixed characteristic and more complex than any single trait. In studies of model organisms, where status creation can be studied without considering long-term memory, rank is very fluid. In cichlid fish, for instance, ranks formed at one time are usually very different from ranks formed by the same fish at a later time.[24] Furthermore, status is a product of both the assets one commands and how those assets are perceived, remembered, and valued by the group. A reputation can be easily cultivated or lost. Those who fail in earlier contests can, for instance, be shunned in ways that prevent them from gaining their status back. Furthermore, the hallmarks of status change according to taste. Standards of beauty, for instance, shift over time, elevating one body type over another depending on prevailing tastes. Rank can also vary within individuals, across social roles and geographic space, as when someone reports high status at their workplace but low status in their neighborhood.

Whatever its sources or dynamics, status is presumed to be important for self-respect, because it is significant for both the individual and the group. Status serves many functions for the individual. High status certainly benefits the individual who enjoys it, granting that person considerable visibility, deference, and influence. Part of this is social, given by others, but part also stems from the personal confidence high status fosters. Status is a resource that can be used, and sometimes expended, but it can also be quickly renewed, especially when status begets more status. In the minds of other people, status is associated with virtue, casting a positive glow over even the most selfish acts.[25] Status also serves several functions for social groups. Status can diminish social conflict, lead to an orderly flow of resources and information, and promote a clear demarcation of authority, all of which serve the interests of a group if not every individual within it.[26]

Something like rank exists in a wide variety of species.[27] In humans, rank is generally regarded as more complex than it is in other animals, but rank can still be observed and studied in nonhuman animals in ways that apply to humans. In nonhuman primates, for instance, rank can be assessed based on behavior, inferring dominant and subordinate roles from fighting, sharing, and grooming, and rank, so conceived, has many of the same consequences among nonhuman primates as among humans. The cross-species significance of status might reflect the evolutionary forces that preserve it. There is, at a minimum, a relationship between status and reproductive fitness. A study of more than thirty nonindustrial populations found that social status is positively associated with men's reproductive success.[28] To be sure, the reproductive success of high-status men may not be as strong today as it was in the past. The benefits of status for reproduction were strongest when those of high status had access to a large number of women, as during the rule of Genghis Khan. Nonetheless, high-income men in the contemporary United States still have more children than very low income men (who often have none).[29] Furthermore, the fitness value of status likely persists even as the determinants of status—whether size, aggressiveness, intelligence, generosity, or appearance—shift over time. The selective pressures on the instinct to maximize status may be strong.

Humans are, in fact, exquisitely attuned to matters of status. Concerns over status are hardly limited to securing a high income or a prized possession—they stretch to even the most mundane interpersonal and environmental factors. Within families, for instance, siblings are sensitive to differences in the relative size of beverages, among many other things. In the workplace, coworkers are even attuned to small differences in office decor, let alone salary.[30] Although attending to such trivial matters might seem irrational, even superficial differences in status are consequential. For one, some goods are in fact limited and will not be available to everyone, including large houses. Furthermore, whether one regards office decor as important or not, slight differences in status are behaviorally consequential. Humans are highly motivated to overcome differences in status when they are apparent. Economist John Harsanyi claims that social status is among the most significant motivating forces, and a long record of psychological research supports his view.[31] For instance, individuals are more proud of accomplishments that boost their social status than they are of accomplishments that are only personally meaningful to them.[32] Furthermore, status is consequential to how others perceive us and how we perceive them. People are more likely to rate those wearing luxury brand shirts, for instance, as more respectable relative to those wearing generic shirts.[33] And attention to sartorial detail need not result in distorted perceptions of who people are. Studies exploring the accuracy of perceived status differences find that individuals are quite accurate in their assessments of status.[34]

The capacity to discern status differences is also reflected in the brain. One account of the evolution of large brains in mammals is that large brains were necessary for coping with complex social problems, a task for which recognizing social status is critical.[35] Some evidence is consistent with the idea that the human brain is hardwired to see status differentials. For one, specific brain areas appear to specialize in facial recognition, which is necessary for managing social relationships. In addition, gray matter volume tends to increase both with increasing social status and social network size.[36] Other studies have established brain areas implicated in discerning hierarchies.[37] The amygdala, for instance, is especially important in what are referred to as "theory of the mind" abilities, a set of skills used for inferring the emotions of other people and guessing their intentions.[38]

Given how social status influences behavior and perception, it is perhaps not surprising that status can also engender strong emotions. Low status, for instance, involves more than the feeling of being less than someone else—status is related, in a wholesale fashion, to perceptions of competence, ability, and worth. Colloquial interpretation of the concept is once again instructive: to be of low status is to feel not just subordinate but that one is a complete "nobody," not even registering on the scale.[39] By the same token, the emotional experience of low status is very similar to the emotional experience of being evaluated by other people, reinforcing its social significance. Being evaluated by other people affects stress hormones more than does a private stressful experience, including performing difficult cognitive tests or watching stressful films.[40]

The same body of research provides evidence linking status to anxiety directly. The brain areas related to perceiving status overlap with those related to anxiety. Studies have linked heightened amygdala activity, for instance, to an increased risk of anxiety disorders.[41] Social anxiety, too, appears to be linked to many of the same regions implicated in the processing of hierarchies.[42] To be sure, the role of status in anxiety is not only a matter of brain activation. It also reflects the kinds of environments that follow high status. Those at the top of a hierarchy experience less stress than those at the bottom. In addition, those at the bottom of the hierarchy sometimes have fewer coping outlets, including less social support, to help them adapt to the stress they experience.[43]

All this is not to suggest that low status always produces higher anxiety. Despite the proximity of regions involved in status perception and anxiety, much of the effect of status on well-being depends on how that status is interpreted and what that status confers. Some evidence, for example, links the receipt of honorific awards to greater longevity. Emmy Award winners tend to live longer than Emmy Award nominees, as do Academy Award–winning actors.[44] But status per se does not explain this pattern. Other contest winners—seemingly of equal significance to those in their respective fields—do not enjoy the same benefits to longevity. Baseball players inducted into the Baseball Hall of Fame, for instance, do not live longer than other professional baseball players. Furthermore, elected presidents and vice presidents live shorter lives than those they ran against, even setting aside presidents who were assassinated.[45] There is also evidence that high-status people respond more severely to threats than do low-status people, even though they generally enjoy greater well-being. In particular, when placed in a task involving social evaluation, high-status people tend to experience more stress than low-status people.[46] This reflects that high-status people believe their status is tenuous, that they fear losing that status, or that they invest more psychologically in their status. In any case, resting on one's laurels does not appear to benefit well-being.

TRENDS IN THE MEANING AND SIGNIFICANCE
OF SOCIAL STATUS

In understanding the role of social status in anxiety, it is important to put status in a broader context. There are good reasons to suspect that status anxiety has become more salient over time. For one, if status anxiety is rooted in social comparison—that is, one's standing is evaluated relative to another person—there may be a growing number of people with whom one can compare. It takes little to produce status differences—status emerges in even small groups based on superficial distinctions. But in the twenty-first century, the potential for identifying someone of higher standing is less constrained by geography or imagination. The same idea applies to growing income inequality. As income inequality grows, the relevance of the tails of distribution increases. The distance between a household in the top 1 percent of income and a household at the median is much larger than it used to be, putting downward pressure on where the average person thinks he or she is situated. By the same token, even a household of modest means might worry that they could quickly fall into a much lower position, recognizing the difficulties of those just below them.

Some evidence more directly points to the growing relevance of social status. There are data, of course, on income over time and there are data on wealth, too. But status is a different concept, and there are fewer direct sources of data. Conventional aspects of status are useful but far from definitive. For instance, surveys reveal that education, income, and occupation are predictive of subjective social status at lower levels of status, though they lose their predictive power at higher levels.[47] Clearer insights on status can be gathered from data on what people purchase.[48] On this point there is abundant evidence for a rise in luxury consumption, marking the emergence of a robust status market. Spending on luxury items has increased over time, including spending on luxury cars, wines, and vacation homes. In addition, Americans are buying larger homes, even as their families grow smaller. Although some of this increase reflects a rise in disposable income and borrowing, the explanation mostly rests with outsized growth of at the top of the distribution. But the consumption of the top 1 percent is not isolated—it changes the consumption of the median household, as families with below-average incomes spend on status items, too, including better televisions and appliances, even if they are unable to purchase the very best.

Another trend consistent with the idea that status is more relevant is change in the sources from which Americans derive their financial satisfaction. Financial satisfaction is a product of financial resources and financial aspirations. Financial aspirations are, in turn, a product of comparisons, both relative to one's prior earnings and relative to the earnings of other people. With this formulation, individuals can derive satisfaction from making more than they did in the past or from making more than others with whom they compare themselves.[49] Historically the former was a major driver of financial satisfaction, and many people reported being satisfied with what they had because their wealth continued to accrue. Over a lifetime, the average employee could expect to earn more than in the past, as real incomes increased steadily over much of the twentieth century. In the late twentieth century, however, real incomes for the median earner were essentially stagnant, likely increasing the relevance of comparisons with other people. In general, individuals assign much greater significance to a loss of income than to a gain of the same amount, referred to as loss aversion.[50] This implies an asymmetry in how status is assessed, especially in the twenty-first century. When incomes are stagnant, individuals will work hard to maintain their current relative position, but when an economy is growing, individuals will have greater confidence they will make more than they did in the past.

EMPIRICAL EVIDENCE ON STATUS AND ANXIETY DISORDERS

Survey data are consistent with the idea of a strong relationship between social status and anxiety disorders. The data for this chapter are drawn from a popular survey question about subjective status. For this question, respondents are presented with an image of ladder with ten rungs and are then asked:

Think of this ladder as representing where people stand in the United States. At the top of the ladder are the people who are the best off—those who have the most money, the most education and the most respected jobs. At the bottom are the people who are the worst off—who have the least money, least education, and the least respected jobs or no job. The higher up you are on the ladder, the closer you are to the people at the very top; the lower you are, the closer you are to the people at the very bottom. Please place a large "X" on the rung where you think you stand at this time in your life, relative to other people in the United States. What is the number to the right of the rung where you placed the "X"?[51]

In another version of the question, respondents are asked where they stand "in their communities," with the caveat that "people define community in different ways." In this version of the question, respondents are not explicitly asked to think about their rank based on income, education, or employment, as they are in the first version.

Figure 8.1 shows the distribution of the U.S.- and community-based ranks. In general, most people place themselves somewhat above the midpoint, and far more people place themselves near the top of the distribution than the bottom. Furthermore, the average placement for the community rank exceeds that for the U.S. rank. Table 8.1 presents average scores over cohort. In addition to the U.S. and community ranks, the table also presents the difference between a respondent's reported rank and the rank expected based on income and education (based on predicted values from a regression model). Of note, younger cohorts are disadvantaged in two ways: they report a lower rank relative to other cohorts, both with respect to the U.S. and community rank, and they also report a lower rank relative to what would be expected based on indicators of their objective status. Conversely, the oldest cohort reports a rank that is almost a half rung higher than what would be expected based on education and income.

Table 8.2 presents models predicting the presence of an anxiety disorder and, in a separate model, a mood disorder. The model is specified based on factors relevant to status, including education, income, and rank. Income is divided into deciles, to match the number of categories of the rank measure and allow for comparisons. The coefficients represent the expected change in the probability of a disorder relative to the reference category, which for income is the first decile and for the ladder score is the first two rungs (very few people place themselves on the bottom rung, necessitating the combination of the two). The model does not include U.S. rank, given the high correlation between U.S. rank and community rank and because community rank, when explored separately, has a stronger relationship with

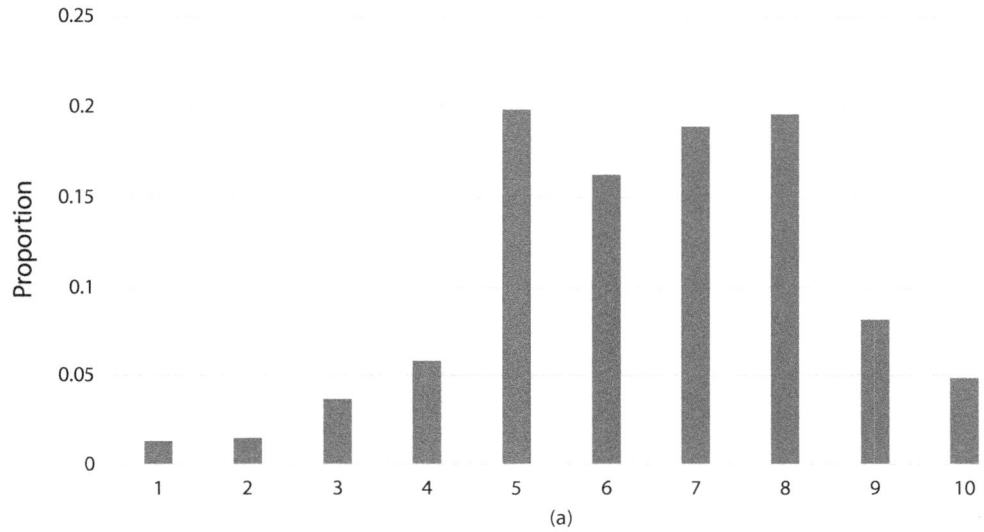

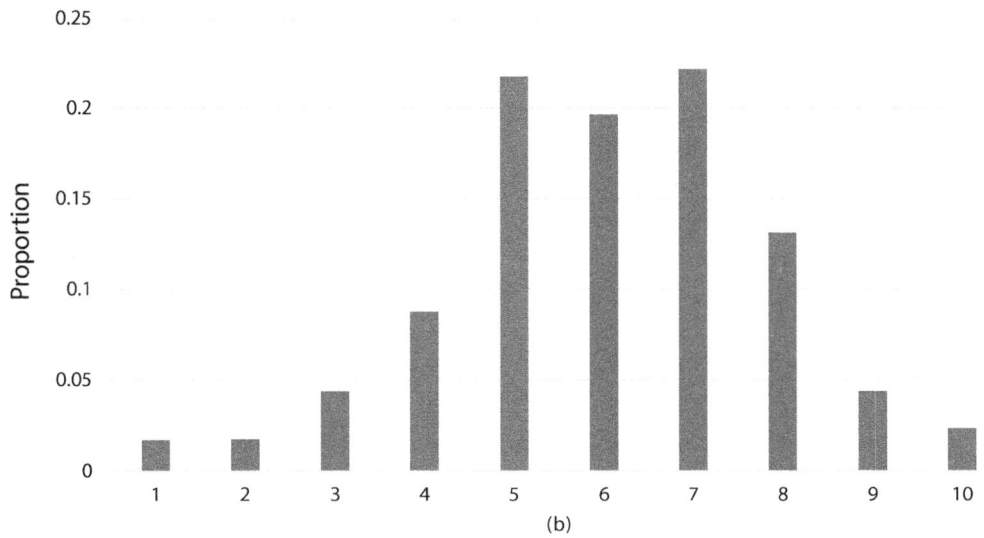

FIGURE 8.1. Distribution of subjective community and U.S. ranks in the United States. *A*. Distribution of Community Rank, *B*. Distribution of U.S. Rank
Source: Collaborative Psychiatric Epidemiological Surveys (Primary Survey, National Comorbidity Survey Replication and National Latino and Asian American Survey, *N* = 10,341)

TABLE 8.1
Average community and U.S. rank by cohort

	Community rank	U.S. rank	Community rank—expected rank	U.S. rank—expected rank
18 to 29	6.206	5.742	−.219	−.187
30 to 44	6.364	5.973	−.223	−.224
45 to 59	6.563	6.189	−.052	−.054
60 and over	6.802	6.235	.440	.412

Source: Margarita Alegria, James S. (James Sidney) Jackson, Ronald C. Kessler, and David Takeuchi, Collaborative Psychiatric Epidemiology Surveys (CPES), 2001–2003 [United States] (Ann Arbor, Mich.: Inter-university Consortium for Political and Social Research [distributor], 2016), https://doi.org/10.3886/ICPSR20240.v8 (primary sruveys: National Comorbidity Survey Replication and National Latino and Asian American Survey, N = 10,341).

anxiety than does U.S. rank. Several things are notable from these sorts of comparisons. First, subjective status matters more than absolute income. Indeed, in the case of both anxiety and mood disorders, the relationship with income is relatively flat, whereas the relationship with status is monotonic and large. Comparisons between the two are somewhat difficult, in that arranging income in deciles results in categories that are evenly spaced with respect to the distribution of income, whereas the community rank scores are not evenly spaced by their distribution. Yet other types of comparisons reach the same conclusion as a straightforward one. Comparisons between standardized coefficients for income and community rank, which adjust for the distribution, reveal a coefficient for community rank that is almost three times larger than for income (−.111 relative to −.033). The same table also presents the relationship between subjective status and mood disorders. Overall, the relationship between status and anxiety is much stronger than the relationship between status and mood disorders. For no row-wise comparison—for example, a community rank of 8 for an anxiety disorder versus a community rank of 8 for a mood disorder—is the mood disorder coefficient numerically larger. If the community rank association is regarded as linear, the relationship with anxiety disorders is much larger than that with mood disorders, at −.025 versus −.018 (with the difference significant at $p < .001$).

TABLE 8.2

Linear probability models of current anxiety and mood disorder with objective and subjective status

	Any current anxiety disorder	Any current mood disorder
Income decile (relative to first)		
Second	−.036 (.019)	−.025 (.015)
Third	−.007 (.019)	−.028 (.017)
Fourth	.006 (.024)	−.037* (.014)
Fifth	−.013 (.021)	−.019 (.016)
Sixth	−.013 (.019)	−.045** (.016)
Seventh	−.037 (.023)	−.059*** (.016)
Eighth	−.032 (.019)	−.041** (.014)
Ninth	−.064*** (.017)	−.076*** (.015)
Tenth	−.037* (.018)	−.053*** (.015)
Community rank (relative to 1 or 2)		
Three	−.068 (.046)	−.066 (.037)
Four	−.179*** (.035)	−.102** (.034)
Five	−.198*** (.036)	−.152*** (.027)
Six	−.215*** (.036)	−.181*** (.029)
Seven	−.247*** (.034)	−.190*** (.030)
Eight	−.249*** (.039)	−.181*** (.028)
Nine	−.248*** (.039)	−.189*** (.031)
Ten	−.281*** (.038)	−.191*** (.030)

* $p < .05$, ** $p < .01$, *** $p < .001$ (standard errors in parentheses).

Source: Margarita Alegria, James S. (James Sidney) Jackson, Ronald C. Kessler, and David Takeuchi, Collaborative Psychiatric Epidemiology Surveys (CPES), 2001–2003 [United States] (Ann Arbor, Mich.: Inter-university Consortium for Political and Social Research [distributor], 2016), https://doi.org/10.3886/ICPSR20240.v8 (primary surveys: National Comorbidity Survey Replication and National Latino and Asian American Survey, $N = 10,341$).

Note: Models also include controls for cohort, race/ethnicity, and education.

TABLE 8.3
Linear probability model of current anxiety on objective with subjective status by cohort

	Any current anxiety disorder
Effects of income by cohort	
18 to 29	−.002
	(.003)
30 to 44	−.009**
	(.003)
45 to 59	−.008**
	(.003)
60 and over	−.003
	(.003)
Effects of community rank by cohort	
18 to 29	−.022***
	(.006)
30 to 44	−.036***
	(.005)
45 to 59	−.021***
	(.004)
60 and Over	−.016**
	(.005)

$* p < .05$, $** p < .01$, $*** p < .001$ (standard errors in parentheses).
Source: Margarita Alegria, James S. (James Sidney) Jackson, Ronald C. Kessler, and David Takeuchi, Collaborative Psychiatric Epidemiology Surveys (CPES), 2001–2003 [United States] (Ann Arbor, Mich.: Inter-university Consortium for Political and Social Research [distributor], 2016), https://doi.org/10.3886/ICPSR20240.v8 (primary surveys: National Comorbidity Survey Replication and National Latino and Asian American Survey, $N = 10,341$).
Note: Model also includes controls for cohort, race/ethnicity, and education.

The idea that younger cohorts are increasingly concerned with status not only implies a lower status among younger cohorts relative to older ones (and relative to objective status). It also implies that status has a stronger relationship with anxiety among younger cohorts, in the sense that they are more sensitive to its significance. Table 8.3 shows cohort-specific associations between anxiety disorders and both income decile and community rank. For simplicity, linear relationships are shown, corresponding to the expected decrease in the probability of an anxiety disorder as a function of a unit increase in the income decile or a one-rung increase in community rank. Community rank is generally more important among younger cohorts, though the only difference that is statistically significant is that between those thirty to forty-four and those sixty and over. Of note, in the youngest cohort, the relationship between income and an anxiety disorder is statistically insignificant, whereas the relationship between community rank and an anxiety disorder is highly significant. In short, the imbalance between objective and subjective status is especially sharp at younger ages. The same pattern is apparent in the oldest cohort as well. In the two middle cohorts, though, both status and income matter for preventing anxiety disorders.

Table 8.4 turns to the role of status in explaining cohort differences in anxiety, consistent with preceding chapters. Although there are significant cohort differences in status, status explains only part of the cohort difference. The first model presents cohort differences adjusted for education and income. And the second model adds community rank. Community rank explains about 11 percent of the cohort difference, even with respect to the difference between the youngest and the oldest cohorts.

This chapter demonstrated the significance of status for understanding anxiety. Although status does not provide a complete explanation for cohort differences, the patterns documented suggest that subjective status is critical to understanding anxiety among the young. This is true in several ways. Younger cohorts report lower status than do older cohorts. Moreover, younger cohorts report lower status than expected based on their objective socioeconomic characteristics. At the same time, perceptions of status matter a great deal more to anxiety than do objective indicators. The relationship between status and anxiety is much larger than that between income and anxiety. And status matters much more for anxiety than it does for depression. For all these reasons, status is critical to understanding the social sources of anxiety. Yet its role in explaining cohort differences is partial at best. Part of the explanation for this pattern reflects the relatively attenuated differences between cohorts. Cohort differences in subjective status never exceed a single rung on the ladder. Furthermore, there is compression across cohorts in the distribution of status, settling around a value that is slightly above the midpoint. Status anxiety is significant and consequential, but it appears that most people find reason to place themselves

TABLE 8.4
Cohort differences in anxiety disorders with and without adjustment for subjective status

Cohort (relative to 60 and over)		
18 to 29	.114***	.101***
	(.012)	(.012)
30 to 44	.142***	.126***
	(.010)	(.009)
45 to 59	.109***	.097***
	(.016)	(.016)
Including community rank	No	Yes

* $p < .05$, ** $p < .01$, *** $p < .001$ (standard errors in parentheses).
Source: Margarita Alegria, James S. (James Sidney) Jackson, Ronald C. Kessler, and David Takeuchi, Collaborative Psychiatric Epidemiology Surveys (CPES), 2001–2003 [United States] (Ann Arbor, Mich.: Inter-university Consortium for Political and Social Research [distributor], 2016), https://doi.org/10.3886/ICPSR20240.v8 (primary surveys: National Comorbidity Survey Replication and National Latino and Asian American Survey, $N = 10,341$).
Note: Both models also include controls for cohort, race/ethnicity, income, and education.

on a rung that affords them some confidence and assurance. The average person places himself or herself somewhat above the midpoint, and few seem to want to place themselves above or below that point. Status might matter the most for the middle-aged, perhaps because that is when status contests are most keen, but even the cohort most affected by status anxiety reports a relatively high rank.

To this point, cohort differences in anxiety appear to be a function of a set of environmental influences. Each influence explains part of the cohort difference. A comprehensive explanation, however, must also address the medical treatment of anxiety. Beyond social and cultural changes that have elevated anxiety, there have been changes in how anxiety is regarded and treated in the health-care system. Even as anxiety has become more common, it has also grown more therapeutically significant, both as a concern for patients and as a target for medical professionals.

Chapter Nine

THE ASCENT OF ANXIETY AS A THERAPEUTIC TARGET

Anxiety is not only a common psychiatric disorder. It is also increasingly common as a therapeutic target. More Americans are seeking treatment for anxiety disorders, and physicians are prescribing more antianxiety medications. Understanding growth in the treatment of anxiety requires more than simply thinking about the growing prevalence of the disorder—anxiety is not simply treated more because it is more common than it used to be. Nor is anxiety treated more than it was simply because there are more medications available to do so. The growing treatment of anxiety also reflects how anxiety is apprehended as a disorder, one that is appropriate for medical intervention and one that is a serious and unique problem. Understanding this change involves considering trends in how physicians perceive the disorder, how patients present with and conceptualize anxiety, and how the treatment of anxiety has evolved. Anxiety has emerged as an important therapeutic target in the minds of physicians, patients, and scientists alike.

A BRIEF HISTORY OF MINOR TRANQUILIZERS

Any account of the medical treatment of anxiety in the twenty-first century requires considering the convoluted history of antianxiety medications, including one of the most popular pharmaceutical treatments of anxiety, benzodiazepines.[1] Benzodiazepines are popular today, and their use is trending upward.[2] But as a category, benzodiazepines are hardly cutting edge. In fact, benzodiazepines were first developed more than a half century ago. The popularity of specific brands, such as Librium, Xanax, and Valium, has waxed and waned, but such medications have never disappeared. Nor is twenty-first century enthusiasm for antianxiety medications entirely unprecedented. Benzodiazepines were preceded by other minor tranquilizers, including meprobamate, which was for a time a best-selling medication under the brand name Miltown. Long before concern over whether it was appropriate to treat sadness with Prozac, the public was debating whether it was proper to treat nerves with Miltown. The history of minor tranquilizers—including all the ongoing cultural wrangling over their appropriateness—is instructive.

The long history of psychiatric medications is one of almost accidental innovations and slow improvements in existing formulas. Nonetheless, the 1950s began a watershed moment, both with respect to the development of effective treatments for certain disorders and the development of medications with less addictive potential. The treatment of anxiety was central to this evolution, as a series of antianxiety medications were introduced, used widely, and eventually replaced by newer competitors. Although antianxiety medications were occasionally met with scientific skepticism, their widespread use at least proved that mental suffering was amenable to pharmaceutical treatment and, at the same time, revealed that the public was more than willing to take such medications.

Miltown was first synthesized in 1950 and launched into production a short time later, following the publication of favorable evaluations in major medical journals.[3] It very quickly became a blockbuster drug, sparking a rise in anti-anxiety medications. By 1965, there were over 50 million prescriptions for anti-anxiety medications.[4] Miltown enjoyed a cultural cachet that had rarely been attached to any other medication. Although Miltown was only indicated for the short-term relief of anxiety, it was used broadly for a variety of psychological ailments, spilling well past the boundaries of what we would now regard as a proper anxiety disorder. Miltown was prescribed primarily by general practitioners and internists rather than psychiatrists, a pattern that continued and was evident even for major tranquilizers.[5]

The popularity of Miltown was born of several things. For one, physicians and psychiatrists were philosophically well-positioned to endorse the pharmaceutical treatment of anxiety. A pharmaceutical approach to emotional suffering is hardly out of place today, though the receptivity of mental health professionals to any psychiatric medication was somewhat surprising at that time. When Miltown was introduced, the dominant approach to the treatment of psychiatric disorders was psychoanalysis. And, at that, much of psychotherapeutic treatment of disorders was dominated by Freudian or neo-Freudian approaches. Even today, psychoanalysis is a competitor of sorts to drugs, though analysis was better positioned to ward off the threat of pharmaceutical encroachment during that earlier period. The field of psychiatry had yet to adopt the biological orientation that prevails today and accepted a more eclectic approach. Yet mental health professionals appear to have absorbed at least two other lessons from psychoanalysis. First, Freud and his followers had effectively taught physicians to take anxiety seriously.[6] Whatever else Freud achieved, he succeeded in convincing practitioners that anxiety was at the center of a host of other psychiatric symptoms. Even a less arcane approach to the understanding mental illness emphasized as much. Early versions of the *Diagnostic and Statistical Manual of Mental Disorders* (*DSM*), for instance, positioned anxiety as a central symptom, even if that positioning was shorn of many of Freud's other ideas. Second, Freud set the stage for appreciating the relevance of mental illness for everyday life, both in how it was manifest and the number of people it affected.[7] For much of psychiatric history, the concept of "mental illness" was reserved for the most severe disorders, including schizophrenia, and psychiatry was practiced mostly in inpatient hospital settings. Freud significantly expanded the concept of psychological dysfunction. He showed how the so-called neurotic disorders could affect virtually anyone and, further, that the symptoms of neurosis spanned a variety of emotions and physiological states. Here, too, the *DSM* formalized this expansive framing by including a section in the manual on "psychophysiologic autonomic and visceral disorders," a category that included respiratory, musculoskeletal, and gastrointestinal "reactions" to psychological issues.[8]

With this understanding, medical professionals could easily appreciate the value of psychiatric medications for their regular ambulatory patients. Drugs like Miltown allowed physicians to treat a complaint that was itself regarded as a serious medical problem, but also to treat adjacent disorders and potentially more serious ones, all without the additional training psychoanalysis would require. If drugs appeared be a quick fix for all manner of dysfunction, it was because physicians had been taught to believe they were. To be sure, there was more than the philosophy of psychoanalysis pushing physicians in this direction. The early scientific evaluations of Miltown were, in fact, cast quite broadly.[9] In 1955, two studies of the drug were published in the *Journal of the American Medical Association*. A study by Lowell Selling reported favorable results for the "anxiety neurosis syndrome," including especially tension, but also reported at least some benefit for treating alcoholism, abdominal discomfort, headache, depression, and behavioral problems in children.[10] A parallel study by Joseph Borrus reported much the same, purporting therapeutic benefits for both acute and chronic anxiety, but also for obsessive-compulsive behavior, and even epilepsy.[11] The clinical value of Miltown was further elevated by the fact that it could treat some of the most common symptoms a general practitioner was likely to see. Evidence collected at the time indicated that, among patients with puzzling symptoms in outpatient settings, it was likely that most suffered from a psychological problem of some sort, while less than 20 percent had only an organic basis for their symptoms.[12] Advertisements for Miltown were hardly blind to this. Marketers recognized the broad potential of the drug and, in contrast to the sort of specific indications that are required in advertisements today, they directly pitched Miltown for a variety of indications, including simple stress and tension.[13]

Enthusiasm for Miltown stretched far beyond the clinic. Scientists, too, recognized the value of anxiolytics and appreciated how antianxiety medications foreshadowed other innovations. Writing in *Science* and *Scientific American* in the 1950s, Harold Himwich accurately anticipated much of what would transpire.[14] For him, drugs like Miltown were only the beginning. They represented "a beachhead which should be steadily extended during the coming years," branching out to disorders that current drugs, through their physiological actions, could not yet treat, including melancholia by way of targeting serotonin.[15] Yet in Miltown he saw something already significant. For Himwich, drugs like Miltown were useful not just for the disordered few, who suffered from specific psychiatric problems, but for the "normal population," who suffered from "intolerable stress."[16] Furthermore, he saw potential in psychiatric medications to make the entire therapeutic process smoother, working hand-in-hand with talk therapy and promoting a more episodic approach to the treatment of suffering. For instance, drugs provided a way for patients on the verge of panic to come to a more "objective evaluation" of their work or financial stress, making them more receptive to therapy.[17] Even the most "ephemeral disturbances" could be treated fruitfully—or, as he put it, "pleasantly dissipated"—by a small dose of a tranquilizer.[18]

Despite fulsome enthusiasm of this sort, pockets of skepticism began to emerge. In fact, critical scientific reviews appeared quite early, a mere three years after the drug was released.[19] Some of the criticism pertained less to Miltown itself but to how studies had evaluated its effectiveness. At the time, the gold standard for the scientific evaluation of pharmaceuticals was shifting to the double-blind, placebo controlled trial, and the earliest evaluations of Miltown were not conducted in this fashion. Although Miltown was hardly alone in being evaluated in a less than ideal way, a review by Victor Laties and Bernard Weiss emphasized the amount of the bias potentially lurking in studies of the drug.[20] They pointed out that the Borrus study, published in the *Journal of the American Medical Association*, had few safeguards against observing a positive result. The study was not blind, for instance. Participating physicians were aware of which patients were taking the medication, and no placebo control was included. In addition, patients receiving the drug were also provided with therapy, suggesting, at least to Laties and Weiss, that the "glowing" effects of Miltown might instead be a "glowing tribute to Borrus's ability as a psychotherapist."[21] The Selling study suffered from similar problems. Like patients in the Borrus study, patients in the Selling study received therapy in addition to Miltown, and no adequate control group was included. Although Selling switched some patients from receiving the drug to receiving a placebo during the course of the study, no information was provided on how these patients were selected, casting doubt on the adequacy of the within-subjects control group.

Yet the skepticism regarding Miltown was largely scientific in nature, at least at the time. It did not extend to all minor tranquilizers and certainly not to the pharmaceutical treatment of anxiety as a philosophical matter. Indeed, the enthusiasm surrounding Miltown was later transferred to newer and seemingly better-tested anxiety medications, including benzodiazepines. Benzodiazepines emerged at about the same time as Miltown, though they slowly took its place when the evidence surrounding their effectiveness became more compelling. Benzodiazepines provided a significant improvement over Miltown, especially with respect to their safety.[22] Scientific credibility and reputation loomed large in this enthusiasm. One doctor gushed that Valium had been subject to "the most rigorous testing of any psychotropic drug in history" by some of the "finest researchers" in the country.[23] By the early 1970s, all the scientific skepticism had finally caught up to Miltown, and its once formidable popularity had faded, but its loss was more than made up for by new and seemingly better alternatives. Indeed, at the time Valium was the single most prescribed brand-name medication in the world.[24] All told there were more than 100 million prescriptions for minor tranquilizers annually, far exceeding the 30 million prescriptions for antidepressants.[25]

Much of the history of psychiatric medication is cyclical. Eventually enthusiasm for benzodiazepines diminished, too, though in this case the change was driven by concerns about both their effectiveness and safety. Enthusiasm was also diminished by a substantial shift in what psychiatric disorders were of most concern to patients and physicians. Although benzodiazepines were safer than their immediate predecessor, they were still associated with dependence. To be sure, some scientists contested the meaning of dependence in scientific demonstrations of this sort. Some scientists, for instance, were quick to highlight a difference between drug *addiction* and therapeutic *dependence* and further argued that the risk of addiction per se varied between specific types of anxiety.[26] Patients treated for panic and agoraphobic disorders, for instance, took benzodiazepines only on an occasional basis with no necessary escalation in dosage. The patients most prone to dependence were those prescribed benzodiazepines for disorders that were less episodic, such as chronic dysphoria, for which the drug was often taken for long periods of time and, at least in some patients, the disorder could occur in the context of alcohol abuse. But distinctions of this sort quickly collapsed as the public moved toward a more conservative approach to the treatment of anxiety.

Other forces pushed the decline of benzodiazepines along. Just as the treatment of anxiety using minor tranquilizers was declining, the treatment of depression using selective serotonin reuptake inhibitors (SSRIs) was expanding. The most significant change in this regard was the development of Prozac in 1987, followed by the marketing of other SSRIs.[27] Not unlike Miltown, SSRIs slowly assumed an omnibus quality, useful for the treatment of distress, not just the treatment of mood disorders. The Food and Drug Administration initially approved SSRIs for the treatment of major depression, but eventually SSRIs were approved for certain anxiety disorders as well, including generalized anxiety disorder.[28] The demon-strated effectiveness of SSRIs was not terribly strong, and their effects were far less immediate than those of a tranquilizer. Nonetheless, SSRIs had some relative advantages. For one, the potential for dependence was less than for benzodiazepines. Some clinicians were concerned about prescription-seeking behavior with respect to tranquilizers. In particular, physicians worried about patients seeking the "high" of drugs like benzodiazepines. This concern was almost entirely absent with respect to SSRIs, whose effects take much longer to realize and do not resemble those of euphoria.[29] In cultural and clinical settings increasingly concerned with abuse, SSRIs were becoming a more attractive option.

THE TREATMENT OF DEPRESSION AND THE OCCLUSION OF ANXIETY

Related to this were parallel shifts in how disorders were regarded by clinicians and patients.[30] A split between anxiety and depression was becoming more apparent, allowing depression to eventually overshadow anxiety, especially in the context of new drugs approved primarily for mood disorders.[31] Depression was increasingly regarded as a biological illness, whereas anxiety was not. The ascent of SSRIs in the treatment of depression certainly played a role in encouraging the view that depression was biological—an inference aided by the idea that a reduction in a specific neurotransmitter was related to the onset of a specific psychiatric disorder—though SSRIs did not act alone in this regard. The clinical presentation of the two disorders likely played a role as well. Unless clinicians are prepared to accept anxiety as a psychiatric disorder or patients are able to articulate their anxiety in a way that facilitates a formal diagnosis, the actual presentation of depression and anxiety in clinical settings can elevate the former while minimizing the latter. Precisely because mood disorders tend to be more episodic over a period of weeks—significant but not situational—they tend to draw more attention. Major depression, for instance, tends to occur in episodes, distinct from periods before and after any onset or remission. Bipolar disorder, too, involves significant fluctuations in mood. Anxiety, meanwhile, is spread far and wide, involving episodes of panic, to be sure, but also chronic low-grade tension and dread.[32] And patients themselves tend to downplay anxiety relative to depression, even when they take it seriously. Patients often attribute their anxiety to character rather than illness, enduring, to be sure, but part of their personality, and therefore, not easily seen as a sign of deterioration. When clinicians ask patients about symptoms such as nervousness, for instance, patients are often inclined to dismiss them with a quick, "I have always been like that."[33] The apparent source of anxiety can also diminish a robust response. A common source of chronic anxiety, for instance, is concern about one's family, which carries the connotation of being positive or at least reasonable.[34]

Part of the difficulty in apprehending anxiety as a disorder also stems from comorbidity. Anxiety often occurs with other disorders, and absent other clues, clinicians tend to focus on diagnosing a single disorder they feel they can treat effectively. This tendency, in turn, accentuates the influence of pharmaceuticals in diagnostic decisions. When SSRIs are more popular than minor tranquilizers, for instance, physicians will, in effect, "see" depression more than they see anxiety. In a particularly illuminating study of biases of this sort, researchers compared the diagnostic decisions of clinicians in natural settings—that is, as they routinely make decisions among the kinds of patients they usually see—with their diagnostic decisions when using a structured clinical interview, that is, when using a script meant to be comprehensive and faithful to published diagnostic criteria.[35] The study found several things. For one, it found that, in general, clinicians overlooked many disorders. In nonstructured interviews, clinicians diagnosed 1.4 disorders on average, whereas in structured interviews they diagnosed 2.3. The study also revealed that clinicians gravitated toward a single disorder much more than was warranted by the symptoms of a case. In a structured interview, only 37 percent of patients were diagnosed with a single disorder, whereas in a natural setting, 65 percent of patients were diagnosed with only one. The study also found that some disorders were more routinely over- or underdiagnosed. Major depressive disorder and dysthymia, for instance, were slightly more frequent in unstructured settings—major depressive disorder was the single most common diagnosis, found in just over half of the nonstructured interviews—whereas every single anxiety disorder (among nine possibilities) was more frequent in the structured setting. Of all the psychiatric disorders, phobic disorders were the most often overlooked and, indeed, were ignored almost altogether. For instance, the prevalence of specific phobias was 0.8 percent in the unstructured setting, but a remarkable 10.4 percent in the structured

setting. Similarly, social phobia was diagnosed in 3.2 percent of unstructured interviews, but 28.6 percent of structured interviews.

THE PERSISTENCE OF MINOR TRANQUILIZERS AND
THE GROWING APPRECIATION OF ANXIETY

Despite all the forces elevating depression and deflating anxiety, anxiety
never went away. Patients still, of course, experienced it. The prevalence of
anxiety disorders did not, in fact, drop. Furthermore, some of the conditions that elevated depression as a therapeutic target have begun to recede.
The diagnosed prevalence of depression rose when the profits of SSRIs
were high, but the patents for many early SSRIs have now expired, and
generic versions have taken their place.[36] Furthermore, the pharmaceutical
treatment of depression has shifted in ways that have fractured the market, splitting the space once held by SSRIs.[37] Antipsychotic medications,
for instance, are now used frequently to treat bipolar disorders, effectively
creating one class of mood disorders treated with increasingly unprofitable
SSRIs and another class treated with medications ordinarily used in the
treatment of psychosis.[38]

The medications used to treat anxiety, meanwhile, never disappeared.
Despite the growth of SSRIs in the 1980s and 1990s, SSRIs never completely
overshadowed minor tranquilizers. Indeed, despite all the wrangling over
their appropriateness and lingering fear of dependence, benzodiazepines
are prescribed with growing frequency.[39] Part of their persistence and
resurgence reflects improvements in their formulation.[40] One criticism of
Valium, for instance, was that the drug took a long time to lose its effect,
resulting in extended periods of fatigue. Recognizing this, newer benzodiazepines have a shorter half-life. Xanax, for instance, was introduced in
1981 and was billed as both safer and shorter-acting than existing benzodiazepines. Perhaps an even bigger part of the resurgence of benzodiazepines
is growing appreciation of their effectiveness, both on their own and relative to other classes of medication. In 1999, a global panel of experts pushed
back on the idea that benzodiazepines were associated with dependence
and recommended the use of benzodiazepines in the treatment of anxiety,
even over prolonged periods of time.[41]

Although benzodiazepines certainly have strong psychoactive effects,
they are clinically attractive for a number of reasons and may be more

clinically attractive than SSRIs.[42] For one, even though both SSRIs and benzodiazepines are used in the treatment of anxiety, SSRIs are less effective. The effects of SSRIs are more unpredictable and their side effects tend to be greater.[43] Furthermore, benzodiazepines are fast acting, whereas SSRIs take weeks to reach full potency, an important consideration given the significance of symptomatic relief for patients.[44] Consumer behavior is consistent with these differences. Drop-out rates for SSRIs in the treatment of depression range between 21 percent and 33 percent, whereas patients tend to take benzodiazepines on a situational basis and often at a lower dosage than prescribed.[45] Harnessing the growing scientific support for the drug, the marketing of benzodiazepines has shifted over time.[46] Whereas benzodiazepines might once have been associated with the alleviation of stress, they are increasingly marketed as fast-acting treatments for specific anxiety disorders. The more tailored marketing has not curtailed the number of prescriptions.

Perhaps the strongest signal of the growing acceptance of benzodiazepines is that Medicare will now pay for them. In 2006, the Medicare Modernization Act established Medicare Part D, the arm of Medicare responsible for prescription drug coverage. At the time of the act's passage, benzodiazepines were excluded, and little discussion was given to expanding coverage. Medicare-eligible patients could still receive coverage for benzodiazepines, but only through supplemental coverage, including Medicaid (which at the time did not have the same restrictions as Medicare), or through a private insurance policy. The history of excluding benzodiazepines from federal programs reflected a long-standing ambivalence about tranquilizers on the part of government.[47] The Omnibus Budget Reconciliation Act of 1990 allowed states to exclude or restrict coverage of benzodiazepines, along with other drugs, such as fertility and weight-loss drugs, under Medicaid. Although at the time no state chose to exclude benzodiazepines outright, about a third imposed some restriction. Their reluctance largely stemmed from concerns about abuse and dependence, which of course concerned clinicians as well. Yet this reluctance slowly evaporated as scientists began to appreciate the value of benzodiazepines. The federal government eventually followed suit. In 2005, Benjamin Cardin (D-MD), along with twenty-three cosponsors, introduced House Resolution 3151, specifically targeting the benzodiazepine exclusion in Medicare.[48] To be sure, some reluctance lingered, as reflected in the text of the resolution, which urged caution in the use of benzodiazepines, hoping to ensure "appropriateness and to avoid abuse" and, in particular, to ensure that the policies regarding prescriptions for benzodiazepine "are consistent with accepted clinical guidelines, are appropriate to individual health histories, and are designed to minimize long term use, guard against over-prescribing, and prevent patient abuse."[49] Ultimately the benzodiazepine exclusion was superseded by the Patient Protection and Affordable Care Act, which took effect in 2013 (and involved other sweeping improvements with respect to mental health care). Yet the resulting change with respect to benzodiazepines was enormous. In its first year of paying for the drug, Medicare—paying on behalf of the elderly and disabled who are covered by the program—paid for nearly 40 million benzodiazepine prescriptions, spending over $377 million in total.[50] Xanax accounted for more than 12 million claims and Klonopin nearly 9 million.

The use of benzodiazepines continues to increase across a variety of indications. In 2003, there were 27.6 million ambulatory-care visits involving benzodiazepines, and in 2015, there were 62.6 million.[51] Approximately half of all visits are associated with primary care physicians rather than specialists. In addition, during this period, coprescribing of benzodiazepines with opioids quadrupled and coprescribing with other sedatives doubled.[52] To be sure, the risks associated with benzodiazepine use are still present—its use has never been considered risk-free. Benzodiazepine overdose mortality increased from 0.58 per 100,000 adults to 3.07 between 1996 and 2013.[53] Part of this increase reflects the fact that few guidelines exist for benzodiazepines, despite their long history. Part also reflects the expansive use of benzodiazepines, especially for back and other kinds of chronic pain. The use of benzodiazepines in anxiety and depression has increased as well, but this increase has been modest relative to their use for pain.[54] It is useful, though, to focus on the identification and treatment of anxiety as a way of understanding why benzodiazepines have retained such therapeutic relevance.

TRENDS IN THE DIAGNOSIS AND TREATMENT OF ANXIETY

For this section I turn to the National Ambulatory Medical Care Survey (NAMCS), a nationally representative survey of physician visits.[55] The survey is useful for multiple reasons. For one, it has been conducted annually for more than a decade. In contrast to the data sets used previously, the NAMCS includes visits among those under the age of eighteen. Furthermore, the survey asks questions about the reasons for the patient's visit, any diagnoses associated with that visit, and any treatment, including prescriptions. The overlap between the reasons for the visit and any resulting diagnostic code is especially informative. The reason for the visit question was explicitly included in the NAMCS to uncover the patient's motivation for seeking care and to provide information on how the patient conceived his or her problem.[56] This can be compared with the actual diagnosis. An International Statistical Classification of Diseases and Related Health Problems (ICD) code was provided for the visit. This diagnostic code may not match the patient's reason for the visit if the physician diagnosed a different problem or did not regard the anxiety as sufficient to warrant a diagnosis. In fact, only 56 percent of those patients who indicated that anxiety was the reason for their visit were given an ICD code for anxiety in the NAMCS. The strength of the correspondence between the reason for the visit and the ICD code provides information on how receptive physicians are to reports of anxiety in their patients.

Figure 9.1 shows trends in the reasons for visiting a physician and the resulting diagnoses associated with that visit. The numbers refer to proportions. Panel A presents anxiety and depression among visits for a mental or behavioral health problem. Panel B presents anxiety and mood disorders among visits associated with a formal ICD code for a psychiatric disorder. Both panels show the growing significance of anxiety, both as a reason for visiting a physician and as a resulting diagnosis. In 2015, among those receiving a psychiatric diagnosis, anxiety was more frequent than depression, at 55 percent relative to 52 percent. Figure 9.2 expands this idea by exploring the intersection of depression and anxiety. The figure corresponds to anxiety and depression diagnoses among visits associated with a psychiatric disorder. The four shaded areas correspond to (1) neither depression nor anxiety as a diagnosis, (2) depression but not anxiety, (3) anxiety but not depression, and (4) both depression and anxiety. This figure also emphasizes the growing importance of anxiety, including anxiety on its own. Although depression without anxiety was the dominant category in the past, anxiety without depression was more common in 2015.

Treatment has increased as well. Figure 9.3 presents the proportion of visits in each year involving a prescription of a benzodiazepine and a

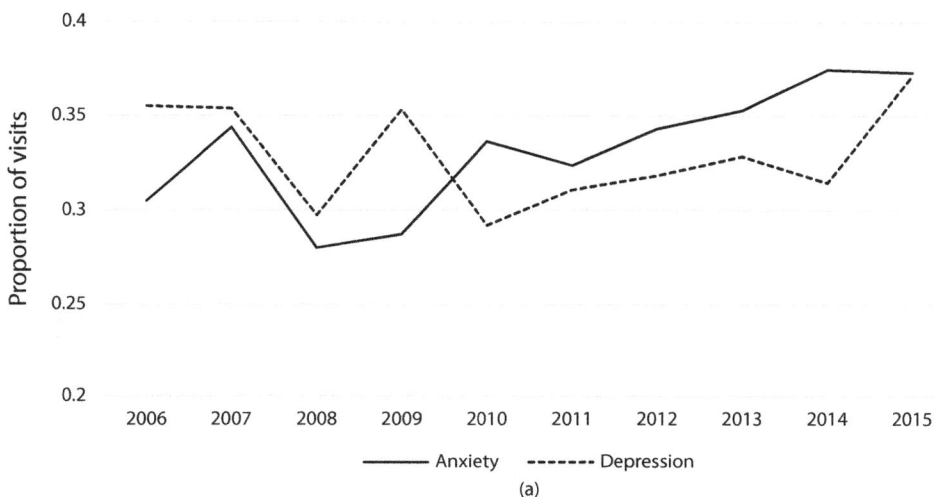

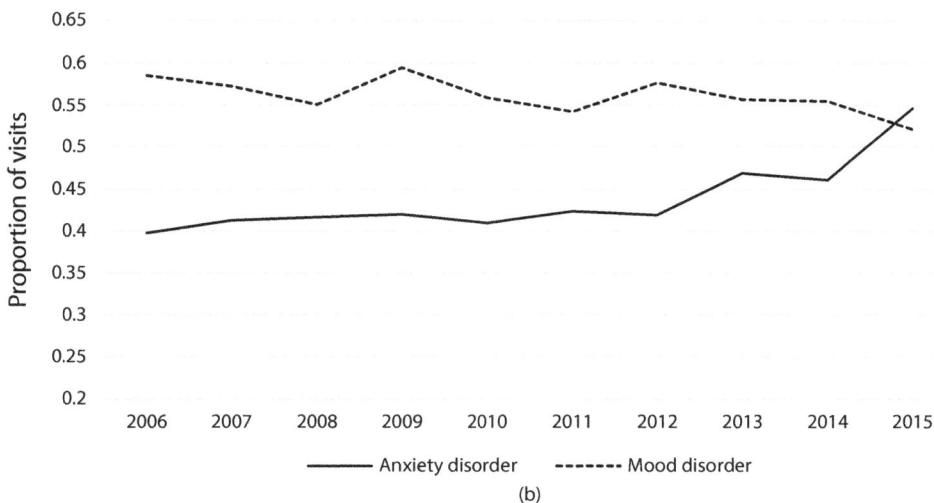

FIGURE 9.1. Trends in anxiety and depression in ambulatory medical care. *A*. Reason for Visit Among those Visiting a Doctor for Mental Health Problems, *B*. Anxiety and Mood Disorders Among those Diagnosed with a Psychiatric Disorder
Source: National Ambulatory Medical Care Survey

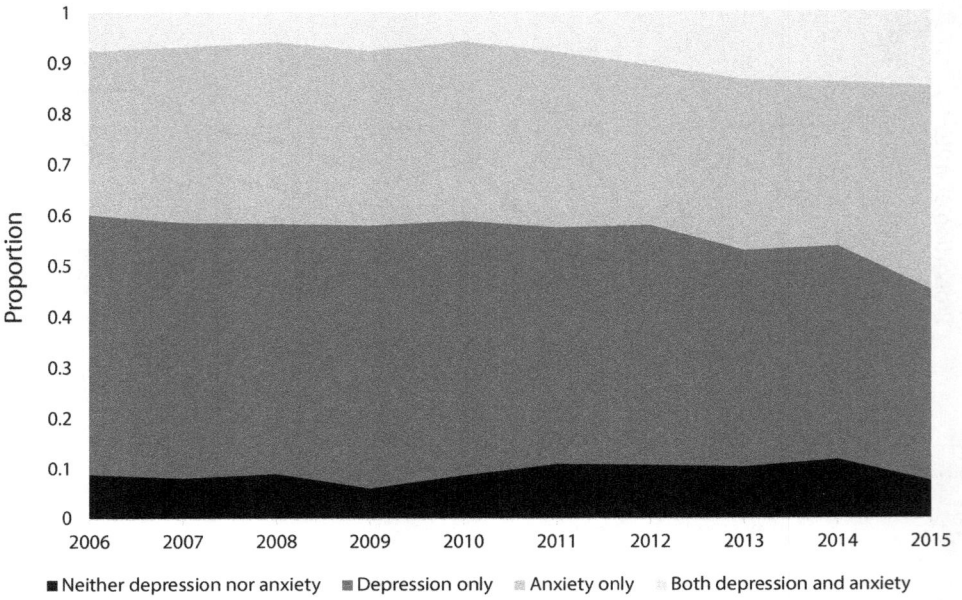

FIGURE 9.2. Trends in diagnoses among visits associated with a psychiatric diagnosis
Source: National Ambulatory Medical Care Survey

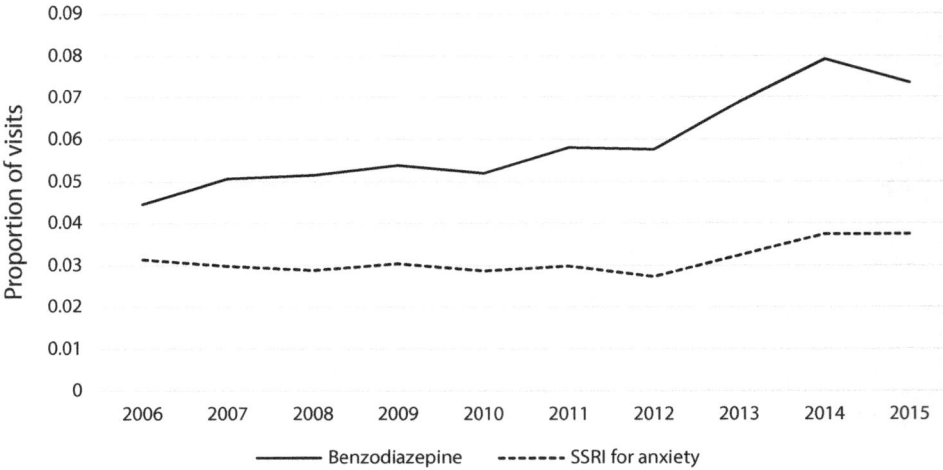

FIGURE 9.3. Trends in antianxiety medication prescriptions
Source: National Ambulatory Medical Care Survey

prescription for one of three SSRIs approved for anxiety (paroxetine, Paxil; sertraline, Zoloft; and venlafaxine, Effexor). In 2014, about 8 percent of ambulatory physician visits involved a prescription for a benzodiazepine, increasing from 4.5 percent in 2006. Although the use of SSRIs for anxiety has increased as well, the dominant anxiety pharmaceutical is consistently a benzodiazepine.

Figure 9.4 explores this increase further. Preceding chapters indicated that the increase in treatment seeking for anxiety could reflect a real increase in the prevalence of anxiety. But it is also possible that physicians have become more receptive to the presentation of anxiety in their patients. Figure 9.2 presents the marginal effects from a model predicting whether the visit resulted in a formal ICD code for anxiety. The probability is modeled as a function of basic demographic characteristics, including sex, age, and race, as well as the total number of ICD codes associated with the visit, assuming that more codes, all else being equal, increase the probability of a psychiatric code. More importantly, the probability is modeled as a function of whether the patient visited the physician because of anxiety. A parallel model explores the probability of a mood disorder ICD code as

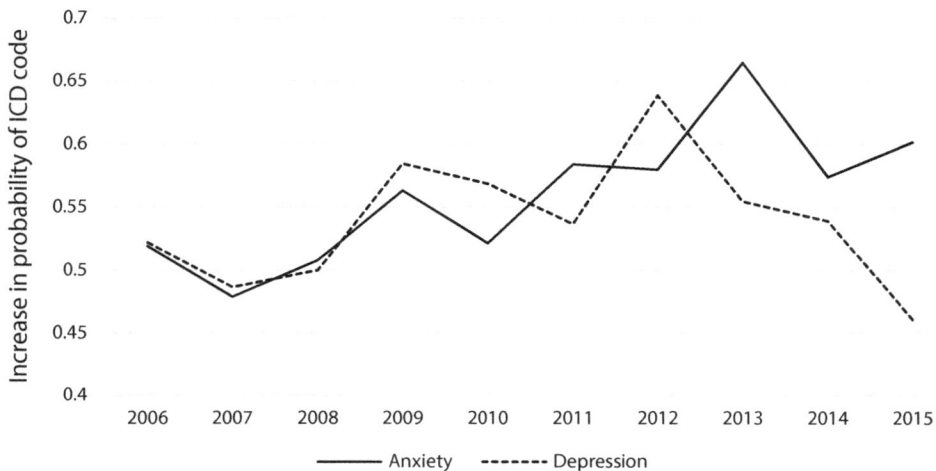

FIGURE 9.4. Summary of effects of anxiety or depression as reason for visit on ICD diagnosis for anxiety or depression
Source: National Ambulatory Medical Care Survey (N = 390,538)

a function of the same factors, but also, in this case, whether the patient visited the physician because of depression. The sample is limited to visits to primary care, where most patients at least initially seek treatment for behavioral problems and where the issue of appropriate sensitivity to psychiatric symptoms is likely to be most acute, as primary care physicians are generally not specialists in mental health. Overall, the average effects of visiting a physician for depression or anxiety on a diagnosis for that specific disorder start around the same place, with an average effect of around .5. In other words, presenting the disorder as a primary complaint increases the probability of a diagnosis by a primary care physician by about .5 points (or about 50 percent of those who present with the disorder are diagnosed with the disorder). Over time, however, anxiety and depression have diverged in this regard. Since 2013, the average effect for anxiety has exceeded that for depression. The models suggest that the magnitude of the anxiety effect has increased significantly, whereas the magnitude of the depression effect has not. In other words, primary care physicians are responding more to reports of anxiety in their patients than to reports of depression.

Table 9.1 turns to a more granular analysis of these trends. The table presents pairs of models, the first with the probability of anxiety as the reason for the visit as the outcome and the second with the probability of a benzodiazepine prescription as the outcome. The table starts by presenting the estimated per-year increase in the probability of each. The first model controls for basic factors—sex, race, and age—and imposes no sample restrictions. Both trends are significant. Over a decade, the expected increase in benzodiazepine prescriptions per physician visit was 3.1 percentage points, while the expected increase in presenting anxiety as a complaint was 1.1 percentage points. An increase in prescriptions for benzodiazepines can be driven by two factors: an increase in diagnoses for anxiety disorders or a growing inclination to use benzodiazepines for an anxiety diagnosis. When the sample is limited to those with a diagnosed anxiety disorder, the year coefficient is no longer significant, suggesting physicians are responding to the presentation of symptoms they are increasingly categorizing as anxiety disorders. The second model suggests that, while younger cohorts are generally more likely to report anxiety, trends in benzodiazepine prescriptions are remarkably consistent over cohorts. The age range of the cohorts is the same as that used in earlier chapters, though the data also include visits by those under the age of eighteen, a useful comparison. The increase is very

TABLE 9.1

Linear probability models of anxiety as reason for visit and benzodiazepine prescription, trend analysis

	Anxiety as reason for visit	Benzodiazepine prescription
Per-year trend	.0011***	.0031***
	(.0002)	(.0005)
Per-year trend by cohort		
0 to 17	.0008**	.0003*
	(.0002)	(.0002)
18 to 29	.0023***	.0031***
	(.0006)	(.0008)
30 to 44	.0014*	.0035***
	(.0005)	(.0008)
45 to 59	.0011**	.0038***
	(.0004)	(.0008)
60 and over	.0008**	.0039***
	(.0002)	(.0008)
Per-year trend by doctor specialty		
Specialist	.0005***	.0031***
	(.0001)	(.0006)
Primary care	.0007**	.0028***
	(.0002)	(.0006)
Psychiatrist	.0025	−.0015
	(.0032)	(.0030)

$^{*}p < .05, ^{**}p < .01, ^{***}p < .001$ (standard errors in parentheses).

Source: United States Department of Health and Human Services, Centers for Disease Control and Prevention, National Center for Health Statistics, National Ambulatory Medical Care Survey (Ann Arbor, Mich.: Interuniversity Consortium for Political and Social Research [distributor]), https://www.icpsr.umich.edu/icpsrweb /NACDA/series/37 ($N = 390,538$).

Note: All models also include controls for gender, cohort, and race/ethnicity.

small for those under the age of eighteen, though the increase is significant for every other age group and, if anything, grows slightly larger with age (though the slope for those age eighteen to twenty-nine is not significantly smaller than the slope for those age sixty and over). The trend in presenting anxiety as a symptom, though, is much more pronounced among the eighteen to twenty-nine cohort, at an increase of 2.3 percentage points per decade versus 0.8 among those sixty and over. The final pair of models explores variation in the magnitude of these trends over three different kinds of physicians: specialists, primary care physicians, and psychiatrists. The medical specialty most appropriate for the treatment of psychiatric disorders is psychiatry, though most patients who receive medical treatment for anxiety receive it, at least initially, through a general practitioner. The increase in prescribing benzodiazepines over time was not, in fact, found among psychiatrists. The increase, instead, was limited to general practitioners and other specialists. In the NAMCS, about 52 percent of benzodiazepine prescriptions came from visits with general practitioners and another 33 percent come from nonpsychiatric specialists, whereas only about 15 percent came from psychiatrists. There are two ways to regard the increase in benzodiazepine prescribing from the standpoint of physician behavior. One interpretation is that the average physician is more likely to prescribe benzodiazepines than in the past, consistent with a growing sensitivity to anxiety as a disorder. Another interpretation, though, is that the increase is due to a change in the composition of the physician workforce. The NAMCS includes information on the physician associated with the visit, and from this it is possible to create indicators of the overall willingness of a given physician to prescribe benzodiazepines. In the data, the maximum number of benzodiazepine prescriptions contributed by a single physician was forty. The average physician prescribed benzodiazepines in 5.8 percent of cases. If the upward trend in benzodiazepine prescribing was driven by an increase in the number of benzodiazepine-inclined physicians rather than an increase in the likelihood of prescribing by the average physician, controlling for the identity of the physician would eliminate the trend. Controls of this sort do not, however, eliminate the increase, suggesting the average physician is more likely to prescribe benzodiazepines than in the past.

The clinical context of anxiety treatment deserves more scrutiny. Very few diagnoses of anxiety (or depression) occur in absence of other diagnoses, especially when visiting a general practitioner. Patients in primary care who have depression or anxiety report, on average, two to three comorbid chronic medical conditions, a rate about twice that found among those not suffering from anxiety or depression.[57] In the NAMCS, only 10 percent of anxiety ICD codes occur stand-alone ICD codes. In general, psychiatric disorders assume a secondary status relative to other conditions and, as a result, physicians often overlook them. For instance, a physician seeking to treat only the most serious condition might focus on cancer or heart disease and neglect anxiety or depression. But if anxiety disorders are becoming more significant as a target for treatment, the crowd out associated with other medical conditions should be less significant. In addition, if anxiety is seen as a more significant medical condition, the crowd out should be less for anxiety than for mood disorders. When presented with multiple conditions, physicians might increasingly elevate anxiety over depression. Table 9.2 explores this possibility using two regression models, the first for whether the visit involved an anxiety ICD code and the second for whether it involved a depression or other mood disorder ICD code. Of note is the inclusion of other ICD codes as predictors of the focal ones. In particular, the models include ICD codes for neoplasms, circulatory problems, and respiratory problems—categories of conditions physicians are likely

TABLE 9.2

Linear probability models of anxiety and mood disorder ICD code with other ICD codes as predictors

	Anxiety ICD code	Depression or mood disorder ICD code
Other ICD codes		
Neoplasms	−.0274***+	−.0419***+
	(.0016)	(.0023)
Circulatory	−.0201***+	−.0285***+
	(.0020)	(.0017)
Respiratory	−.0229***+	−.0272***+
	(.0013)	(.0014)
Number of other ICD codes (relative to one)		
Two	.0296***+	.0227***+
	(.0014)	(.0016)
Three	.0450***+	.0402***+
	(.0022)	(.0024)
Primary care physician	−.0002+	−.0248***+
	(.0019)	(.0024)

* $p < .05$, ** $p < .01$, *** $p < .001$ (standard errors in parentheses).

+ Coefficients significantly different between mood and anxiety disorder equations at $p < .05$.

Source: United States Department of Health and Human Services, Centers for Disease Control and Prevention, National Center for Health Statistics, National Ambulatory Medical Care Survey (Ann Arbor, Mich.: Interuniversity Consortium for Political and Social Research [distributor]), https://www.icpsr.umich.edu/icpsrweb /NACDA/series/37 ($N = 390,538$).

Note: All models also include controls for gender, cohort, year, and race/ethnicity.

to regard as significant and perhaps as superseding psychiatric disorders. In addition, the models include the total number of ICD codes associated with the visit (for a maximum of three) and whether the visit was associated with a primary care physician (as well as controls for basic demographic variables). The idea of a crowd out in diagnostic behavior leads to the expectation that the coefficients for the other ICD codes should be negative: that is, receiving a cancer diagnosis should reduce the likelihood of an anxiety diagnosis, all else equal. At the same time, as the total number of ICD diagnoses increases, the likelihood of also including anxiety in the set should increase as well: that is, psychiatric disorders are more likely to be considered when they are only one of several diagnoses. The models support both kinds of relationships, though comparisons between the models for anxiety and mood disorders are critical. For all three nonpsychiatric ICD codes, the magnitude of the (negative) association is greater for mood disorders than for anxiety disorders. In other words, nonpsychiatric conditions crowd out mood disorders more than they do anxiety disorders.

Although much of this book has focused on reasons for an increase in anxiety over time and between cohorts, it is clear that the growing treatment of anxiety has been abetted by its appeal as a clinical target from the standpoints of patients and providers. Anxiety is presented with greater frequency by patients and treated with more significance by physicians. Furthermore, anxiety is increasingly superseding depression as the most prominent psychiatric complaint. To be sure, patients are especially likely to be diagnosed with *both* mood and anxiety disorders, but pure anxiety disorders are becoming more common than pure mood disorders. These trends are remarkable, given that physicians have historically been better equipped to identify depression than anxiety. One study found detection rates of 34 percent for major depressive disorder, but only 29 percent for generalized anxiety disorder, 14 percent for panic disorder, and 2 percent for social anxiety disorder, in part because physicians almost completely neglect worry as a symptom (even as they recognize stress).[58] The data presented in this chapter suggest that patients themselves may be more forthright in presenting anxiety as a symptom worthy of treatment, perhaps no longer simply discussing worry alone. If anxiety is slowly becoming the signature disorder of the twenty-first century, it is useful to think about what might happen next.

Chapter Ten

THE PAST, PRESENT, AND FUTURE OF FEAR

There are many things to fear, including fear itself. Americans are very anxious, especially recent cohorts, and anxiety is consequential for their lives. Anxiety appears to have increased over time and between cohorts. Americans are more anxious about a variety of topics, but younger cohorts are especially anxious about their social relationships, jeopardizing the emotional support that strong relationships ordinarily afford. And despite an occasional step into an age of melancholia or frayed nerves, America continues to cycle back to describing an age of anxiety, in one form or another. Anxiety has occasionally been overlooked, blended with a variety of other physical and psychological symptoms, and it has sometimes been neglected, regarded merely as part of a mélange of emotional discontent. Yet it has never disappeared altogether. And the idea of an especially anxious era holds recurrent and, it would seem, deeply resonant appeal.

But the idea that anxiety can characterize an *era* betrays a significant assumption about its origins—namely that anxiety is responsive to significant events and, by extension, that it can rise and fall as those events emerge and recede. The events of September 11 exemplify this assumption, though they are not the only examples. Empirical evidence does, in fact, suggest that the events of 9/11 increased the risk of an anxiety disorder.[1] Moreover, evidence suggests that the effects lingered over time, lending credence to the claim that anxiety, at least in the early twenty-first century, might somehow be different in its level and origins. None of this was easily resolved. Following the events, anxiety was further elevated by the government's new security precautions and the ongoing coverage of terrorism.[2] Americans reported more stress in their lives and actively tried to cope in serious ways, by talking to others, turning to religion, and participating in more group activities.[3] These experiences are surely unique and unprecedented in many ways, but the idea of an age of anxiety, whenever it occurs, implies a similarly sharp response to historical circumstance. W. H. Auden began working on *The Age of Anxiety* during World War II. *American Nervousness* was set against a backdrop of rapid technological change.[4] In 2020, the anxiety of the young is often set against the backdrop of social media's harsh glare.

And as I write this, a new source of anxiety has swept the nation. The United States is in the midst of the COVID-19 pandemic, with well over 400,000 deaths and many more infections beyond that. The pandemic has certainty revealed many preexisting inequalities in health, disproportionately affecting marginalized groups already suffering from higher mortality. It also reveals new fears and uncertainty, including fear regarding the risk of infection, but also uncertainty surrounding the consequences of the pandemic for our society and economy, and grief regarding everyone and everything that has already been lost. Scales for assessing coronavirus anxiety have been developed, including items regarding whether the person felt "dizzy, lightheaded, or faint," or had trouble falling asleep, or felt "paralyzed or frozen" when thinking or reading about the coronavirus.[5] More coronavirus anxiety is associated with significant functional impairment, greater alcohol use, more hopelessness, and greater religious coping. And like the other forms of anxiety discussed in this book, coronavirus anxiety is higher among young people, even though their risk of death from infection is lower. In China, the prevalence of anxiety symptoms during the COVID-19 pandemic was 38 percent among those under age thirty-five and 33 percent among those thirty-five and older (with depressive symptoms much less common than anxiety).[6] Although coronavirus anxiety is higher among those who have been infected, it is common among those who are uninfected. The psychological effects of the pandemic are likely to be prolonged.[7]

In general, though, trends in anxiety emerge much more slowly and steadily than responses to the emergence of the pandemic of 2020 or the terrorist attacks of 2001. They reflect the intersection of the person and the environment as much as the effects of any cataclysmic transition. Even the pandemic should be understood in this much broader context: those most at risk for coronavirus anxiety are those who already had significant symptoms before.[8] Events are interpreted in terms of the meaning they hold for the individuals affected by them. The forces propelling anxiety are gradual in most instances, involving slow changes in the family, steady declines in religious participation, and ongoing change in how social relationships are perceived. Social media is new, of course, but the fears surrounding media are long-standing and have little to do with the technological features of the latest platforms.[9] Before the invention of smartphones, for instance, television viewing was at least partly responsible for the decline in social capital.[10] Before the invention of the television, young people spent a considerable amount of time watching movies and listening to the radio. And before the invention of the radio, communities were connected in unprecedented ways by better roads, canals, and railways.[11] Even concerns about the character of recent cohorts have deep historical echoes. Concerns over the narcissism of young people might be especially pronounced today—and gain credence by the obvious self-promoting focus of social media platforms—but concerns about the selfishness of the young were no less pronounced in the 1970s, when critics bemoaned a rising culture of narcissism, or later, when critics counterpoised the self-interest of Generation X against the sacrifice of the Greatest Generation.[12] Slow change in anxiety has been made possible by the fact that the latent risk for an anxiety disorder is very high and probably has been for quite some time. Most Americans report at least one significant fear or worry, one that could eventually develop into a phobia. Far fewer people report a significant episode of sadness in their lifetime. When the right set of personal and environmental influences conspire, anxiety is the likely result.

It is unclear where these trends will go next, though it is unlikely that anxiety can be swiftly alleviated given the forces that have put it into place. Anxiety is at least partly born of uncertainty. Religious involvement alleviates some anxiety, because it provides a degree of confidence in the future. Social status is related to anxiety, in part because it reveals social worth. Family background matters when it provides young people with the confidence to move forward, secure in themselves and their environment. Yet there is a great deal of uncertainty in the twenty-first century. We have already seen two significant economic recessions and a global pandemic, the latter occurring following a remarkably long period of economic growth and exceptionally low unemployment. In many ways life is more predictable now than it was one hundred years ago, but Americans are also more aware of the risks they face, and with two recessions in their lifetime, they might rightly fear their fortune can change.

In addition, the forces that have elevated anxiety in the lexicon of distress are unlikely to disappear anytime soon. For one, public beliefs about mental illness are evolving in ways that likely further enhance the resonance of anxiety. In general, the stigma surrounding mental illness has remained remarkably durable over time. Despite the fact the public now regards most psychiatric disorders as medical conditions, it still fears mental illness, and news coverage of mental illness still tends to focus on violence.[13] The stigma surrounding mental illness remains an impediment to treating psychiatric disorders, in part because potential patients fail to seek help for fear of being rejected by others. There is less research on the stigma surrounding anxiety than other psychiatric disorders, but what research exists suggests the stigma is different in both degree and kind. Anxiety disorders are stigmatizing, to be sure, though they are somewhat less stigmatizing than mood disorders, and the split between the two is especially pronounced in developed countries.[14] Relative to schizophrenia and depression, for instance, anxiety is associated with fewer negative stereotypes, and those who have an anxiety disorder are seen as more likely to recover.[15] Part of the general stigma surrounding mental illness stems from the difficulty other people anticipate when interacting with someone who has a psychiatric disorder. Even short of violence, the public fears those with a mental illness, because they can be awkward to live or work with. But anxiety is different in this regard. In a study conducted in the United Kingdom, 53 percent of adults reported that those with depression were hard to talk to, but only 24 percent reported the same with respect to those with anxiety. The same survey found that 70 percent of adults regarded those with schizophrenia as unpredictable, and 50 percent regarded those with depression as unpredictable, but only 43 percent reported the same about those with anxiety.[16] In addition, evidence indicates that it might be easier to change people's minds with respect to anxiety disorders than many other conditions. In general, learning about mental illness through media portrayals increases stigma insofar as most media portrayals are negative. Yet studies show that those who are exposed to anxiety disorders *only* through the media tend to hold no more stigmatizing views than those who have had direct contact with someone who has an anxiety disorder.[17]

Furthermore, the appeal of anxiety as a clinical target is unlikely to decline. Part of the appeal of treating anxiety stems from the effectiveness of many antianxiety medications, coupled with the apparent ease with which an episode of anxiety can be separated from the idea of a long-term psychiatric disorder, something the public appears to appreciate as well. Benzodiazepines can be used as needed in the treatment of anxiety and alleviate its symptoms rapidly, not unlike many pain-relieving drugs. The plain biological nature of anxiety also likely helps to cast anxiety as situational and treatable. The average American probably has little under-standing of the genetic determinants of psychiatric disorders, though they surely can appreciate that many of the most common symptoms of anxiety are biological in nature, from a racing heart to shortness of breath. These beliefs are consequential. When psychiatric disorders are understood as biological, those who suffer from them are much less likely to blame them-selves for the condition and are more likely to believe that medical treat-ments work.[18]

Efforts to better address and treat anxiety are also well underway. Some of these efforts are driven by the pharmaceutical industry, much like efforts in the late twentieth century to address depression. Direct-to-consumer advertisements of antianxiety medications, for instance, are common and, in addition to their promotional content, include an educational element, effectively teaching the idea that anxiety can sometimes be a disorder. There have also been broad efforts to screen for anxiety, including in school settings. Many school-based programs for anxiety are highly effective, even when they depart from a strict medical approach.[19] Most school-based pro-grams for the treatment of anxiety, for instance, are aimed at nonspecific anxiety and focus on cognitive behavioral therapy. These efforts are being more widely adopted by schools, in part because schools recognize that anxiety is common among students and can undermine test performance. Furthermore, school-based programs are, if anything, more focused on anx-iety than depression and, relative to interventions focused on depression, these programs are more effective across different kinds of administration. Anxiety interventions administered by teachers, for instance, work quite well, even as depression interventions administered by teachers are largely ineffective.[20] Furthermore, universal programs—programs that target all students irrespective of risk or symptoms—work much better for anxiety than depression. Relative to other psychological and behavioral problems, school-based programs for anxiety are perhaps especially effective, but they are part of a broader pattern. Anxiety lends itself well to a variety of treatments and programmatic interventions, even seemingly impersonal ones. Internet-based cognitive behavioral therapy programs, for instance, work well for anxiety. Participants in such programs maintain high expectations regarding their effectiveness.[21] Even if the public occasionally regards anxiety as a natural state, it also recognizes that anxiety is consequential and amenable to amelioration through a variety of means. The capacity to calm an anxious mind does not render anxiety any less significant as a psychological experience.

The diagnostic criteria for most psychiatric disorders will almost certainly be revised again, though here, too, there is no reason to anticipate a decline in the significance attached to anxiety. In fact, some psychiatrists have proposed revising the diagnostic criteria for anxiety disorders in the direction of identifying temperaments as much as disorders. This conceptual shift would potentially expanding the range of treatable psychiatric conditions. Much of this reconsideration has occurred in the context of generalized anxiety disorder (GAD), for which a reframing as a matter of temperament might be especially well suited. Michel Dugas and others, for instance, have proposed that GAD is better characterized by an intolerance of uncertainty rather than simply worry about several things at once.[22] In making the case, they present evidence indicating that intolerance of uncertainty better discriminates between cases and non-cases of GAD than do the symptoms already included in the *DSM*. In the same vein, some have argued that true cases of GAD have less to do with the amount of worry and more with how some people are better able to reduce whatever worry they have.[23] In this case, a better definition of GAD would involve concepts like the controllability of worry, something that varies between individuals and is not uniquely significant in the *DSM* criteria. In the same vein, Hagop Akiskal has argued that GAD is one manifestation of a more general temperament, specifically a chronic disposition to worry.[24] Identifying a disposition is probably no less difficult than identifying the conventional symptoms of GAD, though should the diagnostic criteria for the disorder be revised, such a disposition could be indicated by endorsing statements such as "I am unable to relax," "I cannot help worrying," "I am always worrying about one thing or another," "I am, by nature, a very cautious person," and "I am an insecure person."[25]

Conceptualizing anxiety as a temperament is a significant change—it is not merely a redefinition of GAD. It also may provide a bellwether on how anxiety will be conceptualized in the future. For one, conceptualizing anxiety as a temperament moves anxiety away from the current conception of psychological dysfunction embedded in the *DSM*. Temperamental worry is ordinarily considered a preclinical trait that can be apparent independent of any existing anxiety disorder. In reframing the problem as a temperament, the risk becomes the disease.[26] Furthermore, conceptualizing anxiety as a temperament reduces the relevance of the severity of worry, long a hallmark of the *DSM*'s diagnostic criteria. Temperamental worry need not correspond to significant worry or even be related to any of the other existing symptoms of GAD.[27] It is unclear how the formal classification of anxiety disorders will evolve or whether any of these proposals will gain traction, but proposals of this sort at least open up the possibility of including even more people under the umbrella of "psychologically disordered."

The development of new pharmaceuticals is likely to further elevate the profile of anxiety, especially as the industry focuses on more acute treatments for anxiety. One reason that anxiety is an increasingly attractive target for pharmaceutical development is not just that there is already proof of concept that anxiety can be treated effectively, but that anxiety lends itself well to drug development using the existing scientific tools of the industry. In the *DSM*, psychiatric disorders are generally defined by a set of symptoms that frequently span multiple biological systems. As discussed earlier, this is perhaps especially true of anxiety disorders, in that anxiety, although emotional, also involves behavioral and physiological dimensions, such as arousal, shortness of breath, and a racing heart. These symptoms can be readily measured, and in animal models, scientists can create situations that elevate them, effectively creating something like acute anxiety in non-human animals. To be sure, it is debatable whether this approach has produced significant innovations. In fact, drugs that prove effective in treating the behaviors associated with anxiety in rodents have rarely translated into effective treatments for anxiety disorders in humans.[28] But to the extent that effective anxiety drugs have developed from this approach, it has created a specific kind of drug for a specific kind of anxiety: short-acting drugs useful for treating episodes of fear. Animal experiments have focused on acute anxiety over chronic anxiety by a factor of more than ten to one.[29] Given the reciprocal relationship between how a disorder is defined and how it is treated, it is likely that the type of anxiety that is seen as most significant and amenable to treatment is the type of anxiety that is situational and behavioral in nature.

At a minimum, it is likely that Americans will have just as much to worry about in the latter part of the twenty-first century as they do now. Worry is rooted in concerns about what comes *next*, and our current confidence in the future is surely a sign of anxiety to come. Only 37 percent of Americans believe that children today will grow up to be better off than their parents.[30] When asked to list the top problems they see in their peers, more teens list mental health problems than bullying, alcohol use, or teen pregnancy.[31] Anxiety is certainly critical to apprehending our environments and motivating our behavior, and worry is often born of a truth that has yet to transpire. The science of anxiety has progressed rapidly over the last quarter century, and we know far more about its origins, including within our evolutionary history. Anxiety is common and natural, to be sure. Yet our social and cultural environments might be changing in ways that make us especially anxious and prevent us from alleviating the burden of anxiety altogether.

METHODOLOGICAL APPENDIX

This book relies on many data sources for its original analyses. Several principles guided the selection of data. First, whenever possible, I sought nationally representative surveys. In some instances, this was straightforward. The National Health Interview Survey, for example, was designed to be nationally representative in each year of its administration. In other cases, one data set was combined with others to create especially high-quality data. For instance, the National Survey of American Life oversamples African Americans and Afro-Caribbeans. On its own, the survey is not nationally representative, but when combined with other surveys—some of which oversample other populations—it provides high-quality nationally representative data, especially for otherwise difficult-to-sample subpopulations.

Second, to the extent possible, I sought consistent measures of anxiety and depression, either over different populations or over time. Some surveys, including the Collaborative Psychiatric Epidemiological Surveys, were designed expressly to provide harmonized measures of psychiatric disorders over multiple surveys, based on formal psychiatric nomenclature based on the *Diagnostic and Statistical Manual of Mental Disorders*, 4th edition (*DSM-IV*). These surveys are particularly useful for this book, in that they contain a comprehensive set of specific anxiety disorders. Other surveys, including the National Health Interview Survey, consistently employ dimensional measures of nonspecific psychiatric distress, allowing for an accurate assessment of trends in at least basic symptoms of distress. The principal of consistency is difficult to meet in every instance, however, because the measurement of anxiety has changed, much as the concept itself has evolved. In some chapters, I rely on a survey that employed a more primitive measure of anxiety, though questions of this sort at least ask about worry in a plain fashion and in exactly the same way over two time periods. I will review each data set in detail before turning to a review of some of the basic principles I used for analyzing the data. Of note, all the data used in this study are publicly available. Links are provided in a table at the end of this chapter.

AMERICANS VIEW THEIR MENTAL HEALTH

Americans View their Mental Health (AVMH) is the oldest survey used in this book. AVMH was conducted in 1957 and 1976 among adults 21 and older living in private households. The 1976 version of the survey was a replication of the 1957 survey, in that it asked many of the same questions, using exactly the same wording whenever possible. For reasons outlined in the book, this time span is critical in the history of anxiety, so revisiting the data is still valuable for historical purposes. Sampling for AVMH was based on a multistage probability area design, drawing on sixty-six strata, based on counties, excluding institutionalized populations. Only one randomly selected adult was interviewed within each household. The response rate for the initial survey was high (84 percent), though somewhat lower in 1976 (71 percent). Despite this drop in the response rate, there were no significant differences in the composition of the sample relative to 1976 Current Population Survey data. In contrast to the remaining data sets used in this book, no weighting procedures were used for AVMH, as the data are effectively self-weighting. Previous studies have found only slight differences between weighted and unweighted estimates.[1]

COLLABORATIVE PSYCHIATRIC EPIDEMIOLOGICAL SURVEYS

The Collaborative Psychiatric Epidemiological Surveys (CPES) is a set of three harmonized surveys conducted at approximately the same time, the National Comorbidity Survey Replication (NCS-R), the National Survey

TABLE A.1
Citations for data used in the book

Americans View Their Mental Health

Joseph Veroff, Elizabeth Douvan, and Richard Kulka. Americans View Their Mental Health, 1957 and 1976: Selected Variables. Ann Arbor, Mich.: Inter-university Consortium for Political and Social Research [distributor], 2005. https://doi.org/10.3886/ICPSR07949.v1.

Collaborative Psychiatric Epidemiological Surveys

Margarita Alegria, James S. (James Sidney) Jackson, Ronald C. Kessler, and David Takeuchi. Collaborative Psychiatric Epidemiology Surveys (CPES), 2001–2003 [United States]. Ann Arbor, Mich.: Inter-university Consortium for Political and Social Research [distributor], 2016. https://doi.org/10.3886/ICPSR20240.v8.

National Ambulatory Medical Care Survey

United States Department of Health and Human Services. Centers for Disease Control and Prevention. National Center for Health Statistics. National Ambulatory Medical Care Survey. Ann Arbor, Mich.: Inter-university Consortium for Political and Social Research [distributor]. https://www.icpsr.umich.edu/icpsrweb/NACDA/series/37.

National Health Interview Survey

Lynn A. Blewett, Julia A. Rivera Drew, Miriam L. King, and Kari C. W. Williams. IPUMS Health Surveys: National Health Interview Survey, Version 6.4 [data set]. Minneapolis, Minn.: IPUMS, 2019. https://doi.org/10.18128/D070.V6.4.

of American Life (NSAL), and the National Latino and Asian American Study (NLAAS). All surveys were conducted by the Survey Research Center at the University of Michigan. The CPES was designed primarily to study the prevalence of common psychiatric disorders in the United States, and the CPES links these three surveys to provide the most representative data for doing so. The CPES remains perhaps the best data for estimating the prevalence of psychiatric disorders, providing an especially comprehensive assessment of a wide variety disorders. The CPES also includes questions on social support, social status, religious participation, and other influences of concern in this book. Not all the relevant questions, however, are asked in each version of the survey. For this reason, the sample size of the CPES varies from table to table, reflecting variation in the set of questions used in the models and, thus, variation in what underlying surveys are being deployed.

The three surveys that make up the CPES differ, in that some involve oversampling of specific populations, though in general they are united in involving a four-step sampling procedure: the first involving a primary sample of U.S. metropolitan statistical areas and counties, the second involving smaller geographic areas therein, the third involving housing units within selected area segments, and the fourth involving the random selection of an adult within each unit. The response rate for each of the individual surveys was high, no less than 70 percent and as high as 80 percent for some components of the NCS-R and NLAAS. All analyses using CPES employ survey weights, which adjust for survey nonresponse. The specific weights used vary depending on the specific subsample or set of subsamples used, as per the guidance of the CPES collectors.

The NCS-R is a probability sample of adults in the United States, collected as a replication of the initial National Comorbidity Survey, which was completed in the early 1990s. The NCS-R was administered to English-speaking adults age eighteen and over living in households within the continental United States. It contains two parts, the first involving a diagnostic assessment, administered to 9,282 respondents, and the second involving questions about assorted risk factors, administered to a smaller subsample of 5,692. In this book, respondents participating in this second part are discussed more frequently than respondents only involved in the first, as this book is concerned with the correlates of anxiety as much as anxiety itself. The NCS-R was conducted between February of 2001 and April of 2003 using computer-assisted interview technologies. Most of the interviews occurred in person within the homes of respondents.

The NSAL also focuses on psychiatric disorders, although it was designed to explore racial/ethnic differences in particular and oversamples according to this aim. The NSAL was administered to an English-speaking sample of adults over the age of eighteen living in the continental United States and was conducted from 2001 to 2003. The survey focused on three specific populations: African Americans, Afro-Caribbeans, and non-Hispanic white Americans. The white survey population was unusual relative to the white population in other surveys, because it was drawn predominantly from the universe of white people living in predominantly Black neighborhoods. In total, 6,082 NSAL respondents are represented in CPES, including 3,570 African Americans, 1,621 Afro-Caribbeans, and 891 non-Hispanic whites.

The NLAAS is similar to the other two surveys, although it focuses on Latinx and Asian American populations, two historically understudied groups. The NLAAS samples adults eighteen years of age and older residing in the continental United States and was conducted between May of 2002 and December of 2003. With the goal of speaking to the category of Latinx and Asians, it targeted four specific Latinx populations (Cuban, Mexican, Puerto Rican, and other adults of Latinx descent) and four Asian populations (Chinese, Filipino, Vietnamese, and other adults of Asian descent). It also, however, included a small comparison group of non-Hispanic whites, a group well supplemented by using the entire CPES. Interviews were conducted in the language of the respondent's choice among either English, Spanish, Chinese, Vietnamese, or Tagalog. Interviews were conducted by bilingual interviewers. In total, the sample included 4,864 respondents, with 2,095 Asian, 2,554 Latinx, and 215 non-Hispanic whites.

The central instrument in each of the three surveys is the diagnostic survey, based on the World Health Organization's (WHO) expanded version of the Composite International Diagnostic Interview (CIDI) developed for the World Mental Health (WMH) Survey Initiative (and referred to as the WMH-CIDI rather than the WHO-CIDI).[2] The WMH-CIDI yields diagnoses based on criteria drawn from both *DSM-IV* and the International Statistical Classification of Diseases and Related Health Problems (10th revision), though the estimates provided in this book are based entirely on the *DSM-IV* criteria. The CIDI is a structured lay interview: it is designed to mimic questions a mental health professional might ask in making a diagnosis, but in a survey setting conducted by lay interviewers. It asks questions based on the *DSM-IV*'s symptom-based criteria, asking specific questions about each symptom, from which diagnoses are derived based on whether the respondent met the diagnostic threshold for a specific disorder given the symptoms reported. Diagnoses are coded algorithmically. The CIDI focuses on the most common psychiatric disorders in the United States, including mood and anxiety disorders.

Lay diagnostic interviews are a critical tool in psychiatric epidemiology, though they should not be confused with diagnoses per se, and their validity must be assessed critically. Those who meet the diagnostic threshold for a disorder need not have ever been diagnosed by a professional and, indeed, most people who meet the diagnostic threshold for a disorder never seek treatment for it. In this light, one could question the accuracy of such a measure, but formal tests of validity for the WMH-CIDI have generally been good. Tests of validity for lay diagnoses are based on whether the diagnoses generated by the WMH-CIDI are consistent with those obtained by trained clinical interviewers when conducting semistructured diagnostic interviews with the same respondents. The concordance between these two assessments is generally high, though not perfect. A lack of concordance, however, does not necessarily impugn the validity of the WMH-CIDI (or the *DSM*). Some of the discordance stems from the semistructured interviews rather than from the WMH-CIDI: test–retest concordance between instruments like the WMH-CIDI are generally higher than test–retest concordance between semistructured clinical interviews. The WMH-CIDI can produce estimates of the true prevalence of psychiatric disorders that are, if anything, more faithful to the *DSM-IV*'s criteria, insofar as it structures the diagnoses to be exact with respect to the diagnostic criteria and therefore provides little room for physician bias. Although there has been a good deal of criticism of the *DSM*'s diagnostic criteria, the WMH-CIDI seeks only to replicate what a professional would diagnose if that professional adhered to the *DSM* as intended. It is still possible that clinical interviews can yield diagnoses with greater validity (if not greater reliability). But if so, this only means that mental health professionals employ a more valid definition of psychiatric disorders than is provided in the *DSM*. The WMH-CIDI is comprehensive and reliable, though it is not easy or quick to administer. On average it takes about two hours to administer in general population surveys, though among respondents who screen positive for many disorders (a not uncommon situation), the length of the interview can be much longer.

The authors of the WMH-CIDI constructed the instrument with considerable care, seeking not only to faithfully reflect existing diagnostic criteria, but also to ensure that respondents report their symptoms accurately and completely. Relative to earlier versions of the CIDI, improvements were made to the WMH-CIDI with respect to clarifying symptom questions, defining terms that respondents in earlier versions had a difficult time understanding, training interviewers in the diagnostic criteria the questions were designed to address, and unfolding supplementary or alternative questions when respondents had a difficult time answering an initial one. For instance, in some sections of the interview, respondents are asked to recall when they first experienced a symptom or event. In instances when respondents could not provide a reasonably precise date, they were asked a sequence of questions about the context surrounding the event, such as "Was it before you first started school?" or "Was it before you were a teenager?" and progressing forward or backward in time depending on the experience, as when if not before the respondent was a teenager, "Was it before you turned 20?"[3]

NATIONAL AMBULATORY MEDICAL CARE SURVEY

The National Ambulatory Medical Care Survey (NAMCS) targets a different universe than the other surveys used in this book. The NAMCS is a national probability sample of visits to office-based physicians. It is conducted annually by the National Center for Health Statistics. It includes several exclusions. It excludes federally employed physicians and federally operated facilities. In addition, it excludes visits to specialists in anesthesiology, radiology, and pathology, as those specialists are classified as "patient care" rather than "medical care." The NAMCS uses a multistage probability design, involving three stages: first, a sample of 112 geographic primary sampling units, mostly consisting of counties or groups of counties; second, physician practices within those units; and finally, patient visits within those practices. Physicians selected for the sample are asked to complete patient record forms for a random sample of about thirty visits occurring during a randomly assigned reporting period of one week. The survey was conducted using paper instruments up to 2012, at which point it shifted to computerized data collection. The survey weights for NAMCS adjust for the sample design, as well as nonresponse, weekly visit volume, and physician variation in the number of weeks worked during the year. The NAMCS is limited from the standpoint of providing a true prevalence of anxiety disorders, as it is based on physician visits. But it provides useful information on what kind of symptoms prompt a visit to the physician and how physicians do or do not respond to those symptoms. It is also useful for allowing comparisons between the behaviors of general practitioners and psychiatrists, as both are included in the survey.

NATIONAL HEALTH INTERVIEW SURVEY

The National Health Interview Survey (NHIS) is a long-standing and ongoing data-collection effort designed to monitor the health of Americans. It covers a wide range of health topics, some consistently and some only occasionally, as interest evolves. It is used to evaluate progress toward national health objectives, among other topics. It is conducted by the U.S. Census

Bureau on behalf of the National Center for Health Statistics. Sampling is continuous throughout each year in the survey, though data are compiled into annual files, which are representative of that year. The sampling is based on an area probability design, with the primary sampling unit corresponding to clusters of single counties, several continuous counties, or metropolitan statistical areas. Oversampling has varied over the years. At present there is no oversampling at the household level, though at the selection of adults within the household, persons over the age of sixty-five and racial/ethnic minorities are oversampled. All states and the District of Columbia are included in the sampling frame. The NHIS appears only occasionally in this book, though it is useful for having fielded the K6 measure of nonspecific psychological distress on a regular basis in recent rounds. This measure includes symptoms of anxiety and depression.

BASIC ANALYTIC PRINCIPLES

The analyses presented in this book were guided by several principles. For one, most of the analyses, including regression models, were based on survey weights. Although it is debatable whether survey weights should be used in regression models that are able to control for all aspects upon which oversampling is performed, supplementary analyses indicated that the use of weights did not significantly increase the standard errors of the estimates presented here.[4] In the case of the CPES, weights are even more relevant, as the models are occasionally based on samples drawn from separate surveys, and the NCS-R bases one subsample on whether respondents screen positive for a psychiatric disorder. The CPES includes consolidated weights to address these sampling issues.

Many of the outcomes used in this book are categorical. Respondents either have an anxiety disorder or not. Nonlinear maximum likelihood regression models, such as logit or probit, are ordinarily used in such a situation, as they bound the predicted values of the model between zero and one.[5] Linear regression models, such as ordinary least squares, are not bound in this fashion. Nonlinear models are more efficient than linear models, because the errors in the linear probability model are heteroskedastic. For these reasons, logit models are used frequently for categorical dependent variables. Yet an important feature of this book is to compare coefficients between outcomes and, further, to estimate interactions among independent variables. In such a situation, nonlinear models can be misleading, as the coefficient depends on the level of the dependent variable.[6] For this reason, comparisons of coefficients between equations predicting mood and anxiety disorders can be misleading, as any seemingly significant difference could be driven by differences in the prevalence of the two kinds of disorders rather than any true differences in the magnitude of the effect. A similar problem pertains to interactions, where significant interactions can depend entirely on the level of one of the components. To overcome these problems, I used a linear probability model. A linear probability model produces estimates that do not depend on the margin of the outcome, all else being equal. In addition to allowing for cleaner comparisons between outcomes, the linear probability model also has other attractive features.[7] For one, the coefficients presented in this book have a simple interpretation: they (usually) represent the expected change in the probability of a disorder given a unit change in the independent variable. The probability of the outcome is a linear function of the other covariates. Furthermore, the linear probability model, as used in this book, has few of the biases commonly associated with the linear approach. The linear probability model can involve significant biases when the outcome is rare, but I lessen this possibility by focusing on *any* anxiety disorder rather than the probability of any *specific* anxiety disorder. Combinations of this sort reduce the potential for bias by raising the overall probability of the outcome.

All surveys suffer from some degree of item nonresponse. In most of the data sets used in this study, item nonresponse was limited. Whenever possible, logical imputation was employed to infer a small number of missing values, and when a logical or regression-based imputation was not possible, listwise deletion was used. Listwise deletion can yield less-biased estimates than more sophisticated approaches to missing data, including multiple imputation, especially when data are missing on predictor variables.[8] The impact of missing data is also minimized when using large data sets, as is the case in many of the data sets employed in this book.

VARIABLES

The regression models presented in this book include a few critical variables and employ a variety of control variables. Many of the variables are described in detail in their respective chapters, but others serve a second-order function. Control variables allow the analyst to adjust for the influence of factors that might reasonably confound the relationship between the dependent variable and the focal variable of interest. In general, this book sought to present models reduced only to the most essential variables. Much of the book, for instance, focuses on cohort differences. The book employs, to the extent possible, the same age categories over the entire book, corresponding to ages eighteen to twenty-nine, thirty to forty-four, forty-five to fifty-nine, and sixty and over. Categories of this breadth are common in analysis of the CPES and provide a balance between meaningful cut points with respect to age and sufficiently large sample sizes within each category.

All models control for sex and race/ethnicity. A good deal could be said about sex differences with respect to anxiety. Gender is tied deeply to some of the issues raise in this book, including the ways in which anxiety has or has not been construed as a significant condition. Indeed, some historians argue that at least one reason for the rise of the nervous breakdown in midcentury America is change in gender roles, especially as more women entered the labor force.[9] Gender is also implicated in the onset of anxiety. This book has a narrower focus, though, and the use of gender as only a control variable was motivated by several things.[10] First, gender is relevant to understanding anxiety disorders and their causes in specific and well-known ways. Women consistently report higher rates of anxiety disorders overall. The ratio of women to men for the lifetime prevalence of any anxiety disorder is around 1.7.[11] Women also tend to experience more disabling anxiety than men. But for many of the other empirical issues detailed in this book, there is no significant sex difference. There are no gender differences in the average age of onset for anxiety disorders. Nor are there differences in the chronicity of anxiety disorders. When men and women suffer from an anxiety disorder, the disorder tends to have the same course. Furthermore, though there is a significant sex difference in the lifetime risk of any anxiety disorder, there is no significant gender difference in the lifetime risk of social anxiety disorder. Some of the sex difference in anxiety may be explained by higher levels of stress among women.[12] Women report more adverse childhood events than men.[13] In addition, men and women tend to employ different coping styles. Yet there is little evidence that one style is beneficial over all types of stress in a way that would demand sex-specific models for all the stressors explored in this book. Women may experience more distress associated with friendships, though men may cope better when avoidance is the most effective strategy.[14] The models used in this study adjust for the sex difference in the baseline risk for anxiety disorders, though they do not investigate sex differences in the effects of the key risk factors.

The models also control for race/ethnicity. In general, psychiatric disorders tend to be less common among racial/ethnic minorities. This is also true among anxiety disorders generally, though with some exceptions. Social anxiety disorder tends to be higher among Native Americans than among non-Hispanic whites, though lower among Asians, Hispanics, or African Americans.[15] Post-traumatic stress disorder is more common among African Americans.[16] In general the difference between non-Hispanic whites and minorities is largest for social anxiety disorder.[17] Explorations of race/ethnic differences in vulnerability—whether the effects of stress are larger for one group or another—have generally found few differences. The relationship between life change and psychological distress, for instance, is no greater among African Americans than among whites, even if African Americans are exposed to more stress.[18] For instance, Hurricane Katrina increased depression among residents of New Orleans who were present when the hurricane struck, but no more so among African Americans than whites.[19] The models used in this book adjust for racial/ethnic differences in the risk of anxiety disorders, though they assume a single average effect for the risk factors I explore.

NOTES

1. THE SIGNIFICANCE AND MEANING OF ANXIETY

1. Ronald C. Kessler and Philip S. Wang, "The Descriptive Epidemiology of Commonly Occurring Mental Disorders in the United States," *Annual Review of Public Health* 29, no. 1 (2008): 115–29. This book focuses on data and patterns from the United States, with occasional reference to other countries. Of note, though, anxiety is a worldwide phenomenon. The levels of anxiety vary among countries, but many of the patterns discussed here are cross-nationally consistent. Cohort patterns, for instance, are remarkably consistent. In parts of Asia, anxiety disorders are especially common in the youngest cohort, as they are in the United States. Ronald C. Kessler et al., "Development of Lifetime Comorbidity in the World Health Organization World Mental Health Surveys," *Archives of General Psychiatry* 68, no. 1 (2011): 90–100. In addition, some of the trends discussed in later chapters in an attempt to explain anxiety are found in other regions as well, including Europe. Jason Beckfield, "Remapping Inequality in Europe: The Net Effect of Regional Integration on Total Income Inequality in the European Union," *International Journal of Comparative Sociology* 50, nos. 5–6 (2009): 486–509.
2. Kessler and Wang, "Descriptive Epidemiology."
3. Kessler and Wang, "Descriptive Epidemiology." Prevalence drawn from table 1.
4. George Curtis et al., "Specific Fears and Phobias: Epidemiology and Classification," *British Journal of Psychiatry* 173, no. 3 (1998): 212–17; A. M. Ruscio et al., "Social Fears and Social Phobia in the USA: Results from the National Comorbidity Survey Replication," *Psychological Medicine* 38, no. 1 (2008): 15–28.
5. Kessler and Wang, "Descriptive Epidemiology." Drawn from table 2.
6. Thomas J. Moore and Donald R. Mattison, "Adult Utilization of Psychiatric Drugs and Differences by Sex, Age, and Race," *JAMA Internal Medicine* 177, no. 2 (2017): 274–75.

7. Moore and Mattison, "Adult Utilization of Psychiatric Drugs and Differences by Sex, Age, and Race."

8. Robin Simon and Leda E. Nath, "Gender and Emotion in the United States: Do Men and Women Differ in Self-Reports of Feelings and Expressive Behavior?" *American Journal of Sociology* 109, no. 5 (2004): 1137–76. The comparison is drawn from table A1.

9. Michelle G. Craske et al., "Qualitative Dimensions of Worry in DSM-III-R Generalized Anxiety Disorder Subjects and Nonanxious Controls," *Behaviour Research and Therapy* 27, no. 4 (1989): 397–402.

10. Craske et al., "Qualitative Dimensions of Worry in DSM-III-R Generalized Anxiety Disorder Subjects and Nonanxious Controls."

11. Alan S. Cowen and Dacher Keltner, "Self-Report Captures 27 Distinct Categories of Emotion Bridged by Continuous Gradients," *Proceedings of the National Academy of Sciences of the United States of America* 114, no. 38 (2017): E7900–09. Cowen and Keltner map twenty-seven distinct emotional categories based on reactions to emotionally evocative videos.

12. Scott Stossel, *My Age of Anxiety: Fear, Hope, Dread, and the Search for Peace of Mind* (New York: Knopf, 2013). Stossel, too, reviews the history of claims regarding an era of anxiety, finding special resonance in midcentury America.

13. Rollo May, *The Meaning of Anxiety* (New York: Ronald Press, 1950), 3.

14. May, *The Meaning of Anxiety*, 3.

15. May, *The Meaning of Anxiety*, 3.

16. Ted Halstead, "A Politics for Generation X," *Atlantic*, August 1999, https://www.theatlantic.com/magazine/archive/1999/08/a-politics-for-generation-x/306666.

17. Simon Copland, "Anxiety Is a Way of Life for Gen Y. In an Insecure World, Is It Any Surprise?," *Guardian*, February 24, 2017, https://www.theguardian.com/society/commentisfree/2017/feb/25/anxiety-is-a-way-of-life-for-gen-y-in-an-insecure-world-is-it-any-surprise.

18. Jean M. Twenge, "The Age of Anxiety? The Birth Cohort Change in Anxiety and Neuroticism, 1952–1993," *Journal of Personality and Social Psychology* 79, no. 6 (2000): 1007–21.

19. Twenge bases these comparisons on E. E. Levitt, "A Comparison of Parental and Self-Evaluations of Psychopathology in Children," *Journal of Clinical Psychology* 15 (1959): 402–4.

20. Twenge, "The Age of Anxiety?," 1017.

21. Kessler and Wang, "Descriptive Epidemiology."

22. Steven Pinker, *The Better Angels of Our Nature: Why Violence Has Declined* (New York: Penguin, 2012).

23. Eileen M. Crimmins, "Lifespan and Healthspan: Past, Present, and Promise," *Gerontologist* 55, no. 6 (2015): 901–11.

24. National Center for Health Statistics, *Health, United States, 2018* (Hyattsville, Md., 2019). Calculations based on table 6, which presents leading causes of death.

25. George M. Beard, *American Nervousness: Its Causes and Consequences* (New York: G. P. Putnam's Sons, 1881).

26. May, *The Meaning of Anxiety*.

27. Roxane Cohen Silver et al., "Mental- and Physical-Health Effects of Acute Exposure to Media Images of the September 11, 2001, Attacks and the Iraq War," *Psychological Science* 24, no. 9 (2013): 1623–34.

28. Greg Lukianoff and Jonathan Haidt, *The Coddling of the American Mind: How Good Intentions and Bad Ideas Are Setting up a Generation for Failure* (New York: Penguin, 2018); Christopher Lasch, *The Culture of Narcissism: American Life in an Age of Diminishing Expectations* (New York: Norton, 1978).

29. Christian Smith, *Religion: What It Is, How It Works, and Why It Matters* (Princeton, N.J.: Princeton University Press, 2017).

30. Tak Sang Chow and Hau Yan Wan, "Is There Any 'Facebook Depression'? Exploring the Moderating Roles of Neuroticism, Facebook Social Comparison and Envy," *Personality and Individual Differences* 119 (2017): 277–82.

31. Joseph E. LeDoux, *Anxious: Using the Brain to Understand and Treat Fear and Anxiety* (New York: Viking, 2015), esp. p. 232.

32. Jerome C. Wakefield, "The DSM-5 Debate over the Bereavement Exclusion: Psychiatric Diagnosis and the Future of Empirically Supported Treatment," *Clinical Psychology Review* 33, no. 7 (2013): 825–45; Jerome C. Wakefield and Mark F. Schmitz, "When Does Depression Become a Disorder? Using Recurrence Rates to Evaluate the Validity of Proposed Changes in Major Depression Diagnostic Thresholds," *World Psychiatry* 12, no. 1 (2013): 44–52; Allan V. Horwitz and Jerome C. Wakefield, *The Loss of Sadness: How Psychiatry Transformed Normal Sorrow Into Depressive Disorder* (New York: Oxford University Press, 2007).

33. Howard S. Liddell, "The Role of Vigilance in the Development of Animal Neurosis," in *Anxiety*, ed. P. H. Hoch and J. Zubin (New York: Grune & Stratton, 1950).

34. Jeremy Coplan et al., "The Relationship Between Intelligence and Anxiety: An Association with Subcortical White Matter Metabolism," *Frontiers in Evolutionary Neuroscience* 3, no. 8 (2012): 1–7; Jeremy D. Coplan et al., "Decreased Choline and Creatine Concentrations in Centrum Semiovale in Patients with Generalized Anxiety Disorder: Relationship to IQ and Early Trauma," *Psychiatry Research: Neuroimaging* 147, no. 1 (2006): 27–39.

35. Sigmund Freud, *The Problem of Anxiety* (New York: Norton, 1936).

36. Joseph R. Gusfield, *The Culture of Public Problems: Drinking-Driving and the Symbolic Order* (Chicago: University of Chicago Press, 1981); Peter Conrad, "Medicalization and Social Control," *Annual Review of Sociology* 18 (1992): 209–32.

2. A LATE MODERN HISTORY OF ANXIETY

1. Edward Shorter, *From Paralysis to Fatigue: A History of Psychosomatic Illness in the Modern Era* (New York: Free Press, 1992); Marc-Antoine Crocq, "A History of Anxiety: From Hippocrates to DSM," *Dialogues in Clinical Neuroscience* 17, no. 3 (2015): 319–25; David G. Schuster, "Neurasthenia and a Modernizing America," *Journal of the American Medical Association* 290, no. 17 (2003): 2327–28; Arthur Kleinman, "Neurasthenia and Depression: A Study of Somatization and Culture in China," *Culture, Medicine, and Psychiatry* 6 (1982): 117–90.

2. Megan Barke, Rebecca Fribush, and Peter N. Stearns, "Nervous Breakdown in 20th-Century American Culture," *Journal of Social History* 33, no. 3 (2000): 565–84.

3. George M. Beard, "Neurasthenia, or Nervous Exhaustion," *Boston Medical and Surgical Journal* 80, no. 13 (1869): 217–21; George Miller Beard, *Neurasthenia (Nerve Exhaustion): With Remarks on Treatment* (Reprinted from the *St. Louis Medical*

and Surgical Journal, St. Louis, 1879); George M. Beard, *American Nervousness: Its Causes and Consequences* (New York: G. P. Putnam's Sons, 1881).

4. Charles E. Rosenberg, "The Place of George M. Beard in Nineteenth Century Psychiatry," *Bulletin of the History of Medicine* 36 (1962): 245–59. Rosenberg discusses Beard's reputation and scientific style in detail.

5. Beard, "Neurasthenia, or Nervous Exhaustion."

6. Beard, *American Nervousness*, esp. 2–7.

7. Beard, *American Nervousness*, 8.

8. Beard, *American Nervousness*, 7.

9. Beard, "Neurasthenia, or Nervous Exhaustion," 11.

10. Rosenberg, "The Place of George M. Beard in Nineteenth Century Psychiatry."

11. Shorter, *From Paralysis to Fatigue*.

12. Allan V. Horwitz, *Anxiety: A Short History* (Baltimore, Md.: Johns Hopkins University Press, 2013).

13. Beard, *American Nervousness*, 17.

14. Beard, *American Nervousness*, 176.

15. Scott M. Monroe and Anne D. Simons, "Diathesis-Stress Theories in the Context of Life Stress Research: Implications for the Depressive Disorders," *Psychological Bulletin* 110, no. 3 (1991): 406–25.

16. Paul E. Meehl, "Schizotaxia, Schizotypy, Schizophrenia," *American Psychologist* 17, no. 12 (1962): 827–38; M. Bleuler, "Conception of Schizophrenia Within the Last Fifty Years and Today [Abridged]," *Proceedings of the Royal Society of Medicine* 56, no. 10 (1963): 945–52. In particular, Meehl discusses stress and schizotaxia in the development of schizophrenia.

17. Beard, *American Nervousness*, 26.

18. Beard, *American Nervousness*, 27.

19. Beard, *American Nervousness*, 26.

20. Schuster, "Neurasthenia and a Modernizing America"; Rosenberg, "The Place of George M. Beard in Nineteenth Century Psychiatry"; Andrew Scull, *Madness in Civilization: A Cultural History of Insanity* (Princeton, N.J.: Princeton University Press, 2015).

21. Beard, *American Nervousness*, vii.

22. Beard, *American Nervousness*, vi.

23. Beard, *American Nervousness*, 114.

24. Edward Shorter, *A History of Psychiatry: From the Era of the Asylum to the Age of Prozac* (New York: Wiley, 1997).

25. Thomas A. Ban, "Pharmacotherapy of Mental Illness: A Historical Analysis," *Progress in Neuro-Psychopharmacology and Biological Psychiatry* 25, no. 4 (2001): 709–27; Nancy Tomes, *A Generous Confidence: Thomas Story Kirkbride and the Art of Asylum-keeping, 1840–1883* (New York: Cambridge University Press, 1984).

26. Alexander Wood, "A New Method of Treating Neuralgia by the Direct Application of Opiates to the Painful Points," *Edinburgh Medical and Surgical Journal* 82 (1855): 265–81, 5, 22; reference drawn from Shorter, *A History of Psychiatry*.

27. Beard, *American Nervousness*, 299.

28. Beard, *American Nervousness*, 299.

29. Beard, *American Nervousness*, 299.

30. Beard, *American Nervousness*, ix.

209

31. George Chauncey, *Gay New York: Gender, Urban Culture, and the Makings of the Gay Male World, 1890–1940* (New York: Basic Books, 1994). Chauncey discusses this and other examples of the alignment of homosexuality with psychopathology, as well as the attempts to resist that alignment.
32. Harry Oosterhuis, "Sexual Modernity in the Works of Richard Von Krafft-Ebing and Albert Moll," *Medical History* 56, no. 2 (2012): 133–55.
33. Richard von Krafft-Ebing, "Perversions of the Sexual Instinct: Report of Cases," *Alienist and Neurologist* 9 (1888): 565–81. These examples are drawn from cases III, IV, and I and II, respectively.
34. Charles E. Rosenberg, *No Other Gods: On Science and American Social Thought,* rev. exp. ed. (Baltimore, Md.: Johns Hopkins University Press, 1997).
35. Charles L. Dana, "The Partial Passing of Neurasthenia," *Boston Medical and Surgical Journal* 150, no. 13 (1904): 339–44.
36. Dana, "The Partial Passing of Neurasthenia," 339.
37. Dana, "The Partial Passing of Neurasthenia," 341.
38. Dana, "The Partial Passing of Neurasthenia," 340.
39. For this history, see German E. Berrios and Ivana S. Marková, "The Concept of Neuropsychiatry: A Historical Overview," *Journal of Psychosomatic Research* 53, no. 2 (2002): 629–38; German E. Berrios and Ivana S. Marková , "Assessment and Measurement in Neuropsychiatry: A Conceptual History," *Seminars in Clinical Neuropsychiatry* 7, no. 1 (2002): 3–10.
40. Antonio Egidio Nardi and Rafael Christophe R. Freire, "The Panic Disorder Concept: A Historical Perspective," in *Panic Disorder: Neurobiological and Treatment Aspects,* ed. Antonio Egidio Nardi and Rafael Christophe R. Freire (Cham, Switzerland: Springer International Publishing, 2016); Shorter, *A History of Psychiatry: From the Era of the Asylum to the Age of Prozac.*
41. Pierre Janet, *Les obsessions et la psychasthénie,* 2nd ed. (Paris: Alcan, 1908).
42. Shorter, *From Paralysis to Fatigue,* 226.
43. Shorter, *From Paralysis to Fatigue.* Shorter discusses this transition in detail.
44. Shorter, *From Paralysis to Fatigue,* 227.
45. Shorter, *From Paralysis to Fatigue,* 226.
46. Edward Shorter, *A Historical Dictionary of Psychiatry* (New York: Oxford University Press, 2005), 29.
47. Joseph E. LeDoux, *Anxious: Using the Brain to Understand and Treat Fear and Anxiety* (New York: Viking, 2015).
48. Benjamin Rush, *Medical Inquiries and Observations Upon the Diseases of the Mind* (Philadelphia: Kimber and Richardson, 1812); discussed in German E. Berrios, "Anxiety and Cognate Disorders," in *The History of Mental Symptoms: Descriptive Psychopathology Since the Nineteenth Century,* ed. German E. Berrios (Cambridge: Cambridge University Press, 1996), 263–88.
49. Rush, *Medical Inquiries and Observations Upon the Diseases of the Mind.* See esp. chap. 17, pp. 314–346.
50. Rush, *Medical Inquiries and Observations Upon the Diseases of the Mind,* 324–25.
51. Rush, *Medical Inquiries and Observations Upon the Diseases of the Mind,* 330–31.
52. Rush, *Medical Inquiries and Observations Upon the Diseases of the Mind,* 328.
53. Richard von Krafft-Ebing, *Text Book of Insanity Based on Clinical Observations for Practitioners and Students of Medicine* (Philadelphia: F. A. Davis Company, 1905).

54. Krafft-Ebing, *Text Book of Insanity Based on Clinical Observations for Practitioners and Students of Medicine*, 295, 296.
55. Krafft-Ebing, *Text Book of Insanity Based on Clinical Observations for Practitioners and Students of Medicine*, 296.
56. Krafft-Ebing, *Text Book of Insanity Based on Clinical Observations for Practitioners and Students of Medicine*, 299.
57. Krafft-Ebing, *Text Book of Insanity Based on Clinical Observations for Practitioners and Students of Medicine*, 305.
58. Emil Kraepelin, *Clinical Psychiatry* (New York: Macmillan, 1902).
59. Kraepelin, *Clinical Psychiatry*, 237.
60. Kraepelin, *Clinical Psychiatry*, 240.
61. Kraepelin, *Clinical Psychiatry*, 255.
62. Kraepelin, *Clinical Psychiatry*, 262–63.
63. Kraepelin, *Clinical Psychiatry*, 50.
64. Kraepelin, *Clinical Psychiatry*, 50.
65. Kraepelin, *Clinical Psychiatry*, 50–51.
66. Sigmund Freud, *A General Introduction to Psychoanalysis* (New York: Boni and Liveright, 1920), 340.
67. Frederick Crews, *Freud: The Making of an Illusion* (New York: Metropolitan Books, 2017). Crews provides an especially thorough critique in this book.
68. Sigmund Freud, *The Standard Edition of the Complete Psychological Works of Sigmund Freud*, Vol. 3, ed. James Strachey et al. (London: Hogarth, 1962). See esp. the chapter "On the Grounds for Detaching a Particular Syndrome from Neurasthenia under the Description 'Anxiety Neurosis,' " 85–117.
69. Freud, *The Standard Edition of the Complete Psychological Works of Sigmund Freud*, 3: 90.
70. Freud, *The Standard Edition of the Complete Psychological Works of Sigmund Freud*, 3: 92–94.
71. Freud, *The Standard Edition of the Complete Psychological Works of Sigmund Freud*, 3: 93.
72. Freud, *The Standard Edition of the Complete Psychological Works of Sigmund Freud*, 3:113.
73. Allan Compton, "A Study of the Psychoanalytic Theory of Anxiety. I. The Development of Freud's Theory of Anxiety," *Journal of the American Psychoanalytic Association* 20, no. 1 (1972): 3–44; Allan Compton, "A Study of the Psychoanalytic Theory of Anxiety. II. Developments in the Theory of Anxiety Since 1926," *Journal of the American Psychoanalytic Association* 20, no. 2 (1972): 341–94. Compton discusses the evolution of Freud's thoughts on anxiety.
74. Freud, *The Standard Edition of the Complete Psychological Works of Sigmund Freud*, 3: 99–106.
75. Sigmund Freud, "Inhibitions, Symptoms, and Anxiety," in *The Standard Edition of the Complete Psychological Works of Sigmund Freud*, 20: 87–156, ed. James Strachey (London: Hogarth Press and Institute of Psychoanalysis, 1959).
76. Horwitz, *Anxiety: A Short History*. Horwitz emphasizes this point in his discussion of the legacy of Freud's work.
77. Karen Horney, *The Neurotic Personality of Our Time* (New York: Norton, 1937).
78. Harry Stack Sullivan, *The Interpersonal Theory of Psychiatry* (New York: Norton, 1953).

79. Aaron L. Pincus and Emily B. Ansell, "Interpersonal Theory of Personality," in *Handbook of Psychology*, ed. Irving B. Weiner (New York: Wiley, 2003).
80. James S. House, "Social Psychology, Social Science, and Economics: Twentieth Century Progress and Problems, Twenty-First Century Prospects," *Social Psychology Quarterly* 71, no. 3 (2008): 232–56.
81. Samuel Andrew Stouffer, *The American Soldier: Studies in Social Psychology in World War II* (New York: Wiley, 1965).
82. David Riesman, *The Lonely Crowd: A Study of the Changing American Character* (New Haven, Conn.: Yale University Press, 1976); William H. Whyte Jr, *The Organization Man* (New York: Simon and Schuster, 1956).
83. Rollo May, *The Meaning of Anxiety* (New York: Ronald Press, 1950).
84. May, *The Meaning of Anxiety*, 3.
85. May, *The Meaning of Anxiety*, 4.
86. Edward Shorter, *How Everyone Became Depressed: The Rise and Fall of the Nervous Breakdown* (Oxford: Oxford University Press, 2013). Shorter traces the concept's rise and fall in detail and finds significant parallels between the descriptions of neurasthenia and the nervous breakdown.
87. Frank M. Berger, "Anxiety and the Discovery of the Tranquilizers," in *Discoveries in Biological Psychiatry*, ed. Frank Ayd and Barry Blackwell (Philadelphia: Lippincott, 1970), 115–29; Lowell S. Selling, "Clinical Study of a New Tranquilizing Drug: Use of Miltown (2-Methyl-2-N-Propyl-1, 3-Propanediol Dicarbamate)," *Journal of the American Medical Association* 157, no. 18 (1955): 1594–96.
88. Barry Blackwell, "Psychotropic Drugs in Use Today: The Role of Diazepam in Medical Practice," *Journal of the American Medical Association* 225, no. 13 (1973): 1637–41.
89. Lizabeth Cohen, *A Consumer's Republic: The Politics of Mass Consumption in Postwar America* (New York: Knopf, 2003).
90. Andrea Tone, *The Age of Anxiety: A History of America's Turbulent Affair with Tranquilizers* (New York: Basic, 2009).
91. Tone, *The Age of Anxiety*, xvii.
92. Blackwell, "Psychotropic Drugs in Use Today: The Role of Diazepam in Medical Practice."
93. August B. Hollingshead and Fredrick C. Redlich, *Social Class and Mental Illness: A Community Study* (New York: Wiley, 1958).
94. Hollingshead and Redlich, *Social Class and Mental Illness*, 223–25.
95. Hollingshead and Redlich, *Social Class and Mental Illness*, 224.
96. Hollingshead and Redlich, *Social Class and Mental Illness*, 224.
97. Hollingshead and Redlich, *Social Class and Mental Illness*, 224.
98. Hollingshead and Redlich, *Social Class and Mental Illness*, 224.
99. Hollingshead and Redlich, *Social Class and Mental Illness*, 339.
100. Hollingshead and Redlich, *Social Class and Mental Illness*, 340.
101. May, *The Meaning of Anxiety*, 152.
102. May, *The Meaning of Anxiety*, 345.
103. May, *The Meaning of Anxiety*, 341.
104. Tone, *The Age of Anxiety*.
105. New York Academy of Medicine, Committee on Public Health, "Report on Tranquilizing Drugs," *Bulletin of the New York Academy of Medicine* 33, no. 4 (1957): 282–89. This report is discussed in Tone, *The Age of Anxiety*.

106. New York Academy of Medicine, Committee on Public Health, "Report on Tranquilizing Drugs," 282–83.
107. New York Academy of Medicine, Committee on Public Health, "Report on Tranquilizing Drugs," 283.
108. New York Academy of Medicine, Committee on Public Health, "Report on Tranquilizing Drugs," 283.
109. New York Academy of Medicine, Committee on Public Health, "Report on Tranquilizing Drugs," 289.
110. Tone, *The Age of Anxiety*, 86–89.
111. Allan V. Horwitz and Jerome C. Wakefield, *The Loss of Sadness: How Psychiatry Transformed Normal Sorrow into Depressive Disorder* (New York: Oxford University, 2007). This argument was developed primarily by Horwitz and Wakefield, chiefly in *The Loss of Sadness*.
112. Mark Olfson and Gerald L. Klerman, "Trends in the Prescription of Psychotropic Medications: The Role of Physician Specialty," *Medical Care* 31, no. 6 (1993): 559–64. See esp. table 3.
113. Ramin Mojtabai, "Increase in Antidepressant Medication in the US Adult Population Between 1990 and 2003," *Psychotherapy and Psychosomatics* 77, no. 2 (2008): 83–92.
114. Samuel H. Zuvekas, "Prescription Drugs and the Changing Patterns of Treatment for Mental Disorders, 1996–2001," *Health Affairs* 24, no. 1 (2005): 195–205. See primarily exhibit 3.
115. Mark Olfson and Steven C. Marcus, "National Patterns in Antidepressant Medication Treatment," *Archives of General Psychiatry* 66, no. 8 (2009): 848–56.
116. J. M. Murphy and A. H. Leighton, "Anxiety: Its Role in the History of Psychiatric Epidemiology," *Psychological Medicine* 39, no. 7 (2009): 1055–64.
117. Horwitz and Wakefield, *The Loss of Sadness*, provides a detailed discussion of the rise of depressive disorder, on which my discussion draws.
118. Randall S. Stafford, Ellen A. MacDonald, and Stan N. Finkelstein, "National Patterns of Medication Treatment for Depression, 1987 to 2001," *Primary Care Companion to the Journal of Clinical Psychiatry* 3, no. 6 (2001): 232–35.
119. American Psychiatric Association, *Diagnostic and Statistical Manual of Mental Disorders*, 3rd ed. (Washington, D.C.: American Psychiatric Association, 1980).
120. American Psychiatric Association, *Diagnostic and Statistical Manual of Mental Disorders*, 2nd ed. (Washington, D.C.: American Psychiatric Association, 1968), 39. Hereafter APA, *DSM-II*.
121. APA, *DSM-II*, 36.
122. APA, *DSM-II*, 39.
123. APA, *DSM-II*, 39.
124. APA, *Diagnostic and Statistical Manual of Mental Disorders*, 4th ed. (Washington, D.C.: American Psychiatric Association, 1994). Hereafter APA, *DSM-IV*.
125. APA, *DSM-IV*, 410–11, 16–17.
126. APA, *DSM-IV*, 435–36.
127. APA, *DSM-IV*, 417.
128. Allan V. Horwitz and Jerome C. Wakefield, *All We Have to Fear: Psychiatry's Transformation of Natural Anxieties Into Mental Disorders* (New York: Oxford University Press, 2012).

129. Susan McPherson and David Armstrong, "Social Determinants of Diagnostic Labels in Depression," *Social Science & Medicine* 62, no. 1 (2006): 50–58.
130. Horwitz and Wakefield, *All We Have to Fear.*
131. McPherson and Armstrong, "Social Determinants of Diagnostic Labels in Depression."
132. McPherson and Armstrong, "Social Determinants of Diagnostic Labels in Depression," Table 2.
133. McPherson and Armstrong, "Social Determinants of Diagnostic Labels in Depression."
134. Peter A. Di Nardo et al., "Reliability of DSM-III Anxiety Disorder Categories Using a New Structured Interview," *Archives of General Psychiatry* 40, no. 10 (1983): 1070–74.
135. American Psychiatric Association, *Diagnostic and Statistical Manual of Mental Disorders*, 3rd ed. Rev. (Washington, D.C.: American Psychiatric Association, 1987). Hereafter APA, *DSM-III-R.*
136. APA, *DSM-III-R*, 251.
137. Michelle G. Craske et al., "Qualitative Dimensions of Worry in DSM-III-R Generalized Anxiety Disorder Subjects and Nonanxious Controls," *Behaviour Research and Therapy* 27, no. 4 (1989): 397–402.
138. World Health Organization, *International Statistical Classification of Diseases and Related Health Problems: ICD-10* (Geneva, 1992).
139. Murphy and Leighton, "Anxiety: Its Role in the History of Psychiatric Epidemiology."
140. Karl Rickels and Moira A. Rynn, "What Is Generalized Anxiety Disorder?" *Journal of Clinical Psychiatry* 62, no. 11 (2001): 4–12; T. Slade and G. Andrews, "DSM-IV and ICD-10 Generalized Anxiety Disorder: Discrepant Diagnoses and Associated Disability," *Social Psychiatry and Psychiatric Epidemiology* 36, no. 1 (2001): 45–51.

3. THE EVOLVING SCIENCE OF ANXIETY AND DEPRESSION

1. Peter Tyrer, "Comorbidity or Consanguinity," *British Journal of Psychiatry* 168, no. 6 (1996): 669–71.
2. Ronald C. Kessler et al., "Impairment in Pure and Comorbid Generalized Anxiety Disorder and Major Depression at 12 Months in Two National Surveys," *American Journal of Psychiatry* 156, no. 12 (1999): 1915–23.
3. Paula J. Clayton, "Depression Subtyping: Treatment Implications," Supplement, *Journal of Clinical Psychiatry* 59, no. S16 (1998): 5–12, fig. 2.
4. Ronald C. Kessler et al., "Co-morbid Major Depression and Generalized Anxiety Disorders in the National Comorbidity Survey Follow-Up," *Psychological Medicine* 38, no. 3 (2008): 365–74.
5. Tyrer, "Comorbidity or Consanguinity."
6. Denny Borsboom and Angélique O. J. Cramer, "Network Analysis: An Integrative Approach to the Structure of Psychopathology," *Annual Review of Clinical Psychology* 9, no. 1 (2013): 91–121.
7. Tyrer, "Comorbidity or Consanguinity."
8. American Psychiatric Association, *Diagnostic and Statistical Manual of Mental Disorders*, 4th ed. (Washington, D.C.: American Psychiatric Association, 1994). Hereafter APA, *DSM-IV.*

9. Ronald C. Kessler et al., "Prevalence, Severity, and Comorbidity of 12-Month DSM-IV Disorders in the National Comorbidity Survey Replication," *Archives of General Psychiatry* 62, no. 6 (2005): 617–27.

10. David H. Barlow, *Anxiety and Its Disorders: The Nature and Treatment of Anxiety and Panic* (New York: Guilford, 1988).

11. Clayton, "Depression Subtyping."

12. Peter Tyrer, "The Case for Cothymia: Mixed Anxiety and Depression as a Single Diagnosis," *British Journal of Psychiatry* 179, no. 3 (2001): 191–93.

13. Kenneth S. Kendler et al., "Major Depression and Generalized Anxiety Disorder: Same Genes, (Partly) Different Environments?" *Archives of General Psychiatry* 49, no. 9 (1992): 716–22; Gavin Andrews et al., "Evidence for a General Neurotic Syndrome," *British Journal of Psychiatry* 157, no. 1 (1990): 6–12.

14. J. Emmanuel, S. Simmonds, and P. Tyrer, "Systematic Review of the Outcome of Anxiety and Depressive Disorders," *British Journal of Psychiatry* Supplement, no. 34 (1998): 35–41; Terrie E. Moffitt et al., "Depression and Generalized Anxiety Disorder: Cumulative and Sequential Comorbidity in a Birth Cohort Followed Prospectively to Age 32 Years," *Archives of General Psychiatry* 64, no. 6 (2007): 651–60; H. U. Wittchen et al., "Why Do People with Anxiety Disorders Become Depressed? A Prospective-Longitudinal Community Study," *Acta Psychiatrica Scandinavica* 102(2000): 14–23.

15. Lee Anna Clark and David Watson, "Tripartite Model of Anxiety and Depression: Psychometric Evidence and Taxonomic Implications," *Journal of Abnormal Psychology* 100, no. 3 (1991): 316–36.

16. World Health Organization, *International Statistical Classification of Diseases and Related Health Problems: ICD-10* (Geneva, 1992).

17. World Health Organization, *International Statistical Classification of Diseases and Related Health Problems: ICD-10.*

18. APA, *DSM-IV.*

19. Neeltje M. Batelaan et al., "Mixed Anxiety Depression Should Not Be Included in DSM-5," *Journal of Nervous and Mental Disease* 200, no. 6 (2012): 495–98.

20. Katrin Barkow et al., "Mixed Anxiety–Depression in a 1 Year Follow-up Study: Shift to Other Diagnoses or Remission?" *Journal of Affective Disorders* 79, no. 1 (2004): 235–39.

21. Barkow et al., "Mixed Anxiety–Depression."

22. Tyrer, "The Case for Cothymia."

23. J. Mark G. Williams et al., *Cognitive Psychology and Emotional Disorders* (Oxford, U.K.: Wiley, 1988).

24. Daniel Nettle and Melissa Bateson, "The Evolutionary Origins of Mood and Its Disorders," *Current Biology* 22, no. 17 (2012): R712–R21.

25. Aaron T. Beck, *Cognitive Therapy and the Emotional Disorders* (New York: International Universities Press, 1976); Yair Bar-Haim et al., "Threat-Related Attentional Bias in Anxious and Nonanxious Individuals: A Meta-analytic Study," *Psychological Bulletin* 133, no. 1 (2007): 1–24; Daniel G. Dillon et al., "Peril and Pleasure: An RDoC-inspired Examination of Threat Responses and Reward Processing in Anxiety and Depression," *Depression and Anxiety* 31, no. 3 (2014): 233–49; Andrew Mathews and Colin MacLeod, "Induced Processing Biases Have Causal Effects on Anxiety," *Cognition and Emotion* 16, no. 3 (2002): 331–54; Andrew Mathews, "Why

Worry? The Cognitive Function of Anxiety," *Behaviour Research and Therapy* 28, no. 6 (1990): 455–68.

26. Karin Mogg and Brendan P. Bradley, "Attentional Bias in Generalized Anxiety Disorder Versus Depressive Disorder," *Cognitive Therapy and Research* 29, no. 1 (2005): 29–45.

27. M. Bellew and A. B. Hill, "Negative Recall Bias as a Predictor of Susceptibility to Induced Depressive Mood," *Personality and Individual Differences* 11, no. 5 (1990): 471–80.

28. Colin MacLeod, Andrew Mathews, and Philip Tata, "Attentional Bias in Emotional Disorders," *Journal of Abnormal Psychology* 95, no. 1 (1986): 15–20.

29. Zindel V. Segal et al., "A Priming Methodology for Studying Self-Representation in Major Depressive Disorder," *Journal of Abnormal Psychology* 104, no. 1 (1995): 205–13.

30. Allison J. Ouimet, Bertram Gawronski, and David J. A. Dozois, "Cognitive Vulnerability to Anxiety: A Review and an Integrative Model," *Clinical Psychology Review* 29, no. 6 (2009): 459–70.

31. Michael W. Eysenck et al., "Bias in Interpretation of Ambiguous Sentences Related to Threat in Anxiety," *Journal of Abnormal Psychology* 100, no. 2 (1991): 144–50.

32. Eysenck et al., "Bias in Interpretation of Ambiguous Sentences Related to Threat in Anxiety," table 2.

33. Bar-Haim et al., "Threat-Related Attentional Bias in Anxious and Nonanxious Individuals."

34. Williams et al., *Cognitive Psychology and Emotional Disorders.*

35. Bar-Haim et al., "Threat-Related Attentional Bias in Anxious and Nonanxious Individuals."

36. Lauren S. Hallion and Ayelet Meron Ruscio, "A Meta-analysis of the Effect of Cognitive Bias Modification on Anxiety and Depression," *Psychological Bulletin* 137, no. 6 (2011): 940–58.

37. Karin Mogg and Brendan P. Bradley, "A Cognitive-Motivational Analysis of Anxiety," *Behaviour Research and Therapy* 36, no. 9 (1998): 809–48.

38. Timothy A. Brown, Bruce F. Chorpita, and David H. Barlow, "Structural Relationships Among Dimensions of the DSM-IV Anxiety and Mood Disorders and Dimensions of Negative Affect, Positive Affect, and Autonomic Arousal," *Journal of Abnormal Psychology* 107, no. 2 (1998): 179–92; Auke Tellegen, "Structures of Mood and Personality and Their Relevance to Assessing Anxiety, with an Emphasis on Self-Report," in *Anxiety and the Anxiety Disorders*, ed. A. H. Tuma and J. D. Maser (Hillsdale, N.J.: Erlbaum, 1985).

39. Kenneth S. Kendler et al., "Symptoms of Anxiety and Depression in a Volunteer Twin Population," *Archives of General Psychiatry* 43 (1986): 213–21.

40. David Goldberg, "The Aetiology of Depression," *Psychological Medicine* 36, no. 10 (2006): 1341–47; Michael G. Gottschalk and Katharina Domschke, "Genetics of Generalized Anxiety Disorder and Related Traits," *Dialogues in Clinical Neuroscience* 19, no. 2 (2017): 159–68.

41. Randolph M. Nesse, *Good Reasons for Bad Feelings: Insights from the Frontier of Evolutionary Psychiatry* (New York: Dutton, 2019). Nesse discusses the evolutionary origins of psychiatric disorders, including, but not limited to, anxiety and depression, providing a general explanation for why "bad" feelings can be evolutionarily advantageous.

42. L. Tondo, B. Lepri, and R. J. Baldessarini, "Reproduction Among 1975 Sardinian Women and Men Diagnosed with Major Mood Disorders," *Acta Psychiatrica Scandinavica* 123, no. 4 (2011): 283–89; Arnstein Mykletun et al., "Anxiety, Depression, and Cause-Specific Mortality: The Hunt Study," *Psychosomatic Medicine* 69, no. 4 (2007): 323–31.

43. Allan V. Horwitz and Jerome C. Wakefield, *All We Have to Fear: Psychiatry's Transformation of Natural Anxieties Into Mental Disorders* (New York: Oxford University Press, 2012).

44. Randolph M. Nesse, "Is Depression an Adaptation?" *Archives of General Psychiatry* 57, no. 1 (2000): 14–20. My discussion of the evolutionary origins of anxiety and depression draws extensively from the work of Nesse.

45. John Price et al., "The Social Competition Hypothesis of Depression," *British Journal of Psychiatry* 164, no. 3 (1994): 309–15.

46. Sherry Anders, Midori Tanaka, and Dennis K. Kinney, "Depression as an Evolutionary Strategy for Defense Against Infection," *Brain, Behavior, and Immunity* 31 (2013): 9–22; Dennis K. Kinney and Midori Tanaka, "An Evolutionary Hypothesis of Depression and Its Symptoms, Adaptive Value, and Risk Factors," *Journal of Nervous and Mental Disease* 197, no. 8 (2009): 561–67.

47. Paul W. Andrews and J. Anderson Thomson Jr, "The Bright Side of Being Blue: Depression as an Adaptation for Analyzing Complex Problems," *Psychological Review* 116, no. 3 (2009): 620–54.

48. Andrews and Thomson, "The Bright Side of Being Blue."

49. Charles Darwin, *The Expression of Emotions in Man and Animals* (New York: St. Martin's, 1979).

50. Randolph M. Nesse, "Evolutionary Explanations of Emotions," *Human Nature* 1, no. 3 (1990): 261–89.

51. Isaac fM. Marks and Randolph M. Nesse, "Fear and Fitness: An Evolutionary Analysis of Anxiety Disorders," *Ethology and Sociobiology* 15, no. 5 (1994): 247–61; Nesse, "Evolutionary Explanations of Emotions."

52. Marks and Nesse, "Fear and Fitness," 249.

53. Arnstein Mykletun et al., "Levels of Anxiety and Depression as Predictors of Mortality: The Hunt Study," *British Journal of Psychiatry* 195, no. 2 (2009): 118–25.

54. Richard J. Davidson, "Darwin and the Neural Bases of Emotion and Affective Style," *Annals of the New York Academy of Sciences* 1000, no. 1 (2006): 316–36.

55. Ke Zhao et al., "Neural Responses to Rapid Facial Expressions of Fear and Surprise," *Frontiers in Psychology* 8 (2017): 761.

56. Isaac Marks, *Fears, Phobias and Rituals: Panic, Anxiety, and Their Disorders* (New York: Oxford University Press, 1987); E. J. Gibson and R. D. Walk, "Walking Off a Cliff," in *Introducing Psychological Research: Sixty Studies That Shape Psychology*, ed. Philip Banyard and Andrew Grayson (London: Macmillan Education UK, 1996).

57. Randolph M. Nesse and Eric D. Jackson, "Evolution: Psychiatric Nosology's Missing Biological Foundation," *Clinical Neuropsychiatry: Journal of Treatment Evaluation* 3, no. 2 (2006): 121–31.

58. Rebecca J. Brooker et al., "The Development of Stranger Fear in Infancy and Toddlerhood: Normative Development, Individual Differences, Antecedents, and Outcomes," *Developmental Science* 16, no. 6 (2013): 864–78.

59. Horwitz and Wakefield, *All We Have to Fear: Psychiatry's Transformation of Natural Anxieties into Mental Disorders.*

60. Allan V. Horwitz and Jerome C. Wakefield, *The Loss of Sadness: How Psychiatry Transformed Normal Sorrow Into Depressive Disorder* (New York: Oxford University, 2007).

61. Randolph M. Nesse, "The Smoke Detector Principle," *Annals of the New York Academy of Sciences* 935, no. 1 (2001): 75–85.

62. Nettle and Bateson, "The Evolutionary Origins of Mood and Its Disorders."

63. Frazer Meacham and Carl T. Bergstrom, "Adaptive Behavior Can Produce Maladaptive Anxiety Due to Individual Differences in Experience," *Evolution, Medicine, and Public Health* 2016, no. 1 (2016): 270–85.

64. Thomas R. Insel, "The NIMH Research Domain Criteria (RDoC) Project: Precision Medicine for Psychiatry," *American Journal of Psychiatry* 171, no. 4 (2014): 395–97.

65. Thomas Insel et al., "Research Domain Criteria (RDoC): Toward a New Classification Framework for Research on Mental Disorders," *American Journal of Psychiatry* 167, no. 7 (2010): 748–51.

66. Jordan W. Smoller, *The Other Side of Normal: How Biology Is Providing the Clues to Unlock the Secrets of Normal and Abnormal Behavior.* (New York: William Morrow, 2012). The RDoC is, in this regard, only a reflection of a larger current in psychiatry. Smoller discusses the promise and limits of using biology to adjudicate normal and abnormal.

67. Insel et al., "Research Domain Criteria (RDoC): Toward a New Classification Framework for Research on Mental Disorders," 749.

68. Insel, "The NIMH Research Domain Criteria (RDoC) Project," 396.

69. Thomas Insel, as quoted in Scott Stossel, *My Age of Anxiety: Fear, Hope, Dread, and the Search for Peace of Mind* (New York: Knopf, 2013), 11.

70. RDoC is revised continuously. Its current elements can be found here: https://www.nimh.nih.gov/research-priorities/rdoc/constructs/negative-valence-systems.shtml.

71. Insel et al., "Research Domain Criteria (RDoC)."

72. Lisa M. McTeague and Peter J. Lang, "The Anxiety Spectrum and the Reflex Physiology of Defense: From Circumscribed Fear to Broad Distress," *Depression and Anxiety* 29, no. 4 (2012): 264–81.

73. Kathleen C. Anderson and Thomas R. Insel, "The Promise of Extinction Research for the Prevention and Treatment of Anxiety Disorders," *Biological Psychiatry* 60, no. 4 (2006): 319–21.

74. David L. Walker et al., "Facilitation of Conditioned Fear Extinction by Systemic Administration or Intra-amygdala Infusions of D-Cycloserine as Assessed with Fear-potentiated Startle in Rats," *Journal of Neuroscience* 22, no. 6 (2002): 2343.

75. John F. Cryan and Andrew Holmes, "The Ascent of Mouse: Advances in Modelling Human Depression and Anxiety," *Nature Reviews Drug Discovery* 4(2005): 775–90; William T. McKinney Jr and William. E. Bunney, "Animal Model of Depression: I. Review of Evidence: Implications for Research," *Archives of General Psychiatry* 21, no. 2 (1969): 240–48.

76. Cryan and Holmes, "The Ascent of Mouse," table 1.

77. R. D. Porsolt, M. Le Pichon, and M. Jalfre, "Depression: A New Animal Model Sensitive to Antidepressant Treatments," *Nature* 266, no. 5604 (1977): 730–32.

78. John F. Cryan and Fabian F. Sweeney, "The Age of Anxiety: Role of Animal Models of Anxiolytic Action in Drug Discovery," *British Journal of Pharmacology* 164, no. 4 (2011): 1129–61.

79. Thomas Steckler, Murray B. Stein, and Andrew Holmes, "Developing Novel Anxiolytics: Improving Preclinical Detection and Clinical Assessment," in *Animal and Translational Models for CNS Drug Discovery*, ed. Robert A. McArthur and Franco Borsini (San Diego: Academic Press, 2008).
80. Cryan and Holmes, "The Ascent of Mouse," table 2.
81. D. Caroline Blanchard, Guy Griebel, and Robert J. Blanchard, "The Mouse Defense Test Battery: Pharmacological and Behavioral Assays for Anxiety and Panic," *European Journal of Pharmacology* 463, no. 1 (2003): 97–116.
82. Neal E. Miller, "The Value of Behavioral Research on Animals," *American Psychologist* 40, no. 4 (1985): 423–40.
83. Institute of Medicine, *Science, Medicine, and Animals* (Washington, D.C.: National Academies Press, 1991).
84. Institute of Medicine, National Research Council, *International Animal Research Regulations: Impact on Neuroscience Research: Workshop Summary* (Washington, D.C.: National Academies Press, 2012).
85. Sonia J. Lupien et al., "Effects of Stress Throughout the Lifespan on the Brain, Behaviour and Cognition," *Nature Reviews Neuroscience* 10 (2009): 434.
86. P. Willner, "Validity, Reliability and Utility of the Chronic Mild Stress Model of Depression: A 10-Year Review and Evaluation," *Psychopharmacology* 134, no. 4 (1997): 319–29.
87. Kimberly R. Lezak, Galen Missig, and William A. Carlezon Jr, "Behavioral Methods to Study Anxiety in Rodents," *Dialogues in Clinical Neuroscience* 19, no. 2 (2017): 181–91, 181.
88. Michel Bourin, "Animal Models for Screening Anxiolytic-like Drugs: A Perspective," *Dialogues in Clinical Neuroscience* 17, no. 3 (2015): 295–303.
89. Cryan and Sweeney, "The Age of Anxiety: Role of Animal Models of Anxiolytic Action in Drug Discovery."

4. ANXIETY DISORDERS IN THE UNITED STATES

1. David H. Barlow, *Anxiety and Its Disorders: The Nature and Treatment of Anxiety and Panic*, 2nd ed. (New York: Guilford, 2002).
2. John M. Hettema, Michael C. Neale, and Kenneth S. Kendler, "A Review and Meta-analysis of the Genetic Epidemiology of Anxiety Disorders," *American Journal of Psychiatry* 158, no. 10 (2001): 1568–78.
3. Hettema, Neale, and Kendler, "A Review and Meta-analysis of the Genetic Epidemiology of Anxiety Disorders."
4. Kenneth S. Kendler, L. M. Karkowski, and C. A. Prescott, "Fears and Phobias: Reliability and Heritability," *Psychological Medicine* 29, no. 3 (1999): 539–53.
5. Jude Cassidy et al., "Generalized Anxiety Disorder: Connections with Self-Reported Attachment," *Behavior Therapy* 40, no. 1 (2009): 23–38.
6. Susan Nolen-Hoeksema and Edward R. Watkins, "A Heuristic for Developing Transdiagnostic Models of Psychopathology: Explaining Multifinality and Divergent Trajectories," *Perspectives on Psychological Science* 6, no. 6 (2011): 589–609.
7. Nolen-Hoeksema and Watkins, "A Heuristic for Developing Transdiagnostic Models of Psychopathology: Explaining Multifinality and Divergent Trajectories."

8. Amy Przeworski et al., "Interpersonal Pathoplasticity in Individuals with General-ized Anxiety Disorder," *Journal of Abnormal Psychology* 120, no. 2 (2011): 286–98.
9. Mark A. Whisman, "Marital Distress and DSM-IV Psychiatric Disorders in a Pop-ulation-based National Survey," *Journal of Abnormal Psychology* 116, no. 3 (2007): 638–43; Robert C. Durham, Thérèse Allan, and Christine A. Hackett, "On Predict-ing Improvement and Relapse in Generalized Anxiety Disorder Following Psycho-therapy," *British Journal of Clinical Psychology* 36, no. 1 (1997): 101–19.
10. Lizabeth Roemer, Silvia Molina, and Thomas D. Borkovec, "An Investigation of Worry Content Among Generally Anxious Individuals," *Journal of Nervous and Mental Disease* 185, no. 5 (1997): 314–19, table 1.
11. James S. House, Deborah Umberson, and Karl R. Landis, "Structures and Processes of Social Support," *Annual Review of Sociology* 14(1988): 293–318.
12. Terrie E. Moffitt et al., "Generalized Anxiety Disorder and Depression: Childhood Risk Factors in a Birth Cohort Followed to Age 32," *Psychological Medicine* 37, no. 3 (2007): 441–52.
13. Jesse R. Cougle et al., "Examining the Unique Relationships Between Anxiety Dis-orders and Childhood Physical and Sexual Abuse in the National Comorbidity Survey-Replication," *Psychiatry Research* 177, no. 1 (2010): 150–55.
14. Hans M. Nordahl et al., "Association Between Abnormal Psychosocial Situations in Childhood, Generalized Anxiety Disorder and Oppositional Defiant Disorder," *Australian & New Zealand Journal of Psychiatry* 44, no. 9 (2010): 852–58; Michael J. Shanahan et al., "Environmental Contingencies and Genetic Propensities: Social Capital, Educational Continuation, and Dopamine Receptor Gene DRD2," *Ameri-can Journal of Sociology* 114 (2008): S260–S86.
15. Peter Muris et al., "Worry in Children Is Related to Perceived Parental Rearing and Attachment," *Behaviour Research and Therapy* 38, no. 5 (2000): 487–97.
16. Michelle G. Newman et al., "Worry and Generalized Anxiety Disorder: A Review and Theoretical Synthesis of Evidence on Nature, Etiology, Mechanisms, and Treat-ment," *Annual Review of Clinical Psychology* 9, no. 1 (2013): 275–97.
17. Ronald C. Kessler et al., "Lifetime Prevalence and Age-of-Onset Distributions of DSM-IV Disorders in the National Comorbidity Survey Replication," *Archives of General Psychiatry* 62, no. 6 (2005): 593–602.
18. Kenneth S. Kendler et al., "Major Depression and Generalized Anxiety Disorder: Same Genes, (Partly) Different Environments?" *Archives of General Psychiatry* 49, no. 9 (1992): 716–22.
19. Kendler et al., "Major Depression and Generalized Anxiety Disorder," 721.
20. Kenneth S. Kendler et al., "Life Event Dimensions of Loss, Humiliation, Entrap-ment, and Danger in the Prediction of Onsets of Major Depression and General-ized Anxiety," *Archives of General Psychiatry* 60, no. 8 (2003): 789–96.
21. Robert Finlay-Jones and George W. Brown, "Types of Stressful Life Event and the Onset of Anxiety and Depressive Disorders," *Psychological Medicine* 11, no. 4 (1981): 803–15.
22. Edwin DeBeurs et al., "On Becoming Depressed or Anxious in Late Life: Similar Vulnerability Factors but Different Effects of Stressful Life Events," *British Journal of Psychiatry* 179, no. 5 (2001): 426–31.
23. Kendler et al., "Life Event Dimensions of Loss, Humiliation, Entrapment, and Dan-ger in the Prediction of Onsets of Major Depression and Generalized Anxiety."

24. Nicole K. Phillips et al., "Early Adversity and the Prospective Prediction of Depressive and Anxiety Disorders in Adolescents," *Journal of Abnormal Child Psychology* 33, no. 1 (2005): 13–24.

25. Moffitt et al., "Generalized Anxiety Disorder and Depression."

26. Moffitt et al., "Generalized Anxiety Disorder and Depression"; Terrie E. Moffitt et al., "Depression and Generalized Anxiety Disorder: Cumulative and Sequential Comorbidity in a Birth Cohort Followed Prospectively to Age 32 Years," *Archives of General Psychiatry* 64, no. 6 (2007): 651–60.

27. George W. Brown, T. O. Harris, and M. J. Eales, "Aetiology of Anxiety and Depressive Disorders in an Inner-City Population. II. Comorbidity and Adversity," *Psychological Medicine* 23, no. 1 (1993): 155–65.

28. Brown, Harris, and Eales, "Aetiology of Anxiety and Depressive Disorders in an Inner-City Population. II. Comorbidity and Adversity."

29. Kimberly Christie Burke et al., "Comparing Age at Onset of Major Depression and Other Psychiatric Disorders by Birth Cohorts in Five US Community Populations," *JAMA Psychiatry* 48, no. 9 (1991): 789–95; Peter M. Lewinsohn et al., "Age-Cohort Changes in the Lifetime Occurrence of Depression and Other Mental Disorders," *Journal of Abnormal Psychology* 102, no. 1 (1993): 110–20; Lee N. Robins and Darrel A. Regier, eds., *Psychiatric Disorders in America: The Epidemiological Area Study* (New York: Free Press, 1991).

30. Lewinsohn et al., "Age-Cohort Changes in the Lifetime Occurrence of Depression and Other Mental Disorders."

31. Lewinsohn et al., "Age-Cohort Changes in the Lifetime Occurrence of Depression and Other Mental Disorders."

32. Lewinsohn et al., "Age-Cohort Changes in the Lifetime Occurrence of Depression and Other Mental Disorders."

33. Mark A. Oakley Browne et al., "Lifetime Prevalence and Projected Lifetime Risk of DSM-IV Disorders in Te Rau Hinengaro: The New Zealand Mental Health Survey," *Australian and New Zealand Journal of Psychiatry* 40, no. 10 (2006): 865–74; Kessler et al., "Lifetime Prevalence and Age-of-Onset Distributions of DSM-IV Disorders in the National Comorbidity Survey Replication."

34. Kessler et al., "Lifetime Prevalence and Age-of-Onset Distributions of DSM-IV Disorders in the National Comorbidity Survey Replication."

35. Kessler et al., "Lifetime Prevalence and Age-of-Onset Distributions of DSM-IV Disorders in the National Comorbidity Survey Replication."

36. Andrew S. London and Scott D. Landes, "Cohort Change in the Prevalence of ADHD Among U.S. Adults: Evidence of a Gender-Specific Historical Period Effect," *Journal of Attention Disorders* (2019): 1087054719855689.

37. Joseph Veroff, Elizabeth Douvan, and Richard Kulka, Americans View Their Mental Health, 1957 and 1976: Selected Variables (Ann Arbor, Mich.: Inter-university Consortium for Political and Social Research [ICPSR] [distributor], 2005); Joseph Veroff, Elizabeth Douvan, and Richard A. Kulka, *The Inner American: A Self-Portrait from 1957 to 1976* (New York: Basic, 1981).

38. Andrea Tone, *The Age of Anxiety: A History of America's Turbulent Affair with Tranquilizers* (New York: Basic, 2009), xvii.

39. Veroff, Douvan, and Kulka, *The Inner American: A Self-Portrait from 1957 to 1976*.

40. The scope of worry expanded in other ways. Participants in AVMH were asked to describe the things that worry them most, nominating up to four things. Table 2.4 shows the distribution of worries for each year, categorized by theme. Many concerns are, of course, personal, insofar as they pertain to one's job, for instance, or family. People can also worry about nonpersonal matters, including, as expressed in the survey, politics, national affairs, a growing "lack of morals," and nuclear war. Although 13 percent of Americans worried about such matters in 1957, this had expanded to about 22 percent in 1976. Some of this increase likely reflected the aftereffects of a recession occurring in the early 1970s and Watergate and, indeed, more respondents referred to business conditions and national affairs as a particular kind of nonpersonal problem. Nonetheless, the content of American worry expanded during this interval, stretching beyond personal considerations.

41. Lynn A. Blewett et al., IPUMS Health Surveys: National Health Interview Survey, Version 6.4 [Dataset] (Minneapolis, Minn.: IPUMS, https://doi.org/10.18128/D070.V6.4, 2019).

42. Ronald C. Kessler et al., "Screening for Serious Mental Illness in the General Population," *Archives of General Psychiatry* 60, no. 2 (2003): 184–89.

43. Margarita Alegria et al., *Collaborative Psychiatric Epidemiology Surveys (CPES), 2001–2003, United States* (Ann Arbor, Mich.: Inter-university Consortium for Political and Social Research [Distributor], 2016).

5. FAMILY CHANGE AND COHORT DIFFERENCES IN ANXIETY

1. Frank F. Furstenberg, "Is the Modern Family a Threat to Children's Health?," *Society* 36, no. 5 (1999): 31–37.

2. Claude S. Fischer and Michael Hout, *Century of Difference: How America Changed in the Last One Hundred Years* (New York: Russell Sage Foundation, 2006), 48–49.

3. Andrew J. Cherlin, "Going to Extremes: Family Structure, Children's Well-Being, and Social Science," *Demography* 36, no. 4 (1999): 421–28.

4. Judith S. Wallerstein, Julia Lewis, and Sandra Blakeslee, *The Unexpected Legacy of Divorce: A 25 Year Landmark Study* (London: Fusion, 2002); Judith Rich Harris, *The Nurture Assumption: Why Children Turn Out the Way They Do* (New York: Free Press, 2009).

5. Samuel H. Preston, "Children and the Elderly: Divergent Paths for America's Dependents," *Demography* 21, no. 4 (1984): 435–57.

6. Andrew J. Cherlin, *Marriage, Divorce, Remarriage* (Cambridge, Mass.: Harvard University Press, 1992).

7. Steven Ruggles, "Patriarchy, Power, and Pay: The Transformation of American Families, 1800–2015," *Demography* 52, no. 6 (2015): 1797–823.

8. Sheela Kennedy and Steven Ruggles, "Breaking Up Is Hard to Count: The Rise of Divorce in the United States, 1980–2010," *Demography* 51, no. 2 (2014): 587–98.

9. Kennedy and Ruggles, "Breaking Up Is Hard to Count."

10. Ruggles, "Patriarchy, Power, and Pay."

11. Steven Ruggles, "The Rise of Divorce and Separation in the United States, 1880–1990," *Demography* 34, no. 4 (1997): 455–66.

12. June Carbone and Naomi Cahn, *Marriage Markets: How Inequality Is Remaking the American Family* (New York: Oxford University Press, 2014).
13. Ruggles, "Patriarchy, Power, and Pay," fig. 13.
14. Ronald R. Rindfuss, Karin L. Brewster, and Andrew L. Kavee, "Women, Work, and Children: Behavioral and Attitudinal Change in the United States," *Population and Development Review* 22, no. 3 (1996): 457–82; Ruggles, "Patriarchy, Power, and Pay: The Transformation of American Families, 1800–2015."
15. Arland Thornton, "Changing Attitudes Toward Family Issues in the United States," *Journal of Marriage and the Family* 51, no. 4 (1989): 873–93.
16. Ruggles, "Patriarchy, Power, and Pay."
17. Fischer and Hout, *Century of Difference: How America Changed in the Last One Hundred Years.*
18. Fischer and Hout, *Century of Difference* fig. 4.4.
19. Fischer and Hout, *Century of Difference.*
20. Pew Social Trends, "Parenting in America," accessed August 5, 2020, http://www.pewsocialtrends.org/2015/12/17/1-the-american-family-today/2015.
21. Larry L. Bumpass and R. Kelly Raley, "Redefining Single-Parent Families: Cohabitation and Changing Family Reality," *Demography* 32, no. 1 (1995): 97–109.
22. Maria Cancian, Daniel R. Meyer, and Steven T. Cook, "The Evolution of Family Complexity from the Perspective of Nonmarital Children," *Demography* 48, no. 3 (2011): 957–82.
23. Susan M. McHale, Kimberly A. Updegraff, and Shawn D. Whiteman, "Sibling Relationships and Influences in Childhood and Adolescence," *Journal of Marriage and the Family* 74, no. 5 (2012): 913–30.
24. Bumpass and Raley, "Redefining Single-Parent Families: Cohabitation and Changing Family Reality"; Deborah A. Dawson, "Family Structure and Children's Health and Well-Being: Data from the 1988 National Health Interview Survey on Child Health," *Journal of Marriage and Family* 53, no. 3 (1991): 573–84.
25. Frank F. Furstenberg Jr and Andrew J. Cherlin, *Divided Families: What Happens to Children When Parents Part* (Cambridge, Mass.: Harvard University Press, 1991).
26. Furstenberg, "Is the Modern Family a Threat to Children's Health?"; Anne H. Gauthier, Timothy M. Smeedeng, and Frank F. Furstenberg, "Are Parents Investing Less Time in Children? Trends in Selected Industrialized Countries," *Population and Development Review* 30, no. 4 (2004): 647–71.
27. Suzanne M. Bianchi, "Maternal Employment and Time with Children: Dramatic Change or Surprising Continuity?" *Demography* 37, no. 4 (2000): 401–14.
28. Liana C. Sayer, Suzanne M. Bianchi, and John P. Robinson, "Are Parents Investing Less in Children? Trends in Mothers' and Fathers' Time with Children," *American Journal of Sociology* 110, no. 1 (2004): 1–43.
29. Sabino Kornrich and Frank Furstenberg, "Investing in Children: Changes in Parental Spending on Children, 1972–2007," *Demography* 50, no. 1 (2013): 1–23.
30. Institute of Medicine, National Research Council, *Child Maltreatment Research, Policy, and Practice for the Next Decade: Workshop Summary* (Washington, D.C.: National Academies Press, 2012).
31. Institute of Medicine, National Research Council, *Child Maltreatment Research, Policy, and Practice for the Next Decade: Workshop Summary*, Figure 3.

32. Institute of Medicine, National Research Council, *Child Maltreatment Research, Policy, and Practice for the Next Decade: Workshop Summary.*
33. Tatiana Alina Trifan, Håkan Stattin, and Lauree Tilton-Weaver, "Have Authoritarian Parenting Practices and Roles Changed in the Last 50 Years?" *Journal of Marriage and Family* 76, no. 4 (2014): 744–61.
34. C. Jack Tucker, Jonathan Marx, and Larry Long, " 'Moving On': Residential Mobility and Children's School Lives," *Sociology of Education* 71, no. 2 (1998): 111–29; Sara McLanahan and Gary Sandefur, *Growing Up with a Single Parent: What Hurts, What Helps* (Cambridge, Mass.: Harvard University Press, 1994).
35. Institute of Medicine, National Research Council, *Child Maltreatment Research, Policy, and Practice for the Next Decade: Workshop Summary.*
36. Marcia J. Carlson, Daniel R. Meyer, and Frank F. Furstenberg, "Fifty Years of Family Change: From Consensus to Complexity," *Annals of the American Academy of Political and Social Science* 654, no. 1 (2014): 12–30; Pamela J. Smock and Fiona Rose Greenland, "Diversity in Pathways to Parenthood: Patterns, Implications, and Emerging Research Directions," *Journal of Marriage and Family* 72, no. 3 (2010): 576–93.
37. Anne Case, I. Fen Lin, and Sara McLanahan, "Educational Attainment of Siblings in Stepfamilies," *Evolution and Human Behavior* 22, no. 4 (2001): 269–89.
38. McHale, Updegraff, and Whiteman, "Sibling Relationships and Influences in Childhood and Adolescence," 914.
39. Nina Howe et al., " 'No! The Lambs Can Stay out Because They Got Cozies': Constructive and Destructive Sibling Conflict, Pretend Play, and Social Understanding," *Child Development* 73, no. 5 (2002): 1460–73.
40. Cheryl Slomkowski et al., "Sisters, Brothers, and Delinquency: Evaluating Social Influence During Early and Middle Adolescence," *Child Development* 72, no. 1 (2001): 271–83; McHale, Updegraff, and Whiteman, "Sibling Relationships and Influences in Childhood and Adolescence."
41. Kirstin Stauffacher and Ganie B. DeHart, "Crossing Social Contexts: Relational Aggression Between Siblings and Friends During Early and Middle Childhood," *Journal of Applied Developmental Psychology* 27, no. 3 (2006): 228–40.
42. Ji-Yeon Kim et al., "Longitudinal Linkages Between Sibling Relationships and Adjustment from Middle Childhood through Adolescence," *Developmental Psychology* 43, no. 4 (2007): 960–73; Patricia Noller, "Sibling Relationships in Adolescence: Learning and Growing Together," *Personal Relationships* 12, no. 1 (2005): 1–22.
43. Michael H. Boyle et al., "Differential-Maternal Parenting Behavior: Estimating Within- and Between-Family Effects on Children," *Child Development* 75, no. 5 (2004): 1457–76.
44. Naama Atzaba-Poria and Alison Pike, "Correlates of Parental Differential Treatment: Parental and Contextual Factors During Middle Childhood," *Child Development* 79, no. 1 (2008): 217–32; Alfred Adler, *The Individual Psychology of Alfred Adler: A Systematic Presentation in Selections from His Writings* (New York: Basic, 1956).
45. Kirsten L. Buist, Maja Deković, and Peter Prinzie, "Sibling Relationship Quality and Psychopathology of Children and Adolescents: A Meta-analysis," *Clinical Psychology Review* 33, no. 1 (2013): 97–106.

46. Nicole Campione-Barr, Kelly Bassett Greer, and Anna Kruse, "Differential Associations Between Domains of Sibling Conflict and Adolescent Emotional Adjustment," *Child Development* 84, no. 3 (2013): 938–54.

47. Buist, Deković, and Prinzie, "Sibling Relationship Quality and Psychopathology of Children and Adolescents: A Meta-analysis."

48. Paula Fomby, Joshua A. Goode, and Stefanie Mollborn, "Family Complexity, Siblings, and Children's Aggressive Behavior at School Entry," *Demography* 53, no. 1 (2016): 1–26; Paula Fomby and Andrew J. Cherlin, "Family Instability and Child Well-Being," *American Sociological Review* 72, no. 2 (2007): 181–204.

49. Pew Social Trends, "Parenting in America."

50. Ronald M. Rapee, "Potential Role of Childrearing Practices in the Development of Anxiety and Depression," *Clinical Psychology Review* 17, no. 1 (1997): 47–67; Marie Bee Hui Yap et al., "Parental Factors Associated with Depression and Anxiety in Young People: A Systematic Review and Meta-analysis," *Journal of Affective Disorders* 156(2014): 8–23.

51. In the psychiatric literature, experiences of this sort are considered adverse childhood experiences. there is an extensive literature connecting such experiences to various dimensions of adult health. Melissa T. Merrick et al., "Prevalence of Adverse Childhood Experiences from the 2011–2014 Behavioral Risk Factor Surveillance System in 23 States," *JAMA Pediatrics* 172, no. 11 (2018): 1038–44.

6. THE DECLINE IN RELIGIOUS PARTICIPATION

1. Christian Smith, *Lost in Transition: The Dark Side of Emerging Adulthood* (New York: Oxford University Press, 2011).

2. Paul Vitz and Bruce Buff, "Adolescents in Crisis: Why We Need to Recover Religion," *National Review*, July 27, 2017, https://www.nationalreview.com/2017/07/teen-suicides-depression-anxiety-rising-religion-can-help.

3. Emma Green, "How Will Young People Choose Their Religion?," *Atlantic*, March 20, 2016, https://www.theatlantic.com/politics/archive/2016/03/how-will-young-people-choose-their-religion/474366.

4. Michael Hout and Claude S. Fischer, "Explaining Why More Americans Have No Religious Preference: Political Backlash and Generational Succession, 1987–2012," *Sociological Science* 1, no. 24 (2014): 423–47.

5. Ronald Dworkin, *Religion Without God* (Cambridge, Mass.: Harvard University Press, 2013).

6. This section draws on a framework advanced by Christian Smith. Christian Smith, "Theorizing Religious Effects Among American Adolescents," *Journal for the Scientific Study of Religion* 42, no. 1 (2003): 17–30.

7. Christian Smith, *Religion: What It Is, How It Works, and Why It Matters* (Princeton, N.J.: Princeton University Press, 2017), 152.

8. Allen E. Bergin, "Values and Religious Issues in Psychotherapy and Mental Health," *American Psychologist* 46, no. 4 (1991): 394–403, see esp. table 1.

9. Smith, "Theorizing Religious Effects Among American Adolescents."

10. Smith, *Religion: What It Is, How It Works, and Why It Matters*, 180–81.

11. Smith, *Religion: What It Is, How It Works, and Why It Matters*; Peter C. Hill et al., "Conceptualizing Religion and Spirituality: Points of Commonality, Points of Departure," *Journal for the Theory of Social Behaviour* 30, no. 1 (2000): 51–77.
12. Robert D. Putnam and David E. Campbell, *American Grace: How Religion Divides and Unites Us* (New York: Simon & Schuster, 2010).
13. Kathleen M. Brennan and Andrew S. London, "Are Religious People Nice People? Religiosity, Race, Interview Dynamics, and Perceived Cooperativeness," *Sociological Inquiry* 71, no. 2 (2001): 129–44.
14. Smith, *Religion: What It Is, How It Works, and Why It Matters*, see table 4.2.
15. Smith, *Religion: What It Is, How It Works, and Why It Matters*.
16. Putnam and Campbell, *American Grace*, 139.
17. Putnam and Campbell, *American Grace*.
18. Evelyn L. Lehrer and Carmel U. Chiswick, "Religion as a Determinant of Marital Stability," *Demography* 30, no. 3 (1993): 385–404.
19. Putnam and Campbell, *American Grace*, 447.
20. Sigmund Freud, *The Future of an Illusion* (New York: Liveright, 1928).
21. See Hal Ritter, "Anxiety," *Journal of Religion and Health* 29, no. 1 (1990): 49–53.
22. Rollo May, *The Meaning of Anxiety* (New York: Ronald Press, 1950); Paul Tillich, *Dynamics of Faith* (New York: Harper, 1956).
23. William James, *The Varieties of Religious Experience; a Study in Human Nature* (New York: Longmans, Green, 1902).
24. Putnam and Campbell, *American Grace*.
25. Roger Finke and Rodney Starke, *The Churching of America, 1776–2005: Winners and Losers in Our Religious Economy*, 2nd ed. (New Brunswick, N.J.: Rutgers University Press, 2005).
26. Putnam and Campbell, *American Grace*, 97–98.
27. Art Swift, "Majority in U.S. Still Say Religion Can Answer Most Problems," Gallup: Politics, June 2, 2017, http://news.gallup.com/poll/211679/majority-say-religion-answer-problems.aspx.
28. Putnam and Campbell, *American Grace*, fig. 4.7.
29. Putnam and Campbell, *American Grace*, 208.
30. Hout and Fischer, "Explaining Why More Americans Have No Religious Preference: Political Backlash and Generational Succession, 1987–2012."
31. Claude S. Fischer and Michael Hout, *Century of Difference: How America Changed in the Last One Hundred Years* (New York: Russell Sage Foundation, 2006), 207.
32. Gerald Marwell and N. J. Demerath, " 'Secularization' by Any Other Name," *American Sociological Review* 68, no. 2 (2003): 314–16.
33. Michael Hout and Claude S. Fischer, "Why More Americans Have No Religious Preference: Politics and Generations," *American Sociological Review* 67, no. 2 (2002): 165–90.
34. Fischer and Hout, *Century of Difference*, 208.
35. Hout and Fischer, "Why More Americans Have No Religious Preference: Politics and Generations."
36. Hout and Fischer, "Explaining Why More Americans Have No Religious Preference: Political Backlash and Generational Succession, 1987–2012."
37. Hout and Fischer, "Explaining Why More Americans Have No Religious Preference: Political Backlash and Generational Succession, 1987–2012."

38. Duane F. Alwin, "Cohort Replacement and Changes in Parental Socialization Values," *Journal of Marriage and Family* 52, no. 2 (1990): 347–60.
39. Hout and Fischer, "Explaining Why More Americans Have No Religious Preference: Political Backlash and Generational Succession, 1987–2012."
40. Hout and Fischer, "Explaining Why More Americans Have No Religious Preference: Political Backlash and Generational Succession, 1987–2012."
41. Hout and Fischer, "Explaining Why More Americans Have No Religious Preference: Political Backlash and Generational Succession, 1987–2012." Cohort replacement is discussed in detail between pages 432 and 438, from which my discussion draws.
42. Hout and Fischer, "Explaining Why More Americans Have No Religious Preference: Political Backlash and Generational Succession, 1987–2012."
43. Putnam and Campbell, *American Grace*, 98.
44. Robert N. Bellah et al., *Habits of the Heart: Individualism and Commitment in American Life*, First Perennial Library ed. (New York: Harper & Row, 1986).
45. Kenneth I. Pargament, *The Psychology of Religion and Coping: Theory, Research, Practice* (New York: Guilford, 1997).
46. Smith, *Lost in Transition*.
47. Christian Smith and Patricia Snell, *Souls in Transition: The Religious and Spiritual Lives of Emerging Adults* (New York: Oxford University Press, 2009).
48. Smith, *Lost in Transition*, 237.
49. Smith, *Lost in Transition*, 21.
50. Smith, *Lost in Transition*, 29.
51. Smith, *Religion: What It Is, How It Works, and Why It Matters.*
52. Smith and Snell, *Souls in Transition*, see table 9.7.
53. Smith, *Souls in Transition*, table 9.8.
54. James S. House, Deborah Umberson, and Karl R. Landis, "Structures and Processes of Social Support," *Annual Review of Sociology* 14 (1988): 293–318.
55. Karen Turner, "Secularism Is on the Rise, but Americans Are Still Finding Community and Purpose in Spirituality," *Vox*, June 11, 2019, https://www.vox.com/first-person/2019/6/4/18644764/church-religion-atheism-secularism.

7. UNCERTAIN ATTACHMENTS

1. James S. House, Karl R. Landis, and Debra Umberson, "Social Relationships and Health," *Science* 241, no. 4865 (1988): 540–45.
2. Roy F. Baumeister and Mark R. Leary, "The Need to Belong: Desire for Interpersonal Attachments as a Fundamental Human Motivation," *Psychological Bulletin* 117 (1995): 497–529.
3. Robert D. Putnam, *Bowling Alone: The Collapse and Revival of American Community* (New York: Simon & Schuster, 2000).
4. Eric Klinenberg, *Going Solo: The Extraordinary Rise and Surprising Appeal of Living Alone* (New York: Penguin, 2012).
5. Jean M. Twenge, "Birth Cohort Changes in Extraversion: A Cross-Temporal Meta-analysis, 1966–1993," *Personality and Individual Differences* 30, no. 5 (2001): 735–48.

6. Jean M. Twenge, W. Keith Campbell, and Brittany Gentile, "Increases in Individual-istic Words and Phrases in American Books, 1960–2008," *PLoS ONE* 7, no. 7 (2012): e40181; Jean M. Twenge, "Changes in Masculine and Feminine Traits Over Time: A Meta-analysis," *Sex Roles* 36, no. 5 (1997): 305–25.

7. Pamela Paxton, "Is Social Capital Declining in the United States? A Multiple Indi-cator Assessment," *American Journal of Sociology* 105, no. 1 (1999): 88–127.

8. Vance Packard, *A Nation of Strangers* (New York: McKay, 1972).

9. John T. Cacioppo, "Epidemic of Loneliness," *Psychology Today*, May 3, 2009. *https://www.psychologytoday.com/us/blog/connections/200905/epidemic-loneliness*.

10. Scott Schieman and Heather A. Turner, " 'When Feeling Other People's Pain Hurts': The Influence of Psychosocial Resources on the Association Between Self-Reported Empathy and Depressive Symptoms," *Social Psychology Quarterly* 64, no. 4 (2001): 376–89.

11. Anthony Giddens, *Modernity and Self-Identity: Self and Society in the Late Modern Age* (Stanford, Calif.: Stanford University Press, 1991); Anthony Giddens, *The Con-sequences of Modernity* (Stanford, Calif.: Stanford University Press, 1990).

12. Claude S. Fischer, *Still Connected: Family and Friends in America Since 1970* (New York: Russell Sage Foundation, 2011).

13. Keith N. Hampton et al., *Social Media and the Cost of Caring* (Washington, D.C.: Pew Research Center, 2014).

14. Keith N. Hampton et al., *Social Media and the Cost of Caring*.

15. Klinenberg, *Going Solo*.

16. James S. House, Deborah Umberson, and Karl R. Landis, "Structures and Processes of Social Support," *Annual Review of Sociology* 14 (1988): 293–318.

17. Niall Bolger, Adam Zuckerman, and Ronald C. Kessler, "Invisible Support and Adjustment to Stress," *Journal of Personality and Social Psychology* 79, no. 6 (2000): 953–61.

18. Sidney Cobb, "Social Support as a Moderator of Life Stress," *Psychosomatic Medi-cine* 38 (1976): 300–14.

19. Barbara R. Sarason et al., "Perceived Social Support and Working Models of Self and Actual Others," *Journal of Personality and Social Psychology* 60, no. 2 (1991): 273–87; I. G. Sarason, B. R. Sarason, and E. N. Shearin, "Social Support as Indi-vidual Difference Variable," *Journal of Personality and Social Psychology* 50(1986): 845–55.

20. Fischer, *Still Connected: Family and Friends in America Since 1970*.

21. Adam Isen and Betsey Stevenson, "Women's Education and Family Behavior: Trends in Marriage, Divorce and Fertility," National Bureau of Economic Research Working Paper Series No. 15725, Cambridge, Mass.: National Bureau of Economic Research, 2010.

22. Fischer, *Still Connected*, 26.

23. Fischer, *Still Connected*.

24. National Academies of Sciences, Engineering, and Medicine, *The Integration of Immigrants Into American Society* (Washington, D.C.: National Academies Press, 2015).

25. National Academies of Sciences, Engineering, and Medicine, *The Integration of Immigrants into American Society*, see esp. chap. 8.

26. Chiungjung Huang, "Internet Use and Psychological Well-Being: A Meta-analysis," *Cyberpsychology, Behavior, and Social Networking* 13, no. 3 (2010): 241–49.
27. Robert Kraut et al., "Internet Paradox: A Social Technology That Reduces Social Involvement and Psychological Well-Being?" *American Psychologist* 53, no. 9 (1998): 1017–31.
28. Ethan Kross et al., "Facebook Use Predicts Declines in Subjective Well-Being in Young Adults," *PLoS ONE* 8, no. 8 (2013): e69841.
29. Fischer, *Still Connected*, fig. 4.1.
30. Fischer, *Still Connected*, fig. 4.12.
31. Fischer, *Still Connected*, fig. 3.1.
32. Fischer, *Still Connected*, fig. 3.13.
33. Fischer, *Still Connected*, fig. 5.5.
34. Alfred DeMaris and K. Vaninadha Rao, "Premarital Cohabitation and Subsequent Marital Stability in the United States: A Reassessment," *Journal of Marriage and Family* 54, no. 1 (1992): 178–90.
35. Fischer, *Still Connected*, figs. 6.3, 6.4.
36. Sara H. Konrath et al., "Changes in Adult Attachment Styles in American College Students Over Time: A Meta-analysis," *Personality and Social Psychology Review* 18, no. 4 (2014): 326–48.
37. Konrath et al., "Changes in Adult Attachment Styles in American College Students Over Time: A Meta-analysis."
38. Elizabeth M. Bertera, "Mental Health in U.S. Adults: The Role of Positive Social Support and Social Negativity in Personal Relationships," *Journal of Social and Personal Relationships* 22, no. 1 (2005): 33–48.
39. Bertera, "Mental Health in U.S. Adults: The Role of Positive Social Support and Social Negativity in Personal Relationships," see table 4; see also Karen D. Lincoln et al., "Emotional Support, Negative Interaction and DSM-IV Lifetime Disorders Among Older African Americans: Findings from the National Survey of American Life (NSAL)," *International Journal of Geriatric Psychiatry* 25, no. 6 (2010): 612–21.
40. Jason T. Newsom et al., "The Relative Importance of Three Domains of Positive and Negative Social Exchanges: A Longitudinal Model with Comparable Measures," *Psychology and Aging* 18, no. 4 (2003): 746–54.
41. Amanda L. Forest and Joanne V. Wood, "When Social Networking Is Not Working: Individuals with Low Self-Esteem Recognize but Do Not Reap the Benefits of Self-Disclosure on Facebook," *Psychological Science* 23, no. 3 (2012): 295–302.
42. Hampton et al., *Social Media and the Cost of Caring*.
43. John Bowlby, *Attachment and Loss*, Vol. 2, *Separation, Anxiety and Anger* (New York: Basic Books, 1973).
44. Vivian Zayas et al., "Roots of Adult Attachment: Maternal Caregiving at 18 Months Predicts Adult Peer and Partner Attachment," *Social Psychological and Personality Science* 2, no. 3 (2010): 289–97; Judith A. Feeney and Patricia Noller, "Attachment Style as a Predictor of Adult Romantic Relationships," *Journal of Personality and Social Psychology* 58, no. 2 (1990): 281–91; Jude Cassidy et al., "Generalized Anxiety Disorder: Connections with Self-Reported Attachment," *Behavior Therapy* 40, no. 1 (2009): 23–38.
45. Zayas et al., "Roots of Adult Attachment."

46. Cindy Hazan and Phillip Shaver, "Romantic Love Conceptualized as an Attachment Process," *Journal of Personality and Social Psychology* 52, no. 3 (1987): 511–24; Paula R. Pietromonaco and Lisa Feldman Barrett, "Working Models of Attachment and Daily Social Interactions," *Journal of Personality and Social Psychology* 73, no. 6 (1997): 1409–23.
47. Enrico DiTommaso et al., "Attachment Styles, Social Skills and Loneliness in Young Adults," *Personality and Individual Differences* 35, no. 2 (2003): 303–12.
48. Konrath et al., "Changes in Adult Attachment Styles in American College Students Over Time: A Meta-analysis."
49. Konrath et al., "Changes in Adult Attachment Styles in American College Students Over Time: A Meta-analysis," 333.
50. Shawn M. Bergman et al., "Millennials, Narcissism, and Social Networking: What Narcissists Do on Social Networking Sites and Why," *Personality and Individual Differences* 50, no. 5 (2011): 706–11.
51. George W. Brown, T. O. Harris, and M. J. Eales, "Aetiology of Anxiety and Depressive Disorders in an Inner-City Population. II. Comorbidity and Adversity," *Psychological Medicine* 23, no. 1 (1993): 155–65; David Goldberg et al., "The Influence of Social Factors on Common Mental Disorders. Destabilisation and Restitution," *British Journal of Psychiatry* 156, no. 5 (1990): 704.
52. R. Prudo, T. Harris, and G. W. Brown, "Psychiatric Disorder in a Rural and an Urban Population: 3. Social Integration and the Morphology of Affective Disorder," *Psychological Medicine* 14, no. 2 (1984): 327–45; George W. Brown and Ray Prudo, "Psychiatric Disorder in a Rural and an Urban Population: I. Aetiology of Depression," *Psychological Medicine* 11, no. 3 (1981): 581–99.
53. George W. Brown and Tirril Brown Harris, *Social Origins of Depression: A Study of Psychiatric Disorder in Women* (London: Tavistock, 1978); Robert Finlay-Jones and George W. Brown, "Types of Stressful Life Event and the Onset of Anxiety and Depressive Disorders," *Psychological Medicine* 11, no. 4 (1981): 803–15.

8. STATUS ANXIETY AND GROWING INEQUALITY

1. Stanley Lebergott, *Pursuing Happiness: American Consumers in the Twentieth Century* (Princeton, N.J.: Princeton University Press, 1993); Claude S. Fischer and Michael Hout, *Century of Difference: How America Changed in the Last One Hundred Years* (New York: Russell Sage Foundation, 2006).
2. Fischer and Hout, *Century of Difference*, fig. 6.6.
3. Edward N. Wolff, "Household Wealth Trends in the United States, 1962 to 2013: What Happened Over the Great Recession?" *RSF: The Russell Sage Foundation Journal of the Social Sciences* 2, no. 6 (2016): 24–43.
4. Fischer and Hout, *Century of Difference*, fig. 6.5.
5. Dirk Krueger and Fabrizio Perri, "Does Income Inequality Lead to Consumption Inequality? Evidence and Theory," *Review of Economic Studies* 73, no. 1 (2006): 163–93.
6. Kevin M. White and Samuel H. Preston, "How Many Americans Are Alive Because of Twentieth-Century Improvements in Mortality?" *Population and Development Review* 22, no. 3 (1996): 415–29.

7. Leslie McCall and Christine Percheski, "Income Inequality: New Trends and Research Directions," *Annual Review of Sociology* 36, no. 1 (2010): 329–47; Claudia Goldin and Lawrence F. Katz, "Decreasing (and Then Increasing) Inequality in America: A Tale of Two Half Centuries," in *The Causes and Consequences of Increasing Inequality*, ed. F. Welch (Chicago: University of Chicago Press, 2001).

8. Fischer and Hout, *Century of Difference*.

9. Wolff, "Short Household Wealth Trends in the United States, 1962 to 2013: What Happened Over the Great Recession?"

10. Fischer and Hout, *Century of Difference*.

11. Wolff, "Short Household Wealth Trends in the United States, 1962 to 2013: What Happened Over the Great Recession?"

12. Bruce Western, Deirdre Bloome, and Christine Percheski, "Inequality Among American Families with Children, 1975 to 2005," *American Sociological Review* 73, no. 6 (2008): 903–20.

13. Edward N. Wolff, "Wealth Accumulation by Age Cohort in the U.S., 1962–1992: The Role of Savings, Capital Gains and Intergenerational Transfers," *The Geneva Papers on Risk and Insurance. Issues and Practice* 24, no. 1 (1999): 27–49.

14. Teresa A. Sullivan, Elizabeth Warren, and Jay Lawrence Westbrook, *The Fragile Middle Class: Americans in Debt* (New Haven, Conn.: Yale University Press, 2008).

15. Meta Brown et al., "The Financial Crisis at the Kitchen Table: Trends in Household Debt and Credit," *Current Issues in Economics and Finance* 19, no. 2 (2013): 1–10.

16. Wolff, "Short Household Wealth Trends in the United States, 1962 to 2013," table 5.

17. Wolff, "Short Household Wealth Trends in the United States, 1962 to 2013."

18. Shruti Yamini and Bipin Deokar, "Declining Household Savings," *Economic and Political Weekly* 47, no. 50 (2012): 75–77.

19. Fischer and Hout, *Century of Difference*, fig. 6.7.

20. David Card, "The Effect of Unions on Wage Inequality in the U.S. Labor Market," *ILR Review* 54, no. 2 (2001): 296–315.

21. Titan M. Alon et al., "The Impact of Covid-19 on Gender Equality," National Bureau of Economic Research Working Paper Series No. 26947 (Cambridge, Mass.: National Bureau of Economic Research, 2020).

22. Cecilia L. Ridgeway, "Why Status Matters for Inequality," *American Sociological Review* 79, no. 1 (2013): 1–16.

23. Ivan D. Chase et al., "Individual Differences Versus Social Dynamics in the Formation of Animal Dominance Hierarchies," *Proceedings of the National Academy of Sciences of the United States of America* 99, no. 8 (2002): 5744–49.

24. Chase et al., "Individual Differences Versus Social Dynamics in the Formation of Animal Dominance Hierarchies."

25. Thorstein Veblen, *The Theory of the Leisure Class* (New York: Modern Library, 2001).

26. Ivan D. Chase and W. B. Lindquist, "Dominance Hierarchies," in *The Oxford Handbook of Analytical Sociology*, ed. Peter Hedström and Peter Bearman (Oxford: Oxford University Press, 2009), 566–91.

27. Robert M. Sapolsky, "Social Status and Health in Humans and Other Animals," *Annual Review of Anthropology* 33 (2004): 393–418.

28. Christopher R. von Rueden and Adrian V. Jaeggi, "Men's Status and Reproductive Success in 33 Nonindustrial Societies: Effects of Subsistence, Marriage System,

and Reproductive Strategy," *Proceedings of the National Academy of Sciences of the United States of America* 113, no. 39 (2016): 10824.

29. Rosemary L. Hopcroft, "Sex, Status, and Reproductive Success in the Contemporary United States," *Evolution and Human Behavior* 27, no. 2 (2006): 104–20.

30. Robert H. Frank, *Choosing the Right Pond* (New York: Oxford University Press, 1984).

31. John C. Harsanyi, "A Bargaining Model for Social Status in Informal Groups and Formal Organizations," in *Essays on Ethics, Social Behavior, and Scientific Explanation*, ed. John C. Harsanyi (Dordrecht: Springer Netherlands, 1976); Cameron Anderson, John Angus D. Hildreth, and Laura Howland, "Is the Desire for Status a Fundamental Human Motive? A Review of the Empirical Literature," *Psychological Bulletin* 141, no. 3 (2015): 574–601.

32. Jessica L. Tracy and David Matsumoto, "The Spontaneous Expression of Pride and Shame: Evidence for Biologically Innate Nonverbal Displays," *Proceedings of the National Academy of Sciences of the United States of America* 105, no. 33 (2008): 11655.

33. Rob M. A. Nelissen and Marijn H. C. Meijers, "Social Benefits of Luxury Brands as Costly Signals of Wealth and Status," *Evolution and Human Behavior* 32, no. 5 (2011): 343–55.

34. Anderson, Hildreth, and Howland, "Is the Desire for Status a Fundamental Human Motive? A Review of the Empirical Literature"; Cameron Anderson et al., "Knowing Your Place: Self-Perceptions of Status in Face-to-Face Groups," *Journal of Personality and Social Psychology* 91, no. 6 (2006): 1094–110; Marc A. Fournier, "Adolescent Hierarchy Formation and the Social Competition Theory of Depression," *Journal of Social and Clinical Psychology* 28, no. 9 (2009): 1144–72; Marianne Schmid Mast and Judith A. Hall, "Who Is the Boss and Who Is Not? Accuracy of Judging Status," *Journal of Nonverbal Behavior* 28, no. 3 (2004): 145–65.

35. I. M. Dunbar Robin, "The Social Brain Hypothesis," *Evolutionary Anthropology: Issues, News, and Reviews* 6, no. 5 (1998): 178–90.

36. MaryAnn P. Noonan et al., "A Neural Circuit Covarying with Social Hierarchy in Macaques," *PLoS Biology* 12, no. 9 (2014): e1001940; J. Sallet et al., "Social Network Size Affects Neural Circuits in Macaques," *Science* 334, no. 6056 (2011): 697–700.

37. Caroline F. Zink et al., "Know Your Place: Neural Processing of Social Hierarchy in Humans," *Neuron* 58, no. 2 (2008): 273–83; Noriya Watanabe and Miyuki Yamamoto, "Neural Mechanisms of Social Dominance," *Frontiers in Neuroscience* 9, no. 154 (2015): 1–14; Ralph Adolphs, "Is the Human Amygdala Specialized for Processing Social Information?," *Annals of the New York Academy of Sciences* 985 (2003): 326–40.

38. C. Fine, J. Lumsden, and R. J. R. Blair, "Dissociation Between 'Theory of Mind' and Executive Functions in a Patient with Early Left Amygdala Damage," *Brain* 124, no. 2 (2001): 287–98.

39. Ridgeway, "Why Status Matters for Inequality."

40. Sally S. Dickerson and Margaret E. Kemeny, "Acute Stressors and Cortisol Responses: A Theoretical Integration and Synthesis of Laboratory Research," *Psychological Bulletin* 130, no. 3 (2004): 355–91.

41. Lisa M. Shin and Israel Liberzon, "The Neurocircuitry of Fear, Stress, and Anxiety Disorders," *Neuropsychopharmacology* 35, no. 1 (2010): 169–91.

42. James K. Rilling, James T. Winslow, and Clinton D. Kilts, "The Neural Correlates of Mate Competition in Dominant Male Rhesus Macaques," *Biological Psychiatry* 56, no. 5 (2004): 364–75.

43. Sapolsky, "Social Status and Health in Humans and Other Animals."

44. Donald A. Redelmeier and Sheldon M. Singh, "Survival in Academy Award–winning Actors and Actresses," *Annals of Internal Medicine* 134, no. 10 (2001): 955–62; Bruce G. Link, Richard M. Carpiano, and Margaret M. Weden, "Can Honorific Awards Give Us Clues About the Connection Between Socioeconomic Status and Mortality?" *American Sociological Review* 78, no. 2 (2013): 192–212.

45. Link, Carpiano, and Weden, "Can Honorific Awards Give Us Clues About the Connection Between Socioeconomic Status and Mortality?"

46. Tara L. Gruenewald, Margaret E. Kemeny, and Najib Aziz, "Subjective Social Status Moderates Cortisol Responses to Social Threat," *Brain, Behavior, and Immunity* 20, no. 4 (2006): 410–19.

47. Matthew A. Andersson, "An Odd Ladder to Climb: Socioeconomic Differences Across Levels of Subjective Social Status," *Social Indicators Research* 136, no. 2 (2018): 621–43.

48. Robert H. Frank, *Luxury Fever: Money and Happiness in an Era of Excess* (Bryn Mawr, Penn.: American College, 2000).

49. Benjamin M. Friedman, *The Moral Consequences of Economic Growth* (New York: Knopf, 2005).

50. Richard Thaler, "Toward a Positive Theory of Consumer Choice," *Journal of Economic Behavior & Organization* 1, no. 1 (1980): 39–60.

51. The ladder question is included in numerous surveys, though the text for this version is drawn from the survey used in this chapter. Margarita Alegria, James S. (James Sidney) Jackson, Ronald C. Kessler, and David Takeuchi, Collaborative Psychiatric Epidemiology Surveys (CPES), 2001–2003 [United States] (Ann Arbor, Mich.: Inter-university Consortium for Political and Social Research [distributor], 2016), https://doi.org/10.3886/ICPSR20240.v8)

9. THE ASCENT OF ANXIETY AS A THERAPEUTIC TARGET

1. Mickey C. Smith, *Small Comfort: A History of the Minor Tranquilizers* (New York: Praeger, 1985). Smith provides the first and perhaps most comprehensive history of minor tranquilizers, discussing in particular the "life cycle" of the drugs discussed here and their attendant controversies.

2. Sumit D. Agarwal and Bruce E. Landon, "Patterns in Outpatient Benzodiazepine Prescribing in the United States," *JAMA Network Open* 2, no. 1 (2019): e187399–e99.

3. Andrea Tone, *The Age of Anxiety: A History of America's Turbulent Affair with Tranquilizers* (New York: Basic, 2009); David L. Herzberg, *Happy Pills in America: From Miltown to Prozac* (Baltimore, Md.: Johns Hopkins University Press, 2009). The review presented in this chapter draws from the work of Tone and Herzberg. Tone provides a comprehensive history of tranquilizers, including especially Miltown. Herzberg provides a historical review of a more comprehensive set of psychiatric drugs.

4. Herzberg, *Happy Pills in America*, 207.

5. Hugh J. Parry et al., "National Patterns of Psychotherapeutic Drug Use," *Archives of General Psychiatry* 28, no. 6 (1973): 769–83.

6. Herzberg, *Happy Pills in America*.

7. Herzberg, *Happy Pills in America*, esp. p. 32.

8. American Psychiatric Association, *Diagnostic and Statistical Manual of Mental Disorders* (Washington, D.C.: American Psychiatric Association, 1952).

9. Lowell S. Selling, "Clinical Study of a New Tranquilizing Drug: Use of Miltown (2-Methyl-2-N-Propyl-1, 3-Propanediol Dicarbamate)," *Journal of the American Medical Association* 157, no. 18 (1955): 1594–96; Joseph C. Borrus, "Study of Effect of Miltown (2-Methyl-2-N-Propyl-1, 3-Propanediol Dicarbamate) on Psychiatric States," *Journal of the American Medical Association* 157, no. 18 (1955): 1596–98.

10. Selling, "Clinical Study of a New Tranquilizing Drug: Use of Miltown (2-Methyl-2-N-Propyl-1, 3-Propanediol Dicarbamate)."

11. Borrus, "Study of Effect of Miltown (2-Methyl-2-N-Propyl-1, 3-Propanediol Dicarbamate) on Psychiatric States."

12. M. Ralph Kaufman and Stanley Bernstein, "A Psychiatric Evaluation of the Problem Patient: Study of a Thousand Cases from a Consultation Service," *Journal of the American Medical Association* 163, no. 2 (1957): 108–11.

13. Herzberg, *Happy Pills in America*. Herzberg provides an analysis of the advertisements appearing in the pages of JAMA (p. 34).

14. Harold E. Himwich, "The New Psychiatric Drugs," *Scientific American* 193, no. 4 (1955): 80–87; Harold E. Himwich, "Psychopharmacologic Drugs," *Science* 127, no. 3289 (1958): 59–72.

15. Himwich, "The New Psychiatric Drugs," 86.

16. Himwich, "Psychopharmacologic Drugs," 61.

17. Himwich, "Psychopharmacologic Drugs," 61.

18. Himwich, "Psychopharmacologic Drugs," 61.

19. Victor G. Laties and Bernard Weiss, "A Critical Review of the Efficacy of Meprobamate (Miltown, Equanil) in the Treatment of Anxiety," *Journal of Chronic Diseases* 7, no. 6 (1958): 500–19.

20. Laties and Weiss, "A Critical Review of the Efficacy of Meprobamate (Miltown, Equanil) in the Treatment of Anxiety."

21. Laties and Weiss, "A Critical Review of the Efficacy of Meprobamate (Miltown, Equanil) in the Treatment of Anxiety," 502.

22. H. Angus Bowes, "The Role of Diazepam (Valium) in Emotional Illness," *Psychosomatics* 6, no. 5 (1965): 336–40.

23. Bowes, "The Role of Diazepam (Valium) in Emotional Illness," 336–37.

24. Herzberg, *Happy Pills in America*.

25. Herzberg, *Happy Pills in America*, 39.

26. Carl Salzman, "The APA Task Force Report on Benzodiazepine Dependence, Toxicity, and Abuse," *American Journal of Psychiatry* 148, no. 2 (1991): 151–52.

27. Allan V. Horwitz and Jerome C. Wakefield, *The Loss of Sadness: How Psychiatry Transformed Normal Sorrow Into Depressive Disorder* (New York: Oxford University, 2007). Horwitz and Wakefield discuss the ascent of SSRIs in detail within the context of their critique concerning the definition of major depression in the *DSM*.

28. Haiden A. Huskamp et al., "Generic Entry, Reformulations and Promotion of SSRIs in the U.S.," *PharmacoEconomics* 26, no. 7 (2008): 603–16.

29. Jerrold F. Rosenbaum, "Attitudes Toward Benzodiazepines Over the Years," *Journal of Clinical Psychiatry* 66, no. S2 (2005): 4–8, 5.
30. Rosenbaum, "Attitudes Toward Benzodiazepines Over the Years."
31. Hagop Souren Akiskal, "Toward a Definition of Generalized Anxiety Disorder as an Anxious Temperament Type," *Acta Psychiatrica Scandinavica* 98 (1998): 66–73.
32. Hagop Souren Akiskal, "Anxiety: Definition, Relationship to Depression, and Proposal for an Integrative Model," in *Anxiety and the Anxiety Disorders*, ed. A. Hussain Tuma and Jack D. Maser (Hillsdale, N.J.: Erlbaum, 1985).
33. Akiskal, "Toward a Definition of Generalized Anxiety Disorder as an Anxious Temperament Type," 68.
34. Ronald M. Rapee and David H. Barlow, *Chronic Anxiety: Generalized Anxiety Disorder and Mixed Anxiety-Depression* (New York: Guilford, 1991).
35. Mark Zimmerman and Jill I. Mattia, "Psychiatric Diagnosis in Clinical Practice: Is Comorbidity Being Missed?," *Comprehensive Psychiatry* 40, no. 3 (1999): 182–91.
36. Allan V. Horwitz, "How an Age of Anxiety Became an Age of Depression," *Milbank Quarterly* 88, no. 1 (2010): 112–38; Benjamin G. Druss et al., "Listening to Generic Prozac: Winners, Losers, and Sideliners," *Health Affairs* 23, no. 5 (2004): 210–16.
37. Horwitz, "How an Age of Anxiety Became an Age of Depression."
38. Horwitz, "How an Age of Anxiety Became an Age of Depression."
39. Stephen M. Stahl, "Don't Ask, Don't Tell, but Benzodiazepines Are Still the Leading Treatments for Anxiety Disorder," *Journal of Clinical Psychiatry* 63, no. 9 (2002): 756–57, Table 2.
40. Tone, *The Age of Anxiety: A History of America's Turbulent Affair with Tranquilizers*, esp. pp. 212–13.
41. E. H. Uhlenhuth et al., "International Study of Expert Judgment on Therapeutic Use of Benzodiazepines and Other Psychotherapeutic Medications: 6. Trends in Recommendations for the Pharmacotherapy of Anxiety Disorders, 1992–1997," *Depression and Anxiety* 9, no. 3 (1999): 107–16; American Psychiatric Association, Task Force on Benzodiazepine Dependence, Toxicity, and Abuse, *Benzodiazepine Dependence, Toxicity, and Abuse: A Task Force Report of the American Psychiatric Association* (Washington, D.C.: American Psychiatric Association, 1990).
42. Stahl, "Don't Ask, Don't Tell, but Benzodiazepines Are Still the Leading Treatments for Anxiety Disorder."
43. Vladan Starcevic, "Benzodiazepines for Anxiety Disorders: Maximising the Benefits and Minimising the Risks," *Advances in Psychiatric Treatment* 18, no. 4 (2012): 250–58.
44. S. Pampallona et al., "Patient Adherence in the Treatment of Depression," *British Journal of Psychiatry* 180, no. 2 (2002): 104–09.
45. Patrick P. Gleason et al., "Correlates and Prevalence of Benzodiazepine Use in Community-dwelling Elderly," *Journal of General Internal Medicine* 13, no. 4 (1998): 243–50.
46. Tone, *The Age of Anxiety: A History of America's Turbulent Affair with Tranquilizers*; Andrea Tone, "From Naughty Goods to Nicole Miller: Medicine and the Marketing of American Contraceptives," *Culture, Medicine and Psychiatry* 30, no. 2 (2006): 249–67.
47. Kara Zivin Bambauer, James E. Sabin, and Stephen B. Soumerai, "The Exclusion of Benzodiazepine Coverage in Medicare: Simple Steps for Avoiding a Public Health Crisis," *Psychiatric Services* 56, no. 9 (2005): 1143–46.

48. The text of the bill is available at: https://www.congress.gov/109/bills/hr3151/BILLS -109hr3151ih.pdf.

49. Ibid., 2.

50. Charles Ornstein and Ryann Grochowski Jones, "One Nation, Under Sedation: Medicare Paid for Nearly 40 Million Tranquilizer Prescriptions in 2013," *ProPublica*, June 10, 2015. https://www.propublica.org/article/medicare-paid-for-nearly-40-million -tranquilizer-prescriptions-in-2013.

51. Agarwal and Landon, "Patterns in Outpatient Benzodiazepine Prescribing in the United States."

52. Agarwal and Landon, "Patterns in Outpatient Benzodiazepine Prescribing in the United States."

53. Marcus A. Bachhuber, Sean Hennessy, Chinazo O. Cunningham, and Joanna L. Starrels, "Increasing Benzodiazepine Prescriptions and Overdose Mortality in the United States, 1996–2013," *American Journal of Public Health* 106, no. 4 (2016): 686–88.

54. Agarwal and Landon, "Patterns in Outpatient Benzodiazepine Prescribing in the United States."

55. United States Department of Health and Human Services, Centers for Disease Control and Prevention, National Center for Health Statistics, National Ambulatory Medical Care Survey (Ann Arbor, Mich.: Inter-university Consortium for Political and Social Research [distributor]), https://www.icpsr.umich.edu/icpsrweb /NACDA/series/37.

56. Don Schneider, Linda Appleton, and Thomas McLemore, *A Reason for Visit Classification for Ambulatory Care* (DHEW Publication No. 79-1352, Hyattsville, Md.: U.S. Department of Health, Education, and Welfare, 1979).

57. Alexander S. Young et al., "The Quality of Care for Depressive and Anxiety Disorders in the United States," *Archives of General Psychiatry* 58, no. 1 (2001): 55–61.

58. Monica Vermani, Madalyn Marcus, and Martin A. Katzman, "Rates of Detection of Mood and Anxiety Disorders in Primary Care: A Descriptive, Cross-Sectional Study," *Primary Care Companion to CNS Disorders* 13, no. 2 (2011): PCC.10m01013.

10. THE PAST, PRESENT, AND FUTURE OF FEAR

1. Roxane Cohen Silver et al., "Mental- and Physical-Health Effects of Acute Exposure to Media Images of the September 11, 2001, Attacks and the Iraq War," *Psychological Science* 24, no. 9 (2013): 1623–34; William E. Schlenger et al., "Psychological Reactions to Terrorist Attacks: Findings from the National Study of Americans' Reactions to September 11," *Journal of the American Medical Association* 288, no. 5 (2002): 581–88; Mark A. Schuster et al., "A National Survey of Stress Reactions After the September 11, 2001, Terrorist Attacks," *New England Journal of Medicine* 345, no. 20 (2001): 1507–12.

2. Andrea Tone, *The Age of Anxiety: A History of America's Turbulent Affair with Tranquilizers* (New York: Basic Books, 2009); Patricia Cohen et al., "Current Affairs and the Public Psyche: American Anxiety in the Post 9/11 World," *Social Psychiatry and Psychiatric Epidemiology* 41, no. 4 (2006): 251–60; Schlenger et al., "Psychological Reactions to Terrorist Attacks: Findings from the National Study of Americans' Reactions to September 11."

3. Schuster et al., "A National Survey of Stress Reactions After the September 11, 2001, Terrorist Attacks."

4. eorge M. Beard, *American Nervousness: Its Causes and Consequences* (New York: G. P. Putnam's Sons, 1881).

5. Sherman A. Lee, "Coronavirus Anxiety Scale: A Brief Mental Health Screener for Covid-19 Related Anxiety," *Death Studies* 44, no. 7 (2020): 393–401.

6. Yeen Huang and Ning Zhao, "Mental Health Burden for the Public Affected by the Covid-19 Outbreak in China: Who Will Be the High-Risk Group?," *Psychology, Health & Medicine* (2020): 1–12.

7. Eric D. Miller, "The Covid-19 Pandemic Crisis: The Loss and Trauma Event of Our Time," *Journal of Loss and Trauma* 25, nos. 6–7 (2020): 560–72.

8. Miller, "The Covid-19 Pandemic Crisis: The Loss and Trauma Event of Our Time"; Brenda K. Wiederhold, "Using Social Media to Our Advantage: Alleviating Anxiety During a Pandemic," *Cyberpsychology, Behavior, and Social Networking* 23, no. 4 (2020): 197–98.

9. Aviva Lucas Gutnick et al., *Always Connected: The New Digital Media Habits of Young Children* (New York: Joan Ganz Cooney Center at Sesame Workshop, 2011).

10. Robert D. Putnam, *Bowling Alone: The Collapse and Revival of American Community* (New York: Simon & Schuster, 2000).

11. Claude S. Fischer, *Still Connected: Family and Friends in America Since 1970* (New York: Russell Sage Foundation, 2011).

12. Christopher Lasch, *The Culture of Narcissism: American Life in an Age of Diminishing Expectations* (New York: Norton, 1978).

13. Emma E. McGinty et al., "Trends in News Media Coverage of Mental Illness in the United States: 1995–2014," *Health Affairs* 35, no. 6 (2016): 1121–29.

14. J. Alonso et al., "Association of Perceived Stigma and Mood and Anxiety Disorders: Results from the World Mental Health Surveys," *Acta Psychiatrica Scandinavica* 118, no. 4 (2008): 305–14.

15. Lisa Wood et al., "Public Perceptions of Stigma Towards People with Schizophrenia, Depression, and Anxiety," *Psychiatry Research* 220, no. 1 (2014): 604–08.

16. Wood et al., "Public Perceptions of Stigma Towards People with Schizophrenia, Depression, and Anxiety."

17. Philip J. Batterham et al., "Predictors of Generalized Anxiety Disorder Stigma," *Psychiatry Research* 206, no. 2 (2013): 282–86.

18. Matthew S. Lebowitz, John J. Pyun, and Woo-kyoung Ahn, "Biological Explanations of Generalized Anxiety Disorder: Effects on Beliefs About Prognosis and Responsibility," *Psychiatric Services* 65, no. 4 (2014): 498–503.

19. Alison L. Neil and Helen Christensen, "Efficacy and Effectiveness of School-based Prevention and Early Intervention Programs for Anxiety," *Clinical Psychology Review* 29, no. 3 (2009): 208–15.

20. Neil and Christensen, "Efficacy and Effectiveness of School-based Prevention and Early Intervention Programs for Anxiety."

21. Johanna Boettcher, Babette Renneberg, and Thomas Berger, "Patient Expectations in Internet-based Self-Help for Social Anxiety," *Cognitive Behaviour Therapy* 42, no. 3 (2013): 203–14.

22. Michel J. Dugas et al., "Generalized Anxiety Disorder: A Preliminary Test of a Conceptual Model," *Behaviour Research and Therapy* 36, no. 2 (1998): 215–26.

23. Michelle G. Craske et al., "Qualitative Dimensions of Worry in DSM-III-R Generalized Anxiety Disorder Subjects and Nonanxious Controls," *Behaviour Research and Therapy* 27, no. 4 (1989): 397–402.

24. Hagop Souren Akiskal, "Toward a Definition of Generalized Anxiety Disorder as an Anxious Temperament Type," *Acta Psychiatrica Scandinavica* 98 (1998): 66–73.

25. Akiskal, "Toward a Definition of Generalized Anxiety Disorder as an Anxious Temperament Type," 71–72.

26. Robert A. Aronowitz, "The Converged Experience of Risk and Disease," *Milbank Quarterly* 87, no. 2 (2009): 417–42. Aronowitz writes about the convergence of risk and disease more generally in medicine. If psychiatry is moving in this direction, it is hardly the only specialty to do so.

27. Karl Rickels and Moira A. Rynn, "What Is Generalized Anxiety Disorder?," *Journal of Clinical Psychiatry* 62, no. 11 (2001): 4–12.

28. Guy Griebel and Andrew Holmes, "50 Years of Hurdles and Hope in Anxiolytic Drug Discovery," *Nature Reviews Drug Discovery* 12(2013): 667.

29. Griebel and Holmes, "50 Years of Hurdles and Hope in Anxiolytic Drug Discovery," fig. 5.

30. Pew Research Center, *Global Publics More Upbeat About the Economy* (Washington, D.C., 2017).

31. Pew Research Center, *Most U.S. Teens See Anxiety and Depression as a Major Problem Among Their Peers* (Washington, D.C., 2019).

METHODOLOGICAL APPENDIX

1. Gerald Gurin, *Americans View Their Mental Health: A Nationwide Interview Survey* (New York: Basic, 1960).

2. Ronald C. Kessler and T. Bedirhan Üstün, "The World Mental Health Survey Initiative Version of the World Health Organization Composite International Diagnostic Interview," *International Journal of Methods in Psychiatric Research* 13, no. 2 (2004): 93–121.

3. Kessler and Üstün, "The World Mental Health Survey Initiative Version of the World Health Organization Composite International Diagnostic Interview." The appendix provides many examples of updates in the WMH-CIDI.

4. Christopher Winship and Larry Radbill, "Sampling Weights and Regression Analysis," *Sociological Methods & Research* 23, no. 2 (1994): 230–57.

5. J. Scott Long and Jeremy Freese, *Regression Models for Categorical Dependent Variables Using Stata*, 3rd ed. (College Station, Tex.: Stata Press Publication, Statacorp LP, 2014).

6. Paul D. Allison, "Comparing Logit and Probit Coefficients Across Groups," *Sociological Methods & Research* 28, no. 2 (1999): 186–208.

7. Ottar Hellevik, "Linear Versus Logistic Regression When the Dependent Variable Is a Dichotomy," *Quality & Quantity* 43, no. 1 (2009): 59–74.

8. Paul David Allison, *Missing Data* (Thousand Oaks, Calif.: Sage, 2002).

9. Megan Barke, Rebecca Fribush, and Peter N. Stearns, "Nervous Breakdown in 20th-Century American Culture," *Journal of Social History* 33, no. 3 (2000): 565–84.

10. Carmen P. McLean et al., "Gender Differences in Anxiety Disorders: Prevalence, Course of Illness, Comorbidity and Burden of Illness," *Journal of Psychiatric Research* 45, no. 8 (2011): 1027–35. These authors provide a summary of gender differences in anxiety that is the basis for much of the discussion that follows.

11. McLean et al., "Gender Differences in Anxiety Disorders: Prevalence, Course of Illness, Comorbidity and Burden of Illness."

12. Margaret Altemus, Nilofar Sarvaiya, and C. Neill Epperson, "Sex Differences in Anxiety and Depression Clinical Perspectives," *Frontiers in Neuroendocrinology* 35, no. 3 (2014): 320–30.

13. Altemus, Sarvaiya, and Epperson, "Sex Differences in Anxiety and Depression Clinical Perspectives."

14. Brett J. Deacon et al., "The Anxiety Sensitivity Index—Revised: Psychometric Properties and Factor Structure in Two Nonclinical Samples," *Behaviour Research and Therapy* 41, no. 12 (2003): 1427–49; S. E. Taylor et al., "Biobehavioral Responses to Stress in Females: Tend-and-Befriend, Not Fight-or-Flight," *Psychological Review* 107, no. 3 (2000): 411–29.

15. Bridget F. Grant et al., "The Epidemiology of Social Anxiety Disorder in the United States: Results from the National Epidemiologic Survey on Alcohol and Related Conditions," *Journal of Clinical Psychiatry* 66, no. 11 (2005): 1351–61.

16. Anu Asnaani et al., "A Cross-Ethnic Comparison of Lifetime Prevalence Rates of Anxiety Disorders," *Journal of Nervous and Mental Disease* 198, no. 8 (2010): 551–55.

17. Asnaani et al., "A Cross-Ethnic Comparison of Lifetime Prevalence Rates of Anxiety Disorders."

18. J. A. Neff, "Race and Vulnerability to Stress: An Examination of Differential Vulnerability," *Journal of Personality and Social Psychology* 49, no. 2 (1985): 481–91.

19. Jeanelle S. Ali et al., "Race Differences in Depression Vulnerability Following Hurricane Katrina," *Psychological Trauma: Theory, Research, Practice, and Policy* 9, no. 3 (2017): 317–24.

BIBLIOGRAPHY

Adler, Alfred. *The Individual Psychology of Alfred Adler: A Systematic Presentation in Selections from His Writings*. New York: Basic, 1956.

Adolphs, Ralph. "Is the Human Amygdala Specialized for Processing Social Information?" *Annals of the New York Academy of Sciences* 985 (2003): 326–40.

Agarwal, Sumit D., and Bruce E. Landon. "Patterns in Outpatient Benzodiazepine Prescribing in the United States." *JAMA Network Open* 2, no. 1 (2019): e187399.

Akiskal, Hagop Souren. "Anxiety: Definition, Relationship to Depression, and Proposal for an Integrative Model." In *Anxiety and the Anxiety Disorders*, ed. A. Hussain Tuma and Jack D. Maser, 787–97. Hillsdale, N.J.: Erlbaum, 1985.

——. "Toward a Definition of Generalized Anxiety Disorder as an Anxious Temperament Type." *Acta Psychiatrica Scandinavica* 98 (1998): 66–73.

Alegria, Margarita, James S. Jackson, Ronald C. Kessler, and David Takeuchi. Collaborative Psychiatric Epidemiology Surveys (CPES), 2001–2003, United States. Ann Arbor, Mich.: Inter-university Consortium for Political and Social Research [Distributor], 2016.

Ali, Jeanelle S., Amy S. Farrell, Adam C. Alexander, David R. Forde, Michelle Stockton, and Kenneth D. Ward. "Race Differences in Depression Vulnerability Following Hurricane Katrina." *Psychological Trauma: Theory, Research, Practice, and Policy* 9, no. 3 (2017): 317–24.

Allison, Paul D. "Comparing Logit and Probit Coefficients Across Groups." *Sociological Methods & Research* 28, no. 2 (1999): 186–208.

Allison, Paul David. *Missing Data*. Thousand Oaks, Calif.: Sage, 2002.

Alon, Titan M., Matthias Doepke, Jane Olmstead-Rumsey, and Michèle Tertilt. "The Impact of Covid-19 on Gender Equality." National Bureau of Economic Research Working Paper Series No. 26947. Cambridge, Mass.: National Bureau of Economic Research, 2020.

Alonso, J., A. Buron, R. Bruffaerts, Y. He, J. Posada-Villa, J. P. Lepine, M. C. Angermeyer, et al. "Association of Perceived Stigma and Mood and Anxiety Disorders: Results from the World Mental Health Surveys." *Acta Psychiatrica Scandinavica* 118, no. 4 (2008): 305–14.

Altemus, Margaret, Nilofar Sarvaiya, and C. Neill Epperson. "Sex Differences in Anxiety and Depression Clinical Perspectives." *Frontiers in Neuroendocrinology* 35, no. 3 (2014): 320–30.

Alwin, Duane F. "Cohort Replacement and Changes in Parental Socialization Values." *Journal of Marriage and Family* 52, no. 2 (1990): 347–60.

American Psychiatric Association. *Diagnostic and Statistical Manual of Mental Disorders*. Washington, D.C.: American Psychiatric Association, 1952.

——. *Diagnostic and Statistical Manual of Mental Disorders*. 2nd ed. Washington, D.C.: American Psychiatric Association, 1968.

——. *Diagnostic and Statistical Manual of Mental Disorders*. 3rd ed. Washington, D.C.: American Psychiatric Association, 1980.

——. *Diagnostic and Statistical Manual of Mental Disorders*. 3rd ed. rev. Washington, D.C.: American Psychiatric Association, 1987.

——. *Diagnostic and Statistical Manual of Mental Disorders*. 4th ed. Washington, D.C.: American Psychiatric Association, 1994.

American Psychiatric Association, Task Force on Benzodiazepine Dependence, Toxicity, and Abuse. *Benzodiazepine Dependence, Toxicity, and Abuse: A Task Force Report of the American Psychiatric Association*. Washington, D.C.: American Psychiatric Association, 1990.

Anders, Sherry, Midori Tanaka, and Dennis K. Kinney. "Depression as an Evolutionary Strategy for Defense Against Infection." *Brain, Behavior, and Immunity* 31 (2013): 9–22.

Anderson, Cameron, John Angus D. Hildreth, and Laura Howland. "Is the Desire for Status a Fundamental Human Motive? A Review of the Empirical Literature." *Psychological Bulletin* 141, no. 3 (2015): 574–601.

Anderson, Cameron, Sanjay Srivastava, Jennifer S. Beer, Sandra E. Spataro, and Jennifer A. Chatman. "Knowing Your Place: Self-Perceptions of Status in Face-to-Face Groups." *Journal of Personality and Social Psychology* 91, no. 6 (2006): 1094–110.

Anderson, Kathleen C., and Thomas R. Insel. "The Promise of Extinction Research for the Prevention and Treatment of Anxiety Disorders." *Biological Psychiatry* 60, no. 4 (2006): 319–21.

Andersson, Matthew A. "An Odd Ladder to Climb: Socioeconomic Differences Across Levels of Subjective Social Status." *Social Indicators Research* 136, no. 2 (2018): 621–43.

Andrews, Gavin, Gavin Stewart, Allen Morris-Yates, Phoebe Holt, and Scott Henderson. "Evidence for a General Neurotic Syndrome." *British Journal of Psychiatry* 157, no. 1 (1990): 6–12.

Andrews, Paul W., and J. Anderson Thomson Jr. "The Bright Side of Being Blue: Depression as an Adaptation for Analyzing Complex Problems." *Psychological Review* 116, no. 3 (2009): 620–54.

Aronowitz, Robert A. "The Converged Experience of Risk and Disease." *Milbank Quarterly* 87, no. 2 (2009): 417–42.

Asnaani, Anu, J. Anthony Richey, Ruta Dimaite, Devon E. Hinton, and Stefan G. Hofmann. "A Cross-Ethnic Comparison of Lifetime Prevalence Rates of Anxiety Disorders." *Journal of Nervous and Mental Disease* 198, no. 8 (2010): 551–55.

Atzaba-Poria, Naama, and Alison Pike. "Correlates of Parental Differential Treatment: Parental and Contextual Factors During Middle Childhood." *Child Development* 79, no. 1 (2008): 217–32.

Bambauer, Kara Zivin, James E. Sabin, and Stephen B. Soumerai. "The Exclusion of Benzodiazepine Coverage in Medicare: Simple Steps for Avoiding a Public Health Crisis." *Psychiatric Services* 56, no. 9 (2005): 1143–46.

Ban, Thomas A. "Pharmacotherapy of Mental Illness: A Historical Analysis." *Progress in Neuro-Psychopharmacology and Biological Psychiatry* 25, no. 4 (2001): 709–27.

Bar-Haim, Yair, Dominique Lamy, Lee Pergamin, Marian J. Bakermans-Kranenburg, and Marinus H. van Ijzendoorn. "Threat-Related Attentional Bias in Anxious and Nonanxious Individuals: A Meta-analytic Study." *Psychological Bulletin* 133, no. 1 (2007): 1–24.

Barke, Megan, Rebecca Fribush, and Peter N. Stearns. "Nervous Breakdown in 20th-Century American Culture." *Journal of Social History* 33, no. 3 (2000): 565–84.

Barkow, Katrin, Reinhard Heun, Hans-Ulrich Wittchen, T. Bedirhan Üstün, Michael Gänsicke, and Wolfgang Maier. "Mixed Anxiety–Depression in a 1 Year Follow-up Study: Shift to Other Diagnoses or Remission?" *Journal of Affective Disorders* 79, no. 1 (2004): 235–39.

Barlow, David H. *Anxiety and Its Disorders: The Nature and Treatment of Anxiety and Panic.* 2nd ed. New York: Guilford, 2002.

——. *Anxiety and Its Disorders: The Nature and Treatment of Anxiety and Panic.* New York: Guilford, 1988.

Batelaan, Neeltje M., Jan Spijker, Ron de Graaf, and Pim Cuijpers. "Mixed Anxiety Depression Should Not Be Included in DSM-5." *Journal of Nervous and Mental Disease* 200, no. 6 (2012): 495–98.

Batterham, Philip J., Kathleen M. Griffiths, Lisa J. Barney, and Alison Parsons. "Predictors of Generalized Anxiety Disorder Stigma." *Psychiatry Research* 206, no. 2 (2013): 282–86.

Bachhuber, Marcus A., Sean Hennessy, Chinazo O. Cunningham, and Joanna L. Starrels, "Increasing Benzodiazepine Prescriptions and Overdose Mortality in the United States, 1996–2013," *American Journal of Public Health* 106, no. 4 (2016): 686–88.

Baumeister, Roy F., and Mark R. Leary. "The Need to Belong: Desire for Interpersonal Attachments as a Fundamental Human Motivation." *Psychological Bulletin* 117 (1995): 497–529.

Beard, George M. *American Nervousness: Its Causes and Consequences.* New York: G. P. Putnam's Sons, 1881.

Beard, George Miller. *Neurasthenia (Nerve Exhaustion): With Remarks on Treatment.* St. Louis, 1879.

Beard, George M. "Neurasthenia, or Nervous Exhaustion." *Boston Medical and Surgical Journal* 80, no. 13 (1869): 217–21.

Beck, Aaron T. *Cognitive Therapy and the Emotional Disorders.* New York: International Universities Press, 1976.

Beckfield, Jason. "Remapping Inequality in Europe: The Net Effect of Regional Integration on Total Income Inequality in the European Union." *International Journal of Comparative Sociology* 50, no. 5–6 (2009): 486–509.

Bellah, Robert N., Richard Madsen, William M. Sullivan, Ann Swidler, and Steven M. Tipton. *Habits of the Heart: Individualism and Commitment in American Life.* First Perennial Library ed. New York: Harper & Row, 1986.

Bellew, M., and A. B. Hill. "Negative Recall Bias as a Predictor of Susceptibility to Induced Depressive Mood." *Personality and Individual Differences* 11, no. 5 (1990): 471–80.

Berger, Frank M. "Anxiety and the Discovery of the Tranquilizers." In *Discoveries in Biological Psychiatry*, ed. Frank Ayd and Barry Blackwell, 115–29. Philadelphia: Lippincott, 1970.

Bergin, Allen E. "Values and Religious Issues in Psychotherapy and Mental Health." *American Psychologist* 46, no. 4 (1991): 394–403.

Bergman, Shawn M., Matthew E. Fearrington, Shaun W. Davenport, and Jacqueline Z. Bergman. "Millennials, Narcissism, and Social Networking: What Narcissists Do on Social Networking Sites and Why." *Personality and Individual Differences* 50, no. 5 (2011): 706–11.

Berrios, German E. "Anxiety and Cognate Disorders." In *The History of Mental Symptoms: Descriptive Psychopathology Since the Nineteenth Century*, ed. German E. Berrios, 263–88. Cambridge: Cambridge University Press, 1996.

Berrios, German E., and Ivana S. Marková. "Assessment and Measurement in Neuropsychiatry: A Conceptual History." *Seminars in Clinical Neuropsychiatry* 7, no. 1 (2002): 3–10.

——. "The Concept of Neuropsychiatry: A Historical Overview." *Journal of Psychosomatic Research* 53, no. 2 (2002): 629–38.

Bertera, Elizabeth M. "Mental Health in U.S. Adults: The Role of Positive Social Support and Social Negativity in Personal Relationships." *Journal of Social and Personal Relationships* 22, no. 1 (2005): 33–48.

Bianchi, Suzanne M. "Maternal Employment and Time with Children: Dramatic Change or Surprising Continuity?" *Demography* 37, no. 4 (2000): 401–14.

Blackwell, Barry. "Psychotropic Drugs in Use Today: The Role of Diazepam in Medical Practice." *Journal of the American Medical Association* 225, no. 13 (1973): 1637–41.

Blanchard, D. Caroline, Guy Griebel, and Robert J. Blanchard. "The Mouse Defense Test Battery: Pharmacological and Behavioral Assays for Anxiety and Panic." *European Journal of Pharmacology* 463, no. 1 (2003): 97–116.

Bleuler, M. "Conception of Schizophrenia Within the Last Fifty Years and Today [Abridged]." *Proceedings of the Royal Society of Medicine* 56, no. 10 (1963): 945–52.

Blewett, Lynn A., Julia A. Rivera Drew, Miriam L. King, and Kari C.W. Williams. IPUMS Health Surveys: National Health Interview Survey, Version 6.4 [data set]. Minneapolis, Minn.: IPUMS, 2019. https://doi.org/10.18128/D070.V6.4.

Boettcher, Johanna, Babette Renneberg, and Thomas Berger. "Patient Expectations in Internet-based Self-Help for Social Anxiety." *Cognitive Behaviour Therapy* 42, no. 3 (2013): 203–14.

Bolger, Niall, Adam Zuckerman, and Ronald C. Kessler. "Invisible Support and Adjustment to Stress." *Journal of Personality and Social Psychology* 79, no. 6 (2000): 953–61.

Borrus, Joseph C. "Study of Effect of Miltown (2-Methyl-2-N-Propyl-1, 3-Propanediol Dicarbamate) on Psychiatric States." *Journal of the American Medical Association* 157, no. 18 (1955): 1596–98.

Borsboom, Denny, and Angélique O. J. Cramer. "Network Analysis: An Integrative Approach to the Structure of Psychopathology." *Annual Review of Clinical Psychology* 9, no. 1 (2013): 91–121.

Bourin, Michel. "Animal Models for Screening Anxiolytic-like Drugs: A Perspective." *Dialogues in Clinical Neuroscience* 17, no. 3 (2015): 295–303.

Bowes, H. Angus. "The Role of Diazepam (Valium) in Emotional Illness." *Psychosomatics* 6, no. 5 (1965): 336–40.

Bowlby, John. *Attachment and Loss*. Vol. 2, *Separation, Anxiety and Anger*. New York: Basic, 1973.

Boyle, Michael H., Jennifer M. Jenkins, Katholiki Georgiades, John Cairney, Eric Duku, and Yvonne Racine. "Differential-Maternal Parenting Behavior: Estimating Within- and Between-Family Effects on Children." *Child Development* 75, no. 5 (2004): 1457–76.

Brennan, Kathleen M., and Andrew S. London. "Are Religious People Nice People? Religiosity, Race, Interview Dynamics, and Perceived Cooperativeness." *Sociological Inquiry* 71, no. 2 (2001): 129–44.

Brooker, Rebecca J., Kristin A. Buss, Kathryn Lemery-Chalfant, Nazan Aksan, Richard J. Davidson, and H. Hill Goldsmith. "The Development of Stranger Fear in Infancy and Toddlerhood: Normative Development, Individual Differences, Antecedents, and Outcomes." *Developmental Science* 16, no. 6 (2013): 864–78.

Brown, George W., and Tirril Brown Harris. *Social Origins of Depression: A Study of Psychiatric Disorder in Women*. London: Tavistock, 1978.

Brown, George W., T. O. Harris, and M. J. Eales. "Aetiology of Anxiety and Depressive Disorders in an Inner-City Population. II. Comorbidity and Adversity." *Psychological Medicine* 23, no. 1 (1993): 155–65.

Brown, George W., and Ray Prudo. "Psychiatric Disorder in a Rural and an Urban Population: I. Aetiology of Depression." *Psychological Medicine* 11, no. 3 (1981): 581–99.

Brown, Meta, Andrew Haughwout, Donghoon Lee, and Wilbert van der Klaauw. "The Financial Crisis at the Kitchen Table: Trends in Household Debt and Credit." *Current Issues in Economics and Finance* 19, no. 2 (2013): 1–10.

Brown, Timothy A., Bruce F. Chorpita, and David H. Barlow. "Structural Relationships Among Dimensions of the DSM-IV Anxiety and Mood Disorders and Dimensions of Negative Affect, Positive Affect, and Autonomic Arousal." *Journal of Abnormal Psychology* 107, no. 2 (1998): 179–92.

Buist, Kirsten L., Maja Deković, and Peter Prinzie. "Sibling Relationship Quality and Psychopathology of Children and Adolescents: A Meta-analysis." *Clinical Psychology Review* 33, no. 1 (2013): 97–106.

Bumpass, Larry L., and R. Kelly Raley. "Redefining Single-Parent Families: Cohabitation and Changing Family Reality." *Demography* 32, no. 1 (1995): 97–109.

Burke, Kimberly Christie, Jack D. Burke Jr, Donald S. Rae, and Darrel A. Regier. "Comparing Age at Onset of Major Depression and Other Psychiatric Disorders by Birth Cohorts in Five US Community Populations." *JAMA Psychiatry* 48, no. 9 (1991): 789–95.

Cacioppo, John T. "Epidemic of Loneliness." *Psychology Today*, May 3, 2009. https://www.psychologytoday.com/us/blog/connections/200905/epidemic-loneliness.

Campione-Barr, Nicole, Kelly Bassett Greer, and Anna Kruse. "Differential Associations Between Domains of Sibling Conflict and Adolescent Emotional Adjustment." *Child Development* 84, no. 3 (2013): 938–54.

Cancian, Maria, Daniel R. Meyer, and Steven T. Cook. "The Evolution of Family Complexity from the Perspective of Nonmarital Children." *Demography* 48, no. 3 (2011): 957–82.

Carbone, June, and Naomi Cahn. *Marriage Markets: How Inequality Is Remaking the American Family*. New York: Oxford University Press, 2014.

Card, David. "The Effect of Unions on Wage Inequality in the U.S. Labor Market." *ILR Review* 54, no. 2 (2001): 296–315.

Carlson, Marcia J., Daniel R. Meyer, and Frank F. Furstenberg. "Fifty Years of Family Change: From Consensus to Complexity." *Annals of the American Academy of Political and Social Science* 654, no. 1 (2014): 12–30.

Case, Anne, I. Fen Lin, and Sara McLanahan. "Educational Attainment of Siblings in Stepfamilies." *Evolution and Human Behavior* 22, no. 4 (2001): 269–89.

Cassidy, Jude, June Lichtenstein-Phelps, Nicholas J. Sibrava, Charles L. Thomas, and Thomas D. Borkovec. "Generalized Anxiety Disorder: Connections with Self-Reported Attachment." *Behavior Therapy* 40, no. 1 (2009): 23–38.

Chase, Ivan D., and W. B. Lindquist. "Dominance Hierarchies." In *The Oxford Handbook of Analytical Sociology*, ed. Peter Hedström and Peter Bearman, 566–91. Oxford: Oxford University Press, 2009.

Chase, Ivan D., Craig Tovey, Debra Spangler-Martin, and Michael Manfredonia. "Individual Differences Versus Social Dynamics in the Formation of Animal Dominance Hierarchies." *Proceedings of the National Academy of Sciences* 99, no. 8 (2002): 5744–49.

Chauncey, George. *Gay New York: Gender, Urban Culture, and the Makings of the Gay Male World, 1890–1940.* New York: Basic, 1994.

Cherlin, Andrew J. "Going to Extremes: Family Structure, Children's Well-Being, and Social Science." *Demography* 36, no. 4 (1999): 421–28.

——. *Marriage, Divorce, Remarriage.* Cambridge, Mass.: Harvard University Press, 1992.

Chow, Tak Sang, and Hau Yan Wan. "Is There Any 'Facebook Depression'? Exploring the Moderating Roles of Neuroticism, Facebook Social Comparison and Envy." *Personality and Individual Differences* 119 (2017): 277–82.

Clark, Lee Anna, and David Watson. "Tripartite Model of Anxiety and Depression: Psychometric Evidence and Taxonomic Implications." *Journal of Abnormal Psychology* 100, no. 3 (1991): 316–36.

Clayton, Paula J. "Depression Subtyping: Treatment Implications." Supplement, *Journal of Clinical Psychiatry* 59, no. S16 (1998): 5–12.

Cobb, Sidney. "Social Support as a Moderator of Life Stress." *Psychosomatic Medicine* 38 (1976): 300–14.

Cohen, Lizabeth. *A Consumer's Republic: The Politics of Mass Consumption in Postwar America.* New York: Knopf, 2003.

Cohen, Patricia, Stephanie Kasen, Henian Chen, Kathy Gordon, Kathy Berenson, Judith Brook, and Thomas White. "Current Affairs and the Public Psyche: American Anxiety in the Post 9/11 World." *Social Psychiatry and Psychiatric Epidemiology* 41, no. 4 (2006): 251–60.

Compton, Allan. "A Study of the Psychoanalytic Theory of Anxiety. I. The Development of Freud's Theory of Anxiety." *Journal of the American Psychoanalytic Association* 20, no. 1 (1972): 3–44.

——. "A Study of the Psychoanalytic Theory of Anxiety. II. Developments in the Theory of Anxiety Since 1926." *Journal of the American Psychoanalytic Association* 20, no. 2 (1972): 341–94.

Conrad, Peter. "Medicalization and Social Control." *Annual Review of Sociology* 18 (1992): 209–32.

Coplan, Jeremy, Sarah Hodulik, Sanjay Mathew, Xiangling Mao, Patrick Hof, Jack Gorman, and Dikoma Shungu. "The Relationship Between Intelligence and Anxiety: An

Association with Subcortical White Matter Metabolism." *Frontiers in Evolutionary Neuroscience* 3, no. 8 (2012).

Coplan, Jeremy D., Sanjay J. Mathew, Xiangling Mao, Eric L. P. Smith, Patrick R. Hof, Paul M. Coplan, Leonard A. Rosenblum, Jack M. Gorman, and Dikoma C. Shungu. "Decreased Choline and Creatine Concentrations in Centrum Semiovale in Patients with Generalized Anxiety Disorder: Relationship to IQ and Early Trauma." *Psychiatry Research: Neuroimaging* 147, no. 1 (2006): 27–39.

Copland, Simon. "Anxiety Is a Way of Life for Gen Y. In an Insecure World, Is It Any Surprise?" *Guardian*, February 24, 2017. https://www.theguardian.com/society/commentisfree /2017/feb/25/anxiety-is-a-way-of-life-for-gen-y-in-an-insecure-world-is-it-any -surprise.

Cougle, Jesse R., Kiara R. Timpano, Natalie Sachs-Ericsson, Meghan E. Keough, and Christina J. Riccardi. "Examining the Unique Relationships Between Anxiety Disorders and Childhood Physical and Sexual Abuse in the National Comorbidity Survey- Replication." *Psychiatry Research* 177, no. 1 (2010): 150–55.

Cowen, Alan S., and Dacher Keltner. "Self-Report Captures 27 Distinct Categories of Emotion Bridged by Continuous Gradients." *Proceedings of the National Academy of Sciences of the United States of America* 114, no. 38 (2017): E7900–E7909 201702247.

Craske, Michelle G., Ronald M. Rapee, Lisa Jackel, and David H. Barlow. "Qualitative Dimensions of Worry in DSM-III-R Generalized Anxiety Disorder Subjects and Nonanxious Controls." *Behaviour Research and Therapy* 27, no. 4 (1989): 397–402.

Crews, Frederick. *Freud: The Making of an Illusion.* New York: Metropolitan Books, 2017.

Crimmins, Eileen M. "Lifespan and Healthspan: Past, Present, and Promise." *Gerontologist* 55, no. 6 (2015): 901–11.

Crocq, Marc-Antoine. "A History of Anxiety: From Hippocrates to DSM." *Dialogues in Clinical Neuroscience* 17, no. 3 (2015): 319–25.

Cryan, John F., and Andrew Holmes. "The Ascent of Mouse: Advances in Modelling Human Depression and Anxiety." *Nature Reviews Drug Discovery* 4 (2005): 775–90.

Cryan, John F., and Fabian F. Sweeney. "The Age of Anxiety: Role of Animal Models of Anxiolytic Action in Drug Discovery." *British Journal of Pharmacology* 164, no. 4 (2011): 1129–61.

Curtis, George, William J. Magee, William W. Eaton, Hans-Ulrich Wittchen, and Ronald C. Kessler. "Specific Fears and Phobias: Epidemiology and Classification." *British Journal of Psychiatry* 173, no. 3 (1998): 212–17.

Dana, Charles L. "The Partial Passing of Neurasthenia." *Boston Medical and Surgical Journal* 150, no. 13 (1904): 339–44.

Darwin, Charles. *The Expression of Emotions in Man and Animals.* New York: St. Martin's, 1979.

Davidson, Richard J. "Darwin and the Neural Bases of Emotion and Affective Style." *Annals of the New York Academy of Sciences* 1000, no. 1 (2006): 316–36.

Dawson, Deborah A. "Family Structure and Children's Health and Well-Being: Data from the 1988 National Health Interview Survey on Child Health." *Journal of Marriage and Family* 53, no. 3 (1991): 573–84.

Deacon, Brett J., Jonathan S. Abramowitz, Carol M. Woods, and David F. Tolin. "The Anxiety Sensitivity Index—Revised: Psychometric Properties and Factor Structure in Two Nonclinical Samples." *Behaviour Research and Therapy* 41, no. 12 (2003): 1427–49.

DeBeurs, Edwin, Aartjan Beekman, Sandra Geerlings, Dorly Deeg, Richard Van Dyck, and Willem Van Tilburg. "On Becoming Depressed or Anxious in Late Life: Similar Vulnerability Factors but Different Effects of Stressful Life Events." *British Journal of Psychiatry* 179, no. 5 (2001): 426–31.

DeMaris, Alfred, and K. Vaninadha Rao. "Premarital Cohabitation and Subsequent Marital Stability in the United States: A Reassessment." *Journal of Marriage and Family* 54, no. 1 (1992): 178–90.

Di Nardo, Peter A., Gerald T. O'Brien, David H. Barlow, Maria T. Waddell, and Edward B. Blanchard. "Reliability of DSM-III Anxiety Disorder Categories Using a New Structured Interview." *Archives of General Psychiatry* 40, no. 10 (1983): 1070–74.

Dickerson, Sally S., and Margaret E. Kemeny. "Acute Stressors and Cortisol Responses: A Theoretical Integration and Synthesis of Laboratory Research." *Psychological Bulletin* 130, no. 3 (2004): 355–91.

Dillon, Daniel G., Isabelle M. Rosso, Pia Pechtel, William D. S. Killgore, Scott L. Rauch, and Diego A. Pizzagalli. "Peril and Pleasure: An RDoC-inspired Examination of Threat Responses and Reward Processing in Anxiety and Depression." *Depression and Anxiety* 31, no. 3 (2014): 233–49.

DiTommaso, Enrico, Cyndi Brannen-McNulty, Lynda Ross, and Melissa Burgess. "Attachment Styles, Social Skills and Loneliness in Young Adults." *Personality and Individual Differences* 35, no. 2 (2003): 303–12.

Druss, Benjamin G., Steven C. Marcus, Mark Olfson, and Harold Alan Pincus. "Listening to Generic Prozac: Winners, Losers, and Sideliners." *Health Affairs* 23, no. 5 (2004): 210–16.

Dugas, Michel J., Fabien Gagnon, Robert Ladouceur, and Mark H. Freeston. "Generalized Anxiety Disorder: A Preliminary Test of a Conceptual Model." *Behaviour Research and Therapy* 36, no. 2 (1998): 215–26.

Dunbar Robin, I. M. "The Social Brain Hypothesis." *Evolutionary Anthropology: Issues, News, and Reviews* 6, no. 5 (1998): 178–90.

Durham, Robert C., Thérèse Allan, and Christine A. Hackett. "On Predicting Improvement and Relapse in Generalized Anxiety Disorder Following Psychotherapy." *British Journal of Clinical Psychology* 36, no. 1 (1997): 101–19.

Dworkin, Ronald. *Religion Without God*. Cambridge, Mass.: Harvard University Press, 2013.

Emmanuel, J., S. Simmonds, and P. Tyrer. "Systematic Review of the Outcome of Anxiety and Depressive Disorders." *British Journal of Psychiatry* Supplement, no. 34 (1998): 35–41.

Eysenck, Michael W., Karin Mogg, Jon May, Anne Richards, and Andrew Mathews. "Bias in Interpretation of Ambiguous Sentences Related to Threat in Anxiety." *Journal of Abnormal Psychology* 100, no. 2 (1991): 144–50.

Feeney, Judith A., and Patricia Noller. "Attachment Style as a Predictor of Adult Romantic Relationships." *Journal of Personality and Social Psychology* 58, no. 2 (1990): 281–91.

Fine, C., J. Lumsden, and R. J. R. Blair. "Dissociation Between 'Theory of Mind' and Executive Functions in a Patient with Early Left Amygdala Damage." *Brain* 124, no. 2 (2001): 287–98.

Finke, Roger, and Rodney Starke. *The Churching of America, 1776–2005: Winners and Losers in Our Religious Economy*. 2nd ed. New Brunswick, N.J.: Rutgers University Press, 2005.

Finlay-Jones, Robert, and George W. Brown. "Types of Stressful Life Event and the Onset of Anxiety and Depressive Disorders." *Psychological Medicine* 11, no. 4 (1981): 803–15.

Fischer, Claude S. *Still Connected: Family and Friends in America Since 1970.* New York: Russell Sage Foundation, 2011.

Fischer, Claude S., and Michael Hout. *Century of Difference: How America Changed in the Last One Hundred Years.* New York: Russell Sage Foundation, 2006.

Fomby, Paula, and Andrew J. Cherlin. "Family Instability and Child Well-Being." *American Sociological Review* 72, no. 2 (2007): 181–204.

Fomby, Paula, Joshua A. Goode, and Stefanie Mollborn. "Family Complexity, Siblings, and Children's Aggressive Behavior at School Entry." *Demography* 53, no. 1 (2016): 1–26.

Forest, Amanda L., and Joanne V. Wood. "When Social Networking Is Not Working: Individuals with Low Self-Esteem Recognize but Do Not Reap the Benefits of Self-Disclosure on Facebook." *Psychological Science* 23, no. 3 (2012): 295–302.

Fournier, Marc A. "Adolescent Hierarchy Formation and the Social Competition Theory of Depression." *Journal of Social and Clinical Psychology* 28, no. 9 (2009): 1144–72.

Frank, Robert H. *Choosing the Right Pond.* New York: Oxford University Press, 1984.

——. *Luxury Fever: Money and Happiness in an Era of Excess.* Bryn Mawr, Penn.: American College, 2000.

Freud, Sigmund. *The Future of an Illusion.* New York: Liveright, 1928.

——. *A General Introduction to Psychoanalysis.* New York: Boni and Liveright, 1920.

——. "Inhibitions, Symptoms, and Anxiety." In *The Standard Edition of the Complete Psychological Works of Sigmund Freud,* Vol. 20: 87–156, ed. James Strachey. London: Hogarth Press and Institute of Psychoanalysis, 1959.

——. *The Problem of Anxiety.* New York: Norton, 1936.

——. *The Standard Edition of the Complete Psychological Works of Sigmund Freud,* Vol. 3, ed. James Strachey, Anna Freud, Alix Strachey, and Alan Tyson. London: Hogarth Press, 1962.

Friedman, Benjamin M. *The Moral Consequences of Economic Growth.* New York: Knopf, 2005.

Furstenberg, Frank F. "Is the Modern Family a Threat to Children's Health?" *Society* 36, no. 5 (1999): 31–37.

Furstenberg, Frank F., Jr, and Andrew J. Cherlin. *Divided Families: What Happens to Children When Parents Part.* Cambridge, Mass.: Harvard University Press, 1991.

Gauthier, Anne H., Timothy M. Smeedeng, and Frank F. Furstenberg. "Are Parents Investing Less Time in Children? Trends in Selected Industrialized Countries." *Population and Development Review* 30, no. 4 (2004): 647–71.

Gibson, E. J., and R. D. Walk. "Walking Off a Cliff." In *Introducing Psychological Research: Sixty Studies That Shape Psychology,* ed. Philip Banyard and Andrew Grayson, 319–23. London: Macmillan Education UK, 1996.

Giddens, Anthony. *The Consequences of Modernity.* Stanford, Calif.: Stanford University Press, 1990.

——. *Modernity and Self-Identity: Self and Society in the Late Modern Age.* Stanford, Calif.: Stanford University Press, 1991.

Gleason, Patrick P., Richard Schulz, Nicholas L. Smith, Jason T. Newsom, Patricia D. Kroboth, Frank J. Kroboth, and Bruce M. Psaty. "Correlates and Prevalence of

Benzodiazepine Use in Community-dwelling Elderly." *Journal of General Internal Medicine* 13, no. 4 (1998): 243–50.

Goldberg, David. "The Aetiology of Depression." *Psychological Medicine* 36, no. 10 (2006): 1341–47.

Goldberg, David, Keith Bridges, Diane Cook, Barbara Evans, and David Grayson. "The Influence of Social Factors on Common Mental Disorders. Destabilisation and Restitution." *British Journal of Psychiatry* 156, no. 5 (1990): 704.

Goldin, Claudia, and Lawrence F. Katz. "Decreasing (and Then Increasing) Inequality in America: A Tale of Two Half Centuries." In *The Causes and Consequences of Increasing Inequality*, ed. F. Welch, 37–82. Chicago: University of Chicago Press, 2001.

Gottschalk, Michael G., and Katharina Domschke. "Genetics of Generalized Anxiety Disorder and Related Traits." *Dialogues in Clinical Neuroscience* 19, no. 2 (2017): 159–68.

Grant, Bridget F., Deborah S. Hasin, Carlos Blanco, Frederick S. Stinson, S. Patricia Chou, Rise B. Goldstein, Deborah A. Dawson, et al. "The Epidemiology of Social Anxiety Disorder in the United States: Results from the National Epidemiologic Survey on Alcohol and Related Conditions." *Journal of Clinical Psychiatry* 66, no. 11 (2005): 1351–61.

Green, Emma. "How Will Young People Choose Their Religion?" *Atlantic*, March 20, 2016. https://www.theatlantic.com/politics/archive/2016/03/how-will-young-people -choose-their-religion/474366.

Griebel, Guy, and Andrew Holmes. "50 Years of Hurdles and Hope in Anxiolytic Drug Discovery." *Nature Reviews Drug Discovery* 12 (2013): 667.

Gruenewald, Tara L., Margaret E. Kemeny, and Najib Aziz. "Subjective Social Status Moderates Cortisol Responses to Social Threat." *Brain, Behavior, and Immunity* 20, no. 4 (2006): 410–19.

Gurin, Gerald. *Americans View Their Mental Health: A Nationwide Interview Survey.* New York: Basic, 1960.

Gusfield, Joseph R. *The Culture of Public Problems: Drinking-Driving and the Symbolic Order.* Chicago: University of Chicago Press, 1981.

Gutnick, Aviva Lucas, Michael Robb, Lori Takeuchi, and Jennifer Kotler. *Always Connected: The New Digital Media Habits of Young Children.* New York: Joan Ganz Cooney Center at Sesame Workshop, 2011.

Hallion, Lauren S., and Ayelet Meron Ruscio. "A Meta-analysis of the Effect of Cognitive Bias Modification on Anxiety and Depression." *Psychological Bulletin* 137, no. 6 (2011): 940–58.

Halstead, Ted. "A Politics for Generation X." *Atlantic*, August 1999. https://www.theatlantic .com/magazine/archive/1999/08/a-politics-for-generation-x/306666.

Hampton, Keith N., Lee Rainie, Weixu Lu, Inyoung Shin, and Kristen Purcell. *Social Media and the Cost of Caring.* Washington, D.C.: Pew Research Center, 2014.

Harris, Judith Rich. *The Nurture Assumption: Why Children Turn Out the Way They Do.* New York: Free Press, 2009.

Harsanyi, John C. "A Bargaining Model for Social Status in Informal Groups and Formal Organizations." In *Essays on Ethics, Social Behavior, and Scientific Explanation*, ed. John C. Harsanyi, 204–24. Dordrecht: Springer Netherlands, 1976.

Hazan, Cindy, and Phillip Shaver. "Romantic Love Conceptualized as an Attachment Process." *Journal of Personality and Social Psychology* 52, no. 3 (1987): 511–24.

Hellevik, Ottar. "Linear Versus Logistic Regression When the Dependent Variable Is a Dichotomy." *Quality & Quantity* 43, no. 1 (2009): 59–74.

Herzberg, David L. *Happy Pills in America: From Miltown to Prozac.* Baltimore, Md.: Johns Hopkins University Press, 2009.

Hettema, John M., Michael C. Neale, and Kenneth S. Kendler. "A Review and Meta-analysis of the Genetic Epidemiology of Anxiety Disorders." *American Journal of Psychiatry* 158, no. 10 (2001): 1568–78.

Hill, Peter C., Kenneth Pargament II, Ralph W. Hood Jr, Michael E. McCullough, James P. Swyers, David B. Larson, and Brian J. Zinnbauer. "Conceptualizing Religion and Spirituality: Points of Commonality, Points of Departure." *Journal for the Theory of Social Behaviour* 30, no. 1 (2000): 51–77.

Himwich, Harold E. "The New Psychiatric Drugs." *Scientific American* 193, no. 4 (1955): 80–87.

——. "Psychopharmacologic Drugs." *Science* 127, no. 3289 (1958): 59–72.

Hollingshead, August B., and Fredrick C. Redlich. *Social Class and Mental Illness: A Community Study.* New York: Wiley, 1958.

Hopcroft, Rosemary L. "Sex, Status, and Reproductive Success in the Contemporary United States." *Evolution and Human Behavior* 27, no. 2 (2006): 104–20.

Horney, Karen. *The Neurotic Personality of Our Time.* New York: Norton, 1937.

Horwitz, Allan V. *Anxiety: A Short History.* Baltimore, Md.: Johns Hopkins University Press, 2013.

——. "How an Age of Anxiety Became an Age of Depression." *Milbank Quarterly* 88, no. 1 (2010): 112–38.

Horwitz, Allan V., and Jerome C. Wakefield. *All We Have to Fear: Psychiatry's Transformation of Natural Anxieties Into Mental Disorders.* New York: Oxford University Press, 2012.

——. *The Loss of Sadness: How Psychiatry Transformed Normal Sorrow Into Depressive Disorder.* New York: Oxford University, 2007.

House, James S. "Social Psychology, Social Science, and Economics: Twentieth Century Progress and Problems, Twenty-First Century Prospects." *Social Psychology Quarterly* 71, no. 3 (2008): 232–56.

House, James S., Karl R. Landis, and Debra Umberson. "Social Relationships and Health." *Science* 241, no. 4865 (1988): 540–45.

House, James S., Deborah Umberson, and Karl R. Landis. "Structures and Processes of Social Support." *Annual Review of Sociology* 14 (1988): 293–318.

Hout, Michael, and Claude S. Fischer. "Explaining Why More Americans Have No Religious Preference: Political Backlash and Generational Succession, 1987–2012." *Sociological Science* 1, no. 24 (2014): 423–47.

——. "Why More Americans Have No Religious Preference: Politics and Generations." *American Sociological Review* 67, no. 2 (2002): 165–90.

Howe, Nina, Christina M. Rinaldi, Melissa Jennings, and Harriet Petrakos. "'No! The Lambs Can Stay out Because They Got Cozies': Constructive and Destructive Sibling Conflict, Pretend Play, and Social Understanding." *Child Development* 73, no. 5 (2002): 1460–73.

Huang, Chiungjung. "Internet Use and Psychological Well-Being: A Meta-analysis." *Cyberpsychology, Behavior, and Social Networking* 13, no. 3 (2010): 241–49.

Huang, Yeen, and Ning Zhao. "Mental Health Burden for the Public Affected by the Covid-19 Outbreak in China: Who Will Be the High-Risk Group?" *Psychology, Health & Medicine* (2020): 1–12.

Huskamp, Haiden A., Julie M. Donohue, Catherine Koss, Ernst R. Berndt, and Richard G. Frank. "Generic Entry, Reformulations and Promotion of SSRIs in the U.S." *PharmacoEconomics* 26, no. 7 (2008): 603–16.

Insel, Thomas, Bruce Cuthbert, Marjorie Garvey, Robert Heinssen, Daniel S. Pine, Kevin Quinn, Charles Sanislow, and Philip Wang. "Research Domain Criteria (RDoC): Toward a New Classification Framework for Research on Mental Disorders." *American Journal of Psychiatry* 167, no. 7 (2010): 748–51.

Insel, Thomas R. "The NIMH Research Domain Criteria (RDoC) Project: Precision Medicine for Psychiatry." *American Journal of Psychiatry* 171, no. 4 (2014): 395–97.

Institute of Medicine. *Science, Medicine, and Animals*. Washington, D.C.: National Academies Press, 1991.

Institute of Medicine, National Research Council. *Child Maltreatment Research, Policy, and Practice for the Next Decade: Workshop Summary*. Washington, D.C.: National Academies Press, 2012.

——. *International Animal Research Regulations: Impact on Neuroscience Research: Workshop Summary*. Washington, D.C.: National Academies Press, 2012.

Isen, Adam, and Betsey Stevenson. "Women's Education and Family Behavior: Trends in Marriage, Divorce and Fertility." National Bureau of Economic Research Working Paper Series No. 15725. Cambridge, Mass.: National Bureau of Economic Research, 2010.

James, William. *The Varieties of Religious Experience; a Study in Human Nature*. New York: Longmans, Green, 1902.

Janet, Pierre. *Les obsessions et la psychasthénie*. 2nd ed. Paris: Alcan, 1908.

Kaufman, M. Ralph, and Stanley Bernstein. "A Psychiatric Evaluation of the Problem Patient: Study of a Thousand Cases from a Consultation Service." *Journal of the American Medical Association* 163, no. 2 (1957): 108–11.

Kendler, Kenneth S., Andrew Heath, Nicholas G. Martin, and Lindon J. Eaves. "Symptoms of Anxiety and Depression in a Volunteer Twin Population." *Archives of General Psychiatry* 43 (1986): 213–21.

Kendler, Kenneth S., John M. Hettema, Frank Butera, Charles O. Gardner, and Carol A. Prescott. "Life Event Dimensions of Loss, Humiliation, Entrapment, and Danger in the Prediction of Onsets of Major Depression and Generalized Anxiety." *Archives of General Psychiatry* 60, no. 8 (2003): 789–96.

Kendler, Kenneth S., L. M. Karkowski, and C. A. Prescott. "Fears and Phobias: Reliability and Heritability." *Psychological Medicine* 29, no. 3 (1999): 539–53.

Kendler, Kenneth S., M. C. Neale, R. C. Kessler, A. C. Heath, and L. J. Eaves. "Major Depression and Generalized Anxiety Disorder: Same Genes, (Partly) Different Environments?" *Archives of General Psychiatry* 49, no. 9 (1992): 716–22.

Kennedy, Sheela, and Steven Ruggles. "Breaking Up Is Hard to Count: The Rise of Divorce in the United States, 1980–2010." *Demography* 51, no. 2 (2014): 587–98.

Kessler, Ronald C., Peggy R. Barker, Lisa J. Colpe, Joan F. Epstein, Joseph C. Gfroerer, Eva Hiripi, Mary J. Howes, et al. "Screening for Serious Mental Illness in the General Population." *Archives of General Psychiatry* 60, no. 2 (2003): 184–89.

Kessler, Ronald C., Patricia Berglund, Olga Demler, Robert Jin, Kathleen R. Merikangas, and Ellen E. Walters. "Lifetime Prevalence and Age-of-Onset Distributions of

DSM-IV Disorders in the National Comorbidity Survey Replication." *Archives of General Psychiatry* 62, no. 6 (2005): 593–602.

Kessler, Ronald C., W. Chiu, O. Demler, and E. E. Walters. "Prevalence, Severity, and Comorbidity of 12-Month DSM-IV Disorders in the National Comorbidity Survey Replication." *Archives of General Psychiatry* 62, no. 6 (2005): 617–27.

Kessler, Ronald C., Robert L. DuPont, Patricia Berglund, and Hans-Ulrich Wittchen. "Impairment in Pure and Comorbid Generalized Anxiety Disorder and Major Depression at 12 Months in Two National Surveys." *American Journal of Psychiatry* 156, no. 12 (1999): 1915–23.

Kessler, Ronald C., M. Gruber, J. M. Hettema, I. Hwang, N. Sampson, and K. A. Yonkers. "Co-morbid Major Depression and Generalized Anxiety Disorders in the National Comorbidity Survey Follow-Up." *Psychological Medicine* 38, no. 3 (2008): 365–74.

Kessler, Ronald C., Johan Ormel, Maria Petukhova, Katie A. McLaughlin, Jennifer Greif Green, Leo J. Russo, Dan J. Stein, et al. "Development of Lifetime Comorbidity in the World Health Organization World Mental Health Surveys." *Archives of General Psychiatry* 68, no. 1 (2011): 90–100.

Kessler, Ronald C., and T. Bedirhan Üstün. "The World Mental Health Survey Initiative Version of the World Health Organization Composite International Diagnostic Interview." *International Journal of Methods in Psychiatric Research* 13, no. 2 (2004): 93–121.

Kessler, Ronald C., and Philip S. Wang. "The Descriptive Epidemiology of Commonly Occurring Mental Disorders in the United States." *Annual Review of Public Health* 29, no. 1 (2008): 115–29.

Kim, Ji-Yeon, Susan M. McHale, Ann C. Crouter, and D. Wayne Osgood. "Longitudinal Linkages Between Sibling Relationships and Adjustment from Middle Childhood Through Adolescence." *Developmental Psychology* 43, no. 4 (2007): 960–73.

Kinney, Dennis K., and Midori Tanaka. "An Evolutionary Hypothesis of Depression and Its Symptoms, Adaptive Value, and Risk Factors." *Journal of Nervous and Mental Disease* 197, no. 8 (2009): 561–67.

Kleinman, Arthur. "Neurasthenia and Depression: A Study of Somatization and Culture in China." *Culture, Medicine, and Psychiatry* 6 (1982): 117–90.

Klinenberg, Eric. *Going Solo: The Extraordinary Rise and Surprising Appeal of Living Alone.* New York: Penguin Press, 2012.

Konrath, Sara H., William J. Chopik, Courtney K. Hsing, and Ed O'Brien. "Changes in Adult Attachment Styles in American College Students Over Time: A Meta-analysis." *Personality and Social Psychology Review* 18, no. 4 (2014): 326–48.

Kornrich, Sabino, and Frank Furstenberg. "Investing in Children: Changes in Parental Spending on Children, 1972–2007." *Demography* 50, no. 1 (2013): 1–23.

Kraepelin, Emil. *Clinical Psychiatry.* New York: Macmillan, 1902.

Krafft-Ebing, Richard von. "Perversions of the Sexual Instinct: Report of Cases." *Alienist and Neurologist* 9 (1888): 565–81.

Krafft-Ebing, Richard von. *Text Book of Insanity Based on Clinical Observations for Practitioners and Students of Medicine.* Philadelphia: F. A. Davis Company, 1905.

Kraut, Robert, Michael Patterson, Vicki Lundmark, Sara Kiesler, Tridas Mukophadhyay, and William Scherlis. "Internet Paradox: A Social Technology That Reduces Social Involvement and Psychological Well-Being?" *American Psychologist* 53, no. 9 (1998): 1017–31.

Kross, Ethan, Philippe Verduyn, Emre Demiralp, Jiyoung Park, David Seungjae Lee, Natalie Lin, Holly Shablack, John Jonides, and Oscar Ybarra. "Facebook Use Predicts Declines in Subjective Well-Being in Young Adults." *PLoS ONE* 8, no. 8 (2013): e69841.

Krueger, Dirk, and Fabrizio Perri. "Does Income Inequality Lead to Consumption Inequality? Evidence and Theory." *Review of Economic Studies* 73, no. 1 (2006): 163–93.

Lasch, Christopher. *The Culture of Narcissism: American Life in an Age of Diminishing Expectations.* New York: Norton, 1978.

Laties, Victor G., and Bernard Weiss. "A Critical Review of the Efficacy of Meprobamate (Miltown, Equanil) in the Treatment of Anxiety." *Journal of Chronic Diseases* 7, no. 6 (1958): 500–19.

Lebergott, Stanley. *Pursuing Happiness: American Consumers in the Twentieth Century.* Princeton, N.J.: Princeton University Press, 1993.

Lebowitz, Matthew S., John J. Pyun, and Woo-kyoung Ahn. "Biological Explanations of Generalized Anxiety Disorder: Effects on Beliefs About Prognosis and Responsibility." *Psychiatric Services* 65, no. 4 (2014): 498–503.

LeDoux, Joseph E. *Anxious: Using the Brain to Understand and Treat Fear and Anxiety.* New York: Viking, 2015.

Lee, Sherman A. "Coronavirus Anxiety Scale: A Brief Mental Health Screener for Covid-19 Related Anxiety." *Death Studies* 44, no. 7 (2020): 393–401.

Lehrer, Evelyn L., and Carmel U. Chiswick. "Religion as a Determinant of Marital Stability." *Demography* 30, no. 3 (1993): 385–404.

Levitt, E. E. "A Comparison of Parental and Self-Evaluations of Psychopathology in Children." *Journal of Clinical Psychology* 15 (1959): 402–04.

Lewinsohn, Peter M., Paul Rohde, John R. Seeley, and Scott A. Fischer. "Age-Cohort Changes in the Lifetime Occurrence of Depression and Other Mental Disorders." *Journal of Abnormal Psychology* 102, no. 1 (1993): 110–20.

Lezak, Kimberly R., Galen Missig, and William A. Carlezon Jr. "Behavioral Methods to Study Anxiety in Rodents." *Dialogues in Clinical Neuroscience* 19, no. 2 (2017): 181–91.

Liddell, Howard S. "The Role of Vigilance in the Development of Animal Neurosis." In *Anxiety*, ed. P. H. Hoch and J. Zubin. 183–96. New York: Grune & Stratton, 1950.

Lincoln, Karen D., Robert Joseph Taylor, Kai McKeever Bullard, Linda M. Chatters, Joseph A. Himle, Amanda Toler Woodward, and James S. Jackson. "Emotional Support, Negative Interaction and DSM-IV Lifetime Disorders Among Older African Americans: Findings from the National Survey of American Life (NSAL)." *International Journal of Geriatric Psychiatry* 25, no. 6 (2010): 612–21.

Link, Bruce G., Richard M. Carpiano, and Margaret M. Weden. "Can Honorific Awards Give Us Clues About the Connection Between Socioeconomic Status and Mortality?" *American Sociological Review* 78, no. 2 (2013): 192–212.

London, Andrew S., and Scott D. Landes. "Cohort Change in the Prevalence of ADHD Among U.S. Adults: Evidence of a Gender-Specific Historical Period Effect." *Journal of Attention Disorders* (2019): 1087054719855689.

Long, J. Scott, and Jeremy Freese. *Regression Models for Categorical Dependent Variables Using Stata.* 3rd ed. College Station, Tex.: Stata Press Publication, Statacorp LP, 2014.

Lukianoff, Greg, and Jonathan Haidt. *The Coddling of the American Mind: How Good Intentions and Bad Ideas Are Setting up a Generation for Failure*. New York: Penguin, 2018.

Lupien, Sonia J., Bruce S. McEwen, Megan R. Gunnar, and Christine Heim. "Effects of Stress Throughout the Lifespan on the Brain, Behaviour and Cognition." *Nature Reviews Neuroscience* 10 (2009): 434.

MacLeod, Colin, Andrew Mathews, and Philip Tata. "Attentional Bias in Emotional Disorders." *Journal of Abnormal Psychology* 95, no. 1 (1986): 15–20.

Marks, Isaac. *Fears, Phobias and Rituals: Panic, Anxiety, and Their Disorders*. New York: Oxford University Press, 1987.

Marks, Isaac fM., and Randolph M. Nesse. "Fear and Fitness: An Evolutionary Analysis of Anxiety Disorders." *Ethology and Sociobiology* 15, no. 5 (1994): 247–61.

Marwell, Gerald, and N. J. Demerath. " 'Secularization' by Any Other Name." *American Sociological Review* 68, no. 2 (2003): 314–16.

Mast, Marianne Schmid, and Judith A. Hall. "Who Is the Boss and Who Is Not? Accuracy of Judging Status." *Journal of Nonverbal Behavior* 28, no. 3 (2004): 145–65.

Mathews, Andrew. "Why Worry? The Cognitive Function of Anxiety." *Behaviour Research and Therapy* 28, no. 6 (1990): 455–68.

Mathews, Andrew, and Colin MacLeod. "Induced Processing Biases Have Causal Effects on Anxiety." *Cognition and Emotion* 16, no. 3 (2002): 331–54.

May, Rollo. *The Meaning of Anxiety*. New York: Ronald Press, 1950.

McCall, Leslie, and Christine Percheski. "Income Inequality: New Trends and Research Directions." *Annual Review of Sociology* 36, no. 1 (2010): 329–47.

McGinty, Emma E., Alene Kennedy-Hendricks, Seema Choksy, and Colleen L. Barry. "Trends in News Media Coverage of Mental Illness in the United States: 1995–2014." *Health Affairs* 35, no. 6 (2016): 1121–29.

McHale, Susan M., Kimberly A. Updegraff, and Shawn D. Whiteman. "Sibling Relationships and Influences in Childhood and Adolescence." *Journal of Marriage and the Family* 74, no. 5 (2012): 913–30.

McKinney, William T., Jr, and William. E. Bunney. "Animal Model of Depression: I. Review of Evidence: Implications for Research." *Archives of General Psychiatry* 21, no. 2 (1969): 240–48.

McLanahan, Sara, and Gary Sandefur. *Growing Up with a Single Parent: What Hurts, What Helps*. Cambridge, Mass.: Harvard University Press, 1994.

McLean, Carmen P., Anu Asnaani, Brett T. Litz, and Stefan G. Hofmann. "Gender Differences in Anxiety Disorders: Prevalence, Course of Illness, Comorbidity and Burden of Illness." *Journal of Psychiatric Research* 45, no. 8 (2011): 1027–35.

McPherson, Susan, and David Armstrong. "Social Determinants of Diagnostic Labels in Depression." *Social Science & Medicine* 62, no. 1 (2006): 50–58.

McTeague, Lisa M., and Peter J. Lang. "The Anxiety Spectrum and the Reflex Physiology of Defense: From Circumscribed Fear to Broad Distress." *Depression and Anxiety* 29, no. 4 (2012): 264–81.

Meacham, Frazer, and Carl T. Bergstrom. "Adaptive Behavior Can Produce Maladaptive Anxiety Due to Individual Differences in Experience." *Evolution, Medicine, and Public Health* 2016, no. 1 (2016): 270–85.

Meehl, Paul E. "Schizotaxia, Schizotypy, Schizophrenia." *American Psychologist* 17, no. 12 (1962): 827–38.

Merrick, Melissa T., Derek C. Ford, Katie A. Ports, and Angie S. Guinn. "Prevalence of Adverse Childhood Experiences from the 2011–2014 Behavioral Risk Factor Surveillance System in 23 States." *JAMA Pediatrics* 172, no. 11 (2018): 1038–44.

Miller, Eric D. "The Covid-19 Pandemic Crisis: The Loss and Trauma Event of Our Time." *Journal of Loss and Trauma* 25, nos. 6–7 (2020): 560–72.

Miller, Neal E. "The Value of Behavioral Research on Animals." *American Psychologist* 40, no. 4 (1985): 423–40.

Moffitt, Terrie E., Avshalom Caspi, Honalee Harrington, Barry J. Milne, Maria Melchior, David Goldberg, and Richie Poulton. "Generalized Anxiety Disorder and Depression: Childhood Risk Factors in a Birth Cohort Followed to Age 32." *Psychological Medicine* 37, no. 3 (2007): 441–52.

Moffitt, Terrie E., HonaLee Harrington, Avshalom Caspi, Julia Kim-Cohen, David Goldberg, Alice M. Gregory, and Richie Poulton. "Depression and Generalized Anxiety Disorder: Cumulative and Sequential Comorbidity in a Birth Cohort Followed Prospectively to Age 32 Years." *Archives of General Psychiatry* 64, no. 6 (2007): 651–60.

Mogg, Karin, and Brendan P. Bradley. "Attentional Bias in Generalized Anxiety Disorder Versus Depressive Disorder." *Cognitive Therapy and Research* 29, no. 1 (2005): 29–45.

——. "A Cognitive-Motivational Analysis of Anxiety." *Behaviour Research and Therapy* 36, no. 9 (1998): 809–48.

Mojtabai, Ramin. "Increase in Antidepressant Medication in the US Adult Population Between 1990 and 2003." *Psychotherapy and Psychosomatics* 77, no. 2 (2008): 83–92.

Monroe, Scott M., and Anne D. Simons. "Diathesis-Stress Theories in the Context of Life Stress Research: Implications for the Depressive Disorders." *Psychological Bulletin* 110, no. 3 (1991): 406–25.

Moore, Thomas J., and Donald R. Mattison. "Adult Utilization of Psychiatric Drugs and Differences by Sex, Age, and Race." *JAMA Internal Medicine* 177, no. 2 (2017): 274–75.

Muris, Peter, Cor Meesters, Harald Merckelbach, and Paulette Hülsenbeck. "Worry in Children Is Related to Perceived Parental Rearing and Attachment." *Behaviour Research and Therapy* 38, no. 5 (2000): 487–97.

Murphy, J. M., and A. H. Leighton. "Anxiety: Its Role in the History of Psychiatric Epidemiology." *Psychological Medicine* 39, no. 7 (2009): 1055–64.

Mykletun, Arnstein, Ottar Bjerkeset, Michael Dewey, Martin Prince, Simon Overland, and Robert Stewart. "Anxiety, Depression, and Cause-Specific Mortality: The Hunt Study." *Psychosomatic Medicine* 69, no. 4 (2007): 323–31.

Mykletun, Arnstein, Ottar Bjerkeset, Simon Overland, Martin Prince, Michael Dewey, and Robert Stewart. "Levels of Anxiety and Depression as Predictors of Mortality: The Hunt Study." *British Journal of Psychiatry* 195, no. 2 (2009): 118–25.

Nardi, Antonio Egidio, and Rafael Christophe R. Freire. "The Panic Disorder Concept: A Historical Perspective." In *Panic Disorder: Neurobiological and Treatment Aspects*, ed. Antonio Egidio Nardi and Rafael Christophe R. Freire. 1–8. Cham, Switzerland: Springer International Publishing, 2016.

National Academies of Sciences, Engineering, and Medicine. *The Integration of Immigrants Into American Society*. Washington, D.C.: National Academies Press, 2015.

National Center for Health Statistics. *Health, United States, 2018*. Hyattsville, Md., 2019.

Neff, J. A. "Race and Vulnerability to Stress: An Examination of Differential Vulnerability." *Journal of Personality and Social Psychology* 49, no. 2 (1985): 481–91.

Neil, Alison L., and Helen Christensen. "Efficacy and Effectiveness of School-based Prevention and Early Intervention Programs for Anxiety." *Clinical Psychology Review* 29, no. 3 (2009): 208–15.

Nelissen, Rob M. A., and Marijn H. C. Meijers. "Social Benefits of Luxury Brands as Costly Signals of Wealth and Status." *Evolution and Human Behavior* 32, no. 5 (2011): 343–55.

Nesse, Randolph M. "Evolutionary Explanations of Emotions." *Human Nature* 1, no. 3 (1990): 261–89.

——. *Good Reasons for Bad Feelings: Insights from the Frontier of Evolutionary Psychiatry*. New York: Dutton, 2019.

——. "Is Depression an Adaptation?" *Archives of General Psychiatry* 57, no. 1 (2000): 14–20.

——. "The Smoke Detector Principle." *Annals of the New York Academy of Sciences* 935, no. 1 (2001): 75–85.

Nesse, Randolph M., and Eric D. Jackson. "Evolution: Psychiatric Nosology's Missing Biological Foundation." *Clinical Neuropsychiatry: Journal of Treatment Evaluation* 3, no. 2 (2006): 121–31.

Nettle, Daniel, and Melissa Bateson. "The Evolutionary Origins of Mood and Its Disorders." *Current Biology* 22, no. 17 (2012): R712–R21.

New York Academy of Medicine, Committee on Public Health. "Report on Tranquilizing Drugs." *Bulletin of the New York Academy of Medicine* 33, no. 4 (1957): 282–89.

Newman, Michelle G., Sandra J. Llera, Thane M. Erickson, Amy Przeworski, and Louis G. Castonguay. "Worry and Generalized Anxiety Disorder: A Review and Theoretical Synthesis of Evidence on Nature, Etiology, Mechanisms, and Treatment." *Annual Review of Clinical Psychology* 9, no. 1 (2013): 275–97.

Newsom, Jason T., Masami Nishishiba, David L. Morgan, and Karen S. Rook. "The Relative Importance of Three Domains of Positive and Negative Social Exchanges: A Longitudinal Model with Comparable Measures." *Psychology and Aging* 18, no. 4 (2003): 746–54.

Nolen-Hoeksema, Susan, and Edward R. Watkins. "A Heuristic for Developing Transdiagnostic Models of Psychopathology: Explaining Multifinality and Divergent Trajectories." *Perspectives on Psychological Science* 6, no. 6 (2011): 589–609.

Noller, Patricia. "Sibling Relationships in Adolescence: Learning and Growing Together." *Personal Relationships* 12, no. 1 (2005): 1–22.

Noonan, MaryAnn P., Jerome Sallet, Rogier B. Mars, Franz X. Neubert, Jill X. O'Reilly, Jesper L. Andersson, Anna S. Mitchell, et al. "A Neural Circuit Covarying with Social Hierarchy in Macaques." *PLoS Biology* 12, no. 9 (2014): e1001940.

Nordahl, Hans M., Adrian Wells, Craig A. Olsson, and Ottar Bjerkeset. "Association Between Abnormal Psychosocial Situations in Childhood, Generalized Anxiety Disorder and Oppositional Defiant Disorder." *Australian & New Zealand Journal of Psychiatry* 44, no. 9 (2010): 852–58.

Oakley Browne, Mark A., J. Elisabeth Wells, Kate M. Scott, and Magnus A. McGee. "Lifetime Prevalence and Projected Lifetime Risk of DSM-IV Disorders in Te Rau Hinengaro: The New Zealand Mental Health Survey." *Australian and New Zealand Journal of Psychiatry* 40, no. 10 (2006): 865–74.

Olfson, Mark, and Gerald L. Klerman. "Trends in the Prescription of Psychotropic Medications: The Role of Physician Specialty." *Medical Care* 31, no. 6 (1993): 559–64.

Olfson, Mark, and Steven C. Marcus. "National Patterns in Antidepressant Medication Treatment." *Archives of General Psychiatry* 66, no. 8 (2009): 848–56.

Oosterhuis, Harry. "Sexual Modernity in the Works of Richard Von Krafft-Ebing and Albert Moll." *Medical History* 56, no. 2 (2012): 133–55.

Ornstein, Charles, and Ryann Grochowski Jones. "One Nation, Under Sedation: Medicare Paid for Nearly 40 Million Tranquilizer Prescriptions in 2013." *ProPublica*, June 10, 2015. https://www.propublica.org/article/medicare-paid-for-nearly-40-million-tranquilizer-prescriptions-in-2013.

Ouimet, Allison J., Bertram Gawronski, and David J. A. Dozois. "Cognitive Vulnerability to Anxiety: A Review and an Integrative Model." *Clinical Psychology Review* 29, no. 6 (2009): 459–70.

Packard, Vance. *A Nation of Strangers*. New York: McKay, 1972.

Pampallona, S., P. Bollini, G. Tibaldi, B. Kupelnick, and C. Munizza. "Patient Adherence in the Treatment of Depression." *British Journal of Psychiatry* 180, no. 2 (2002): 104–09.

Pargament, Kenneth I. *The Psychology of Religion and Coping: Theory, Research, Practice*. New York: Guilford, 1997.

Parry, Hugh J., Mitchell B. Balter, Glen D. Mellinger, Ira H. Cisin, and Dean I. Manheimer. "National Patterns of Psychotherapeutic Drug Use." *Archives of General Psychiatry* 28, no. 6 (1973): 769–83.

Paxton, Pamela. "Is Social Capital Declining in the United States? A Multiple Indicator Assessment." *American Journal of Sociology* 105, no. 1 (1999): 88–127.

Pew Research Center. *Global Publics More Upbeat About the Economy*. Washington, D.C., 2017.

Pew Research Center. *Most U.S. Teens See Anxiety and Depression as a Major Problem Among Their Peers*. Washington, D.C., 2019.

Pew Social Trends. "Parenting in America." December 17, 2015. http://www.pewsocial trends.org/2015/12/17/1-the-american-family-today.

Phillips, Nicole K., Constance L. Hammen, Patricia A. Brennan, Jake M. Najman, and William Bor. "Early Adversity and the Prospective Prediction of Depressive and Anxiety Disorders in Adolescents." *Journal of Abnormal Child Psychology* 33, no. 1 (2005): 13–24.

Pietromonaco, Paula R., and Lisa Feldman Barrett. "Working Models of Attachment and Daily Social Interactions." *Journal of Personality and Social Psychology* 73, no. 6 (1997): 1409–23.

Pincus, Aaron L., and Emily B. Ansell. "Interpersonal Theory of Personality." In *Handbook of Psychology*, ed. Irving B. Weiner. 209–29. New York: Wiley, 2003.

Pinker, Steven. *The Better Angels of Our Nature: Why Violence Has Declined*. New York: Penguin, 2012.

Porsolt, R. D., M. Le Pichon, and M. Jalfre. "Depression: A New Animal Model Sensitive to Antidepressant Treatments." *Nature* 266, no. 5604 (1977): 730–32.

Preston, Samuel H. "Children and the Elderly: Divergent Paths for America's Dependents." *Demography* 21, no. 4 (1984): 435–57.

Price, John, Leon Sloman, Russell Gardner, Paul Gilbert, and Peter Rohde. "The Social Competition Hypothesis of Depression." *British Journal of Psychiatry* 164, no. 3 (1994): 309–15.

Prudo, R., T. Harris, and G. W. Brown. "Psychiatric Disorder in a Rural and an Urban Population: 3. Social Integration and the Morphology of Affective Disorder." *Psychological Medicine* 14, no. 2 (1984): 327–45.

Przeworski, Amy, Michelle G. Newman, Aaron L. Pincus, Michele B. Kasoff, Alissa S. Yamasaki, Louis G. Castonguay, and Kristoffer S. Berlin. "Interpersonal Pathoplasticity in Individuals with Generalized Anxiety Disorder." *Journal of Abnormal Psychology* 120, no. 2 (2011): 286–98.

Putnam, Robert D. *Bowling Alone: The Collapse and Revival of American Community*. New York: Simon & Schuster, 2000.

Putnam, Robert D., and David E. Campbell. *American Grace: How Religion Divides and Unites Us*. New York: Simon & Schuster, 2010.

Rapee, Ronald M. "Potential Role of Childrearing Practices in the Development of Anxiety and Depression." *Clinical Psychology Review* 17, no. 1 (1997): 47–67.

Rapee, Ronald M., and David H. Barlow. *Chronic Anxiety: Generalized Anxiety Disorder and Mixed Anxiety-Depression*. New York: Guilford, 1991.

Redelmeier, Donald A., and Sheldon M. Singh. "Survival in Academy Award–winning Actors and Actresses." *Annals of Internal Medicine* 134, no. 10 (2001): 955–62.

Rickels, Karl, and Moira A. Rynn. "What Is Generalized Anxiety Disorder?" *Journal of Clinical Psychiatry* 62, no. 11 (2001): 4–12.

Ridgeway, Cecilia L. "Why Status Matters for Inequality." *American Sociological Review* 79, no. 1 (2013): 1–16.

Riesman, David. *The Lonely Crowd: A Study of the Changing American Character*. New Haven, Conn.: Yale University Press, 1976.

Rilling, James K., James T. Winslow, and Clinton D. Kilts. "The Neural Correlates of Mate Competition in Dominant Male Rhesus Macaques." *Biological Psychiatry* 56, no. 5 (2004): 364–75.

Rindfuss, Ronald R., Karin L. Brewster, and Andrew L. Kavee. "Women, Work, and Children: Behavioral and Attitudinal Change in the United States." *Population and Development Review* 22, no. 3 (1996): 457–82.

Ritter, Hal. "Anxiety." *Journal of Religion and Health* 29, no. 1 (1990): 49–53.

Robins, Lee N., and Darrel A. Regier, eds. *Psychiatric Disorders in America: The Epidemiological Area Study*. New York: Free Press, 1991.

Roemer, Lizabeth, Silvia Molina, and Thomas D. Borkovec. "An Investigation of Worry Content Among Generally Anxious Individuals." *Journal of Nervous and Mental Disease* 185, no. 5 (1997): 314–19.

Rosenbaum, Jerrold F. "Attitudes Toward Benzodiazepines Over the Years." *Journal of Clinical Psychiatry* 66, no. S2 (2005): 4–8.

Rosenberg, Charles E. *No Other Gods: On Science and American Social Thought*. Rev. exp. ed. Baltimore, Md.: Johns Hopkins University Press, 1997.

——. "The Place of George M. Beard in Nineteenth Century Psychiatry." *Bulletin of the History of Medicine* 36 (1962): 245–59.

Ruggles, Steven. "Patriarchy, Power, and Pay: The Transformation of American Families, 1800–2015." *Demography* 52, no. 6 (2015): 1797–823.

——. "The Rise of Divorce and Separation in the United States, 1880–1990." *Demography* 34, no. 4 (1997): 455–66.

Ruscio, A. M., T. A. Brown, W. T. Chiu, J. Sareen, M. B. Stein, and R. C. Kessler. "Social Fears and Social Phobia in the USA: Results from the National Comorbidity Survey Replication." *Psychological Medicine* 38, no. 1 (2008): 15–28.

Rush, Benjamin. *Medical Inquiries and Observations Upon the Diseases of the Mind*. Philadelphia: Kimber and Richardson, 1812.

Sallet, J., R. B. Mars, M. P. Noonan, J. L. Andersson, J. X. O'Reilly, S. Jbabdi, P. L. Crox-son, et al. "Social Network Size Affects Neural Circuits in Macaques." *Science* 334, no. 6056 (2011): 697–700.

Salzman, Carl. "The APA Task Force Report on Benzodiazepine Dependence, Toxicity, and Abuse." *American Journal of Psychiatry* 148, no. 2 (1991): 151–52.

Sapolsky, Robert M. "Social Status and Health in Humans and Other Animals." *Annual Review of Anthropology* 33 (2004): 393–418.

Sarason, Barbara R., Gregory R. Pierce, Edward N. Shearin, Irwin G. Sarason, Jennifer A. Waltz, and Leslie Poppe. "Perceived Social Support and Working Models of Self and Actual Others." *Journal of Personality and Social Psychology* 60, no. 2 (1991): 273–87.

Sarason, I. G., B. R. Sarason, and E. N. Shearin. "Social Support as Individual Difference Variable." *Journal of Personality and Social Psychology* 50 (1986): 845–55.

Sayer, Liana C., Suzanne M. Bianchi, and John P. Robinson. "Are Parents Investing Less in Children? Trends in Mothers' and Fathers' Time with Children." *American Journal of Sociology* 110, no. 1 (2004): 1–43.

Schieman, Scott, and Heather A. Turner. " 'When Feeling Other People's Pain Hurts': The Influence of Psychosocial Resources on the Association Between Self-Reported Empathy and Depressive Symptoms." *Social Psychology Quarterly* 64, no. 4 (2001): 376–89.

Schlenger, William E., Juesta M. Caddell, Lori Ebert, B. Kathleen Jordan, Kathryn M. Rourke, David Wilson, Lisa Thalji, et al. "Psychological Reactions to Terrorist Attacks: Findings from the National Study of Americans' Reactions to September 11." *Journal of the American Medical Association* 288, no. 5 (2002): 581–88.

Schneider, Don, Linda Appleton, and Thomas McLemore. *A Reason for Visit Classification for Ambulatory Care.* DHEW Publication No. 79–1352. Hyattsville, Md.: U.S. Department of Health, Education, and Welfare, 1979.

Schuster, David G. "Neurasthenia and a Modernizing America." *Journal of the American Medical Association* 290, no. 17 (2003): 2327–28.

Schuster, Mark A., Bradley D. Stein, Lisa H. Jaycox, Rebecca L. Collins, Grant N. Marshall, Marc N. Elliott, Annie J. Zhou, et al. "A National Survey of Stress Reactions After the September 11, 2001, Terrorist Attacks." *New England Journal of Medicine* 345, no. 20 (2001): 1507–12.

Scull, Andrew. *Madness in Civilization: A Cultural History of Insanity.* Princeton, N.J.: Princeton University Press, 2015.

Segal, Zindel V., Michael Gemar, Catherine Truchon, Manal Guirguis, and Leonard M. Horowitz. "A Priming Methodology for Studying Self-Representation in Major Depressive Disorder." *Journal of Abnormal Psychology* 104, no. 1 (1995): 205–13.

Selling, Lowell S. "Clinical Study of a New Tranquilizing Drug: Use of Miltown (2-Methyl-2-N-Propyl-1, 3-Propanediol Dicarbamate)." *Journal of the American Medical Association* 157, no. 18 (1955): 1594–96.

Shanahan, Michael J., Stephen Vaisey, Lance D. Erickson, and Andrew Smolen. "Environmental Contingencies and Genetic Propensities: Social Capital, Educational Continuation, and Dopamine Receptor Gene DRD2." *American Journal of Sociology* 114 (2008): S260–86.

Shin, Lisa M., and Israel Liberzon. "The Neurocircuitry of Fear, Stress, and Anxiety Disorders." *Neuropsychopharmacology* 35, no. 1 (2010): 169–91.

Shorter, Edward. *From Paralysis to Fatigue: A History of Psychosomatic Illness in the Modern Era.* New York: Free Press, 1992.

——. *A Historical Dictionary of Psychiatry.* New York: Oxford University Press, 2005.

——. *A History of Psychiatry: From the Era of the Asylum to the Age of Prozac.* New York: Wiley, 1997.

——. *How Everyone Became Depressed: The Rise and Fall of the Nervous Breakdown.* Oxford: Oxford University Press, 2013.

Silver, Roxane Cohen, E. Alison Holman, Judith Pizarro Andersen, Michael Poulin, Daniel N. McIntosh, and Virginia Gil-Rivas. "Mental- and Physical-Health Effects of Acute Exposure to Media Images of the September 11, 2001, Attacks and the Iraq War." *Psychological Science* 24, no. 9 (2013): 1623–34.

Simon, Robin, and Leda E. Nath. "Gender and Emotion in the United States: Do Men and Women Differ in Self-Reports of Feelings and Expressive Behavior?" *American Journal of Sociology* 109, no. 5 (2004): 1137–76.

Slade, T., and G. Andrews. "DSM-IV and ICD-10 Generalized Anxiety Disorder: Discrepant Diagnoses and Associated Disability." *Social Psychiatry and Psychiatric Epidemiology* 36, no. 1 (2001): 45–51.

Slomkowski, Cheryl, Richard Rende, Katherine J. Conger, Ronald Simons, and Rand Conger. "Sisters, Brothers, and Delinquency: Evaluating Social Influence During Early and Middle Adolescence." *Child Development* 72, no. 1 (2001): 271–83.

Smith, Christian. *Lost in Transition: The Dark Side of Emerging Adulthood.* New York: Oxford University Press, 2011.

——. *Religion: What It Is, How It Works, and Why It Matters.* Princeton, N.J.: Princeton University Press, 2017.

——. "Theorizing Religious Effects Among American Adolescents." *Journal for the Scientific Study of Religion* 42, no. 1 (2003): 17–30.

Smith, Christian, and Patricia Snell. *Souls in Transition: The Religious and Spiritual Lives of Emerging Adults.* New York: Oxford University Press, 2009.

Smith, Mickey C. *Small Comfort: A History of the Minor Tranquilizers.* New York: Praeger, 1985.

Smock, Pamela J., and Fiona Rose Greenland. "Diversity in Pathways to Parenthood: Patterns, Implications, and Emerging Research Directions." *Journal of Marriage and Family* 72, no. 3 (2010): 576–93.

Smoller, Jordan W. *The Other Side of Normal: How Biology Is Providing the Clues to Unlock the Secrets of Normal and Abnormal Behavior.* 1st ed. New York: William Morrow, 2012.

Stafford, Randall S., Ellen A. MacDonald, and Stan N. Finkelstein. "National Patterns of Medication Treatment for Depression, 1987 to 2001." *Primary Care Companion to the Journal of Clinical Psychiatry* 3, no. 6 (2001): 232–35.

Stahl, Stephen M. "Don't Ask, Don't Tell, but Benzodiazepines Are Still the Leading Treatments for Anxiety Disorder." *Journal of Clinical Psychiatry* 63, no. 9 (2002): 756–57.

Starcevic, Vladan. "Benzodiazepines for Anxiety Disorders: Maximising the Benefits and Minimising the Risks." *Advances in Psychiatric Treatment* 18, no. 4 (2012): 250–58.

Stauffacher, Kirstin, and Ganie B. DeHart. "Crossing Social Contexts: Relational Aggression Between Siblings and Friends During Early and Middle Childhood." *Journal of Applied Developmental Psychology* 27, no. 3 (2006): 228–40.

Steckler, Thomas, Murray B. Stein, and Andrew Holmes. "Developing Novel Anxio-
lytics: Improving Preclinical Detection and Clinical Assessment." In *Animal and
Translational Models for CNS Drug Discovery*, ed. Robert A. McArthur and Franco
Borsini, 117–32. San Diego: Academic Press, 2008.

Stossel, Scott. *My Age of Anxiety: Fear, Hope, Dread, and the Search for Peace of Mind.*
New York: Knopf, 2013.

Stouffer, Samuel Andrew. *The American Soldier: Studies in Social Psychology in World
War II.* New York: Wiley, 1965.

Sullivan, Harry Stack. *The Interpersonal Theory of Psychiatry.* New York: Norton, 1953.

Sullivan, Teresa A., Elizabeth Warren, and Jay Lawrence Westbrook, *The Fragile Middle
Class: Americans in Debt* (New Haven, Conn.: Yale University Press, 2008).

Swift, Art. "Majority in U.S. Still Say Religion Can Answer Most Problems." Gallup: Politics, June 2, 2017. http://news.gallup.com/poll/211679/majority-say-religion-answer
-problems.aspx.

Taylor, S. E., L. C. Klein, B. P. Lewis, T. L. Gruenewald, R. A. R. Gurung, and J. A.
Updegraff. "Biobehavioral Responses to Stress in Females: Tend-and-Befriend, Not
Fight-or-Flight." *Psychological Review* 107, no. 3 (2000): 411–29.

Tellegen, Auke. "Structures of Mood and Personality and Their Relevance to Assessing
Anxiety, with an Emphasis on Self-Report." In *Anxiety and the Anxiety Disorders*, ed.
A. H. Tuma and J. D. Maser. 681–706. Hillsdale, N.J.: Erlbaum, 1985.

Thaler, Richard. "Toward a Positive Theory of Consumer Choice." *Journal of Economic
Behavior & Organization* 1, no. 1 (1980): 39–60.

Thornton, Arland. "Changing Attitudes Toward Family Issues in the United States."
Journal of Marriage and the Family 51, no. 4 (1989): 873–93.

Tillich, Paul. *Dynamics of Faith.* New York: Harper, 1956.

Tomes, Nancy. *A Generous Confidence: Thomas Story Kirkbride and the Art of Asylum-
keeping, 1840–1883.* New York: Cambridge University Press, 1984.

Tondo, L., B. Lepri, and R. J. Baldessarini. "Reproduction Among 1975 Sardinian Women
and Men Diagnosed with Major Mood Disorders." *Acta Psychiatrica Scandinavica*
123, no. 4 (2011): 283–89.

Tone, Andrea. *The Age of Anxiety: A History of America's Turbulent Affair with Tranquilizers.* New York: Basic, 2009.

——. "From Naughty Goods to Nicole Miller: Medicine and the Marketing of American
Contraceptives." *Culture, Medicine and Psychiatry* 30, no. 2 (2006): 249–67.

Tracy, Jessica L., and David Matsumoto. "The Spontaneous Expression of Pride and
Shame: Evidence for Biologically Innate Nonverbal Displays." *Proceedings of the
National Academy of Sciences* 105, no. 33 (2008): 11655.

Trifan, Tatiana Alina, Håkan Stattin, and Lauree Tilton-Weaver. "Have Authoritarian
Parenting Practices and Roles Changed in the Last 50 Years?" *Journal of Marriage
and Family* 76, no. 4 (2014): 744–61.

Tucker, C. Jack, Jonathan Marx, and Larry Long. " 'Moving On': Residential Mobility
and Children's School Lives." *Sociology of Education* 71, no. 2 (1998): 111–29.

Turner, Karen. "Secularism Is on the Rise, but Americans Are Still Finding Community and Purpose in Spirituality." *Vox*, June 11, 2019. https://www.vox.com/first
-person/2019/6/4/18644764/church-religion-atheism-secularism.

Twenge, Jean M. "The Age of Anxiety? The Birth Cohort Change in Anxiety and Neuroticism, 1952–1993." *Journal of Personality and Social Psychology* 79, no. 6 (2000): 1007–21.

——. "Birth Cohort Changes in Extraversion: A Cross-Temporal Meta-analysis, 1966–1993." *Personality and Individual Differences* 30, no. 5 (2001): 735–48.

——. "Changes in Masculine and Feminine Traits Over Time: A Meta-analysis." *Sex Roles* 36, no. 5 (1997): 305–25.

Twenge, Jean M., W. Keith Campbell, and Brittany Gentile. "Increases in Individualistic Words and Phrases in American Books, 1960–2008." *PLoS ONE* 7, no. 7 (2012): e40181.

Tyrer, Peter. "The Case for Cothymia: Mixed Anxiety and Depression as a Single Diagnosis." *British Journal of Psychiatry* 179, no. 3 (2001): 191–93.

——. "Comorbidity or Consanguinity." *British Journal of Psychiatry* 168, no. 6 (1996): 669–71.

Uhlenhuth, E. H., Mitchell B. Balter, Thomas A. Ban, and Kenneth Yang. "International Study of Expert Judgment on Therapeutic Use of Benzodiazepines and Other Psychotherapeutic Medications: 6. Trends in Recommendations for the Pharmacotherapy of Anxiety Disorders, 1992–1997." *Depression and Anxiety* 9, no. 3 (1999): 107–16.

United States Department of Health and Human Services. Centers for Disease Control and Prevention. National Center for Health Statistics. National Ambulatory Medical Care Survey. Ann Arbor, Mich.: Inter-university Consortium for Political and Social Research [distributor]. https://www.icpsr.umich.edu/icpsrweb/NACDA/series/37.

Veblen, Thorstein. *The Theory of the Leisure Class.* New York: Modern Library, 2001.

Vermani, Monica, Madalyn Marcus, and Martin A. Katzman. "Rates of Detection of Mood and Anxiety Disorders in Primary Care: A Descriptive, Cross-Sectional Study." *Primary Care Companion to CNS Disorders* 13, no. 2 (2011): PCC.10m01013.

Veroff, Joseph, Elizabeth Douvan, and Richard Kulka. Americans View Their Mental Health, 1957 and 1976: Selected Variables. Ann Arbor, Mich.: Inter-university Consortium for Political and Social Research (ICPSR) [distributor], 2005.

Veroff, Joseph, Elizabeth Douvan, and Richard A. Kulka. *The Inner American: A Self-Portrait from 1957 to 1976.* New York: Basic, 1981.

Vitz, Paul, and Bruce Buff. "Adolescents in Crisis: Why We Need to Recover Religion." *National Review*, July 27, 2017. https://www.nationalreview.com/2017/07/teen-suicides-depression-anxiety-rising-religion-can-help.

von Rueden, Christopher R., and Adrian V. Jaeggi. "Men's Status and Reproductive Success in 33 Nonindustrial Societies: Effects of Subsistence, Marriage System, and Reproductive Strategy." *Proceedings of the National Academy of Sciences of the United States of America* 113, no. 39 (2016): 10824.

Wakefield, Jerome C. "The DSM-5 Debate Over the Bereavement Exclusion: Psychiatric Diagnosis and the Future of Empirically Supported Treatment." *Clinical Psychology Review* 33, no. 7 (2013): 825–45.

Wakefield, Jerome C., and Mark F. Schmitz. "When Does Depression Become a Disorder? Using Recurrence Rates to Evaluate the Validity of Proposed Changes in Major Depression Diagnostic Thresholds." *World Psychiatry* 12, no. 1 (2013): 44–52.

Walker, David L., Kerry J. Ressler, Kwok-Tung Lu, and Michael Davis. "Facilitation of Conditioned Fear Extinction by Systemic Administration or Intra-amygdala Infusions of D-Cycloserine as Assessed with Fear-potentiated Startle in Rats." *Journal of Neuroscience* 22, no. 6 (2002): 2343.

Wallerstein, Judith S., Julia Lewis, and Sandra Blakeslee. *The Unexpected Legacy of Divorce: A 25 Year Landmark Study.* London: Fusion, 2002.

Watanabe, Noriya, and Miyuki Yamamoto. "Neural Mechanisms of Social Dominance." *Frontiers in Neuroscience* 9, no. 154 (2015): 1–14.

Western, Bruce, Deirdre Bloome, and Christine Percheski. "Inequality Among American Families with Children, 1975 to 2005." *American Sociological Review* 73, no. 6 (2008): 903–20.

Whisman, Mark A. "Marital Distress and DSM-IV Psychiatric Disorders in a Population-based National Survey." *Journal of Abnormal Psychology* 116, no. 3 (2007): 638–43.

White, Kevin M., and Samuel H. Preston. "How Many Americans Are Alive Because of Twentieth-Century Improvements in Mortality?" *Population and Development Review* 22, no. 3 (1996): 415–29.

Whyte, William H., Jr. *The Organization Man.* New York: Simon and Schuster, 1956.

Wiederhold, Brenda K. "Using Social Media to Our Advantage: Alleviating Anxiety During a Pandemic." *Cyberpsychology, Behavior, and Social Networking* 23, no. 4 (2020): 197–98.

Williams, J. Mark G., Fraser N. Watts, Colin MacLeod, and Andrew Mathews. *Cognitive Psychology and Emotional Disorders.* Oxford, U.K.: Wiley, 1988.

Willner, P. "Validity, Reliability and Utility of the Chronic Mild Stress Model of Depression: A 10-Year Review and Evaluation." *Psychopharmacology* 134, no. 4 (1997): 319–29.

Winship, Christopher, and Larry Radbill. "Sampling Weights and Regression Analysis." *Sociological Methods & Research* 23, no. 2 (1994): 230–57.

Wittchen, H. U., R. C. Kessler, H. Pfister, M. Höfler, and R. Lieb. "Why Do People with Anxiety Disorders Become Depressed? A Prospective-Longitudinal Community Study." *Acta Psychiatrica Scandinavica* 102 (2000): 14–23.

Wolff, Edward N. "Household Wealth Trends in the United States, 1962 to 2013: What Happened Over the Great Recession?" *RSF: The Russell Sage Foundation Journal of the Social Sciences* 2, no. 6 (2016): 24–43.

——. "Wealth Accumulation by Age Cohort in the U.S., 1962–1992: The Role of Savings, Capital Gains and Intergenerational Transfers." *Geneva Papers on Risk and Insurance. Issues and Practice* 24, no. 1 (1999): 27–49.

Wood, Alexander. "A New Method of Treating Neuralgia by the Direct Application of Opiates to the Painful Points." *Edinburgh Medical and Surgical Journal* 82 (1855): 265–81.

Wood, Lisa, Michele Birtel, Sarah Alsawy, Melissa Pyle, and Anthony Morrison. "Public Perceptions of Stigma Towards People with Schizophrenia, Depression, and Anxiety." *Psychiatry Research* 220, no. 1 (2014): 604–08.

World Health Organization. *International Statistical Classification of Diseases and Related Health Problems: ICD-10.* Geneva, 1992.

Yamini, Shruti, and Bipin Deokar. "Declining Household Savings." *Economic and Political Weekly* 47, no. 50 (2012): 75–77.

Yap, Marie Bee Hui, Pamela Doreen Pilkington, Siobhan Mary Ryan, and Anthony Francis Jorm. "Parental Factors Associated with Depression and Anxiety in Young People: A Systematic Review and Meta-analysis." *Journal of Affective Disorders* 156 (2014): 8–23.

Young, Alexander S., Ruth Klap, Cathy D. Sherbourne, and Kenneth B. Wells. "The Quality of Care for Depressive and Anxiety Disorders in the United States." *Archives of General Psychiatry* 58, no. 1 (2001): 55–61.

Zayas, Vivian, Walter Mischel, Yuichi Shoda, and J. Lawrence Aber. "Roots of Adult Attachment: Maternal Caregiving at 18 Months Predicts Adult Peer and Partner Attachment." *Social Psychological and Personality Science* 2, no. 3 (2010): 289–97.

Zhao, Ke, Jia Zhao, Ming Zhang, Qian Cui, and Xiaolan Fu. "Neural Responses to Rapid Facial Expressions of Fear and Surprise." *Frontiers in Psychology* 8 (2017): 761.

Zimmerman, Mark, and Jill I. Mattia. "Psychiatric Diagnosis in Clinical Practice: Is Comorbidity Being Missed?" *Comprehensive Psychiatry* 40, no. 3 (1999): 182–91.

Zink, Caroline F., Yunxia Tong, Qiang Chen, Danielle S. Bassett, Jason L. Stein, and Andreas Meyer-Lindenberg. "Know Your Place: Neural Processing of Social Hierarchy in Humans." *Neuron* 58, no. 2 (2008): 273–83.

Zuvekas, Samuel H. "Prescription Drugs and the Changing Patterns of Treatment for Mental Disorders, 1996–2001." *Health Affairs* 24, no. 1 (2005): 195–205.

INDEX

abuse: alcohol, 45, 186; cohort differences in, 103–4; maltreatment and, 70, 100; neglect and, 103–8, 126, 128; physical, 67, 100; prescription drug, 32, 170–71, 174–75; religion and, 128; sexual, 67, 100, 106

adaptation, 9, 20. *See also* evolution

adolescence, 72, 102, 106

adversity, early life, 70; consequences of, 104–9; religion and, 128

age, 71–75; age of onset distributions and, 74, 87, 91; trends and, 77–79; versus period and cohort effects, 71–75

"age of anxiety," 1–3, 5, 71, 185–86; versus "age of depression," 7–9

Akiskal, Hagop, 190

American Nervousness, 15–20, 186

amygdala: activity of, 60, 154–55; deficient activation of, 60

animal models of anxiety and depression, 61–63, 191

antisocial reactions, 31

apprehension as characteristic of anxiety, 6, 10, 12, 60

arousal, 59, 191; autonomic, 62

attachment style, 138–48; fearful style, 139, 141, 143, 148; insecure style, 139, 140, 141, 143–48; preoccupied dismissing style, 141; preoccupied style, 139, 141

attention processes in anxiety and depression, 46–50, 53, 62

attitudes, 72, 97–98, 114

Auden, W. H., 3, 186

autoimmune disease, 54

avoidance, 10, 23, 53, 60, 203

Barlow, David, 65–66

Batelaan, Neeltje, 44–45

Bateson, Melissa, 46

Beard, George Miller, 6, 15–22, 26, 30

benzodiazepines, 2, 12, 63, 165–66, 169–71, 173–76, 178–82, 189. *See also* prescriptions

biological influences, general, 65–67, 154–57

bipolar disorder, 37, 87, 91, 171; depression and, 41

birth trauma, 26

Borrus, Joseph, 168, 169

GPSR Authorized Representative: Easy Access System Europe, Mustamäe tee
50, 10621 Tallinn, Estonia, gpsr.requests@easproject.com

www.ingramcontent.com/pod-product-compliance
Lightning Source LLC
Chambersburg PA
CBHW032121020426
42334CB00016B/1033